NORTHERN GETAWAY

Northern Getaway

Film, Tourism, and the Canadian Vacation

DOMINIQUE BRÉGENT-HEALD

McGill-Queen's University Press
Montreal & Kingston • London • Chicago

ISBN 978-0-2280-1392-1 (cloth)
ISBN 978-0-2280-1393-8 (paper)
ISBN 978-0-2280-1486-7 (ePDF)
ISBN 978-0-2280-1487-4 (ePUB)

Legal deposit fourth quarter 2022
Bibliothèque nationale du Québec

This book has been published with the help of a grant from the Canadian Federation for the Humanities and Social Sciences, through the Awards to Scholarly Publications Program, using funds provided by the Social Sciences and Humanities Research Council of Canada.

Funding was also received from the Faculty Publications Subvention Program of Memorial University of Newfoundland.

Financé par le gouvernement du Canada | Funded by the Government of Canada | Canada | Conseil des arts du Canada | Canada Council for the Arts

We acknowledge the support of the Canada Council for the Arts.

Nous remercions le Conseil des arts du Canada de son soutien.

Library and Archives Canada Cataloguing in Publication

Title: Northern getaway: film, tourism, and the Canadian vacation/ Dominique Brégent-Heald.

Names: Brégent-Heald, Dominique, 1973– author.

Description: Includes bibliographical references and index.

Identifiers: Canadiana (print) 20220250480 | Canadiana (ebook) 20220250502 | ISBN 9780228013921 (hardcover) | ISBN 9780228013938 (softcover) | ISBN 9780228014867 (PDF) | ISBN 9780228014874 (ePUB)

Subjects: LCSH: Canada—In motion pictures. | LCSH: Travelogues (Motion pictures)—Canada—History and criticism. | LCSH: Tourism and motion pictures—Canada. | LCSH: Motion picture industry—Canada—History. | LCSH: Tourism—Canada—History. | LCSH: Tourism—Social aspects—Canada.

Classification: LCC PN1995.9.C33 B74 2022 | DDC 791.43/65871—dc23

This book was typeset by Marquis Interscript in 10.5/13 Sabon.

Contents

Figures

Acknowledgments

After receiving a one-year SSHRC Standard Research Grant, I put on hold the project that became *Northern Getaway* to complete my first book, *Borderland Films: American Cinema, Mexico, and Canada during the Progressive Era*. In the spring of 2016, I was awarded a SSHRC Insight Grant for this project, and I am grateful for this federal funding, which enabled me to conduct archival research and disseminate preliminary findings at various conferences. Because of this support, I was fortunate enough to visit various archives across Canada and the United States, which are listed in the bibliography. I wanted to express my gratitude to all the hardworking archivists and librarians who ensured that my research trips were always efficient and productive. Specifically, I benefitted from the assistance of the staff members of provincial archives in Nova Scotia, New Brunswick, Ontario, Saskatchewan, Alberta, and British Columbia who helped me locate and navigate a wealth of primary materials and motion pictures. Closer to home, the lovely people at Document Delivery at Memorial University's Queen Elizabeth II Library tracked down many obscure works for me, and for that I am much obliged.

I am also indebted to the University of Toronto's Media Archives and its Gordon Sparling Collection, which was indispensable for my understanding of Canada's early film history, particularly the Montreal-based Associated Screen News. Moreover, the knowledgeable staff at the Glenbow Archives in Calgary guided my research regarding the filmmaker William J. Oliver. I would be remiss if I did not express my utmost gratefulness to the archivists and reference librarians at Library and Archives Canada who granted me access to a host of audio-visual materials and provided me with seemingly countless files pertaining to the Canadian Government Motion Picture Bureau, the (Dominion)

Parks Branch, the Canadian Travel Bureau, the National Film Board, the Canadian Cooperation Project, the (Dominion) Department of Trade and Commerce, Crawley Films, and microfilms of the *Canadian Moving Picture Digest*.

In the United States, my thanks go to the staff at the National Archives at College Park, Maryland ("Archives II"), where I screened Canadian-themed productions in its Ford [Motor Company] film collection. Additionally, thanks to those individuals who retrieved hundreds of documents connected to the US Office of War Information, which helped me contextualize the role of tourism films in wartime US-Canadian relations. In Washington, DC, I depended on the kindness of those working in the Library of Congress's Moving Image Research Center and its Manuscript Division, which house numerous early tourism films and educational catalogues, respectively. One of the great pleasures of researching this book was returning to the Cinematic Arts Library at the University of Southern California, in Los Angeles, and the Margaret Herrick Library at the Academy of Motion Picture Arts and Sciences in Beverly Hills, which maintains the Motion Picture Association Correspondence Files, various production records, and pressbooks that enriched my comprehension of the Canadian Cooperation Project, as well as the conception and marketing for Canadian-themed feature films and travelogues produced in Hollywood.

In addition, so much of this book has been informed by conversations with friends and colleagues, including Liz Czach; Zoë Druick, who graciously read a draft of chapter 5 and offered constructive comments; and Jennifer VanderBurg. I similarly owe a debt of gratitude to John Sandlos for providing feedback on an early draft of chapter 3. I have also benefitted from research assistance by the following graduate students: Norman Potter, Andy Post, Ashley Ring, Nakita Ryan, and Aileen Worrall. Kudos to my colleagues and the academic staff in the Department of History at Memorial for all their help and support. My appreciation also goes out to the anonymous reviewers whose thoughtful suggestions have made this monograph much stronger. I would like to extend a special thanks to Jonathan Crago at McGill-Queen's University Press, who has been most supportive and patient, as well as John Parry for his careful copy editing. Thanks also to Memorial University for providing financial assistance via a Publication Subvention Grant. Above all, this book would have not been possible without the love of my friends (especially my Golden Girls and 416 Besties) and family – children, husband, mother, sister, in-laws, and fur kids!

NORTHERN GETAWAY

Introduction

Jane gave a blissful sigh as the travelogue ended and the lights in the theater bloomed into brightness.

"Bali!" she said. "Isn't it lovely! Wouldn't that be a wonderful place to go on our honeymoon?"

"Listen, dear," said John. "I don't think you're going to make a very practical wife. We've been engaged three weeks, and during that time you've wanted to go to Switzerland, the South Seas, Panama, and Iceland for our honeymoon."

Picture Play Magazine, June 1935[1]

The above discussion, appearing in a fan magazine, speaks to the power of film as an advertisement for tourist travel. The unfolding of carefully curated moving images of island paradises, mountain peaks, and glaciers before Jane's eyes while she sits comfortably in a darkened theatre provoked emotional attachments that, in turn, pushed her to desire these locales for a honeymoon. Beyond functioning as a surrogate for travel, these appealing environments as seen on the larger-than-life silver screen ultimately translated into a tangible yearning to visit these locations. For such "average" American tourists as John and Jane, however, Europe, South America, and the South Pacific were prohibitively expensive holiday destinations. But for most US holidaymakers, Canada figured as an attainable and enticing place to vacation.

Canada's status as Americans' northern getaway was not inevitable, nor did government officials and tourism-industry leaders take the development and strength of the Dominion's tourism sector for granted. From the first moving images of Niagara Falls and the Canadian Rockies and Selkirks at the turn of the twentieth century through the end of the 1950s, when made-for-television programming had become the primary visual medium for tourism promotion, film offered a ground-breaking method to promote Canada as the leading foreign tourist destination for the US market. This statement raises questions that *Northern Getaway* seeks to answer, while motivating further research and debate on the interplay between film and tourism in the two countries' history more broadly. For example, in what ways have the economic and discursive synergies between film and tourism helped to shape national identity and cultural representations? Did the drive to sell Canada as a tourist destination influence sociopolitical relations in North America? How did the exhibition and aesthetics of films in the service of tourism promotion in Canada change over time?

During the first half of the twentieth century, a Gordian knot of private and public tourist interests at the Dominion and provincial levels in Canada, and at times in collaboration with the American film industry, wagered that film – a product and expression of modernizing society – presented a cutting-edge means through which to construct and circulate what tourism stakeholders refer to today as a particular destination brand in the collective mind of the American tourist. An effective branding strategy is one that establishes a unique identity or core message to distinguish a particular place from other locations by building on its perceived strengths, guiding visitors' expectations of it, and fostering prospective visitors' emotive connections with it. Such branding normally includes stressing its key attributes, such as natural or built attractions, cultural components, and accessibility to and within the destination.[2]

Only recently have tourist organizations and marketers begun to recognize the potential of film, as well as video, television, and media culture, to develop and/or sustain a particular destination image to attract visitors.[3] *Northern Getaway* demonstrates that Canada was an innovator in harnessing the potential of motion pictures to shape and disseminate a recognizable destination brand. This was accomplished through what I call "tourism films." Given that tourism is largely an intangible product and highly experiential, it is not surprising that the parameters for tourism films are equally nebulous. As National Film Board (NFB) Secretary Alan Field observed in 1948:

> One question that often arises is what exactly is a tourist film. No concrete definition exists for a "tourist film." All films, other than specialized or technical films, have some interest for people who wish to come to Canada or are planning to visit this country ... Any list of films taken at random – *Great Lakes*, *Niagara Frontier*, *A City Sings*, *Gaspe Codfishermen*, *Montreal*

> *by Night*, *Red Runs the Fraser*, *Trappers of the Sea*, *The New North* – all of these made for a variety of purposes have interest for potential tourists to Canada.[4]

This begs the question: can every film with Canadian content shown in the United States or elsewhere be considered a tourism film? The short answer is yes, depending on its purpose and context. Tourism was omnipresent in Canadian film during the first half of the twentieth century, and the nation's efforts to encourage tourism through film culture were eclectic and often experimental. As this book explores, travelogues (also known as scenics or travel pictures) dealing with modes of mobility, host–guest relationships, urban settings, natural landscapes, and/or historical sites openly encouraged tourism. Yet elements of travel promotion were present in productions that trade journals and catalogues classified under such umbrella groupings as educational (particularly the subcategory of geography), industrial, or apropos of the agricultural or resource economy.[5] Moreover, tourism films transected such traditional binaries as non-fiction/fiction productions; amateur/professional filmmaking; 16-mm (non-theatrical)/35-mm (theatrical) films; and public/private sponsorship. The intersection between film and tourism can also be seen in the ways in which tourism stakeholders publicized Hollywood celebrities who fished, golfed, and vacationed in various locales throughout the country.

In *Northern Getaway*, I define tourism films broadly as cinematic representations that stimulate recreational travel to a particular location. Their function, whether intentional or inadvertent, resulted in the formation of a destination brand. Over the course of the first half of the twentieth century, tourism films were responsible for marking Canada as a northern getaway where American visitors could experience a short, restorative vacation from the exigencies of the day-to-day world while still having the benefit of contemporary amenities. Tourism films produced a consistent and sustained pattern of settler-colonial representations that celebrated Canada's seemingly unspoiled natural landscapes, abundant wildlife, and recreational opportunities while revealing how these attributes were integrated into intricate networks of industrialism, consumerism, and technological change. The legacy of these tourism films carries through to the present day, playing a central role in what Daniel Francis refers to as Canada's "organizing myths" to promote an "idealized version" of the nation.[6] Indeed, recent Destination Canada brand guidelines continue to market the nation's "natural wonders," "accessible adventures," "wide variety of wildlife," and "vibrant cities."[7] Tourism films thus offered spectators an aesthetically pleasing visual experience of travel and mobility resulting in a distinctive tourist perspective – that is, one that demonstrates how spectators *should* relate to Canada and closing off possibilities for alternative ways-of-seeing and knowing.

THE TOURISM FILM IN CANADA: A BRIEF TOUR

Northern Getaway demonstrates that Canada was a pioneer in the use of the tourism film as a form of advertisement or marketing in the first half of the twentieth century. While the focus of this book is the interconnected relationship between tourism and film in the Canadian context, it aims to provide a departure point for elucidating (or disrupting) the general phenomenon of film as a driver for tourism and destination branding. Motion pictures and modern tourism in North America both emerged in step with the consumerist economy and mass culture that began to coalesce in the late nineteenth century. Moving images of travel dominated cinema's foundational period, characterized by the production of "actualities," presenting novel settler-colonial/imperial ways of seeing the world. Thomas Edison, for one, proclaimed that motion pictures imparted "knowledge of distant lands, customs and peoples," serving as a "connective force" that informally links disparate groups of strangers and resulting in "imagined communities."[8] Exhibitors screened these films in a variety of pedagogical and cultural-exhibition venues, frequently accompanied by a lecturer. In Canada, transportation companies seized upon this new technology, working with such US-based film companies as Edison and Biograph to promote tourism and/or colonization along their rail or steamship routes.

Over the following several decades, the film and tourism industries matured into economic powerhouses alongside the broader processes of industrial capitalism, the growth of new technologies and transportation systems, namely the automobile, and the ongoing commercialization of leisure. Spectators increasingly viewed motion pictures in dedicated settings as the film industry transitioned into producing longer, narrative-based films. Tourism films did not vanish but rather acclimatized to increasingly specialized production methods, as well as the amalgamating distribution and exhibition systems of the

American film industry. In this evolving cinematic landscape, devotees of the burgeoning visual-instruction movement championed travel subjects as pedagogical tools, while business and industry recognized that the sponsored film was a superior means of advertising. This was in keeping with contemporaneous theories proposing that individuals retained more through images than through words; that is, the intensity and realism of moving pictures produced a peculiar cognitive state favourable to learning and/or consumption.

Believing that the experience of viewing motion pictures would incentivize travel, government agencies within Canada increasingly invested in film production to promote tourism, as seen in the Dominion's establishment in 1917–18 of the Exhibits and Publicity Bureau, which in 1923 became the Canadian Government Motion Picture Bureau (CGMPB). By being presented as educational films, as opposed to direct advertisements, tourism films furnished the illusion of instruction. As journalist and "authority on advertising and scientific merchandising" Frederick J. Haskin touted, "Canada is the first government to advertise itself commercially by the films."[9] The Dominion Parks Branch also expanded its film production during the interwar period to attract American tourists, while the CGMPB increasingly turned to 16-mm production, which circulated in such non-theatrical settings as schools and community groups.

The National Film Board (NFB), set up in 1939 under John Grierson, absorbed the CGMPB in 1941. Its documentary approach, which Fanning Hearon described as a "new type of film which moves in the mist between fairyland fiction and schoolhouse dullness," seemed anathema to the tourism film.[10] Nevertheless, the onset of the Second World War and the need for US currency called for novel approaches to promoting tourism by producing documentary-style films, setting the stage for a postwar travel boom. Furthermore, the Canadian Travel Bureau (CTB), founded in 1935 as a centralized agency to "sell Canada" to American tourists, facilitated an overall program after the war of 16-mm tourism films directed at the US market.

Together with these state-sponsored efforts, public and private tourist interests in Canada continually sought the involvement of US film interests (both commercial and amateur) to spur tourism. These informal liaisons culminated in the Canadian Cooperation Project (1948–58), in which Hollywood made a direct commitment to encourage tourism into Canada, with the goal of reversing the country's postwar shortage of American dollars. As tourism scholars Nigel

Morgan and Annette Pritchard have noted, highlighting a destination in a motion picture is the ultimate form of placing a tourism product. Due to cinema's ability to reach an audience of millions, an appearance in a mainstream film provided the city, province, or country in question a much wider variety of tourism-driven publicity activities before, during, and after the picture's release than could the more traditional advertising methods.[11] By the mid-1950s, television broadcasting had largely replaced film as the preferred medium for promoting tourism in Canada. Although travelogues continued to be produced, and travel-lecture circuits still featured the motion pictures of amateur and professional filmmakers, the "Golden Age" of Canadian tourism films was over.[12]

FILM AND TOURISM: APPROACHES

Despite their shared legacy, film and tourism's historical and conceptual intersections within Canada are little understood. To comprehend this evolving interrelationship, *Northern Getaway* is indebted to several existing traditions of academic inquiry in film history/studies and tourism research. Since the study of film emerged as an academic discipline in the 1960s, scholars in North America have tended to examine commercial feature-length narrative motion pictures, as opposed to marginal forms of film practice, including tourism films. Moreover, a range of theoretical approaches, including auteurism, critical race studies, feminist and queer theory, Marxism, postcolonialism, postmodernism, poststructuralism, psychoanalysis, reception theory, and semiotics, have shaped the study of film. The traditional emphasis on textual analysis and the formalist criticism of film as an art form have mostly ignored broader cultural, ideological, and institutional contexts. Over the past two decades, historical approaches to film have revitalized the study of cinema as a site of social interaction by recognizing that film is not just an aesthetic object or text but also a cultural force. Rather than studying individual films or filmmakers, proponents of the "new cinema history" and "new film history" consider the wider circumstances and conditions of production, distribution, and reception by drawing evidence from a range of filmic and extra-filmic sources. New cinema history also frequently encompasses data-driven analysis to uncover broader patterns in film culture. Such initiatives as the History of Moviegoing, Exhibition, and Reception (HoMer), established in 2004 as an international and multidisciplinary network of researchers, illustrate diverse theories and methods for examining "cinema as a site of cultural and social exchange."[13]

Meanwhile, the focus on historical conditions and contexts has also helped expand scholarship about various film forms outside mainstream cinema.[14] Since the early 2000s, film studies have looked at a kaleidoscopic range of non-Hollywood-style productions from around the world. The inclusive and emergent subfield of non-theatrical film encompasses studies of advertising, amateur, educational, industrial, and sponsored pictures. These are small-gauge films (i.e., smaller than the standard theatrical 35-mm format) distributed outside conventional commercial theatrical networks, through venues that include churches, classrooms, and clubs, and typically free of charge.

Beginning in 1982, archivist, writer, and filmmaker Rick Prelinger championed the preservation and study of what he termed "orphan films" – ephemeral or disposable film product that had heretofore been overlooked in film analysis. The Library of Congress in 2002 acquired his collection of over 50,000 amateur, educational, and industrial films. The Internet Archive subsequently partnered with Prelinger to digitize thousands of these discarded productions.[15] Dan Streible has likewise pioneered the study of non-theatrical motion pictures. Since 1999, he has organized the annual Orphan Film Symposium (held in various cities), which embraces "all manner of films outside the commercial mainstream" and provides a forum for collectors, enthusiasts, preservationists, and scholars to resurrect these undervalued films.[16] In their edited collection, Charles Acland and Haidee Wasson have also explored the cultural importance of non-theatrical motion pictures as "useful cinema" – "a body of films and technologies that perform tasks and serve as instruments in an ongoing struggle for aesthetic, social and political capital." Borrowing from Tony Bennett's concept of "useful culture," they approach these so-called lesser films not for their artistic or entertainment purpose but rather for their utility. In other words, these are functional films created for a specific purpose or to perform a particular task. Acland and Wasson's formulation of "useful cinema" therefore considers institutional frameworks, be they corporate, educational, or governmental, and how they have conceptualized and deployed the film medium to serve their interests.[17]

By concentrating on how institutional agents (such as the CGMPB, Parks Branch, CTB, NFB, and railways) have exploited the film medium to sell Canada to American tourists, *Northern Getaway* sits comfortably within historical studies of non-theatrical and useful films. This book examines the production, circulation, and consumption of tourism films, which were central to non-theatrical film exhibition, to figure out how these productions have functioned as complex nexuses of North American culture, economy, and society. Beyond providing theatrical entertainment, tourism films screened in classrooms, community halls, and exhibition grounds promoted tourism (sometimes obliquely), frequently under the pretense of education or visual instruction. Yet *Northern Getaway* also considers films promoting tourism in Canada that were circulated in commercial theatres. The study of film and tourism in Canada thus straddles both the theatrical and the non-theatrical worlds – sometimes part of the Hollywood standard, and sometimes operating directly in opposition to it.

While the history of the tourism film in Canada has been heretofore overlooked, scholars have begun to explore the travelogue in American cinema. A key tenet of this US research is the genre's emphasis on pleasure and mobility. Travelogues offer spectators vicarious access to historical sites, natural landmarks, and urban spaces around the world. Lynne Kirby considers the historical and theoretical connections, predominantly shared conceptions of time and space, between the railways and the early cinema. Railway companies frequently financed motion pictures to boost travel along their routes, which helped shape a peculiar modern sensibility, most notably transforming or annihilating time and space.[18] Moreover, contributors to Jeffrey Ruoff's anthology *Virtual Voyages* (2006) examine the critical and enduring role of travelogues in the history of cinema, from illustrated-travel lecturers of the 1890s through the classical Hollywood era to epic IMAX theatres, while also considering such themes as colonialism, imperialism, and technology.[19] In *Education in the School of Dreams* (2013), Jennifer Peterson (a contributor to *Virtual Voyages*) examines the pivotal role of the travelogue genre to cinema's transitional era, 1907–15. She suggests that films of travel constructed a "poetic reverie" by opening new worlds remotely, encouraging a sense of wonder, and providing moviegoers with a fleeting oppositional space to transcend the pressures of their day-to-day lives. Beyond their aesthetic and entertaining qualities, they served as a tool of social and cultural uplift during the Progressive era (1880s–1910s).[20]

These discussions of "armchair tourism" – the consumption of spatial and cultural spaces beyond one's familiar environs from the comfort and safety of the theatre – emphasize the cinematic experience as a form of *virtual* mobility. This filmic replication of tourism encounters often stemmed from a scopophilic (love of looking) desire for the foreign, the exotic, or the "Other." As Anne Friedberg shows, developments in architecture, consumer culture, transportation, and visual technologies enabled this "mobilized virtual gaze," which she argues "is not a direct perception but a *received* perception mediated through representation."[21] Giuliana Bruno similarly positions moving images as a form of sightseeing or *site-seeing*, while Ellen Strain suggests that the cinema and other media technologies fetishize a mobile immersive (yet distant) experience that positions spectators as tourists.[22] Although *Northern Getaway* recognizes the imaginary possibilities of cinematic tourism, it considers the more practical use of fiction and non-fiction films intended to stimulate travel to Canada. The usefulness of the tourism film did not necessarily translate into an absence of amusement value or creativity. The exaggerated qualities of the filmic experience potentially fuelled a desire for the experiences witnessed on screen, thus fashioning unique forms of spectatorship. Moving images of Canada offered spectators an aesthetically pleasing visual experience of travel and mobility, generating a peculiarly modern tourist perspective.[23]

In addition to responding to this growing body of work on new film history, useful films, and travelogues, *Northern Getaway* is informed by an area of academic inquiry centred on film-induced tourism or simply "film tourism." Early investigations into this phenomenon looked at how different forms of media (oral, literary, and visual) influenced tourists' desire to visit a particular place, and recommended further research into the possibilities of film to promote destinations as tourist sites.[24] Consequently, social scientists Dwayne Baker, Roger Riley, and Carlton S. Van Doren produced several collaborative data-driven articles in the 1990s examining the motivational drivers behind film-related tourism, as well as the advantages and potential drawbacks of movie-induced tourism in the United States.[25]

Sue Beeton wrote the first book-length study of the subject in *Film-Induced Tourism* (2005). The Australian-based researcher studied the phenomenon of a "pilgrimage" to a location following the release of a motion picture made or set in that particular setting and used a theoretical framework that combines business management, postmodern discourse, psychology, and tourism research. Beyond considering theatrical movies, typically a one-time experience, she also explores the long-term effects of DVDs, television programs, and "off location" film-related tourist activities, including film festivals, premières, studio tours, and synergistic theme parks/rides based on movies, as they relate to such concepts as authenticity, social representations, and the tourist gaze. Through participant-observation case studies centred on Australia, New Zealand, and the United Kingdom, Beeton discusses how film-induced tourism could boost the economies of listless rural and urban communities while emphasizing the need for strategic planning to manage the social and environmental ramifications of increased tourism.[26]

Subsequently, conceptual research into film and tourism has mushroomed in several disciplines, mostly in the social sciences, that use both quantitative and qualitative approaches.[27] Some scholars, for instance, examine the interrelationship of film and tourism with notions of authenticity, that is, fictional or "real" film locations as tourist destinations.[28] Sociologist Rodanthi Tzanelli attempts to unpack the ideological power of Hollywood in constructing exotic destinations that shape popular versions of ethnic and national cultures. She also recognizes global, national, and local counter-hegemonic resistance to "cinematic tourism."[29] Another rich area of research involves studies of landscapes and concepts of space and place. As Martin Lefebvre argues, cinema has "the unique ability to call forth both space and time, picture and narrative, into its mode of representation and, therefore, into the representation of landscape." As Lefebvre makes clear, not "every depiction of exterior or natural space is a *landscape*." Setting, he tells us, refers "to spatial features that are necessary for all event-driven films, whether fiction or documentary," and landscape is "space freed from eventhood."[30]

Beyond these theoretical reflections, other researchers have concentrated on the real-world impacts of film-induced tourism, as destinations around the globe have recognized the potential benefits of incorporating film in marketing campaigns ranging from encouraging informal travel to commercialized packaged tours. This research has tended to use case studies to discern the economic bottom-line of a specific film(s) for the benefit of destination-marketing organizations (DMOs), rather than assessing media-induced tourism as a sociocultural practice. For example, given the popularity of the *Harry Potter* movies and the *Downton Abbey* television series, VisitBritain adopted "sophisticated techniques to engage the tourist capitalising on links between film and place" via an interactive map featuring some of the country's most recognized filming locations.[31] Tim Edensor examines *Braveheart* (dir.

by Mel Gibson, 1995) and its effect on tourism and Scottish identity, while more recently researchers have observed Ireland's cachet as a film-tourism destination following HBO's television series *Game of Thrones* (2011–19) and *Star Wars: The Force Awakens* (dir. by J.J. Abrams, 2015).[32] In particular, the global success of *The Lord of the Rings* franchise as an ongoing tourism motivator in New Zealand has created significant scholarly and industry interest.[33] Similarly, media-driven tourism has generated economic activity throughout Asia, which has produced a growing literature on this phenomenon.[34]

Hence scholarship on film tourism breaks down roughly into two parallel tracks – theoretical discussions of film's conceptual similarities to tourism and analyses of the power of film to encourage tourism.[35] Most of this research considers contemporary motion pictures or television programs from a social-sciences perspective, examining the advantages and disadvantages of film-induced tourism, as well as its short-term economic, environmental, and social outcomes. Yet what of the deeper themes, patterns, and processes of change associated with film tourism in the past? What does the synergistic relationship between film and tourism reveal about the role of public and private institutions in national life? Does an analysis of the production and dissemination of tourism films lay bare the economic motivations and shared social values of hegemonic state authority? What can we learn about cultural activities, leisure patterns, and attitudes towards class, ethnicity, gender, race, and sexuality from a study of film tourism over a longer period? These are some of the queries *Northern Getaway* seeks to probe within the Canadian context.

THE CANADIAN CONTEXT

Despite pioneering the use of motion pictures to promote tourism, Canada has been largely absent from academic discussions on film tourism, while the tourism film remains underexplored within Canadian film history. Since Peter Morris's seminal monograph on film in Canada prior to the NFB – *Embattled Shadows* (1978) – there have been valuable studies on aspects of cinema in or about Canada.[36] In *Now Playing* (2008), Paul S. Moore examines early movie-going and distribution practices in English Canada, while Peter Lester's dissertation, "Cultural Continuity and Technological Indeterminacy" (2008), focuses on 16-mm itinerant exhibition in the interwar period.[37] André Gaudreault, Germain Lacasse, Louis Pelletier, and Pierre

Véronneau each explore various aspects of Quebec cinema in the late nineteenth and early twentieth centuries.[38] Other research has considered the contribution of women to early Canadian film culture.[39] The NFB has been the object of study for many film scholars, especially its first commissioner, John Grierson, institutional practices, social themes, and activism.[40] Meanwhile, the literature on the Canadian Cooperation Project has emphasized the historical development of feature-film policy in Canada, American cultural imperialism, and broader discourses of cultural production and national identity.[41] This heterogeneous historiography has, however, largely overlooked the key role that tourism has played in Canada's film history and beyond.

Perhaps this is because the academic study of tourism in Canada, though expanding, is still in its infancy. One of the earliest studies of Canadian tourism is E.J. Hart's investigation of the Canadian Pacific Railway (CPR's) promotional activities to attract tourists at the turn of the twentieth century.[42] This has been followed by critical investigations at the intersection of tourism and environmental studies vis-a-vis evolving notions of the wilderness, national parks, and the exclusion of Indigenous communities.[43] With notable pan-Canadian exceptions – Alan Gordon's monograph on living history museums in Canada (*Time Travel* [2017]), Daniel Francis's lavishly illustrated popular history of Canadian tourism and immigration propaganda between the 1870s and the Second World War (*Selling Canada* ([2011]), J.I. Little's essays on the nineteenth-century construction of Canadian landscapes (*Fashioning the Canadian Landscape* [2018]), and Alisa Apostle's dissertation on the CTB ("The Display of a Tourist Nation" [2001]) – most historians have concentrated on a particular province/region in terms of such themes as authenticity, consumer culture, heritage, identity, and promotion and marketing.[44]

Although *Northern Getaway* considers the filmic creation of tourism landscapes at the regional, provincial, and even municipal levels, it is *national* in scope, though not comprehensive.[45] The book aims to demonstrate how tourism films, in an effort to anticipate the desires and needs of the targeted American (white and middle-to-upper class) tourist market, constructed larger – albeit overlapping, selective, and varied – Canadian cultural identities. As Renisa Mawani explains, "Tourist attractions are ... places in which the nation is constituted."[46] Tourism films, though a unique representational practice, function similarly as a form of national self-definition, helping to reframe what it meant to be Canadian within North America.

An examination of the ways in which tourism films have shaped and redefined the national imaginary not only reveals critical interconnections between the film and tourism industries, but also provides insights into how the state, in conjunction with the private sector, envisioned itself in the first half of the twentieth century in ways that would appeal to potential tourists. Tourism films fashioned a visual (and later visual-aural) lexicon of symbols that distinguished Canada from other competing locations, thus reinforcing concepts of collective identity. Filmic discourses developed and disseminated a vision of Canada as a desirable destination for the US market by emphasizing scenic beauty, a wealth of undomesticated non-human animals, and outdoor activities and by incorporating elements of Indigeneity to convey an anti-modernist image while paradoxically characterizing Canada as a technologically and industrially advanced settler-colonial country.

The justification for this cultural construction was often financial in nature – boosters at the local, regional, and national levels saw American tourist dollars as a universal panacea for the economy. How the nation marketed itself offers a window into not only how tourism films, both government-sponsored and private filmmaking ventures, rhetorically framed Canada as a destination to the *outside* world but in the process also elucidates the ways in which film has helped to foment positive attitudes *within* Canada towards tourism by associating the industry with prosperity, progress, and international goodwill. Tourism films thus perpetuated, to borrow Michael Billig's phrase, "banal nationalism," which he defines as mundane or unconscious reminders of national belonging in everyday life that are typically taken for granted.[47]

The unfolding process of forming national identity through filmic tourism narratives, as well as using national discourse to promote tourism, ties in with the idea of "nation branding." Though a relatively new term, the concept dates back to the nineteenth century, when nation-states began to employ various forms of advertising to advance their particular cultural, economic, or political agendas.[48] Branding discourses and practices, while often frustratingly elusive and intangible, construct and communicate nationhood, which may not only expand tourism, but also enhance the nation's stature abroad, advance the national economy, and enrich diplomatic relations.[49] Employing a cultural approach to this phenomenon in the Canadian context, *Northern Getaway* reveals the historical processes by which tourism films commodified certain representations that marketed "brand Canada" to American tourists. As Eric G.E. Zuelow reminds us, tourism does not function within "a geographically bounded" area but rather illuminates "larger transnational connections."[50] While *Northern Getaway* contends with the largely one-directional flow of tourists from the United States into Canada, it embraces a transnational approach to film and tourism cultures that emphasizes collaborations, influences, and intermedial links that can transcend the centralizing power of nation-states and the paradigm of national cinema.[51]

Most recently, scholars recognize that the bond between tourism and nationhood has evolved under the conditions of settler colonialism, understood as an enduring societal structure, which necessitates persistent fortification through discursive means. Tourism draws from and perpetuates what anthropologist Patrick Wolfe terms the settler-colonial "logic of elimination": the removal of Indigenous peoples from their ancestral homelands, followed by the frequent appropriation and commodification of their cultural formations.[52] As Margaret Werry argues, "Settlers declare their newfound national identity by presenting those they have displaced as their symbolic surrogates, nostalgically borrowing the authenticity of Indigenous belonging, profiting from the traffic in Indigenous images and property, and buttressing the racial distinctions between primitivism and modernity that undergird the whole edifice of the nation."[53]

Canada's history is similarly marked by the physical removal and sociocultural exclusion of First Nations peoples under the Euro-Canadian-centric pretext of development, conservation, and tourism. Consequently, representations of space and place in the dominant culture are based on the false concept of *terra nullius* (nobody's land), making seemingly empty landscapes available for the fleeting pleasure of settler-colonial tourists. *Northern Getaway* acknowledges that film is equally complicit in these practices of erasure and re-creation in the ways that it deletes, absorbs, and re-inscribes a romanticized version of the "imaginary Indian" into Canada's destination brand. The ability of settler colonialism to "cover its tracks" renders the trauma associated with these processes of colonial displacement and substitution invisible.[54] Rather than revealing these landscapes as sites of dispossession and recognizing the legacy of Indigenous expulsion, tourism films formulated a shared language that characterized these places as vacationlands for settler tourists that persists through to today.[55]

MAPPING THE *NORTHERN GETAWAY*

In tracing the early history of the tourism film in Canada, this study relies primarily on a rich vein of extra-filmic documentation to elucidate the economic, political, and social contexts of tourism films. In addition to harnessing archival materials, I have digitally excavated a wealth of primary material from catalogues, newspapers, and periodicals available through HathiTrust, the Internet Archive, and the Media History Digital Library. The viewing of tourism films, however, proved more challenging, given the paucity of extant film prints. Since they were produced with a specific, fleeting goal and circulated for a short period to remain timely, most were destroyed or are simply lost. Thanks to the efforts of media preservationists and archivists, who recognized the significance of these audio-visual records of Canadian culture and society, a few have been preserved at Library and Archives Canada, the Library of Congress, and several provincial archives.[56] This has enabled me to screen several of the films discussed herein.

Northern Getaway considers the content of tourism films; the specific contexts and conditions of their production, distribution, and circulation; and their cultural and institutional functions. It examines a diverse body of works, such as Canadian-themed travelogues and feature films produced within the commercial US film industry; government-produced and/or -sponsored films made within Canada; small-gauge (e.g., 16-mm) and 35-mm productions; and amateur moviemakers alongside professionals. It recognizes that these differences affected budget and financing, exhibition venues (theatrical/non-theatrical), methods of distribution and dissemination, and intended audience. Yet despite these variances in production, circulation, and exhibition, all tourism films share a common purpose – *to actuate travel*.

While *Northern Getaway* assumes a very inclusive view of tourism films and covers a large body of productions (albeit by no means exhaustive), there are some restrictions. Expedition, exploration, and mountaineering motion pictures are largely excluded, as they present adventure activities and remote locations that would challenge the average tourist. Moreover, although tourism films may contain ethnographic elements, *Northern Getaway* does not consider documentary pictures as a practice of visual anthropology. Finally, the book omits "home movies," due to their limited audience of primarily friends and family and their casual production values. It does, however, include amateur or non-professional filmmakers who engaged in cine tourism. Unlike the people who made impromptu home movies, the creators of personal tourism films engaged in months of research and pre-planning, often aided by private and/or public tourism publications or consultation with publicity bureaux. The resulting motion pictures circulated in wider non-theatrical contexts, such as film clubs and contests.

The individuals behind the scenes within this largely uncharted corpus of tourism films are typically anonymous. Except for such celebrity travelogue filmmakers as Burton Holmes or James A. FitzPatrick, the creators of most are unknown. While I have endeavoured to identify the filmmaker(s) responsible for productions, in *Northern Getaway* their purposefulness takes precedence over authorship. Since non-theatrical tourism films tended to be financed by industry or government agencies, their aesthetics and rhetoric served the specific interests of the sponsoring institution(s), as opposed to the creative or ideological intentions of the filmmaker. As Yvonne Zimmerman notes, a sponsored production contradicts "the idea of film as the work of an author, of film as art."[57] Likewise, specific details surrounding theatrical and non-theatrical spectators are frustratingly elusive. We can only speculate about how individuals engaged with the film product, resulting in a lacuna surrounding reception. Evidence regarding whether a particular tourism film encouraged travel is fragmentary, a gap that frustrated tourism boosters at the time as well.

Northern Getaway attempts to piece together the disjointed and neglected trajectory of the tourism film in Canada, and the intertwined histories of film and tourism in North America more broadly. Chapter 1 considers the emergence of Canadian tourism films during the American cinema's early and transitional periods (1896–1913). Scenics, often sponsored by railway companies and frequently accompanied by a lecture, proffered novel ways of experiencing Canada by cultivating spatial and visual perceptions that emphasized immediacy, mobility, and speed. Chapter 1 also traces the advertising and educational possibilities of Canadian tourism films in the context of changing production and exhibition practices in the film industry, the rise of the story film, and debates over shifting social values during the Progressive era. Chapter 2 explores the expansion of state involvement in filmmaking as a medium for propaganda and advertising during a wave of nationalism that coincided with and followed the First World War. Armed with psychological studies on the perceived receptivity of film spectators, government agencies commissioned and/or produced "useful films" to promote tourism while framing these productions as part of the emergent visual-education movement. In particular, it considers the CGMPB, founded 1923, and its Seeing Canada series, which promoted the nation's recreational and industrial attributes throughout the United States.

Chapter 3 centres on how the Parks Branch between the wars used film as a publicity medium to attract American tourists. The Calgary-based filmmaker William J. Oliver conveyed the parks' institutional and settler-colonial priorities, emphasizing landscapes accessible by automobiles, outdoor leisure activities, and wildlife preservation, as well as motion pictures featuring Grey Owl (né Archie Belaney). Chapter 4 looks at the establishment of the CTB in 1935 under D. Leo Dolan, alongside Hollywood studios' increased production of 35-mm tourism films of Canada in sound and/or colour. While the CTB lacked the funds to produce travelogues, the CGMPB turned more and more to 16-mm production and the robust field of non-theatrical distribution, which offered Canada a novel market for its tourism campaign.

Chapter 5 details the National Film Board (NFB's) expansion during the Second World War and its involvement in tourism promotion, born of a dire need for US dollars during the postwar currency crisis, by nurturing amateur filmmakers. It also discusses the ways in which Hollywood studios produced Canadian-themed tourism films during the war to boost morale and enhance intercultural diplomacy between the two countries. Chapter 6 demonstrates that the wartime relationship created the conditions for deeper cross-border cooperation during postwar reconstruction. Canada's ongoing shortage of US dollars and the increasingly frigid Cold War geopolitical climate precipitated the Canadian Cooperation Project, which represented the apex of nearly four decades of private-public efforts to use film to promote Canada to American tourists. *Northern Getaway* concludes with a discussion of the rise of tourism-related television programming in Canada and the retirement of D. Leo Dolan, and it provides a summary of the main arguments and themes of the book.

1

The Wonders of Canada

Film and Tourism during the Progressive Era

It was the scenic picture that gave cinematography its start.

Moving Picture World, 9 July 1910[1]

In his 1910 essay bemoaning the rising popularity of the "punk melodrama," exhibitor H.F. Hoffman praised the ongoing pull of scenic views that had dominated the first fifteen years or so of the motion-picture trade. He wrote about the "fashionable people" held captive by the offerings of such celebrity illustrated-travel lecturers as Burton Holmes and Lyman H. Howe. Even without an accompanying lecture, he noted, a program of scenics held "the undivided attention" of the audience for two hours. Theatregoers at New York City's 5,200-seat Hippodrome, for example, paid the premium price of one dollar to gaze upon "the sensible scenic picture," thus sidestepping the crass commercialism of lurid melodramas at the five- and ten-cent houses. Hoffman singled out *Wonders of Canada* (1906) as "the most talked-of picture" of the evening.[2]

The film, released by the Charles Urban Trading Company, based in London, and made available to the US market via Chicago's Kleine Optical Company, celebrates the Dominion's agricultural, industrial, and natural bounties. As Terry Ramsaye later quipped in his 1925 history of the American cinema, "If the adolescent picture patron were set on the high road to hell by the *Gaieties of Divorce* he would in turn be brought back on snowshoes by the *Wonders of Canada*."[3] Hoffman himself had exhibited the film to offset the potentially detrimental impact of sensational melodramas on the city's youth. His admiration of this seemingly lofty production, however, belies its materialist underpinnings. The American-born producer Charles Urban cobbled it together from scenes featured in his company's Living Canada series sponsored by the Canadian Pacific Railway (CPR).

The CPR, Canada's largest transportation company, had arranged with Urban's Bioscope Company of Canada to produce more than thirty motion pictures to attract investment and stimulate tourism and settlement to areas served by the railway. Between 1900 and 1902, F. Guy Bradford, Clifford Denham, and Joseph Rosenthal filmed "scenic shots" between Quebec and British Columbia for these CPR-backed productions.[4] As Denham later recalled, "The railroad scenes were taken from a flat car pushed by an engine and the others were usually picked out by Tourist Bureaus, etc., as we visited different cities in turn."[5] Though likely unbeknownst to them, spectators seeing *Wonders of Canada* were thus watching a *tourism film* – a motion picture intended to trigger or actuate recreational travel.

In discussing "What People Want," Hoffman also posited a false dichotomy between the melodrama and the scenic. The evolving film industry broadly categorized scenics, along with industrial, science, and topical films, as educational subjects to indicate instructive entertainment. While Hoffman derided exhibitors for catering "to the intelligence of an amusement loving public" with repeated showings of melodramas, the CPR had been sponsoring motion pictures that combined elements of the story film with the scenic genre, which indicates the elastic line between "non-fiction" and "fiction" in Canadian tourism films.[6] Notably, *Hiawatha, the Messiah of the Ojibway* (dir. by Joseph Rosenthal, 1903), part of the Living Canada series, was both an adaptation of Henry Wadsworth Longfellow's epic poem *The Song of Hiawatha* (1855) and a promotion for the railway's summer tours to Ontario's Upper [Great] Lakes region (i.e., Lakes Superior, Michigan, and Huron). Moreover, the same year that Hoffman penned "What People Want" (1910), the CPR contracted the Edison Manufacturing Company to produce a series of experimental films that were hybrids of the scenic and melodrama genres. This conceptual fuzziness points to the innovative ways in which early tourism films proffered new ways of seeing and experiencing Canada's heterogeneous landscapes as tourist destinations in the pre-automobile era. It also highlights the importance of Canadian tourism films within the context of debates over the function and meaning of cinema and movie-going in American culture and society. While moral reformers sought to regulate the film industry and its product, they held that scenics could delight and edify a wide-ranging demographic.

This chapter explores the various ways in which tourism stakeholders, particularly the CPR, collaborated with emergent film companies to boost travel into Canada during the American cinema's early and transitional periods, roughly 1896–1913. This timeframe coincided with the Progressive era, which spanned from the 1880s to the First World War and was characterized by the spirit of reform and a desire to impose order in the aftermath of rapid industrialization and urbanization. Stemming from proto-cinematic illustrated-travel lectures and magic-lantern shows, moving images of travel intersected with the rise of imperialism, industrialized forms of transportation, mass consumerism, and settler colonialism. Canadian tourism films were part of this "Cult of the Travelogue," that is, the demand for "interesting and instructive" motion pictures.[7] Most notably, Niagara Falls and the Canadian Rockies and Selkirks experienced tremendous growth both as film subjects and as tourism destinations, which developed out of such intertwined movements as anti-modernism, romanticism, and notions of the sublime. Other early non-fiction films focused on nature and wildlife alongside opportunities for hunting and fishing in the Maritimes and the Dominion of Newfoundland. The advent of story films and melodramas in the early 1900s would also incorporate visual and thematic elements established by the scenic genre functioning as indirect tourism promotion. Hence, Canadian tourism films were as much about educating and entertaining American audiences as about encouraging them to see the wonders of Canada for themselves.

VISUAL CULTURE AND TRAVEL

The roots of the Canadian tourism film stem from magic-lantern exhibits and illustrated-travel lectures, which often featured projected photographic views of landscapes, cityscapes, and architecture from foreign lands or destinations closer to home. The centrality of travel and visual culture, particularly scientific developments in photomechanical reproduction, arose from a catholic desire to know the world, or, as Burton Holmes often quipped, speaking from the perspective of a privileged settler colonial, "to possess the world."[8] Casting large-scale luminous images transferred to small plates of glass onto a large canvas or wall, lanternists re-created the illusion of movement through various mechanical slides or dissolving-view effects enabled by a stereopticon, a combination of two or more magic lanterns placed one above the other. Narration, special effects, and music accompanied touring exhibits – making for multi-sensory screen entertainments that offered audiences enhanced visual experiences.[9]

Lecturers carefully crafted, memorized, and rehearsed the accompanying scripts, which typically described a location, its history, and the life and customs of its peoples. Since many travel lecturers physically visited the sites represented in their shows, they frequently inserted personal anecdotes, adding an air of authenticity and authority.[10] According to the *Optical Lantern and Cinematograph Journal*, a British trade periodical, the combination of oration and visual images both informed and amused audiences, marking the illustrated-travel lecture as "a powerful factor in modern civilization." The article also recognized the genre's more pragmatic use for tourism publicity: "Fashionable pleasure resorts, which seek to draw visitors, and have publicity and advertising associations for placing the charms of their localities before the public would be well-advised if they had good sets of photographic lantern slides prepared, showing the beauties of their golf links, their hunting scenes, their local steamboats, motor cars, diagrammatic slides of their health statistics, their archaeology, their natural history, flora, fauna, geology, and general attractions from an artistic point of view."[11]

With the 1896 debut of projected motion pictures in North America, illustrated-travel lecturers quickly began to incorporate this new visual technology – either in place of or in addition to still coloured photographic slides. Burton Holmes's advertising booklet for his 1897–98 touring season boasted that he had the first motion pictures of travel ever made.[12] His camera operator/projectionist Oscar Depue interjected these films "when movement is essential to complete and vivify the impressions produced by the spoken words and colored illustrations."[13] In his talks, Holmes became the virtual tour guide, transforming his patrons, most of them from the cultural (or aspiring) elite, into fellow travellers by using the present tense and first-person plural in his narration. Rather than locating images to illuminate the show's oral components, he produced both words and images "in support of a global audiovisual conception."[14] Beyond a form of "armchair tourism," this approach potentially shaped audience members' future travel-making decisions.

A contemporary of Holmes's, Lyman H. Howe, reputedly as early as December 1896 included motion pictures in his performances, which catered to the "better classes" and/or upwardly mobile middle-class patrons. Unlike Holmes, he used existing scenics produced by such early film companies as Edison and Charles Urban. Although he neither photographed these subjects nor personally journeyed to these places, he routinely billed himself as "America's Greatest Traveller."[15] In addition to showing foreign views of such locations as Egypt, Europe, and India, he routinely featured moving pictures of North American tourist destinations, specifically the Grand Canyon, Niagara Falls, the Rockies, and Yellowstone. These were intended to both titillate and edify audiences.

During an engagement at New York's Hippodrome Theatre, for example, Howe held his audience in rapt attention with "wonderfully clever and well timed effects," which made the images seem more real. According to one film critic, "When we went to Niagara, we shivered at the icy grandeur of Winter, and felt the roll and roar of the great waters in Summer ... So, too, as the train tore through the Frazer [*sic*] River Can[y]on of the Rockies ... there were the accompanying toots and rattle of the locomotives, the tumultuous swirl of tumbled waters." Howe was doing "a great public service in dignifying the motion picture." The critics' comments point to the experience of "consuming" scenics, which cultivated spatial and visual perceptions that emphasized immediacy, speed, and mobility, as both a part and a symptom of modernity. Moreover, Howe remarked that the "educative," "entertaining," and "inspiring" program charmed a diverse audience, which speaks to the elevated status of visual representations of travel in this period. "The travel note is a safe one to strike in cosmopolitan New York," he concluded, "where all sorts and conditions of men from all parts of the world are gathered together." Howe's "high class motion photography" of tourism destinations thus advanced the motion-picture industry while the place of film culture was being contested during the Progressive era.[16]

Beyond Holmes and Howe, early audiences encountered moving images of travel in a variety of contexts, delivered by a heterogeneous group of professional and amateur presenters, which speaks to how inclusive exhibition was in this period. Constantly on the move, the most successful travel lecturers arranged to use a church or lodge hall in exchange for a percentage of the receipts, or rented an auditorium or opera house. Itinerant lecturers presented an evening's worth of refined amusement by packaging together an eclectic mix of stereopticon views and moving pictures into a meaningful program, often bolstered by illustrated songs, sometimes performed by local talent, and even live-action entertainment. These public speakers did not merely orate, but also edited and wrote material, interpreting and artfully arranging fleeting sequences of moving and still images into extended and sometimes elaborate narratives, enhanced with sound effects, musical accompaniment, and description.[17]

Most illustrated-travel lecturers were educated, experienced, prosperous white men (with the notable exceptions of such women as Bernyce Childs and Mary Schäffer), who exuded an air of authority, expertise, and privilege.[18] This aura intrigued audiences that "eschewed the world of commercial amusement not for religious reasons but because they insisted on cultural elitism."[19] This discourse of respectability and refinement contrasted with other forms of commercialized leisure, such as amusement parks, dance halls, and vaudeville houses, hinting at Progressive-era cultural divides. These latter heterosocial and consumption-based forms of mass culture challenged the Victorian cultural consensus of refinement, restraint, and "separate spheres" that excluded middle-to-upper-class women from the public realm. Reformers, predominantly middle-class Protestants, endeavoured to regulate these newfangled recreational outlets typically frequented by wage-earning urban immigrants.[20]

Reacting to these perceived threats to the dominant social order, many reformers argued that the emergence of nickelodeons (five-cent theatres, *fl.* c. 1905–15) further corrupted labouring and/or foreign-born communities, especially women and children, leading many civic leaders, politicians, and clergy members to clamour for regulation.[21] By characterizing film culture as a cheap amusement and a potentially transgressive activity, cultural elites and moral reformers attempted to control the working class and/or new immigrants as part of their expansive push to impose order and stability. To counter cinema's detractors and forestall censorship by states and municipalities, the film industry opted for gentrification, "cleaning up" film culture so that it would appeal to, or at least appease, the discriminating tastes of the middle class. This would be a multi-pronged strategy in which tourism films would play a central role.[22]

Following the surge of five-cent theatres and converted storefronts between 1905 and 1907, entrepreneurs constructed motion-picture theatres, which offered more amenities and charged higher admission prices, as part of the drive to uplift film exhibition. Exhibitors featured a rotating program of six to eight one- and two-reel films (a reel lasting roughly ten to twelve minutes). These programs included a mix of fictional narratives or story films and "educational" films (i.e., nonfiction). Even though the emergence and rapid expansion of motion-picture venues transformed film culture in the early 1900s, scenics maintained a meaningful role. Scenics served as a venerable form of entertainment and edification for cultured patrons (or those staking out elite status) while potentially elevating the masses. Both Canadian tourism interests and the American film industry recognized early on, to quote producer Charles Urban, "the value of the living picture as an educator" and promoter.[23]

MODERN TOURISM AND THE ROMANTIC SPIRIT

At a time when social and cultural elites sought to regulate film content, the privileged status of the modern tourism industry imbued scenics with prestige and cultural legitimacy. For many Americans, the allure of travel in the nineteenth century arose from their country's increasing engagement in global affairs and imperial expansion. With improvements in steamship lines, numbers of well-to-do Americans embarked on a version of the eighteenth-century British "grand tour" – an edifying, whirlwind journey through the cultural centres of Europe, the Middle East, and parts beyond.[24] Scenics, a powerful form of "visual imperialism," allowed a wider swath of their compatriots to consume these destinations at home. Moving images of travel operated in a dynamic arena "where dominant ideologies compete for attention of dominant and subordinate groups alike, where the use of the visual medium as a cultural apparatus is coded with cultural biases" surrounding class, gender, and race.[25]

Moneyed American tourists also engaged in domestic versions of the grand tour. Pilgrimages to such "sacred places" as the White Mountains of New Hampshire, Yellowstone Canyon, and Yosemite Valley expressed the rising tide of nationalist pride and American exceptionalism. An emergent middle class also began to take advantage of the expanding, increasingly affordable, and accessible US and Canadian tourism infrastructure. Rapid industrialization and the growth of corporate capitalism after the Civil War expanded the numbers of professionals and white-collar workers. The separation between work and leisure time, declining hours of labour, and increased wages provided novel opportunities for commercialized leisure and travel.[26]

Tourism stakeholders in Canada encouraged these American travellers to include such locales as the St Lawrence region, Ontario's Muskoka lakes, and the Upper Great Lakes in their journeys. Close to the US border, these were wild yet tame places where settler-colonial visitors could commune with nature and "primeval" peoples without eschewing modern conveniences.[27] The apex of the grand tour through New England, New York state, and Upper Canada/Ontario and Lower Canada/Quebec was typically a visit to Niagara Falls. Realizing its economic potential, boosters on both sides of the border marketed Niagara as a post-nuptial resort for newlyweds, fostering the notion that the cataract uniquely blended romance and passion.[28]

Although Niagara Falls, northern Ontario, and Quebec continued to be a tourist draw, emphasis gradually shifted westward to the Canadian Rockies, which extend from southwest Alberta to the Liard River in northern British Columbia, and to the Selkirks in southeast British Columbia. The completion of the transcontinental CPR in 1885 (passenger service began in June 1886), and later branch and spur lines connecting to the US system, facilitated both settlement and tourism in western Canada.[29] The Dominion deemed agricultural development of the western interior a vital enterprise, integral to the nation's future. The CPR vigorously propagandized the government's colonization policies, particularly in the prairies. Canadian agents travelled to the United States, the British Isles, and northern Europe to recruit "desirable" immigrants, chiefly farmers, agricultural labourers, and domestic servants, by highlighting the potential for success and minimizing possible hardships.[30]

In conjunction with pushing colonization, the CPR saw cultivating recreational travel as a way to help relieve its debts and assure prosperity. Economic motives and nationalist ambitions spurred development and resource exploitation and subsequently removed or constrained Indigenous communities. As per the logics of settler colonialism, the CPR, an agent of the nation-state, then re-inscribed "vanishing Indians" as tourist attractions. It frequently invoked their imagery in its publicity and in its sponsorship, together with local businesses, of the annual Banff Indian Days. Featuring mostly Stoney Nakoda performers from the nearby Morley reserve, the ethnographic festival entertained railway tourists from as early as 1887 through to its demise in the 1970s.[31]

Striving to penetrate the thriving travel market in the United States, the CPR stepped up its publicity efforts there to convince potential visitors that a trip through the Canadian west was preferable to a

European vacation or a domestic railway excursion. William Van Horne, CPR president beginning in 1888, provided free passes to prominent artists and photographers to capture the region's towering peaks and valleys, rocky chasms, hot springs, glacial rivers, and crystal-blue lakes, as well as its deluxe tourist establishments that the CPR was constructing therein.[32] In its promotional materials, the CPR thus recognized the value of visual culture to advance its own corporate interests while linking the western landscape, the railway, and the nation's settler-colonial identity. Moreover, as early as 1888, the railway began offering packaged "summer tours" and issued guidebooks with detailed instructions for tourists. US visitors quickly and consistently became the largest national group staying in CPR hotels.[33]

Certainly, the CPR had been actively developing the tourism infrastructure along the rail routes by establishing Swiss-style luxury resorts and restaurant stops. Throughout its early publicity, it emphasized the scenery of the "Canadian Alps," which resembled "fifty or sixty Switzerlands rolled into one," the recreational opportunities (e.g., fishing, mountaineering, trail riding), the cutting-edge facilities, and the curative potential of nature, particularly hydrotherapy.[34] Additionally, the rail journey became as much a part of the tourist experience as was the destination. Although faster than many other forms of transportation, as Catherine Cocks reminds us, the relatively slow pace of trains in this period "complemented and encouraged the leisurely contemplation of beautiful landscapes."[35] In contrast to the bare-bones carriages designated for emigrant passage, first-class tourists consumed Canada's moving vistas from within the CPR's well-appointed dining and observation cars.

Such intertwined movements as romanticism and anti-modernism provided the cultural foundation for tourism in Canada during the pre-automobile era. Since the mid-nineteenth century, romanticists have imbued the wilderness with deep symbolic meaning; natural landscapes were places of metaphysical regeneration and scenic grandeur that enabled intense experiences in the viewer. Anti-modernism was a reaction to rapid urbanization and mechanization and manifested itself in the therapeutic pursuit of intense physical and spiritual experiences in pre-industrial artisanship, "primitive" cultures, and natural environments. Canada's seemingly pristine landscapes countered the Progressive era's relentless drive for bureaucracy, efficiency, order, and scientific management. The concomitant perception that the wilderness was eroding due to market capitalism's unfettered expansion, with the budding tourism industry complicitous, precipitated a drive to conserve natural resources for their expressive and material value.[36]

The romantic aesthetics of the sublime (something that evokes beauty and terror) and the picturesque (a metaphor for "nature in progress") often shaped depictions of landscapes' restorative and inspirational potential. These iconographic representations turned these places into scenery – landscapes that could enhance Canada's burgeoning tourism industry and its national culture.[37] Railways, bridges, factories, hydroelectric power plants, and steamships were also drawing tourists to what David Nye terms the "technological sublime."[38] Niagara Falls is a case in point, standing not only as a natural wonder but also as an icon of progress and industry, where visitors marvelled at such manufactured triumphs as the *Maid of the Mist* ferry, steel suspension bridges, trains, the Shredded Wheat factory located on the New York side of the Niagara River, and eventually the Sir Adam Beck Generating Station, the world's largest when it opened in late 1921.[39] Likewise, the CPR (aided and abetted by the nation-state) surmounted the west's sometimes-impenetrable topography, harsh climate, and "bigness" with technology, thereby creating new ways of seeing the environment informed by mobility and its compression of time and space. A new transportation framework consisting of tunnels, climbing mountain passes, and hillside cuttings not only moved tourists through the awesome landscape but became tourist attractions themselves.[40]

CANADIAN TOURISM FILMS: FROM SCENICS TO STORY FILMS

Canadian tourism films produced during the early and transitional periods of American cinema (approximately 1890s–1914) drew from various forms of visual culture, such as lanternslides, paintings, pamphlets, photographs, and posters, which celebrated both the natural and the technological sublime. Romantic landscape painting (i.e., the "great picture" genre) and nascent marketing and publicity efforts by commercial tourism entities, particularly transportation companies, inspired the iconography of early Canadian motion pictures.[41] Yet the intense experience of cinema likely intensified audience desire for the places witnessed on screen. In particular, films of such tourism regions as Niagara Falls and the Canadian Rockies and Selkirks evinced modernism along with residual romanticism, celebrating seemingly pristine natural landscapes as an antidote to stifling urban-industrial society while touting updated tourist infrastructure.[42]

As a new technology, motion pictures helped construct modern tourist subjectivities rooted in increased access and mobility and heightened visual representation. This in turn diverted attention away from settler colonialism's elision of Indigenous peoples and cultures. Canadian tourism films privileged settler-colonial narratives of seemingly unspoiled natural landscapes integrated into a web of consumerism, industrialism, and technological change. With their emphasis on graphic verisimilitude combined with movement, they were a product and expression of modernizing society, shaping these spaces as tourist destinations and addressing settler-colonial spectators as prospective tourists.

Moving pictures did not simply project these images for spectators to admire but encouraged them to visit these locations. As *Moving Picture World* reported in 1908, "The value of advertising nowadays is recognized as much by nations and governments as by private individuals," and "The Canadian Government has shown that it does not mean to let slip any proper method of making known the advantages and resources" to the outside world.[43] The first Canadian tourism films were transnational constructions – produced, distributed, and exhibited by US or British film companies mostly to narrativize and visualize the promotional-tourism landscape of the nation-state. Initially mostly panoramic views and train films, Canadian-themed story films would by 1903 also incorporate elements of the scenic, which was valuable for both film and tourism more broadly. Tourism interests, particularly the railways, employed motion pictures to boost travel by romanticizing sublime landscapes, heralding technological progress, and celebrating the settler-colonial nation-state.

Given its lauded status as a tourist destination and its relative proximity to early filmmaking in New York and New Jersey, Niagara Falls became the "Mecca of all early motion picture cameramen."[44] Probably New York brothers Grey and Otway Latham obtained the first American moving images of the tourist landmark in 1896. That same year, Edison cameraman William Heise, accompanied in all likelihood by James White, ventured to Niagara Falls on a filming excursion. Although Heise photographed the cataract from a dozen camera positions, the results apparently did not do it justice. As a result, Edison distributed only four scenes, most notably *Niagara Falls, Gorge* (1896).[45] Described as "a panoramic picture obtained from the rear end of a swiftly moving train on the Niagara Gorge railway," the film juxtaposed the speed of transportation technology with the rushing waters of the waterfalls, whirlpools, and rapids.[46] It attempted to reconcile the location's awe-inspiring nature graphically with industrial and commercial encroachment, setting a pattern for future productions.

Between 1895 and 1935, electric trolley cars ran from Prospect Park in Niagara Falls, New York, along a gentle grade down the side of the gorge. Following the river's course, they passed the Whirlpool Rapids, the Grand Whirlpool, and the Devil's Hole before terminating in Lewiston, New York. This Great Gorge Route offered scenes "so wild, so beautiful and so new, that it seems almost beyond belief that it exists so close to civilization."[47] *Niagara Falls, Gorge* similarly not only aimed to thrill viewers but also positioned the railway as a lure in and of itself. As one commentator observed, "In this view the stone bluffs of the gorge, the telegraph poles, rail fences and the waters of the great river go rushing by with incredible swiftness, but yet plain enough for one to note everything in a general way, just as though seated in an observation car. The Whirlpool rapids are in sight one moment and lost to view the next, their whirling eddies and foam-flecked waves sparkling in the sun's rays, forming a very beautiful picture."[48] This account reinforces the site's natural and technological sublimity, as well as the power of the directed gaze from the perspective of a railway observation car (figure 1.1).

In early December 1896, Heise and White returned to the area and improved on their previous effort. Edison announced its New Niagara Falls Series in its January 1897 catalogue. "All taken on the latest and most improved clear stock," these were not to be "confounded with former negatives, which were not entirely satisfactory." Of the seven copyrighted films, three displayed perspectives of the American Falls. *American Falls from Bottom of Canadian Shore* (1896), which depicted the mist rising and gradually settling over the cascade, provided "the best general view of Niagara." The other two subjects similarly captured its organic beauty while explicitly evoking a modern tourist subjectivity. *American Falls from Above, American Side* (1896) offered a "glittering ice background and a group of photographers preparing to take pictures." The three men stand in the foreground overlooking the precipice as they gesticulate, which likely conveyed a sense of immediacy to the viewer. *American Falls from Incline Railroad* (1896) similarly conflates tourism and film spectatorship. According to the catalogue, the film "has the most popular point of view, as the

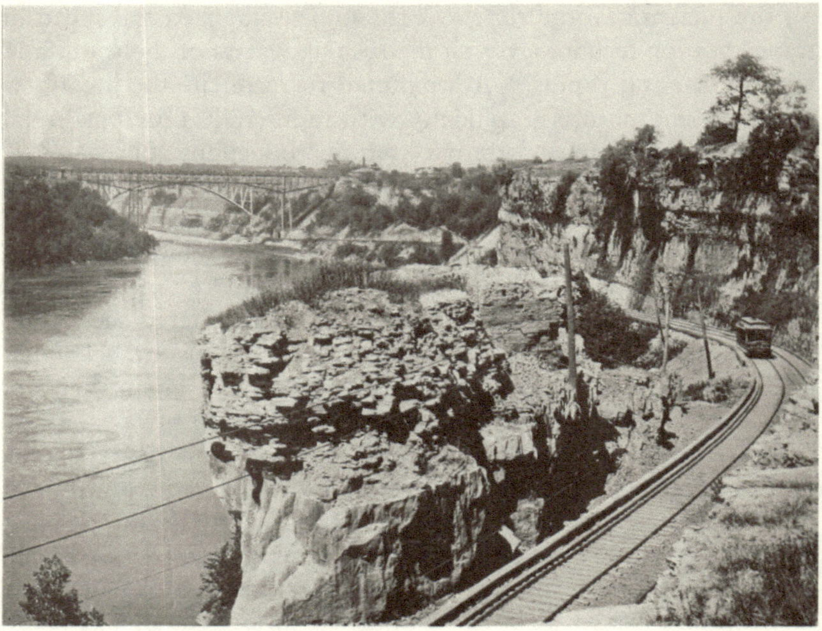

1.1 The Niagara Gorge Railroad, 1900

facilities afforded by this railroad are most convenient for the general tourist." Additionally, two moving pictures showed the Canadian Horseshoe Falls from Luna Island and Table Rock, respectively, with images of "the foaming and white-capped" waters. The remaining productions, *Rapids at Cave of the Winds* (1896) and *Whirlpool Rapids from Bottom of Canadian Shore* (1896), "the most turbulent and dangerous spot in the entire gorge," also focused on the water effects caused by the restless rapids.[49]

Over the next decade or so, Edison produced an assortment of scenics highlighting the kinetic energy of the area's aquatic features with the mobility of such technologies as cameras and railways. Many of these implemented what Edison described as "a new departure in the recording of panoramic pictures." Dubbed "circular panoramas," they used slow panning and a mobile tripod head that produced an effect resembling the large-scale painted moving panoramas of the mid-nineteenth century. For example, James White filmed *Circular Panorama of Niagara Falls* (1901) from Goat Island, "beginning with the camera pointed up the Rapids above the Horseshoe Falls, and slowly revolved from left to right until the entire Horseshoe is shown, with the Canadian shore in the background." *Circular Panorama of the American Falls* (1901) opened with "the camera pointed toward the Canadian shore" and turned slowly "from left to right until a close view of the Suspension Bridge and the whirlpool below the Falls [is] shown."[50]

In other Edison films, the camera was placed at the front end of a rapidly moving train, providing animated views from start to finish. The company boasted that *Panoramic View of the Gorge Railroad* (1901) would make a lasting impression on the audience not only due to its display of "a remarkably picturesque strip of scenery" but also because of "the combined motion of the train in one direction and the water in the opposite direction … sending beautiful masses of spray and foam many feet in the air."[51] *Panorama of Lewiston Suspension Bridge at Queenstown* starts at Queenston, Ontario, where a train car speeds across the wire suspension bridge along the American shore overlooking the Niagara River and arrives at Lewiston, "a familiar spot to all Niagara Falls tourists." Completed in 1899 to replace the original structure built in 1851–52 but destroyed by high winds in 1864, the Queenston-Lewiston Suspension Bridge spanned the Niagara River, linking the southern termini of the electric [US] Niagara Gorge Railroad with Canada's Niagara Falls Parks and River Railway. This feat of engineering enabled "the tourist to make a complete circuit of the most interesting portion of the gorge without a change of car."[52] Edison's film emphasized how both the bridge and the motion-picture camera enhanced tourist access by providing a bird's-eye perspective of the Niagara River, the rapids, and unique rock formations.

Not to be outdone, the American Mutoscope Company (known popularly as Biograph), one of Edison's main filmmaking rivals, also filmed scenics of Niagara that celebrated both the natural and the technological sublime. In the autumn of 1896, W.K.L. Dickson wedded expressive scenes of the landscape with current forms of tourist transportation.[53] Biograph promised "embracing views of the cataract from all of the more interesting points, with several turning panoramas covering the whole extent of this wonderful phenomenon of nature, from the beginning of the upper rapids, across the Canadian and American Falls and as far down as the cantilever bridge."[54] For at least one spectator, the viewing experience was transcendent: "To see Niagara taken with all its water drops in paroxysm … the rapids full of delugers outdeluged, drowners drowning, furies flying, is to arrest the heart and make science-devout the audience which came only to leer at lewdness. Gods they never feared. But knowledge in its apparitions makes them worshipers."[55]

In 1899, Biograph returned to the area to secure more tourist views. *Niagara Falls Station* (1899) "is the view which passengers have of the Falls, as they ride by on the Michigan Central trains." Audiences could also witness *Whirlpool Rapids* (1899), as "they are seen from the front of a car on the Great Gorge Road." Meanwhile, *The Approach to Niagara* (1899) was "taken from the front of a locomotive running at rapid speed near Queenstown Heights, Ontario."[56] For this film, Frederick S. Armitage and his crew mounted the camera, which, with its electric apparatus and motors, weighed several hundred pounds, on a high platform on a fast-moving locomotive car to capture the whole scenery of the Niagara River. He employed this method to obtain landscape or panoramic views intended to mimic what the rider would see from the train.

In an interview, Armitage described a harrowing episode as he filmed the gorge, rapids, and falls along the twists and turns of the Great Gorge Route "for the enjoyment of the admiring public." Apparently, when "the car struck an unusually sharp curve" it reared up, "balanced in the air for a minute and then went over on her side ... We saved ourselves by jumping off at the right time. But if that car had gone off the track at almost any of the other points where she had threatened to do so, the whole outfit would have been plunged into the rapids." Armitage took this near-death incident in stride: "To travel sixty miles an hour lashed to the pilot of an engine, sharing your narrow rest with the camera and being compelled to keep that camera in operation, is an experience of which one instalment will satisfy the ordinary man. But risks must be run where it is a question of satisfying the public's appetite for entertainment."[57]

Armitage's sensationalist account communicates the undercurrents of excitement and angst accompanying the rapid technological shifts of the transition to modernity. In his cultural history of US railways in the early nineteenth century, Wolfgang Schivelbusch demonstrates that, despite the seemingly smooth changeover to industrialized travel, "certain residues of anxiety remained." Many travellers feared train accidents or crashes.[58] Yet Armitage highlights the commercial exploitation of audiences' desire for sensory thrills. The emphasis on speed, sensationalism, and hyper-stimulus of the senses – a "barrage of powerful impressions, shocks, and jolts" – as Ben Singer contends, is characteristic of the subjective experience of modernity in that period.[59] The energetic approach of motion pictures intensified viewers' perception by stimulating the senses. Railway films re-created the feeling of travelling as a projectile – being hurtled through space at a dizzying speed. Moreover, sound effects during screenings often simulated the noises of an oncoming train, such as the ringing of bells and whistles, and the blowing of steam, which intensified the heightened presence of mind.[60]

Film historian Stephen Bottomore discusses intense audience reactions to early train films – what Russian film theorist Yuri Tsivian calls the "train effect" – when early spectators, not yet able to fully process projected moving images on a grand scale, initially experienced fear. While reports of spectators panicking at the sight of an approaching train were exaggerated, they were not entirely apocryphal.[61] The sensory overload of spectacular railway films potentially compounded this apprehension surrounding travel. Playing on this trepidation, train films could appear erratic, unstable, and even dangerous, leaving passengers/spectators vulnerable to trauma – a condition of modern life. Yet because viewers experienced the ride vicariously in the comfort and safety of a stable setting, such fears surrounding the power of modern technologies, both the railway and film, became enjoyable experiences. Railway-tourism films thus helped alter "the ways in which people negotiated their world."[62] By offering spectators a visual experience of mobility, train-centric motion pictures helped reinforce a tourist perspective.

Tourism films of Niagara both evoked and shaped modern consciousness through their emphasis on movement and the compression of time and space. While some motion pictures focused on a passing locomotive as it sliced through a still landscape, others were taken from the passenger's perspective. This transformed Niagara's visual landscape by creating kinematic panoramas of the scenery. In *Niagara Falls Station* (1899), for example, the screen's rectangular shape mimicked the window of a compartment, reproducing what Schivelbusch has called "panoramic perception."[63] Meanwhile, in *The Approach to Niagara* (1899) and *Panoramic View of the Gorge Railroad* (1901), viewers could experience Niagara from the viewpoint of the locomotive itself.

Following the immense success of *The Haverstraw Tunnel* (1897), which Biograph cameraman G.W. (Billy) Bitzer filmed from the head of the train, camera operators increasingly shot from the front of a speeding train, known as the cowcatcher, or by a camera mounted on the rear observation platform.[64] These phantom rides offered a thrilling optical perspective that differed from what a typical train passenger would see outside his or her window.[65] This highly subjective point of view and use of visual spectacle was characteristic of modernity's gestalt shift of perception. Hence, the synergy between film and train travel in depictions of Niagara Falls was both an agent and an indication of a peculiarly modern sensibility by simulating movement and confirming technical advance and progress. The early tourism film revealed the profound impact of an expanding tourism culture, technological forms of mobility, and a novel sensory-perceptual environment. Railway travel both evoked and helped shape modern consciousness. With their photographic realism and ability to project speed, movement, and images, railway films stood witness to the reorientation of space and time associated with distinctly modern modes of perception.

In addition to the filmic one-upmanship surrounding the Edison and Biograph films of Niagara, which resulted in increasingly striking views, the rival companies competed in their production of railway films of the Canadian west that similarly attempted to resolve the contradiction between nature and the machine, thus encouraging modern forms of spectatorship, defined by time–space compression, panoramic perception, and hyper-stimulating thrills. The emergence of Canadian tourism films overlapped with the heyday of transcontinental rail travel, occasioning a spate of scenics sponsored by or made in cooperation with railway companies. As Arthur Edwin Krows notes in his early history of the non-theatrical film, railway agents solicited such business and quickly learned "what films may do for them" in terms of boosting ridership.[66] Most notably, the CPR recognized that the marriage of motion pictures and locomotives provided potential tourists with access to sublime visions of Canadian tourist landscapes, ideally resulting in actual travel plans.

A product of nation-building initiatives, the CPR quickly became a leader in its use of film as a cutting-edge promotional tool to herald technological progress, mobility, and settler-colonial expansion by enabling the state to extend and consolidate through settlement and tourism along the transcontinental route. In 1898, the CPR sponsored a cinematograph lecture tour of England called "Ten Years in Manitoba," which emphasized the scenic, agricultural, and industrial advantages of the Canadian west to encourage immigration. James S. Freer, an established lecturer originally from England who had settled in Brandon, Manitoba, to farm, presented these filmic scenes of settler-colonial life. Richard A. Hardie, who debuted an Edison Vitascope in Winnipeg in 1896, probably made these films, which included *Arrival of C.P.R. Express at Winnipeg*; *Harnessing the Virgin Prairie Harvesting Scene with Train Passing*; and *Pacific and Atlantic Mail Trains* (figure 1.2).[67]

In addition to working with such British film enterprises as Charles Urban and the Hepworth Manufacturing Company, the CPR collaborated with US-based film companies to promote tourism.[68] In the autumn of 1899, it teamed up with Biograph on "a series of panoramic views taken in the Canadian Rockies over the line of the Canadian Pacific Railroad." Filmed by Billy Bitzer, these subjects maintained, according to the Biograph catalogue, "a stereoscopic quality which has occasioned the most enthusiastic praise wherever the pictures have been shown. The scenery is the most magnificent on the North American continent." Shot "as if one were riding on the cowcatcher of a locomotive running at high speed," these subjects offered spectators a thrilling ocular experience that "even tourists riding on the line are not privileged to enjoy."[69] Biograph's series whisked viewers through darkened tunnels, whipped them around sharp turns overlooking steep cliffs, and carried them over narrow bridges at a breakneck pace.

Undoubtedly, competition between Biograph and Edison drove progressively more ambitious railway films, resulting in more expeditions to Canada's western mountains, realized with the CPR's keen participation. Not to be outdone, in 1901 Edison assigned a camera operator, probably Robert K. Bonine, to shoot in the Canadian Rockies along the CPR line. Edison's catalogue proclaimed that its "series of panoramic Rocky Mountain views" were "of the highest photographic quality and unusual interest." Several of these pictures, including *Panoramic View of Kicking Horse Cañon*; *Panoramic View of Lower Kicking Horse Cañon*; and *Panoramic View of the Canadian Pacific R.R. Near Leauchoil, B.C.* were phantom rides, taken from the front of the moving train.[70]

As Biograph did with its series, Edison claimed that the striking surroundings would excite spectators, as would the high speed, sharp curves, and alpine heights. The catalogue description for *Panoramic View of Upper Kicking Horse Cañon* announced that "as a panoramic mountain picture this is the most thrilling, as the audience imagines while they are being carried along with the picture, the train will be toppled over thousands of feet into the valley below." Similarly, the summary for *Panoramic View Near Mt. Golden on the Canadian Pacific R.R.*

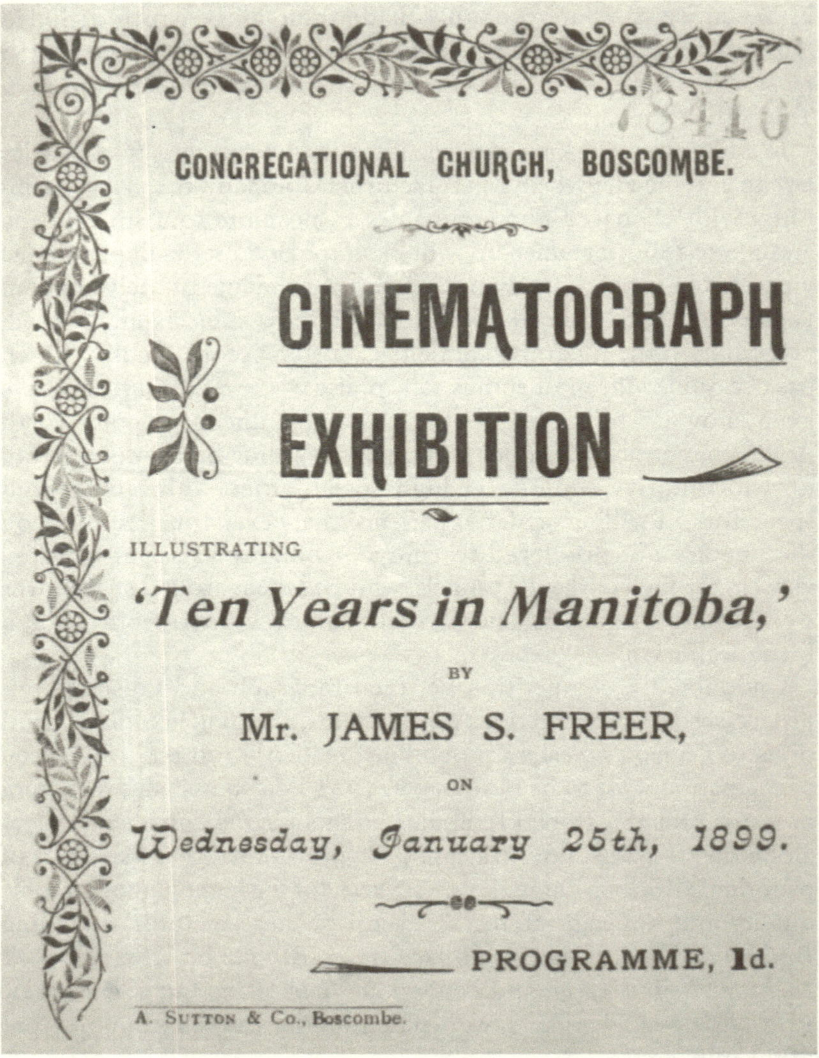

1.2 James Freer, *Congregational Church, Boscombe: Cinematograph Exhibition Illustrating Ten Years in Manitoba*, 25 January 1899

declared, "One minute you are running straight into the mountain of rock, and then when you expect to be dashed into it, suddenly turn and skirt the very side of this mountain over trestles, bridges, and finally stop where in front of you can be seen Mt. Hector at a distance of about 12 miles."[71] The Biograph and Edison films also emphasized the built environment of the railways – such elements as bridges, depots, roundhouses, tracks, and tunnels – as modern-day feats of engineering that provided access to the seemingly authentic, pre-industrial landscape.

While the phantom ride might have lost its novel effect, a new device for showing motion pictures briefly gave it a new lease on life. Between 1904 and roughly 1912, Hale's Tours, presentation sites designed to simulate the passenger car of a train, garnered considerable attention throughout North America and Europe. These multimedia presentations simulated train travel not only to such foreign destinations as China, Japan, and Switzerland, but also to Niagara Falls and the Rocky/Selkirk Mountains, with material Hale secured from existing Edison and Biograph productions. For instance, a 1906 bulletin promoting the exhibition of "attractive railroad pictures" proclaimed: "Biograph pictures are generally considered by far the most desirable for Hale Tour Cars." The ad announced "four splendid scenes on the picturesque Canadian Pacific near Banff," namely *Down Kicking Horse Slide, C.P.R.R.*; *Frazer Canon* [*sic*], *East of Yale, C.P.R.R.*; *The Gap, C.P.R.R.*; and *Under the Shadow of Mt. Stephen, C.P.R.R.*, which Billy Bitzer had filmed in 1899. Using the CPR's name, written as "C.P.R.R." (with "R.R." the US short form for "railroad"), in promotional materials indicated that the filmmakers and exhibitors recognized the tourism film as a marketing tool.[72]

These novelty movie-rides transformed motion-picture enthusiasts literally into passengers by offering a multi-sensory experience, coordinating images, mechanical movement, and sound to simulate train travel.[73] Hale's Tours offered kinaesthetic views from a commercialized tourist perspective. The camera position in a particular film would switch from showing twin ribbons of steel or iron, as seen from the front or rear of the train, to revealing to passengers/spectators the surrounding features of the landscape or tourist landmarks. Sometimes the film would cut to the car's interior to expose the parallel social interactions of train travel.[74] The motion pictures emphasized the process of travel as well as the destination(s), while the film spectators and railway passengers alike travelled within these circuits of consumption.

Hence, railway films cinematically promoted the "iron horse" as a technological agent of economic advancement, as a portent of civilization, and as the consolidator of the settler-colonial nation-state, without acknowledging that the construction of the transcontinental line helped to destroy as much as it created. As Christopher Gittings articulates, such productions presented "a colonizing narrative in which the territory of the Dominion of Canada is represented as a passive and fertile terrain" awaiting the domination of non-Indigenous settlers and travellers.[75] The railway accelerated the dispossession of Indigenous peoples, displaced local communities, affected the environment, reshaped the topographical landscape, and precipitated a series of unanticipated cultural, political, and social transformations. Although this history of destruction and conquest occupies the spaces off-screen, these tourism films ultimately reveal what Peter Limbrick describes as "the uneasy, unequal status of the settler colonial societies and empires that produce and are produced by them."[76]

Progressive-era tourism films about hunting and fishing in the Maritimes and Newfoundland (not then part of Canada) further shaped audience understandings of Canada's settler-colonial landscapes, as well as human relationships with non-human animals. In the late nineteenth and early twentieth centuries, spending time in the Canadian wilderness seemingly offered privileged groups of hunters and fishers a taste of what US President Theodore Roosevelt termed the "strenuous life," which counteracted the pitfalls of "over-civilization" and the perceived feminization of modern culture. The establishment of such magazines as *Forest and Stream* and *Rod and Reel* encouraged sporting tourism by reinforcing to a wider audience articulations of "primitive masculinity," marked by athleticism, ruggedness, and self-reliance.[77] Early wildlife films appealed largely to this middle-class, urban, and masculine tourist sensibility (or to working-class social aspirations) by constructing anti-modern encounters with the natural world informed by modern, mediated bureaucratization and commercialized recreation. Wildlife-tourism films "faithfully" represented nature and non-human animals while masking filmic construction by author and editor. According to Greg Mitman, the tension between authenticity and artifice lies at the heart of wildlife pictures.[78]

Although these films evolved into a separate genre, with its own codes, conventions, and rules, the line between scenics and wildlife pictures was blurry, as both promoted the centrality of nature tourism in Canada's national identity.[79] For instance, in 1906 Biograph produced a series of nature-tourism films for a sportsmen's show in Boston put on by the New England Forest, Fish, and Game Association. Billy Bitzer's *Moose Hunt in New Brunswick* (1906) opens on the platform at the Union railway station in Portland, Maine, as a party of sharply dressed male hunters board the Bull Moose Special bound for Saint

John, New Brunswick. A picturesque jaunt on the railway is followed by a trek by horse and wagon to the moose-hunting grounds. The *Boston Herald* remarked that the film demonstrated "the uniqueness of the road" and the "general character of the country," as much about the railway journey as about hunting – not surprising, given that Harrie B. Coe of the Maine Central Railroad was a member of the group.[80]

Biograph later released a similar picture showing a hunting party that departs Portland, Maine, for Millertown, Newfoundland, where it is met by local guides. *A Caribou Hunt* (1907) depicts "real camp life in the wilderness," followed by the pursuit and taking of several caribou.[81]

Moose Hunt in New Brunswick and *A Caribou Hunt* demonstrate the interconnectedness of the film and tourism industries and their shared commercial interests in the wilderness, as well as the impact of centralized wildlife conservation and modern resource management. Depicting seemingly abundant fish and wild game, attentive and knowledgeable guides, and an efficient transportation network, these nature-tourism films upheld the two dominions' reputation as a paradise for elite cross-border hunters and anglers in need of reinvigoration.[82]

While probably not intending to address the era's environmental debates, these "educational" productions embraced the Progressive era's conservationist and preservationist ethos. Fearing that rapid industrialization and urbanization were depleting North America's natural resources, conservationists advocated the scientific management of wildlife, forests, and the land for their economic value and efficient use by future generations. Preservationists sought to protect the wilderness from further industrial encroachment. Both the United States and Canada tightened federal control over wildlife and fish stocks. Restrictive game and fish laws, along with the expropriation of land to create national parks and game preserves, favoured bourgeois hunters and sport fishing over local subsistence trappers and fishers and pushed Indigenous communities out of their traditional hunting and fishing grounds. Indigenous and settler-colonial backwoodsmen subsequently became guides in the new tourist economy, offering elite sportsmen their wilderness skills and other essential services, such as paddling, portaging, cooking, and setting up camp.[83]

By the time that Biograph released these productions in 1906, filmmakers had been increasingly using motion pictures to relate fictional narratives. Scenics and other "educational" pictures were not, however, relegated to the dustbin of film history. Trade journals consistently emphasized that patrons, including "tired businessmen," children, and small-town audiences, loved travelogues.[84] Industry champions of scenics seemed careful not to appear to be imposing pedagogical motion pictures on passive and uncritical theatregoers. According to Frederic J. Haskin, filmgoers continued to "demand travel scenes. They must be had, and they must be filled with adventure and perhaps have a bit of romance tucked in between – for ever since time began all the world has loved the lover and sympathized with him in his joys and sorrows."[85]

Nevertheless, as Haskin's remarks insinuate, the boundary between fiction and non-fiction was far from rigid. Scenics frequently injected fictionalized elements of romance and adventure, as well as humour, pathos, and anthropomorphized wildlife, while Canadian-themed story films integrated elements of the travelogue. In other words, just as scenics deployed narrative devices and staged scenes to construct meaning, story films relayed aspects of the landscape, along with its recreational advantages, which marked Canada as an appealing tourist destination. Therefore the industry-wide rise of storytelling films in 1903–04, which altered production and exhibition practices, did not signal the demise of the travelogue but rather continued to shape the contours of film culture.[86]

Hiawatha, the Messiah of the Ojibway (1903), part of the Charles Urban Company's Living Canada series, illustrates this conflation between fiction and non-fiction characteristic of many Canadian tourism films. In his seminal history of cinema in Canada up to 1939, Peter Morris identifies *Hiawatha* as the country's first narrative film.[87] The fifteen-minute work, which documents the annual "Indian Passion Play" performed by the Garden River First Nation in Desbarats, Ontario (fifty-four kilometres east of Sault Ste Marie), is more closely akin to a pseudo-ethnographic scenic. In an eastern counterpart to Banff Indian Days, each summer between 1901 and 1918 the CPR sponsored the pageant for settler tourists. Based on Longfellow's fictional account of the "vanishing" culture of the Lake Superior Ojibwa, the play also toured major cities in the United States and Europe. Although Anishinaabe men and women were performing Indianness for paying settler-colonial spectators, they "claimed the stage at least in part as a space of their own shaping" in subtle "assertions of indigenous language, song, drum, and humor" at a time when government policies had forbidden public displays of their culture (figure 1.3).[88]

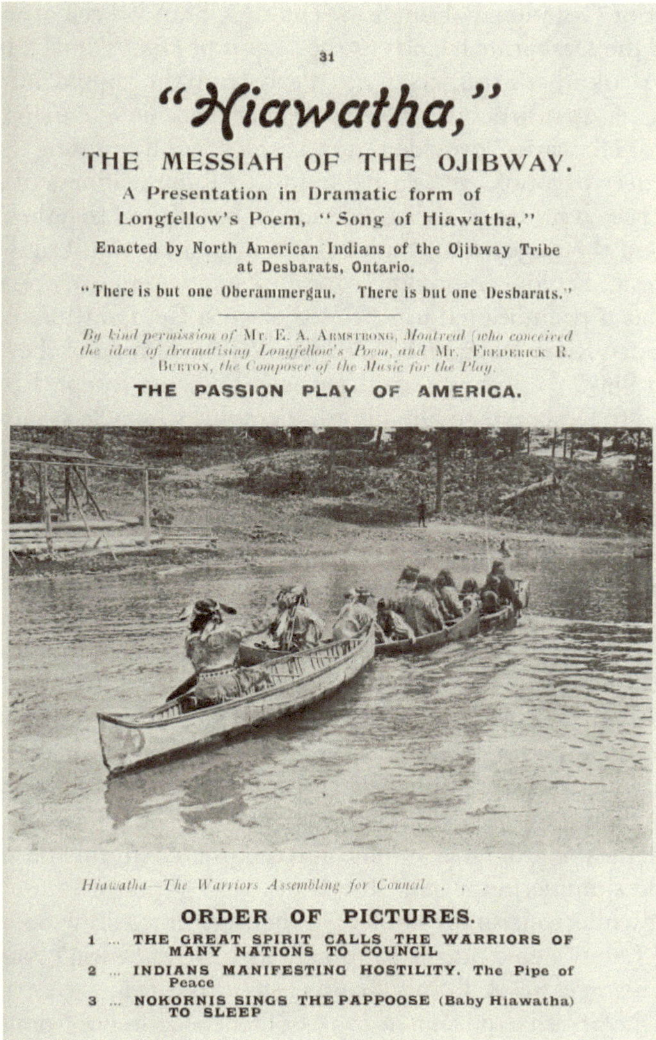

31

"Hiawatha,"

THE MESSIAH OF THE OJIBWAY.

A Presentation in Dramatic form of Longfellow's Poem, "Song of Hiawatha,"

Enacted by North American Indians of the Ojibway Tribe at Desbarats, Ontario.

"There is but one Oberammergau. There is but one Desbarats."

By kind permission of Mr. E. A. Armstrong, *Montreal (who conceived the idea of dramatising Longfellow's Poem, and* Mr. Frederick R. Burton, *the Composer of the Music for the Play.*

THE PASSION PLAY OF AMERICA.

Hiawatha—The Warriors Assembling for Council . . .

ORDER OF PICTURES.

1 ... THE GREAT SPIRIT CALLS THE WARRIORS OF MANY NATIONS TO COUNCIL

2 ... INDIANS MANIFESTING HOSTILITY. The Pipe of Peace

3 ... NOKORNIS SINGS THE PAPPOOSE (Baby Hiawatha) TO SLEEP

1.3 *Hiawatha, the Messiah of the Ojibway*, 1903

The CPR, as Fenn Stewart argues, had employed Hiawatha as a "racial shorthand" to convey northern Ontario's "wildness" and "Indianness."[89] In addition to the pageant, the railway company based its advertising campaign largely around Longfellow's cultural appropriation of the Anishinaabe, who had been physically removed from the land and then symbolically re-inscribed as a national myth in the context of Canadian colonialism. The CPR branded the area in and around the Desbarats Islands as the "Land of Hiawatha," a popular summer colony for tourists, particularly from the United States. For instance, a CPR brochure advertised that a scenic excursion to the "Land of Hiawatha" provided "good fishing, good shooting ... exquisite scenery of a bold and varied kind ... All the wildness of Nature and all the comforts of civilization are to be enjoyed together."[90]

Beyond the pageant and textual publicity material, Louis Oliver Armstrong, a colonization officer for the CPR, was an early proponent of film as a promotional tool. Together with George Kabaosa from the Garden River Reserve, he spearheaded the filming of the "Indian Passion Play" to promote local tourism. Director Joseph Rosenthal travelled to Desbarats to film the ethnographic spectacle as part of the CPR-sponsored Living Canada series. Although there is no complete extant copy, it appears that the production unfolds as a series of twenty animated tableaux rather than a coherent narrative. The Charles Urban catalogue's detailed summary emphasizes the authenticity of Indigenous performances, characteristic of ethnographic films. Describing the festivities after Hiawatha and Minnehaha wed, the synopsis states: "There is no stage manager, no cue is sounded, but one part follows another with the utmost ease and naturalness." Given the film company's background in producing "educational" films, this account unsurprisingly emphasizes the verisimilitude of the natural surroundings over its fictional elements: "The picture stamps indelibly upon the mind of every beholder, a perpetual memory, odorous with the unnameable fragrance of pine and cedar and balsam and shelving rock and shimmering water."[91]

Meanwhile, tourism promoters in the Maritimes drew on another of Longfellow's epic poems to romanticize Nova Scotia's Annapolis Valley. *Evangeline: A Tale of Acadie* (1847) is a tragic love story set against the British expulsion in 1755 of French Catholics from Acadia, mythologized as a pastoral, pre-industrial, and picturesque land populated by simple folk.[92] Longfellow's invented A[r]cadia, as Ian MacKay and Robin Bates explain, brought about "the wholesale reorganization of an actual landscape in order to make it conform to a bestselling historical romance."[93] By 1900, the Dominion Atlantic Railway and the Yarmouth Steamship Company were marketing Grand Pré, the heroine's village, and its surroundings as the "Land of Evangeline" – a quaint destination for middle-class New Englanders seeking to avoid cramped resorts closer to home.[94]

The Land of Evangeline inspired multiple scenic-story hybrid films. Progressive-era film companies recognized that adapting such notable works of fiction could raise cinema's cultural legitimacy, assuage moral reformers, engage a middle-class clientele, and increase profits. Moreover, audience familiarity with such a well-known story could help the creators construct narrative coherence during the American cinema's transitional period.[95] With its vaguely historical framework and picturesque scenery, *Evangeline* appropriated the conventions of the tourism film and the film industry's discourse of uplift.[96] For instance, in 1907 Biograph produced *An Acadian (Arcadian) Elopement: A Romance in the Land of Evangeline*, a one-reel (715 feet) romantic comedy, in which a New Yorker vacationing in Nova Scotia "wins the heart of a pretty Quaker maiden" and persuades her to elope. Their honeymoon provides a loose narrative for what is essentially a scenic. The couple travel by railway, eat clam chowder at a restaurant, and visit a beach "where a novel scene is shown of natives opening clams for the market." They then meander along "Lover's Lane … through which no doubt the beautiful Evangeline strolled in the Summer twilight with her gallant Gabriel." Although *Elopement* was filmed probably in New England, promotional materials characterized Nova Scotia as a pleasing playground for American tourists. "Lovers of Longfellow," exclaimed the Biograph bulletin, "are here transported to the beautiful scenes so dear to him, the Normandie of the New World with its blossomy fields, and lanes shaded with masses of pendulous foliage, colored with ephemeral clusters of wild flowers."[97]

A year later, the New York–based Kalem Company released an adaptation of Longfellow's poem as "told in pictures" – "a splendid specialty for Sunday shows." It offered exhibitors an optional, accompanying "lecturette" – a descriptive script like those developed by illustrated-travel lecturers for showing scenics, indicating the blurry line between scenics and story pictures in Canadian tourism films.[98] Subsequently, Kalem released other Canadian-themed story films that drew from the deep-rooted scenic tradition. Unlike most film companies, which shot outdoor pictures in the Fort Lee–Coytesville area of New Jersey, Kalem, during the summer of 1909, sent to Canada a stock company supervised by Toronto-born director Sidney Olcott "in search of the picturesque."[99] *Moving Picture World* praised Kalem's "decided leaning toward Canadian themes," stating that "the scenic embellishments" of its upcoming releases "are particularly beautiful and the Canadian scenes full of primitive splendor."[100]

Other story films took place in Niagara Falls, where honeymoon trips serve as a pretext for tourism promotion.[101] In Edison's *The Honeymoon at Niagara Falls* (dir. by Edwin S. Porter, 1906), the camera follows a bridal couple "in their explorations of the American and Canadian sides." *Variety* averred that the scenes were "interesting," but also "instructive," and "should prove a drawing card, especially with a 'matinee house.'"[102] Edison also offered to sell the 1,000-foot film in its entirety, or each of the eight scenes individually, to make its "beautiful scenery combined with comedy" available for various exhibition settings and suitable for tourism advocacy.[103] Thanhouser's *A Niagara Honeymoon* (1912) similarly constructs its narrational elements to highlight various views of the great cataract. Promotional pieces boasted that this "scenic gem" took the spectator "to every point of the famous Falls," where "the situations are worked out in the localities that citizens of every nation pay large money to see. From far and wide they come to look at Niagara Falls, and far and wide they will welcome heartily the best moving picture ever taken there."[104]

While tourism promotion in these scenic-story films was largely secondary to landscape and leisure opportunities, in 1910 the CPR sponsored an experimental series of melodramas to underscore western Canada's agricultural and scenic advantages, probably in response to the boom in recreational travel in the American west, as boosters positioned domestic tourism as an expression of national citizenship and republicanism. In 1910, the Great Northern Railway (GNR) adopted the "See America First" slogan in promoting Glacier National Park in the Montana–Alberta borderlands along the railway's Minneapolis– Seattle trunk line.[105] As the GNR endeavoured to keep tourists within US borders, the CPR aspired to lure them north. It is plausible that the GNR's advertising strategy, which equated travel to Glacier National Park as an act of patriotism rather than consumerism, spurned the CPR to produce a new type of scenic-melodrama hybrid to sell the Canadian west.[106]

The CPR, at the behest of J.S. (John Stoughton) Dennis, an engineer who headed its irrigation department in Calgary, contracted Edison to produce a film series to secure "pictures of typical Canadian scenery" and shoot "against these Canadian backgrounds typical Canadian stories, especially prepared."[107] Accordingly, Edison supplied one of its stock companies, including the husband-and-wife acting team of Herbert Prior and Mabel Trunnelle, camera operator Henry Cronjager, and director J. Searle Dawley. Although the level of CPR involvement in devising the film synopses is unclear, it supplied a special train, a steamship, mountain guides, and first-class accommodations.[108]

According to Norman S. Rankin, a Calgary-based publicity agent for the railway, the rationale for this shrewd venture was that "the great mass of the public who nightly attend the moving picture halls want to be amused and entertained, not instructed, and if they are to be educated it must be in a subtle, delicate manner, absorbed, as it were, unconsciously, through the interest that the story itself creates in the minds of the audience."[109] This notion of the unconscious indicates an awareness of what American cultural historian T.J. Jackson Lears calls "suggestion psychology," which was popular in advertising circles prior to the First World War.[110] Influenced by the writings of psychologist Walter Dill Scott, the relatively new advertising and marketing industries turned to psychology, believing that an appeal to the consumer's emotions was more effective than trying to convince the logical mind.[111] With its emphasis on pathos, overwrought emotion, moral polarization, and sensationalism, melodrama seemed an ideal vehicle to evoke an emotional response in spectators as consumers/tourists.[112]

Beginning in June 1910, Dawley and company filmed for two months between Montreal and Victoria. These thirteen one-reel films – three "educational" productions and ten scenic-melodrama hybrids – aimed to promote tourism and colonization. The three "nonfiction" efforts vary in theme and location. *A Trip over the Rocky and Selkirk Mountains in Canada* (dir. by J. Searle Dawley, 1910) "represents artistically the glories of the Rockies" and "gives a good idea of what scenic wonders present themselves to the eye of the traveler."[113] *The Life of a Salmon* (dir. by J. Searle Dawley, 1910) is at once a science film, an industrial subject, and a scenic. It opens in Capilano Canyon (North Vancouver) and focuses on the life stages of salmon, the trapping of the silver horde on the Fraser River, and the delivery of fish to the cannery for processing. The conclusion features a canoe race in Victoria's inner harbour crewed by Indigenous peoples (likely Coast Salish) employed at the canneries, while a group of settler colonials cheers them on. The backdrop is the château-style Empress Hotel, which the CPR opened in 1908 as part of its commitment to provide top-quality tourist accommodations. The Empress quickly became a landmark for the city, a sort of symbolic crossroads for the British Empire, as well as a towering reminder of the ongoing colonization of First Nations territory.[114]

Finally, *A Wedding Trip from Montreal through Canada to Hong Kong* (dir. by J. Searle Dawley, 1910) promoted the CPR's diverse operations: its impressive Windsor Station in downtown Montreal; its deluxe passenger rail cars; the Hot Sulphur Swimming Pool at its spectacular Banff Springs Hotel; and the majestic RMS *Empress of India*, one of its three ocean liners, heading to Hong Kong. These tourist locations provide a setting for the amusing mishaps that befall fictional newlyweds "Dearie" and "Lovey." As the film combines elements of the scenic and comedy genres, the interest of the audience is "divided between the ludicrous actions of the pair and the magnificent scenery along the way." For at least one observer, however, the film's fuzzy categories proved frustrating. "It was not a dramatic, not a comedy, not a scenic, not an industrial, not even an entertaining picture," wrote J.M.B. from Chicago.[115]

The other ten productions in Edison's series were melodramas that more successfully synthesized the scenic's conventions to create inventive storytelling, which promoted Canada for tourism and settlement. Edison called *An Unselfish Love: A Story of Western Canada* (dir. by J. Searle Dawley, 1910) "the first of [its] long expected Canadian pictures," produced with the CPR's cooperation. Set in Strathmore, a railway boomtown, the film highlights southern Alberta's up-to-date agricultural practices. With scenes showing "ploughing with a threshing engine" and "ditch irrigation," it affords "a clear impression of the development now in progress there."[116] Hearing of western Canada's wonderful opportunities, an American named John boards a train bound for Alberta to seek his fortune. This occurs after the father of the girl he loves (Mabel) refuses her hand in marriage because he's poor. John secures a tract of irrigated farmland, and quickly prospers. He and Mabel are reunited at the conclusion. Therefore, just as John has integrated himself into the prairies, *An Unselfish Love* seamlessly knits together melodramatic and promotional elements into a coherent storytelling whole. "We desire to put on record the very effective use which the Canadian Pacific Railroad [*sic*] is making of the moving picture," observed *Moving Picture World*. In addition to telling "a strong, interesting, dramatic story," the Edison film "gives a clear idea of the marvellous farming possibilities of that country." The "educational value of the picture" ultimately strengthened "the attraction" of the narrative (figure 1.4).[117]

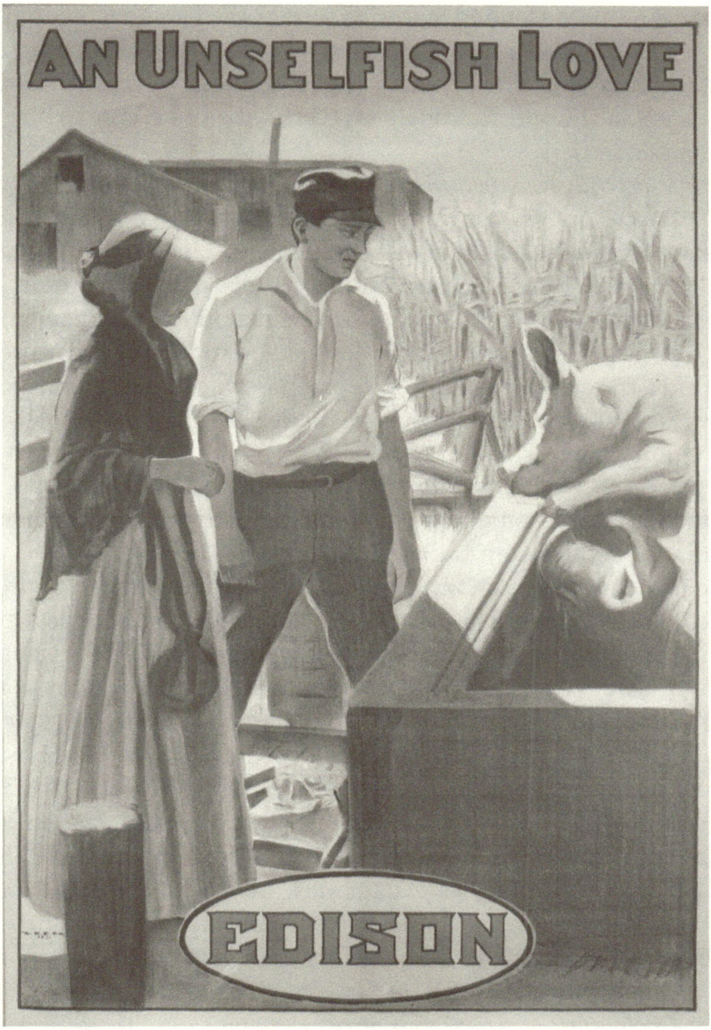

1.4 Edison Manufacturing Co. advertisement, 1910

An Unselfish Love makes clear that John succeeds because farming in the region advanced after the CPR in 1905 completed major irrigation projects, which had opened the area to massive, non-Indigenous settlement. John's fictional achievement, in turn, represents the success of the nation-state's colonizing project in the Canadian west. Certainly, in the wake of Edison's release of the production, settlers flooded in, primarily from the United States, as well as the United Kingdom. The year 1910–11 saw a peak in sales of tickets to Strathmore, and the CPR built two extra passing tracks to cope. By 1912, nearly all CPR lands in the surrounding area were sold and colonized by non-Indigenous settlers.[118]

The Song that Reached his Heart: A Story of the Lumber Regions of Western Canada (dir. by J. Searle Dawley, 1910) more candidly appeals to a tourist sensibility by framing the Canadian Pacific northwest as a space of regeneration to recuperate from urbanized life in the east. Mabel Trunnelle plays Miss Bennett, a neuraesthenic singer who travels to British Columbia via the CPR for her health, probably to demonstrate to potential female rail passengers that women could easily travel alone safely.[119] Upon her arrival, Bennett reforms a rough-hewn lumberman who had once been her childhood sweetheart. The film positions a settler woman as the harbinger of civilization, who heralded the last, triumphant phase of interlaced processes of tourism, colonialism, and nation-building in western Canada.[120]

Two other CPR-Edison melodramas, *The Little Station Agent* (dir. by J. Searle Dawley, 1910) and *The Swiss Guide* (dir. by J. Searle Dawley, 1910), take place "in that region of grandeur and beauty, the Canadian Rockies." According to reviewers, the alpine setting functions as more than a simple milieu for staging the action; it provides a conspicuous visual experience that nearly overshadows the narrative elements. The "complicated love story" in *The Swiss Guide*, for instance, "will scarcely attract more attention than the scenery. The artistic service performed by this company in this direction is by no means slight. To be able to produce hundreds of miles distant such accurate representations of mountain scenery is an achievement of which any firm may be proud." As a scenic-melodrama hybrid, the film's authentic scenic components thus contrast with the artificiality of its melodramatic elements.[121]

The Little Station Agent similarly takes place in "the grandeur of the Canadian Rockies."[122] Trunnelle plays the lone operator of a secluded railway depot whose quick thinking saves a runaway train with hundreds of people on board, including her sweetheart, from running off a mountain slope. As Shelagh J. Squire shows, a gendered workforce was essential to the CPR tourism infrastructure. These female employees destabilized traditional gender identities without challenging the patriarchal order. Trunnelle's unnamed character embodies this Progressive-era "new woman" that contrasted with the Victorian-era "cult of womanhood," which had exalted piety and domesticity.[123] *Moving Picture World* reinforced this discourse, remarking that Trunnelle not only capers about "as occasion demands with great agility," but also "does not mind getting thoroughly wet through on a Canadian snow field in the course of a picture drama."[124]

Trunnelle's robust performance in *The Little Station Agent*, as well as the other CPR-Edison films, presaged such serial queens as Pearl White and Helen Holmes. Producers targeted these action-fuelled melodramas largely to women, a demographic coveted by the era's film industry. American cinema's cultural legitimacy, as Shelley Stamp demonstrates, was often "yoked with the industry's campaign to build its female audience, since women, middle-class women in particular, embodied the same respectability tradesmen sought for motion pictures: social propriety, refined manners, and impeccable taste."[125] By setting Trunnelle's daring escapades in the breathtaking Canadian Rockies, these CPR-Edison films could appeal to the perceived desires of female filmgoers while addressing them as prospective tourists.

Arguably, *The Little Station Agent*'s thrills, action, and stirring sense of peril might undermine its potency as a tourist ad. Despite the success of the heroine's herculean efforts, the "imminent danger of wrecking a fast train with hundreds of people on board" could heighten anxieties regarding CPR travel. The associate editor of *Motography* calls it "no small feat to induce a great railroad company to place its tracks and box-cars at the disposal of a photoplay producer in order that he might create sensational entertainment for distant multitudes. Three box-cars running wild down a mountain slope with the hero lying insensible on top! Whew!"[126] While this depiction could discourage people from visiting or settling in the region, the danger was part of the melodramatic mode, and probably appealed to the potential tourist/spectator's sense of adventure.

Likewise, *Riders of the Plains* (dir. by J. Searle Dawley, 1910) and *More Than His Duty* (dir. by J. Searle Dawley, 1910) conceivably stimulated audiences by portraying the Canadian northwest as rife with crime. Although this may seem puzzling in a series promoting tourism and colonization, in each production the Royal North-West Mounted Police (RNWMP), or Mounties, impose law and order in a spectacular show of (settler male) state authority, making the west safe for colonization and/or tourism.[127] Moreover, in marketing these Mountie melodramas, Edison emphasized the CPR's ultimate goal of showcasing the sublime landscape. For example, an advertisement for *More Than His Duty* proclaims it to be "a gripping story, taken at the posts of the

Royal Mounted, *scenically* beautiful and dealing with the finest and best disciplined body of men in the world."[128] *Moving Picture World* also remarked on the film's deft alchemy of story and scenery:

> Scenically it is beautiful beyond description, opening a region little known in this portion of the world and therefore arousing unusual interest ... The scenery forms a magnificent background and has been selected with an artist's appreciation of the most suitable points from which to make the exposures. Introducing and illustrating the heroism of this magnificent body of men produced in the actual setting where they do their work, the picture is in a different class from 'the usual thing' and one which attracts through its dramatic, photographic and educational qualities.[129]

In keeping with the goal of promoting tourism and settlement, the Edison-CPR melodramas emphasize the overcoming of obstacles and adversity. In an article in *Man-to-Man*, a monthly dedicated to western Canada, CPR publicity agent Norman Rankin explains that the pictures show "the struggling farmer ... the premium that Western Canada offers for home-making and independence"; the cowboy becoming a prosperous "cattle king" after "many hair-breadth escapes"; the hunter stalking a treacherous grizzly before bringing him "to earth at last"; or the mountaineer making his perilous way up the slope to the summit. The films, "illustrated with the most picturesque and appropriate scenery," ultimately demonstrate to "the piscatorial enthusiast," to "the sportsman and hunter," to "the Alpine climber," and to "the tourist and traveller the beauties of mountain, wood and valley, prairie, crag and torrent, and the comfort and luxury of modern hotel, train, boat, and steamer."[130]

Ergo the CPR-Edison scenic-melodramas occupied a complex space in-between the actual (albeit-constructed) tourist landscape and the diegetic world occupied by the story's characters and events. This experiment met, if not exceeded, expectations. In a full-page article previewing the series, *Moving Picture World* praises the filmmakers' weaving together "fidelity to nature," "local color," "territorial idiosyncrasies," and "pictorial excellence" to create relatable and original stories that also functioned as effective tourism advertisements: "To our wonderment and surprise, are the beautiful Canadian Alps which seem to vie in scenic splendour with the Swiss and Austrian

Alps. You have lofty snow mountains, great snow fields, glaciers, crevasses, Swiss-looking chalets, Swiss guides and beautiful hotels. You can have all the Alpine adventure that you want in Canada. You can recover from consumption [tuberculosis] there ... So why go to Europe to do these things?" If the common purpose of these "splendid" views was to "show the moving picture public throughout the world what a wonderful place this young Canada is ... we shouldn't be a bit surprised if these beautiful pictures did not largely attract immigrants from the United States into Canada; a process that is going on all the time and will largely ... bring about some interesting political developments."[131] Therefore, the overarching goal of branding Canada as a northern getaway seamlessly circulated across each motion picture. Blurring the lines between promotion and the fictional narrative, the series compelled spectators to imagine themselves as tourists or settlers, ideally propelling them to plan an actual trip or a permanent move.

The advent of Canadian tourism films at the turn of the twentieth century relied on a confluence of interrelated cultural, historical, and social phenomena connected to consumerism, modernization, and settler colonialism during the pre-automobile era. A climate of one-upmanship also played a role; the rivalry between such trailblazers as Edison and Biograph resulted in novel views of the Dominion's tourist landmarks, specifically Niagara Falls and the Rockies/Selkirks. These scenics visually fused the natural and technological sublime while offering Progressive-era audiences what we would describe today as edutainment. The film industry ventured that the scenic genre's professed ability to inform and entertain would raise the industry's profile. Moreover, the comfort and convenience of increasingly gentrified exhibition venues allayed any residual anxieties about industrialized travel or traumas associated with the transition to modernity. Fundamentally, the combined effect of these touristic and filmic discourses operated within a complex settler-colonial discourse of nation-building and offered spectators modern experiences of travel and mobility.

Although film companies continued to produce and exhibit travelogues on a large scale until the 1950s, after 1903–04 they increasingly used motion pictures to relate fictional narratives. Regional tourism destinations, including the "Land of Hiawatha" and the "Land of Evangeline," provided enticing settings for story films, thereby helping to establish the early stages of their destination brands. Meanwhile, scenics integrated narrative devices to produce emotional responses that could potentially stimulate travel – this at a time when filmmakers, through trial and error, worked towards arranging storytelling elements into a reliable cinematic language. They wove into scenics such staged comedic and dramatic elements as amorous shenanigans during a Canadian honeymoon or the suspense of the chase and pathos of the kill in a hunting picture. By 1910, the Edison-CPR series would push the boundaries of the scenic and melodrama by experimenting with various narrative and aesthetic forms to spark the spectators' imagination and shape the modern tourist consciousness.

Ultimately, J.S. Dennis, who ran the CPR's irrigation department, was astute in proposing a collaboration with Edison to produce a series of scenic-melodramas that would represent the "very highest class of advertising" for tourism to Canada.[132] As motion-picture journalist Ernest A. Dench would aver in his 1916 guidebook on advertising through film, that medium represented the ideal way for railway companies to advertise their lines for vacations. While printed matter "appeals to the brain," the business of tourism "demands that the mental strain be non-existent." Potential travellers are "more than likely to throw your expensive literature away unused when you expect them to use their brains to imagine things. With motion pictures you don't have to – everything is taken in by the eyes."[133] By this time, the Canadian government was ready to embark on a more formalized approach to engaging filmgoers as prospective tourists through the "eye gate."

2

Through the "Eye Gate"

The Emergence of Government-Sponsored/ Produced Canadian Tourism Films

As a perceiver, the sense of sight is worth nearly seven times as much as all the other senses combined.

Reel and Slide, March 1918[1]

In an article touting visual teaching aids as a practical and efficient method of instruction, Morton A. Bassett argues that "experimental psychologists" consider sight the most retentive of all the senses. Moving images excel in their ability to hold the viewer's attention and create "mental pictures."[2] Throughout the Progressive era, the film industry had similarly heralded scenics as conducive to learning to counter detractors who labelled cinema a cheap amusement. As an exhibitor from Chicago claimed, "The biograph is doing more to educate the lower classes in art, travel and history than any other agency before the public."[3] Likewise, the advertising industry increasingly accepted the idea that people retained more from moving images than from words, thus fostering a mindset conducive to consumption. Business organizations seized upon film as a media delivery mechanism to make clear and lasting impressions. According to Jack W. Speare, advertising manager of the Todd Protectograph Company, film is "the one medium that is indelible, that sinks in so deep that it can never be entirely erased from memory."[4] Building on these intersecting theories, by the end of the First World War, the Canadian government would also fully embrace motion pictures as an effective publicity agent to promote tourism.

Since about 1900, scenics and later story films had offered new ways of seeing Canada as a tourist destination. These were produced by film companies based outside the Dominion. Following a series of "made in Canada" films released 1912–14, the outbreak of war in August 1914 precipitated greater state involvement, buoyed by a wave of nationalism. This narrative of the war and its aftermath as a crossroads for Canada's film industry is a familiar one. As Peter Morris and others demonstrate, during this period Canadians left behind aspirations of a domestic feature-film industry and surrendered to the consolidating Hollywood studio system as the primary purveyor of filmic entertainment. Instead, the Dominion focused on producing instructional films distributed largely through non-theatrical circuits.[5] While Canada apparently eschewed commercialism in favour of pedagogy, the spate of government-sponsored and/or -produced tourism films indicates a concurrent commitment to advertising through film.

The state's role in generating tourism films intertwined with the overlapping spheres of visual education, cinematographic advertising, and wartime propaganda. In 1918, the Dominion government created the Exhibits and Publicity Bureau within its Department of Trade and Commerce to promote Canada, particularly by producing motion pictures. Re-organized in 1923 as the Canadian Government Motion Picture Bureau (CGMPB), the agency publicized the nation's recreational attributes and its industry and manufacturing until the National Film Board (NFB) absorbed it in 1941. State-sponsored motion pictures repurposed First World War propaganda techniques to brand Canada in ways believed to be enticing to American tourists.

Inspired by the relatively new field of visual education, many economic, political, and social leaders came to grasp the tremendous influence and efficacy of moving images vis-à-vis learning and retention. Building on Progressive-era efforts by educators and social reformers to teach through film, the visual-instruction movement, as editor Nelson L. Greene explained in the inaugural 1922 issue of the *Educational Screen*, sought "to broaden and deepen … education in school, church, club and community center" through motion pictures.[6] Meanwhile, proponents of cinematographic advertising celebrated film as a superior medium to sell everything from "farming machinery" to "an expensive travel tour."[7] Government officials speculated that viewing their tourism films would actuate vacation travel. Yet, by not appearing as blatant commercials, these productions avoided potentially alienating viewers. Government-produced scenics straddled the interconnected categories of educational films and screen advertising within the conceptual framework of what Charles Acland and

Haidee Wasson have dubbed "useful cinema."[8] Yet the Dominion recognized the power of Hollywood film product to generate interest and attract visitors. The CGMPB thus encouraged the shooting of Canadian-themed features on location to obliquely promote a positive destination image and motivate travel-making decisions.

VISUAL EDUCATION AND CINEMATOGRAPHIC ADVERTISING

The advent of motion pictures at the turn of the twentieth century coincided with a growing movement in Canada and the United States to make education more accessible and effective at cultivating productive citizens.[9] A diverse category of progressive educators endorsed student-centred learning that allowed students more creativity and freedom. Traditional education, by contrast, emphasized "textbook-bounded instruction," drilling, and rote memorization. Among these activists, social-efficiency educators sought to streamline the transmission and reception of knowledge. Most advocates of visual instruction fell into this sub-group of pedagogical reformers.[10]

Many Progressive-era educators embraced the notion that the "eye gate" was the most direct way to reach young students and adult learners. Ruth Dolesé, a former public-school art teacher, championed film's didactic capabilities: "Our greatest men and most prominent writers have long claimed that education 'through the eye' is more lasting, more thought-producing than any other method. How many of our great teachers have striven for years to bring before the world the truth that 'Seeing is Believing.'"[11] *Moving Picture World* even conjectured, "The time is slowly but surely coming" when the motion picture will "take the place of the antiquated blackboard in the school and college."[12] To quantify film's purported teaching capabilities, proponents of visual education turned to the emergent social sciences. F.D. (Frederick Dean) McClusky, an instructor at the University of Illinois (1922–25), called for scientific research "to establish with a large degree of certainty the educational value" of the moving picture and other forms of visual instruction.[13] Given film's pedagogical potential, in January 1911 *Moving Picture World* inaugurated a new weekly feature, "In the Educational Field," with a view to both "lead and follow the motion picture in its advance along all lines calculated to increase its value and progress in the entire field of educational work."[14]

Concerted efforts to develop the use of motion pictures in education stemmed from university and college extension programs, which increased access to higher education through correspondence courses and other community engagement. Such outreach dates back to the US land-grant colleges (founded 1862) and their public-service mandate.[15] In 1915, the National University Extension Association (NUEA) was established, with twenty-two participating institutions (eighteen state or land-grant institutions and four research universities).[16] Its inaugural meeting took place at the land-grant University of Wisconsin (UW) at Madison, which had since 1907 maintained one of the largest extension programs in the country and served as an exemplar. Deeply indebted to Progressive-era reformist thought, the "Wisconsin Idea" posited that every modern postsecondary institution should, according to Charles Van Hise (UW president 1903–18), "carry to the people the knowledge which they can assimilate for their betterment along all lines."[17]

Within its Department of General Information and Welfare, UW organized the Bureau of Visual Instruction, with William H. Dudley as director 1913–29. Lending out free of charge its extensive circuit of moving pictures on a wide range of subjects, the Bureau encouraged film's teaching possibilities for adults not formally enrolled in a school. Speaking before the NUEA in 1915, Dudley stated that "the opportunities for constructive educational work through the use of the lantern slide and motion picture film, – and education of all the people, – are too great to be made simply an incidental thing."[18]

After the First World War, American visual instruction professionalized, as seen in the National Academy of Visual Instruction (NAVI), founded in 1920, the Visual Instruction Association of America (VIAA) in 1922, and the National Education Association's Department of Visual Instruction (NEA DVI) in 1923. Their overarching goal was to "stimulate a far more intelligent use of visual aids" in schools and other non-theatrical venues, such as churches, clubs, and welfare societies[19] by creating equipment standards, standardizing practice and procedure, training staff, and establishing dedicated screening facilities, described as "a visual education laboratory."[20] Dudley Grant Hays, director of visual education in Chicago schools and president 1922–25 of NAVI thought that such institutionalization would equip teachers to develop minds, cultivate imagination, and foster "keen observation, accurate perception, and sound reasoning"[21] (figure 2.1).

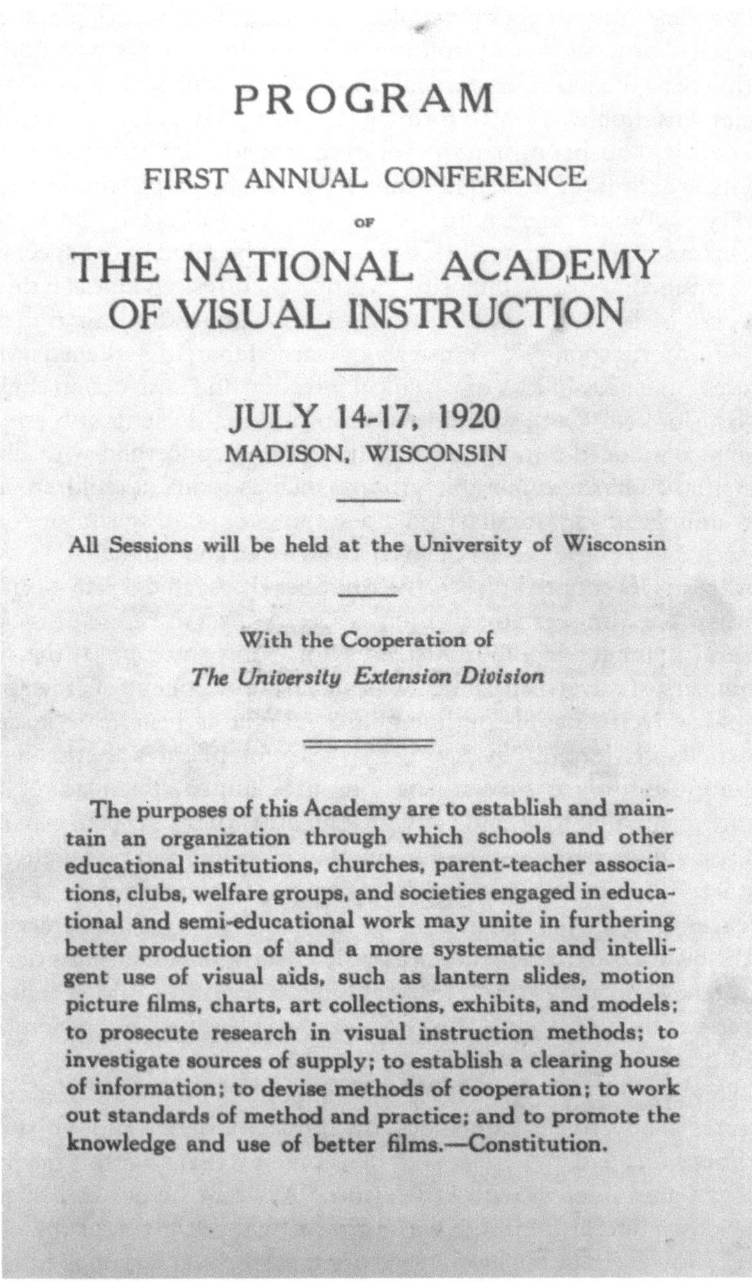

PROGRAM

FIRST ANNUAL CONFERENCE

OF

THE NATIONAL ACADEMY OF VISUAL INSTRUCTION

JULY 14-17, 1920
MADISON, WISCONSIN

All Sessions will be held at the University of Wisconsin

With the Cooperation of
The University Extension Division

The purposes of this Academy are to establish and maintain an organization through which schools and other educational institutions, churches, parent-teacher associations, clubs, welfare groups, and societies engaged in educational and semi-educational work may unite in furthering better production of and a more systematic and intelligent use of visual aids, such as lantern slides, motion picture films, charts, art collections, exhibits, and models; to prosecute research in visual instruction methods; to investigate sources of supply; to establish a clearing house of information; to devise methods of cooperation; to work out standards of method and practice; and to promote the knowledge and use of better films.—Constitution.

2.1 National Academy of Visual Instruction First Conference Program, July 1920

Drawing from the era's psychology theories, the advertising industry similarly harnessed visual education's notion that the eye was a direct pathway to the brain. As early as 1904, Walter Dill Scott argued that visual sensation was key to forming the "mental imagery" advertising needed.[22] The prominent psychologist and film theorist Hugo Münsterberg later articulated film's "kinematoscopic rendering of reality … Whatever in nature or in social life interests the human understanding or human curiosity comes to the mind of the spectator with an incomparable intensity." Motion pictures' vividness induced a sort of hypnotic mindset, creating "starting points for imitation and other motor responses." Münsterberg warned that, in darkened movie houses, "the possibilities of psychical infection and destruction cannot be overlooked." Still, while the notion of a highly suggestible *mass* audience induced a moral panic among those concerned with film's potential to harm vulnerable groups, such as women, children, and new immigrants, particularly in cities, the *individual* spectator could be seen as an empty vessel open to knowledge and uplift.[23]

Advertisers counted on "the possibilities of psychical infection" of the captive filmgoer to sell their wares. Watterson G. Rothacker, general manager of the Industrial Film Company, one of the first producers of advertising films, was an early proponent of cinematographic advertising. He outlined film's marketing benefits in a series of articles in *Motography* (1911–13). "Motion pictures are the up-to-the-minute thing in advertising!" he proclaimed. Their adaptable nature meant that they could advertise an array of products to generate interest and actuate sales. His discussion of "scenic and travel moving pictures" illustrates this point. According to Rothacker, films "create a yearning to see the original of the subject. Their graphic depictions of the beauties of scenery are decidedly effective in actuating a desire. Thus, they encourage travel by disclosing its pleasures, and benefit the advertiser by suggesting a trip over the road identified in the pictures" (figure 2.2).[24]

Likewise, in Ernest A. Dench's 1916 handbook on the use of motion pictures in advertising campaigns, the British journalist and self-styled authority on all matters related to film contends that with this medium one can gain interest with little effort. "At home he or she can toss your costly literature in the waste-basket without giving it the once over"; however, "at the motion-picture theater the situation is entirely different, for your audience is already waiting to be tackled. Their attention is literally glued to the screen."[25] In promoting tourism

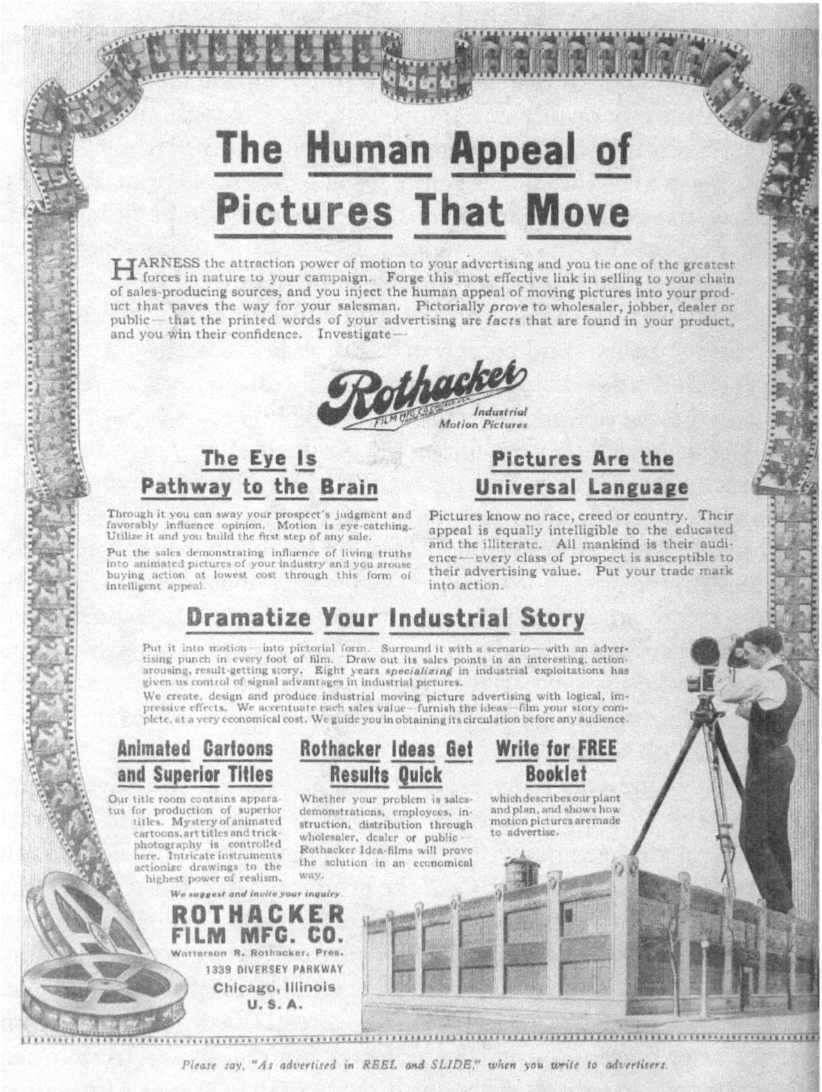

2.2 Rothacker Industrial Motion Pictures, *Reel and Slide* (May-June 1918), back-page advertisement through film, Dench surmises that the usual distributing of printed materials fails to lure visitors. Adopting the viewpoint of the "man in the street," he asks: "It is all very well of you to inform me of the advantages of your city or pleasure resort, but how on earth am I to know whether it was not written by somebody with a tendency to exaggerate? Again, I have to picture things before my eyes from cold print. Why not, therefore, have this done for me?" Dench concludes that "it is for this precise purpose that the motion picture has made itself conspicuous as an advertising medium – one differing from all others."[26]

E.J. Clary concurred that film was "the ideal method" to advertise tourism due to its "pulling power" and wide circulation. Calling it "playground advertising," he argued that audiences were likely unaware they were watching a promotional film because they believed it was educational. Resort films, he continued, "need not bear any earmarks of an ad. They become scenics." Clary offers a hypothetical scenario: a tired businessman in need of rest and relaxation who is at a theatre or some other venue. Although he thinks he is watching a "scenic" on the great outdoors, he is in reality engaging with a sponsored tourism ad. Already open to consumption, he is responsive to film's "peculiar psychology" to reach the "mind's eye" and is thus more willing to take the next step of booking a trip to experience at first hand the alluring "delights, pleasures and conveniences" of the places represented on screen.[27]

Not everyone was convinced of film's potential for advertising. One American expert claimed that, while film was "the greatest publicity medium in the world," as it familiarized more people with a brand, it did not necessarily *sell* the product.[28] In other words, large audiences did not automatically translate into sales. According to *Reel and Slide*, viewers' resentment of film advertising might outweigh any possible benefits – a captive audience is not necessarily a passive one. It related a cautionary tale of a YMCA secretary who returned from France after screening for US soldiers a film "designed to take the audience on a trip through the most picturesque sections of America by automobile. It made the trip all right, but the name of the sightseeing car was the most prominent object in every scene, and it wasn't long before the dough-boys became disgusted and left before the trip was completed." She reckoned: "If the producers of that film had shown the auto in the first scene with whatever advertising they wished to give, and had shown it again with publicity at the end of the film, they would have put their message across without difficulty and would have won the favor of their audience. But their anxiety to advertise caused them to overdo things to their cost."[29]

Regardless, "if done on the right lines," as Dench asserted, "a film does not appear to be an ad. Motion-picture fans ... have become so accustomed to seeing scenics and educationals that they would not realize the true object of city boosters and Chambers of Commerce." So long as the film was kept to about a reel in length, "audiences will stand this without a murmur of protest, since they appreciate one good extra reel on the program. It matters little whether they realize that it is advertising disguised."[30] Watterson G. Rothacker equally affirmed: "Motion pictures are the most subtle form of advertising. The consumer's busy instinct is aroused while he is being entertained."[31] In Canada, Dominion-government officials likewise believed that motion pictures could function as "living advertisements" of the country to attract investment, build up trade, and expand tourism by creating unconscious desire and influencing the viewing public's travel decisions.[32]

In the spring of 1916, under director and co-founder Francis Holley, the Washington, DC-based Bureau of Commercial Economics arranged "useful" exhibitions of instructive subjects that were of the "greatest possible interest to the public generally and of educationally interested persons especially." Holdings of the Bureau – a charitable organization – included films of the "Canadian Rockies, the Forests of British Columbia, Evangeline Country, [and the] Land of Hiawatha." Holley arranged to have these films "philanthropically" displayed to expose the public to the "pleasure spots which nature has provided."[33] At the invitation of Prime Minister Sir Robert Borden, he toured Canada "to investigate the possibilities of making motion pictures descriptive of travel, industry and all the natural resources of the Dominion" to be displayed throughout the United States. Since the Bureau's Department of Public Instruction boasted that it reached approximately two million spectators per month, the Dominion recognized a tremendous opportunity to "advertise Canada."[34]

Canadian Minister of Trade and Commerce Sir George Foster (served 1911–21) hired Essanay Film MFG Co. to produce a series of films as "the picturization of Canada." John Murray Gibbon, the CPR's general publicity agent (1913–45) had recommended the Chicago-based outfit, which had recently produced scenics for the railway, including *A Trip through the Canadian Rockies* and *Camping in the Canadian Rockies*. Charles F. Stark, manager of Essanay's commercial department since 1912, oversaw Trade and Commerce's motion-picture "advertising campaign." Foster summoned Stark to Ottawa to outline the task at hand, which was to have filmgoers leave the theatre exclaiming: "Gee, Canada must be a great country ... I think I'll go there." Given "carte blanche" to capture the Dominion's natural resources, scenery, and industry, by November 1916 Essanay accumulated 42,000 feet of film that visually imparted "the story of Canada" to film exchanges throughout the world (figure 2.3).[35]

Essanay distributed these one-reel films as parts of its Wonders of Nature and Science "educational" films. The ambiguity between instruction and advertising was likely deliberate. From the outset, Trade and Commerce envisioned that these motion pictures would inform viewers of the Dominion's natural attributes, unique landscapes, major cities, and industries from coast to coast.[36] In so doing, they would also highlight "many of the scenes familiar to tourists." Even those Essanay films primarily showcasing industry and agriculture still invoked a tourist sensibility. *The Water Powers of Eastern Canada* (1918), for instance, ostensibly about the region's hydro industry, depicted "the artistic side of Canada" by including "picturesque vistas" of countless falls, rapids, and rivers in Ontario and Quebec.[37] By emphasizing the edifying value of the moving pictures, government officials could shrewdly accentuate Canada's "scenic beauty" so as to "stimulate the interest of the people not only in the Dominion, but in foreign lands."[38]

Although the Essanay venture demonstrated the value of sponsored film production, Trade and Commerce calculated that producing in-house would be cheaper and more efficient. Deputy Minister F.C.T. O'Hara complained that Essanay's progress had been slow. Moreover, even though the department did 90 per cent of the work, Essanay received 65 per cent of the earnings. The department paid the firm $32,571.35 – more than a third of its total expenditures that year, which totalled $92,832.98 in October 1919. By contrast, it could equip an Ottawa-based film plant for only $3,000–$4,000.[39] Believing that the medium "lends itself to effective and economic distribution of information as no other form of publicity," Minister Foster concluded that Trade and Commerce should invest in domestic film production and coordinate all the government's motion-picture publicity work to build on growing interest in the Dominion's products and destinations.[40] Such a desire was not new but emanated from the intense patriotism of the 1910s, which resulted in Canada creating motion pictures for propaganda and publicity.

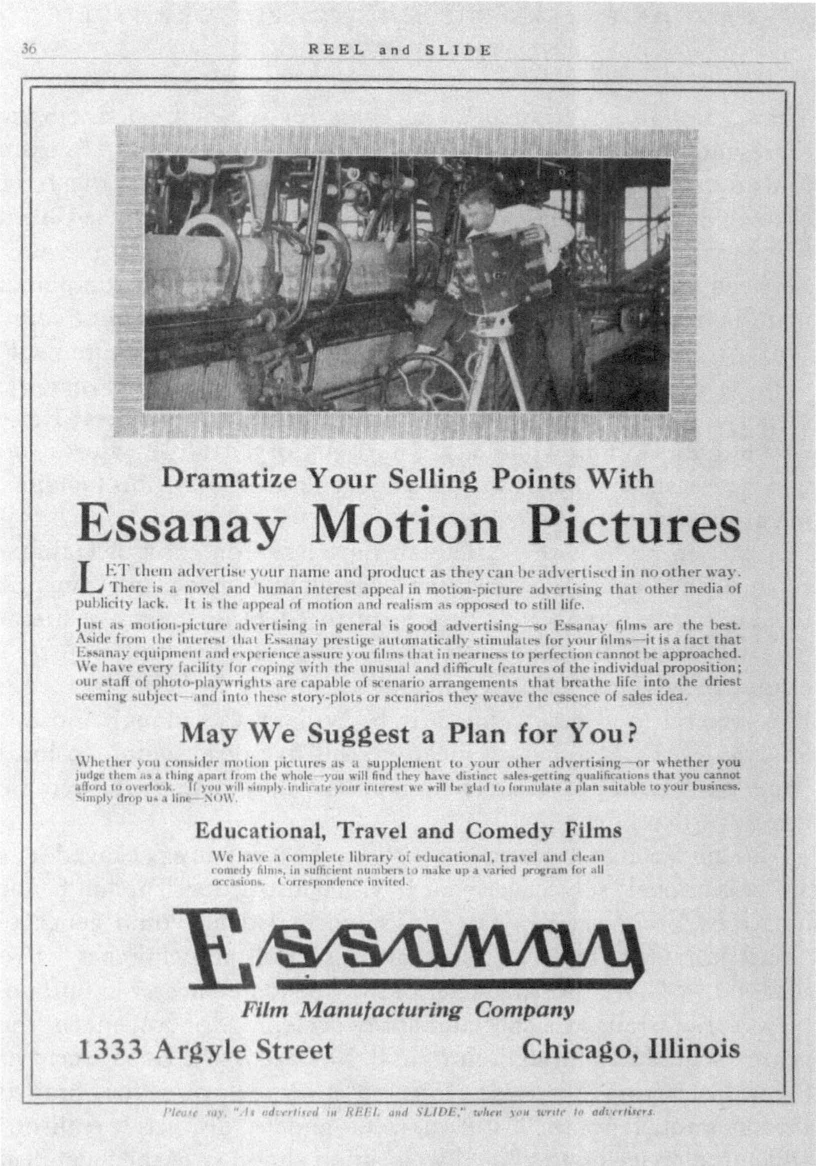

36 REEL and SLIDE

Dramatize Your Selling Points With

Essanay Motion Pictures

LET them advertise your name and product as they can be advertised in no other way. There is a novel and human interest appeal in motion-picture advertising that other media of publicity lack. It is the appeal of motion and realism as opposed to still life.

Just as motion-picture advertising in general is good advertising—so Essanay films are the best. Aside from the interest that Essanay prestige automatically stimulates for your films—it is a fact that Essanay equipment and experience assure you films that in nearness to perfection cannot be approached. We have every facility for coping with the unusual and difficult features of the individual proposition; our staff of photo-playwrights are capable of scenario arrangements that breathe life into the driest seeming subject—and into these story-plots or scenarios they weave the essence of sales idea.

May We Suggest a Plan for You?

Whether you consider motion pictures as a supplement to your other advertising—or whether you judge them as a thing apart from the whole—you will find they have distinct sales-getting qualifications that you cannot afford to overlook. If you will simply indicate your interest we will be glad to formulate a plan suitable to your business. Simply drop us a line—NOW.

Educational, Travel and Comedy Films

We have a complete library of educational, travel and clean comedy films, in sufficient numbers to make up a varied program for all occasions. Correspondence invited.

Essanay

Film Manufacturing Company

1333 Argyle Street Chicago, Illinois

Please say, "As advertised in REEL and SLIDE," when you write to advertisers.

2.3 Essanay Industrial advertisement, *Reel and Slide*, March 1918

CANADA ENTERS THE MOTION PICTURE FIELD AND THE BATTLEFIELD

The Canadian government's eagerness for self-defined cinematic representations and its longing to control the production of tourism films date back to a surge in nationalism resulting from the 1911 election debate over the Liberals' proposed reciprocity with the United States, which brought the protectionist Conservatives to power.[41] Between 1912 and 1914, several private domestic film companies materialized, aided by American or British capital. *Moving Picture World* trumpeted the nation's "entry into the motion picture field" with "a strong bid for showing her natural resources and majestic scenery to the world in purely Canadian motion pictures."[42] These new interests in film would generate a mix of narrative features and non-fiction short subjects showcasing scenic attributes, thus functioning as tourism films.

A case in point is the Canadian Bioscope Company of Halifax, established late in 1912, depicting "Canadian, historic, and romantic incidents."[43] Its explicit commitment to adapting works of literature and/or historical subjects was in step with the film industry's efforts to advance its own cultural legitimacy. In February 1914, Bioscope released *Evangeline* (dir. by William Cavanaugh and E.P. Sullivan, 1913). Filmed on location, this five-reeler would, a local paper surmised, provide the Annapolis Valley with "considerable free advertising."[44]

Though basing the feature on fiction, the company packaged it as an "educational" subject germane to visual instruction. The "authentic locations," remarked reviewer George Blaisdell, would generate "marked interest for entertainments in schools and churches."[45] To that end, W.G. Kaliska, manager of the Allendale Theater in Buffalo, New York, arranged a special matinee screening for students at the nearby school and brought in John B. Mallard of the Department of Public Instruction to provide a lecture.[46] *Motion Picture News* praised the film's adherence to "historical facts" and its "distinctive realism," which the reviewer attributed to location shooting in the "identical surroundings ... where the experiences which the poem relates were originally supposed to have been enacted."[47]

As a "faithful" adaptation of the epic poem and a "truthful" recreation of Acadian history, *Evangeline* not only served a didactic function, but also supported the region's burgeoning tourist economy.

In its Longfellow-based concoction of Acadia, the Annapolis Valley was "unsurpassed for beauty and grandeur," according to Canadian Biograph Vice President and General Manager H. Thomas Oliver.[48] Civic leaders and local business interests wagered that the buzz surrounding the film would enable them to capitalize on the fictitious world of Evangeline and lure tourism and development. In an early instance of a tie-in, the Newfoundland-based Red Cross Line (New York, Newfoundland & Halifax Steamship Co.) advertised its northern cruises aboard luxurious modern steamers from New York City to Halifax, "the land of Evangeline," in the September 1914 issue of *Motion Picture Magazine*, which, unlike most film-related periodicals, was aimed at audiences, not exhibitors.[49] By this time, however, the start of war (at least for Canada) would hurt recreational travel between the Maritimes and New England in the U-boat–infested waters of the Gulf of St Lawrence and the North Atlantic (figures 2.4 and 2.5).

The onset of overseas hostilities, however, did not hinder Canadian tourism overall. James B. Harkin, the first commissioner (1911–36) of the Dominion Parks Branch, asserted that the war produced uniquely favourable circumstances. American citizens, he claimed, ostensibly neutral, could "spend huge sums upon travel and recreation. At the present time, for all practical purposes, the only field open to them is Canada and the United States." Harkin anticipated that after the war thousands of tourists would want to travel to Europe. It was imperative that "during the war every possible effort should be made to attract tourists to the Canadian mountains in order that when the call of the battlefields sets in" the call of the mountains "shall be strong."[50] Hence, during the summer of 1915 Canadian hotels, resorts, and transportation systems prepared for the projected invasion of those American tourists who normally vacationed in Europe. Believing that the increased business would ground a healthy tourism industry when peace came, the provincial and Dominion governments encouraged this northward trend. The Department of Immigration instructed its officers not to interfere with "bona-fide tourist traffic" by not requiring passports at the border.[51]

Beyond stimulating more American vacationers, the war accelerated the domestic audience's desire for Canadian representations on screen and stimulated a nationalist practice of filmgoing.[52] While most motion pictures continued to emanate from the United States, more Canadian

Made in Annapolis Valley amongst the Actual Scenes Described in the Poem

EVANGELINE

Capt. H. H. B. HOLLAND, President — JOHN STRONG, Treasurer — T. J. PAYNE, Secretary — H. T. OLIVER, Vice Pres. & Gen. Manager

CANADIAN BIOSCOPE CO., Limited

PRESENTS

The Film Classic from Beginning to End

EVANGELINE

(ADAPTED FROM LONGFELLOW'S IMMORTAL POEM)

FIVE REELS

TINTED AND TONED

Stirring

Enthralling

Impressive

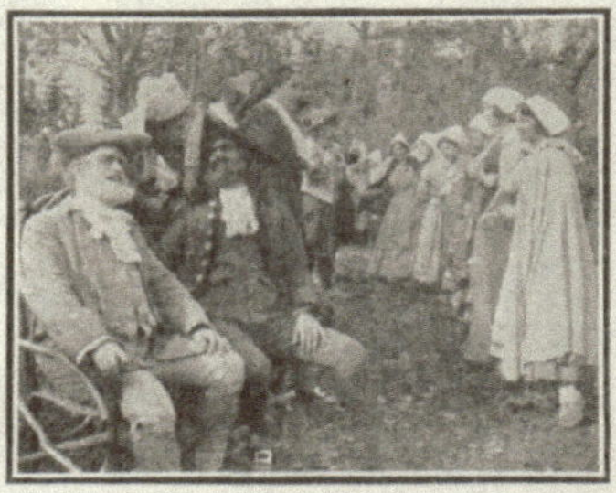

Star Cast

Perfect Photography

Natural Scenery

"Merrily, Merrily Whirled the Wheels of the Dizzying Dances"

Beautiful Paper, 1s, 3s, 6s, 12s. *Heralds, Photos, Slides*

Made by GREENWICH LITHO CO.

STATE RIGHTS NOW SELLING

Address

1209 Candler Building 220 West 42nd Street, New York City

Phone, 3559 Bryant

CLARENCE SCHOTTENFELS, Sales and Advertising Manager

EVANGELINE

Made in Annapolis Valley amongst the Actual Scenes Described in the Poem

In writing to advertisers please mention "THE MOTION PICTURE NEWS"

2.4 Advertisement for *Evangeline*, *Motion Picture News*, 31 January 1914

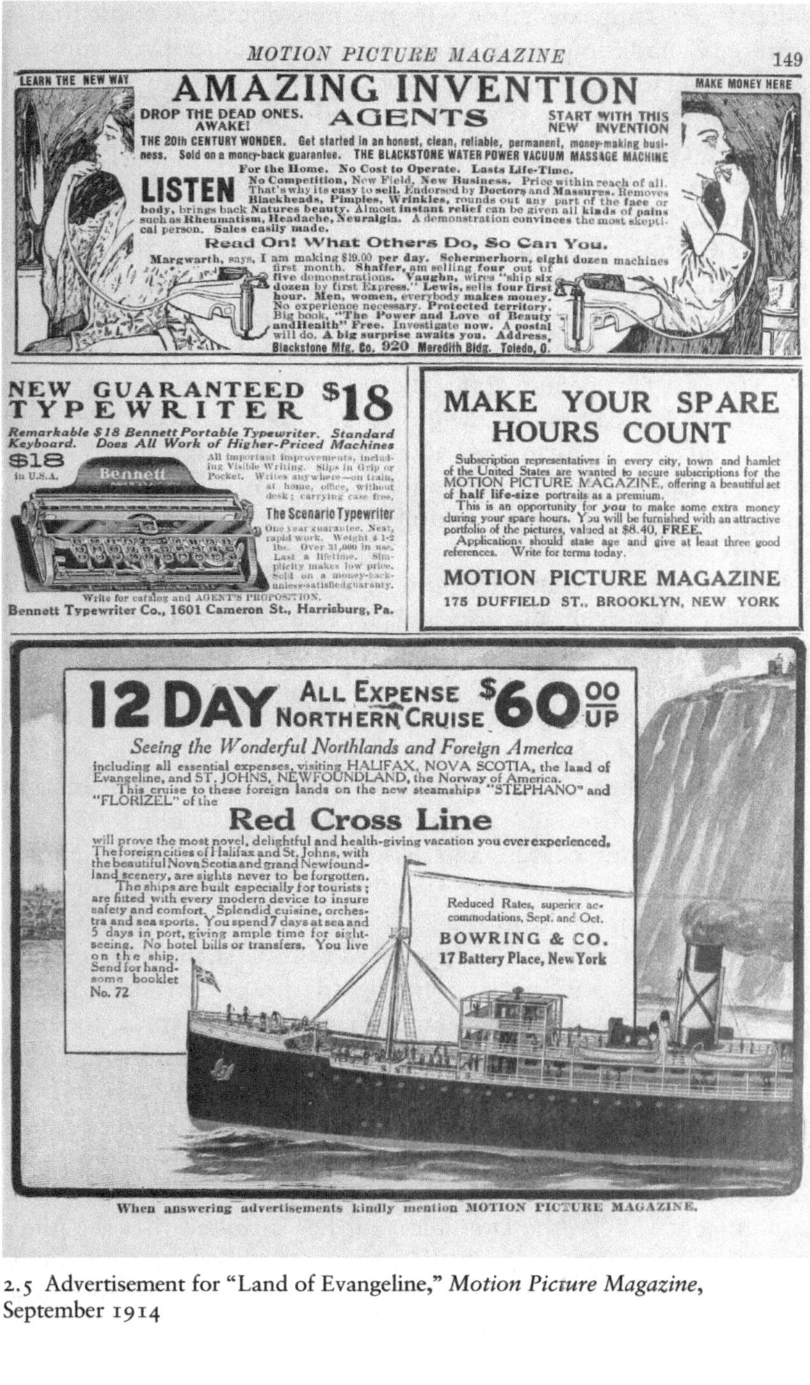
MOTION PICTURE MAGAZINE 149

LEARN THE NEW WAY

AMAZING INVENTION

MAKE MONEY HERE

DROP THE DEAD ONES. AWAKE!

AGENTS

START WITH THIS NEW INVENTION

THE 20th CENTURY WONDER. Get started in an honest, clean, reliable, permanent, money-making business. Sold on a money-back guarantee. THE BLACKSTONE WATER POWER VACUUM MASSAGE MACHINE

For the Home. No Cost to Operate. Lasts Life-Time.

LISTEN No Competition, New Field, New Business. Price within reach of all. That's why its easy to sell. Endorsed by Doctors and Massures. Removes Blackheads, Pimples, Wrinkles, rounds out any part of the face or body, brings back Natures beauty. Almost instant relief can be given all kinds of pains such as Rheumatism, Headache, Neuralgia. A demonstration convinces the most skeptical person. Sales easily made.

Read On! What Others Do, So Can You.

Margwarth, says, I am making $19.00 per day. Schermerhorn, eight dozen machines first month. Shaffer, am selling four out of five demonstrations. Vaughn, wires "ship six dozen by first Express." Lewis, sells four first hour. Men, women, everybody makes money. No experience necessary. Protected territory. Big book, "The Power and Love of Beauty andHealth" Free. Investigate now. A postal will do. A big surprise awaits you. Address, Blackstone Mfg. Co. 920 Meredith Bldg. Toledo, O.

NEW GUARANTEED TYPEWRITER $18

Remarkable $18 Bennett Portable Typewriter. Standard Keyboard. Does All Work of Higher-Priced Machines

$18 in U.S.A.

Bennett

All important improvements, including Visible Writing. Slips in Grip or Pocket. Writes anywhere—on train, at home, office, without desk; carrying case free.

The Scenario Typewriter

One year guarantee. Neat, rapid work. Weight 4 1-2 lbs. Over 31,000 in use. Last a lifetime. Simplicity makes low price. Sold on a money-back-unless-satisfiedguaranty.

Write for catalog and AGENT'S PROPOSITION.

Bennett Typewriter Co., 1601 Cameron St., Harrisburg, Pa.

MAKE YOUR SPARE HOURS COUNT

Subscription representatives in every city, town and hamlet of the United States are wanted to secure subscriptions for the MOTION PICTURE MAGAZINE, offering a beautiful set of **half life-size** portraits as a premium.

This is an opportunity for *you* to make some extra money during your spare hours. You will be furnished with an attractive portfolio of the pictures, valued at $8.40, **FREE.**

Applications should state age and give at least three good references. Write for terms today.

MOTION PICTURE MAGAZINE

175 DUFFIELD ST., BROOKLYN, NEW YORK

12 DAY ALL EXPENSE NORTHERN CRUISE $60.00 UP

Seeing the Wonderful Northlands and Foreign America

including all essential expenses, visiting HALIFAX, NOVA SCOTIA, the land of Evangeline, and ST. JOHNS, NEWFOUNDLAND, the Norway of America.

This cruise to these foreign lands on the new steamships "STEPHANO" and "FLORIZEL" of the

Red Cross Line

will prove the most novel, delightful and health-giving vacation you ever experienced. The foreign cities of Halifax and St. Johns, with the beautiful Nova Scotia and grand Newfoundland scenery, are sights never to be forgotten.

The ships are built especially for tourists; are fitted with every modern device to insure safety and comfort. Splendid cuisine, orchestra and sea sports. You spend 7 days at sea and 5 days in port, giving ample time for sightseeing. No hotel bills or transfers. You live on the ship. Send for handsome booklet No. 72

Reduced Rates, superior accommodations, Sept. and Oct.

BOWRING & CO.

17 Battery Place, New York

When answering advertisements kindly mention MOTION PICTURE MAGAZINE.

2.5 Advertisement for "Land of Evangeline," *Motion Picture Magazine*, September 1914 military views appeared. As a self-governing dominion of the British Empire, Canada imported war-related newsreel footage from the United Kingdom, splicing in the activities of Canadian soldiers, to encourage enlistment and to stimulate patriotism.[53] Furthermore, with Ottawa's cooperation, such new commercial film companies as Montreal's Canadian Animated Weekly and Dominion General Film Corporation, Toronto's Conness-Till Company, and Windsor's All Red Feature Company produced newsreels that focused on the activities of Canadian troops. Wartime actualities propagated ideas and images to shape and control public opinion in ways intended to encourage patriotism and self-sacrifice and inform the public about Canada's war effort.[54] This demonstrates the era's synergy between the state, private film companies, and the growth of advertising, education, and propaganda. As Jonathan Rose notes, government elites employ advertising to "bind the polity to the state" – a purposeful form of delivery "designed to elicit some behavioral or attitudinal change on the part of the public."[55]

By 1918, the Dominion would become more directly involved in producing moving pictures as "powerful factors in educational and commercial work."[56] The Department of Soldiers' Civil Re-establishment (DSCR) sponsored *Canada's Work for Wounded Soldiers* (dir. by William J. Craft, 1918). This five-reel film examines hospital care and rehabilitation for convalescing and disabled soldiers to inform the "men in khaki of the advantages the government was placing at their disposal." The DSCR distributed the film to theatres free of all booking charges and disseminated posters, lobby photographs, and newspaper stories – the type of publicity normally reserved for fictional features.[57]

The work was enthusiastically received in Canada, the United States, and the United Kingdom, pointing to the potential of future government-sponsored propaganda. The *Toronto World*, for one, praised the film for offering "instruction, interest, and sometimes amusement."[58] The motion picture was also shown to educators from the [US] Federal Board of Vocational Training, who appreciated its "pointers" on career rehabilitation for veterans and later presented the film in the United States for educational purposes.[59] Looking ahead to imminent victory, the Dominion further surmised that the film's excellent "scenic features," which incorporated "the lakes and mountains of British Columbia" and "the picturesque farm life of prairie and dairy farm," would benefit tourism.[60]

Indeed, this government-sponsored production augured Canada's leadership in the burgeoning postwar visual-education movement, in which the tourism film would play a key role. Public agencies would apply the experience gained from wartime propaganda and cinematic techniques used in films such as *Canada's Work for Wounded Soldiers* to motion pictures that advertised Canada to the American tourism market.[61] According to Henry MacMahon, special correspondent for *Reel and Slide*, the first journal dedicated to educational and industrial motion pictures, "The war has called the attention of film men to useful pictures," which "will be the salvation of the industry in the stressful times now coming."[62] Some of these "useful" films advertised goods and services, as well as nations seeking trade and tourists.

Ontario was the first provincial government to produce such items for propaganda and publicity. In early 1917, its Department of Agriculture commissioned a series of instructional films on farm activities for exhibition in non-theatrical venues, including fairs, farmers' gatherings, public schools, and YMCAs. In May of that year, the government created the Ontario Motion Picture Bureau (OMPB) under Sidney C. Johnston, a vegetable specialist from its Department of Agriculture. Johnston passed away at the age of twenty-eight on 21 November 1918, and his assistant, William Dawson, replaced him.

Believing that motion pictures could get "inside the heads of their spectators," as Charles Tepperman explains, Dawson mobilized film to instruct the province's farming community on agricultural matters, as well as social relations and hygiene.[63] Equipped with Pathéscope projectors, 45 departmental representatives fanned out delivering illustrated lectures to rural districts. In 1918–19, 82 subjects were shown 1,956 times to 700,000 people all over the province.[64] To boost attendance, some shows added comedies and dramas featuring such stars as Charlie Chaplin and Toronto-born Gladys Smith, better known as Mary Pickford. The OMPB surmised that the presence of commercial film product would increase audience "receptivity" to the "educational influences" of its productions.[65] That is, the immersive cinematic medium activated an attentive mind and thus stimulated associative cognition.

Although it is unclear whether OMPB officials were familiar with educational and advertising theories of the "eye gate," the Bureau privileged non-theatrical film in its efforts to modernize rural Ontario. Its agricultural productions showed government officials the medium's efficacy and value at distributing information about the province's resources both within Ontario and beyond. In his annual financial report of 1919, Treasurer Thomas W. McGarry, who was also responsible for the film industry, remarked:

> That the work being carried on by the Ontario Government in motion picture educational propaganda is becoming widely known and appreciated is evidenced by the fact that letters of inquiry have been received from the Departments of Agriculture of Nova Scotia and New Brunswick, the Manitoba Agricultural College, the Extension Department of the University of Alberta, the National Board of Review of Motion Pictures, New York; the Lincoln Park Co., Worcester, Massachusetts; Eaths, Mills & Bell Co., St. Paul, Minnesota, and the Community Picture Bureau, New York.[66]

McGarry envisioned that motion pictures made under "official auspices" or purchased from outside sources should be "intended to advertise the Province of Ontario far and wide." Several of these "agricultural propaganda films" were loaned to the US government and probably influenced its campaign to employ motion pictures to teach modern, efficient agricultural techniques to American farmers.[67] *Moving Picture World* also remarked that the American film industry had taken "considerable interest" in Ontario's "unusual" circulating of "instructive films."[68] A feature article in *Reel and Slide* praised the province's adoption of "visual education work," claiming that it was "more thoroughly progressive" than anywhere else in the world.[69]

Given the educational-film program's "excellent results" in publicizing the province's agriculture and industry, the OMPB surmised that film would be equally effective in promoting its scenery and tourism facilities in a likely record-breaking first-postwar summer of US visitors. In early 1919, the OMPB produced *Ontario's Playgrounds* to highlight the "beauty spots" of Muskoka, the Lake of Bays district, and Algonquin Park.[70] At the 41st annual Canadian National Exhibition (CNE) in Toronto, 23 August–6 September 1919, the government screened *Ontario's Playgrounds* free of charge as part of "a continuous educational film program" targeted at American vacationers. Although the CNE was primarily a domestic, national event, as Chester W. Martin of the US consulate in Toronto pronounced, it was "in a sense international, and it is almost as much interest to the country south of the boundary as it is to you people of

Canada." Speaking at the fair's "America Day" luncheon, Martin added: "The coming together of the people of the two countries annually" gives "us an opportunity to know something of your great resources and material attainments."[71]

Hence, the CNE was a fitting locale for moving images to reveal "the vastness, wealth and great possibilities of Ontario" and offered "a strong appeal to tourists both of Canada and other countries through the wonders of Algonquin Park." More than a travelogue to entertain and inform CNE visitors, *Ontario's Playgrounds* served as a novel way to advertise the burgeoning postwar tourism industry, that is, to lure "the great mass of citizens who have not been fortunate to take a trip into the north." During the CNE's transportation day, the OMPB showed the film for railway officials from Montreal, Toronto, Boston, Chicago, Detroit, and New York City. If any of the latter had "hesitated in the past to send their tourists into Ontario," opined Toronto's *Globe*, "these pictures will doubtless overcome all that." Presenting the province's "beauty spots" alongside "some of the sporting features, [and] camping scenes," the OMPB production "made the [Algonquin] park so alluring that the first temptation of the visitors was to take the earliest train north."[72]

Hence, by emphasizing its abstract educational interest regarding Ontario's resources, the province had astutely banked on film for advertising to increase tourist traffic and reaped the benefits. Summer travel exploded in 1919, as evidenced by reports of Toronto hotels unable to cope with the steady stream of travellers, largely American, returning from "growingly popular holidays in Muskoka Lakes district, Algonquin Park and other parts of the Ontario and Quebec 'wilds.'"[73] Nevertheless, the OMPB could not take sole credit. Ontario presented useful pictures at the CNE that summer in "a happy spirit of co-operation" with free film screenings put on by the Dominion's Trade and Commerce Department. Visitors were treated to moving pictures depicting Canada's scenic and industrial attractions, often accompanied by lectures given by D.W. Johnson, the OMPB's director of publicity.[74]

Certainly, war's end intensified calls for more Canadian motion pictures. *Educational Film Magazine* made this explicit: "Canada had received an advertisement that time will never efface in the gallant work done by Canadian lads on Flanders Fields." The "peoples of the earth" were "already talking Canada as a result of the Dominion's effort overseas in the great war." Therefore, the time was ripe to build on this global goodwill and "put the movies to work for Canada."[75] Riding the momentum of wartime propaganda, government agencies invested in film sponsorship/production to promote tourism while framing these motion pictures as educational.

"MOTION PICTURE PROPAGANDA"

In the autumn of 1917, Anita Maris Boggs, co-founder and dean of the Department of Public Instruction at the Bureau of Commercial Economics in Washington, DC, wrote to Deputy Minister of Trade and Commerce F.C.T. O'Hara in Ottawa asking him to shed light on a "state secret" after she had encountered hearsay about the Dominion's coming "motion picture propaganda." The rumour was true, O'Hara replied. His department was developing a motion-picture branch to advertise the country abroad.[76] Reacting to Essanay's expensive (though rewarding) series of "educational" films and the nationalist crusade for expanded Canadian film content, Trade and Commerce championed greater investment in domestic film production and the coordination of the nation's motion-picture publicity efforts under one roof.

An order-in-council in September 1918 established the Exhibits and Publicity Bureau within Trade and Commerce to produce "propaganda and advertising" primarily through motion pictures.[77] Minister Sir George Foster wanted this film agency to expedite the "reconstruction work of the country." His department prepared "for the great commercial struggle that would follow in the wake of peace" by initially appropriating $150,000 to develop and extend trade by publicizing Canada by exhibiting motion pictures in the United States, as well as in Australia, Britain, China, Japan, and New Zealand.[78] Sustained domestic film production was intended to stimulate interest in Canadian products and destinations, thereby attracting external trade and tourists.

The *Globe* heralded this new scheme, calling Canada "a picture propaganda pioneer." While the United States concentrated on "made-for-amusement" films, the Dominion was making "rapid strides of progress" and promises to "lead the world" in the manufacture of films that are "more useful than entertaining." As a department official later proclaimed, Canada "was on the ground floor in national film advertising ... before many other countries had awakened to the possibilities of the screen."[79] Not everyone was so sanguine. H. Norton

DeWitt, president of Pathéscope Company of Canada, wrote to Acting Minister of Trade and Commerce Alexander K. Maclean to protest the department's making and distributing of motion pictures "in competition with Canadian producers" of education, industrial, and scenic films. Pathéscope had proposed to produce motion pictures for the department for a flat price per foot of film and include all expenses for the camera operators. The director of the Exhibits and Publicity Bureau, B.E. Norrish, however, favoured centralizing production into an in-house film plant, which permitted greater control over publicity.[80]

Norrish, a civil engineer and chief draughtsman of the Dominion Water Power Branch, had overseen the Essanay film unit during its Canadian filming stint and also had observed the productivity of the Ford Motor Company's in-house film department.[81] This practical experience, together with his science background (a master of science from Queen's University), made him see the moving picture as an effectual means of education and advertising. In a paper delivered to the Convention of the Society of Motion Picture Engineers, he argued that "seven-eighths of all knowledge is acquired and understood only after there has been a mental picture of it formed, and the motion picture provides a very quick means of doing this. In describing the industries of a country, for example, the motion picture gives the student a much clearer perception than could possibly be obtained through any text."[82]

Norrish apparently took as gospel that the intensity and realism of moving images would take hold of audiences, producing a subjective state favourable to learning and/or consumption. Privileging the "eye gate" over the "ear gate," he gambled that the Exhibits and Publicity Bureau's films would produce a singular state of consciousness conducive to retaining knowledge about Canada's industries and tourism sites, leading to positive impressions about its factories, farms, and scenery, motivating people to trade with and/or travel to the Dominion. This logic was in keeping with theories on promoting tourism through cinematographic advertising, which could be passed off as educational. The association of scenics with (or as a synonym for) "educationals" during the Progressive era undergirded this correlation.

One year after the Bureau's establishment, the *Globe* reported that it had exhibited around the world over 100,000 feet of film "depicting Canada as a land of magic beauty and vast resources." *The Most Picturesque Spot in North America* (1918), for example, presents a settler-colonial male tourist photographing the lakes, mountains, forests, and wildflowers of Alberta's Bow River Valley. It also shows a tony couple enjoying the Rockies' CPR Château Lake Louise's boating, cuisine, riding, and manicured grounds. In keeping with the verisimilitude of the film medium and the significance of the eye gate, an intertitle informs viewers: "Beyond imagination! This background was made to fit the eye!" This is reinforced throughout via multiple iris shots of various sizes to frame the scenery and focus the viewer's gaze on the picture. Heralding the "call of Mother Nature," such images, as the *Globe* articulated, proclaimed "in words stronger and louder than man: 'See Canada First.'"[83] This phrase was an explicit retort to the widespread "See America First" campaign, which "promoted tourism as a ritual of American citizenship," and signalled that the Dominion was promoting tourism forcefully through cinematographic advertising (figure 2.6).[84]

Industry insiders applauded the Dominion's foray into film production. W.A. Bach, a well-known figure in Toronto advertising circles and former publicity manager of the Canadian Universal Film Corporation, observed throughout the nation "a wonderful awakening of a national spirit," which has started "a recrudescence of the production fever in Canada." He predicted that 1919 would be "the biggest year for the Canadian motion picture industry." To elucidate his point, Bach singled out the Dominion's upcoming production of "some remarkably fine motion picture scenics depicting the beauties of various parts of the country ... in conjunction with a world-wide propaganda campaign."[85] Bach was doubtlessly referring to the Exhibits and Publicity Bureau's series of one- and two-reel made-in-Canada scenics known as Seeing Canada.

The Bureau's first catalogue from 1920 contained 39 subjects, including the sponsored Essanay films, as well as scenic-industrials ranging from airplane manufacture and shipbuilding to salmon fishing and the harvesting of maple and apple trees.[86] It also featured motion pictures based on "6,000 feet of the finest negative of the Canadian Rockies that has been prepared to date," which Trade and Commerce purchased from the American-born alpinist Byron Harmon, who had settled in Banff in 1903.[87] Additional items were created in partnership with other Dominion agencies, most notably the Parks Branch, set up in 1911 within the Department of the Interior. The Parks Branch encouraged tourism as a source of revenue and endorsed film as a publicity method.[88] For instance, several early Seeing Canada productions flaunted Banff as a premier winter resort, with skating, skiing, and

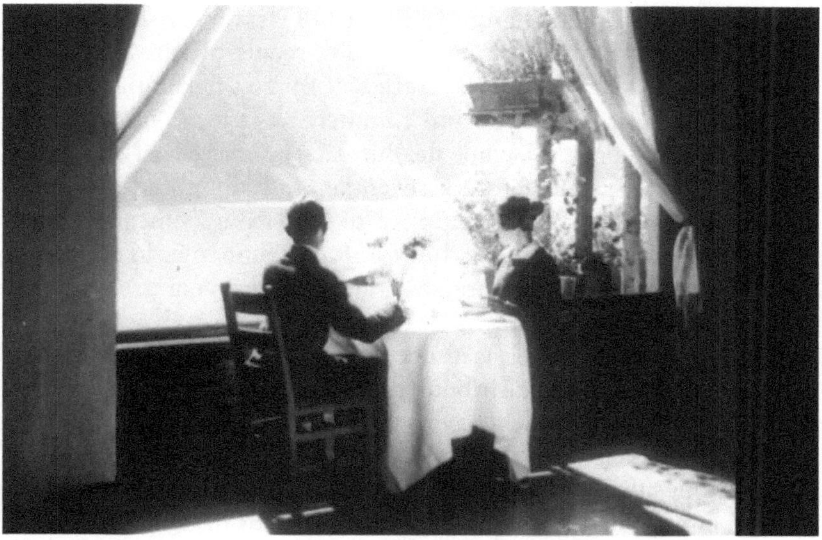

2.6 Exhibits and Publicity Bureau, *The Most Picturesque Spot in North America*, 1918

snowshoeing (*Prince of the Playgrounds*); displayed alpine climbing in Yoho National Park (*In the Yoho Valley* and *Campfires among the Snow Peaks*); and took viewers into the heart of Jasper Park via a "rare educational film as well as a scenic beauty film" (*World of Scenic Wonders*).[89]

Provincial governments recognized how the made-in-Canada series raised profiles, leading to collaborations. In 1920, the premier of New Brunswick invited Norrish to present his promotional films at a Fredericton theatre to MLAs to show them "the importance of the motion picture as a means of advertising the Province." Members of the Fredericton Board of Trade and Tourist Association were also in attendance. The Exhibits and Publicity Bureau later released two scenics – *A Fish and Bear Tale* and *Along the St. John River, New Brunswick* – in cooperation with the New Brunswick Tourist Association and the provincial government.[90]

Despite being unable to demonstrate tangible results quickly, the Bureau averred that its useful films were fruitful. Norrish cited as proof the millions of viewers exposed to the Dominion's agricultural, industrial, and scenic attributes; prints were shown an average of three times a day to a conservative estimate of 500 people per screening and reached approximately 5.6 million potential American tourists each week. In his report to Deputy Minister O'Hara, Norrish concluded that the US distribution of the Bureau's "scenic pictures" had "the effect of increasing our tourist traffic."[91] By 1925, Thomas A. Low, Dominion minister of trade and commerce 1923–25, informed the House of Commons that, while the Bureau was not yet self-sustaining, Seeing Canada was generating revenue. He highlighted the series' impact as "a medium of advertising ... to the encouragement of tourist traffic." He added, "There are thirty or forty companies in the United States to whom our films are sold, and we receive a great deal of advertising in that way."[92]

The Bureau initially released one of its Seeing Canada films every other week through such distributing agencies as the Canadian Universal Film Company. By the end of its first full year of operation, over 600 prints were in theatrical circulation in the United States, being shown alongside Outing-Chester travel-scenics and Ford Educational Weekly films. Norrish was pleased to report that his Bureau's output compared favourably to these commercial American productions.[93] In addition, the Bureau expanded its non-theatrical distribution throughout the United States, often via the Washington-based Bureau of Commercial Economics, into boards of trade, chambers of commerce, church organizations, hunting and fishing associations, and Rotary and other community clubs. An official lecturer, such as D.W. Johnson, frequently accompanied the presentations.[94]

The Bureau also recognized that new audiences created by the postwar expansion of US educational-film-distribution agencies might be responsive to propaganda and advertising.[95] Building on networks formed by such trailblazers as Charles Urban and George Kleine, the Bureau circulated Seeing Canada films in the United States via college and university extension divisions, museums, public and school libraries, states' departments of education, and the YMCA. Schools purchased these films or rented or borrowed them in circuits, with one institution passing them to the next during the academic year according to the established route and schedule. Alternatively, the special-order distribution system allowed educators to reserve a film for a specific date, typically via the school system's visual-instruction department.[96] University and college extension programs typically distributed films to off-campus groups and organizations, often extending into remote or rural areas. Motion pictures and lantern slides on a wide range of subjects, covering agriculture, history, industry, literature, science, and travel, were loaned for free or for a small fee.

The University of Wisconsin at Madison maintained one of the largest circulating libraries of motion pictures. By academic 1921–22, William H. Dudley, director of its Bureau of Visual Instruction, claimed to have 3,500 reels available for both "formal classroom work" and "civic and community organizations," that is, community welfare organizations, farmer's clubs, and women's clubs.[97] Its catalogue for that year included a package labelled "Canadian Travel" with 99 lantern slides of the Canadian Rockies and three one-reel films, *The Canadian Rockies*, *Famous Locks at Sault Sainte Marie*, and *Water Power Tributary to Montreal, Canada*. For literary instruction, the Bureau also rented out Canadian Bioscope's five-reel feature *Evangeline* (1913).[98] The deputy minister at Canada's Department of Trade and Commerce later reported that it had also deposited Seeing Canada prints in such US extension divisions as the University of Arizona, University of California, University of Colorado, University of Indiana, University of Iowa, University of Kansas, University of Minnesota, University of Missouri, University of Oregon, University of Texas, and University of Utah.[99]

Likewise, North Dakota Agricultural College's Visual Instruction Service, under A.P. Hollis (director 1918–24), which was part of its Extension Division, included a scenic on the Canadian Rockies and suggested it for history or geography classes.[100] This was not an anomaly: US visual-education libraries typically listed Canadian tourism films under the heading of geography, as can be seen in educational catalogues circulated during this period. For example, the *1001 Films* catalogue, an early reference guide to non-theatrical productions first published in 1920 by *Moving Picture Age*, typically listed tourism films under their geography category, including five one-reel "educational" films produced by the Ford Motor Company featuring Canada. These works explicitly privileged a tourist perspective by offering scenic views, highlighting recreational possibilities (boating, golfing, riding, swimming) and sightseeing via Ford automobiles (figure 2.7).[101]

Specialists in visual instruction repeatedly cited the exceptional value of moving images when they distributed content for geography courses. An article in *Reel and Slide* reported, "Perhaps no branch of instruction offers such excellent opportunities for visualization as does geography. The class is enabled to see, in life like pictures, localities which, heretofore, have been described only in the motionless illustrations of the text book."[102] The tourism industry surmised that visual instruction of geography content could instill a longing to visit some

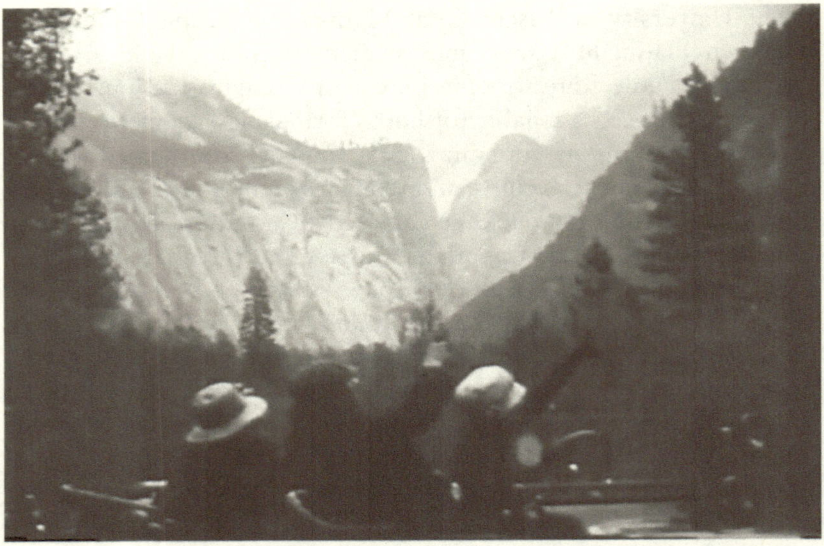

2.7 Ford Educational Weekly, *Nature's Echo: With the Canadian Rockies as the Host*, 1919

day. To that end, public and private organizations connected to tourism donated scenics to non-theatrical distribution agencies as educational. Schoolchildren and adult learners provided a sizable market for motion pictures that discreetly advertised their sponsors. Most schools gratefully accepted free or low-cost scenics, which were rebranded as geography, travel, or transportation films, as they did not tax the limited resources of the school system.[103]

Therefore, most motion pictures distributed for instruction by Trade and Commerce's Exhibits and Publicity Bureau were educational in the broadest sense. Some leaders in visual education saw the travelogue, essentially an ad for the tourism industry, being repurposed in geography lessons. Anna Verona Dorris, both the director of Visual Education for the Berkeley Public Schools and an assistant professor of geography at San Francisco State University, held that, although visual instruction enhanced the teaching of modern geography, most "motion-picture material has been produced primarily for commercial purposes. Much of it has considerable educational value, but it must be adapted to school purposes, re-arranged, classified, re-titled, and in general made over to meet the needs of school children."[104] According to W.M. Gregory of the Cleveland School of Education, "Most of the so-called educational film consists of material that has been stripped from cast-off commercial film and retitled ... for school purposes." As well, "Frequently the only film entering a school is that produced for advertising."[105] F.D. McClusky, arguably the most strident critic, cautioned educators about the propaganda surrounding free motion pictures in the classroom.[106] He saw their preponderance as "a drug on the market," which "has seriously hampered the work of non-theatrical commercial interests."[107]

RAYMOND S. PECK AND THE CANADIAN GOVERNMENT MOTION PICTURE BUREAU

The individual largely responsible for expanding the non-theatrical distribution of Seeing Canada films into the United States was Raymond S. Peck, chief film editor at the Exhibits and Publicity Bureau, who became its director in the summer of 1920. B.E. Norrish had left the Bureau to become general manager of the new Associated Screen News of Canada (ASN), headquartered in Montreal. Tied to the CPR, ASN initially produced films for Canadian industry, but soon expanded to deliver a wide range of scenic pictures covering Canada as it carried out assignments for transportation companies and tourist agencies.[108] Most notably, between 1921 and 1929, ASN produced *Kinograms*, a series of theatrically released travelogues promoting CPR railway and steamship routes. Norrish claimed that these "scenics are made up to a high technical standard, aimed at fitting them to appear on the same screen with the best feature dramatic productions." With such titles as *Quebec, Old and New* (1921), *Canada's Last West* (1924), *The Classic Nipigon* (1926), and *Niagara* (1929), *Kinograms* occupied filmic terrain similar to the Bureau's Seeing Canada series, using film "to encourage travel, colonization and industrial development."[109] Moreover, ASN was contracted to supply a Canadian section of Pathé News. These Canadian-themed newsreels also held "supreme publicity value," circulating throughout the United States and the United Kingdom, reaching even "into the farthest corners where the motion picture has penetrated."[110]

As the Bureau's new director, Raymond S. Peck, who had considerable experience in publicity and film exchanges, oversaw a team of ten field cameramen spread out across the country shooting new "scenic-industrial reels" for bi-monthly theatrical and non-theatrical release, adding to the Seeing Canada subjects already in circulation.[111] One of Peck's first initiatives was an ambitious program for the new Canadian National Railways (CNR), incorporated 6 June 1919 following amalgamation of the Canadian Northern, the Grand Trunk Pacific, the Intercolonial, and the National Transcontinental railways, and as of January 1923 it would also include the Grand Trunk. With films illustrating elements of Canada's tourist attractions from the Bay of Fundy to Prince Rupert, the series would "produce a composite picture of the 'National Way.'" The following summer, the Bureau sent a cameraman to shoot scenes along Ontario's Nipigon River, the excavation of dinosaurs in Alberta, and Jasper National Park. Another cinematographer filmed in Quebec City, Montreal, Toronto, London, Hamilton, and Windsor for the Grand Trunk, while a colleague shot scenics in the Maritimes. To narrate these pictures, the CNR employed lecturers to address various educational bodies and chambers of commerce, reaching "thousands of people of the highest type."[112]

In 1923, Peck changed his agency's name to the Canadian Government Motion Picture Bureau (CGMPB) to indicate that it mostly produced films.[113] As its chief, Peck believed in "the tremendous national and international potentialities that are inherent in the narrow ribbon of celluloid" for acquainting the world with the Dominion's opportunities for "the home-seeker, the capitalist, and the tourist." He told the Society of Motion Picture Engineers that Canada, "through the aggressive and appealing use of the motion picture, is placing her wares in the world's 'shop window.'" To illustrate, he praised his agency's films for shaping international opinion of "the Dominion as a tourists' holiday land."[114] While quantifying its impact on tourism was, he admitted, challenging, he cited specific examples. Namely, after a Canadian government official asked a group of American tourists "how and why they had selected Jasper Park as their tourist objective," the party declared "they had seen or been shown some Canadian Government motion pictures dealing with Jasper Park and were 'sold' on the Jasper Park trip."[115]

Nevertheless, Peck saw film's publicity power as a double-edged sword. Certainly, the Bureau's cinematographic advertising campaign boosted tourism. "When it is realized that the fourth industry of Canada is the tourist industry," he informed the Associated Motion Picture Advertisers (AMPA) in New York, "the value of motion pictures to the Dominion can readily be appreciated."[116] Yet "a certain type of screen drama" could harm tourism by exhibiting "Canada as a vast, barren tract of snow and ice, cut into furrows by malemutes [sled dogs] driven by Indians or Eskimos with handsome, dashing members of the Northwest Mounted Police 'getting their man' amid the depths of snow and ice. All this is mighty romantic and colorful, but it is not typically true of Canada."[117]

Peck's derision of a "certain type of screen drama" refers to the popular Canadian-themed fictional dramas produced by the American film industry. From the 1910s and into the 1950s, most US-based studios produced motion pictures categorized as north-woods or northwest (melo)dramas that diverged from Westerns or other outdoor adventure films due to their Canadian setting. Although many were filmed in northern California, they modelled the northland, an imagined region referring to the Canadian northwest, Klondike, and northern Ontario/Quebec, according to romantic notions of the sublime. Narratives were temporally situated in the eighteenth and nineteenth centuries and featured such colourful stock characters as voyageurs (French-Canadian fur traders), lumberjacks, miners, Mounties, "Indians," and "half-breeds." North-woods melodramas were typically settler-colonial tales celebrating virile (Anglo-Saxon) masculinity, often in the form of the Mountie, succeeding against all odds – an unforgivable climate, wild animals, and criminal elements.[118]

Filmmakers typically derived these regional representations of Canada from popular novels and short stories by such authors as Rex Beach, Ralph Connor, James Oliver Curwood, Jack London, Robert Service, and Stewart Edward White, but especially Curwood. Throughout the early twentieth century, the prolific Michigan-born author shaped the genre by fashioning the imagined literary/cinematic geography of "God's Country." Before achieving recognition as an author and later film scenarist and producer, Curwood had been hired by the Dominion government to promote, in a series of magazine articles, the settlement of white (ideally northern European) American farmers in Canada's western interior as part of its "Last Best West" advertising campaign. Government and railway officials also paid Curwood, an avid outdoorsman, to inject advertising messages obliquely into his writings to stimulate tourism to Canada. As he transitioned into the film industry by the mid-1910s, his name was already a branded commodity, strategically linked to the Canadian northwest in the cultural marketplace. Red-blooded motion pictures that bore his name indirectly advertised Canada as a desirable destination to American moviegoers (figure 2.8).[119]

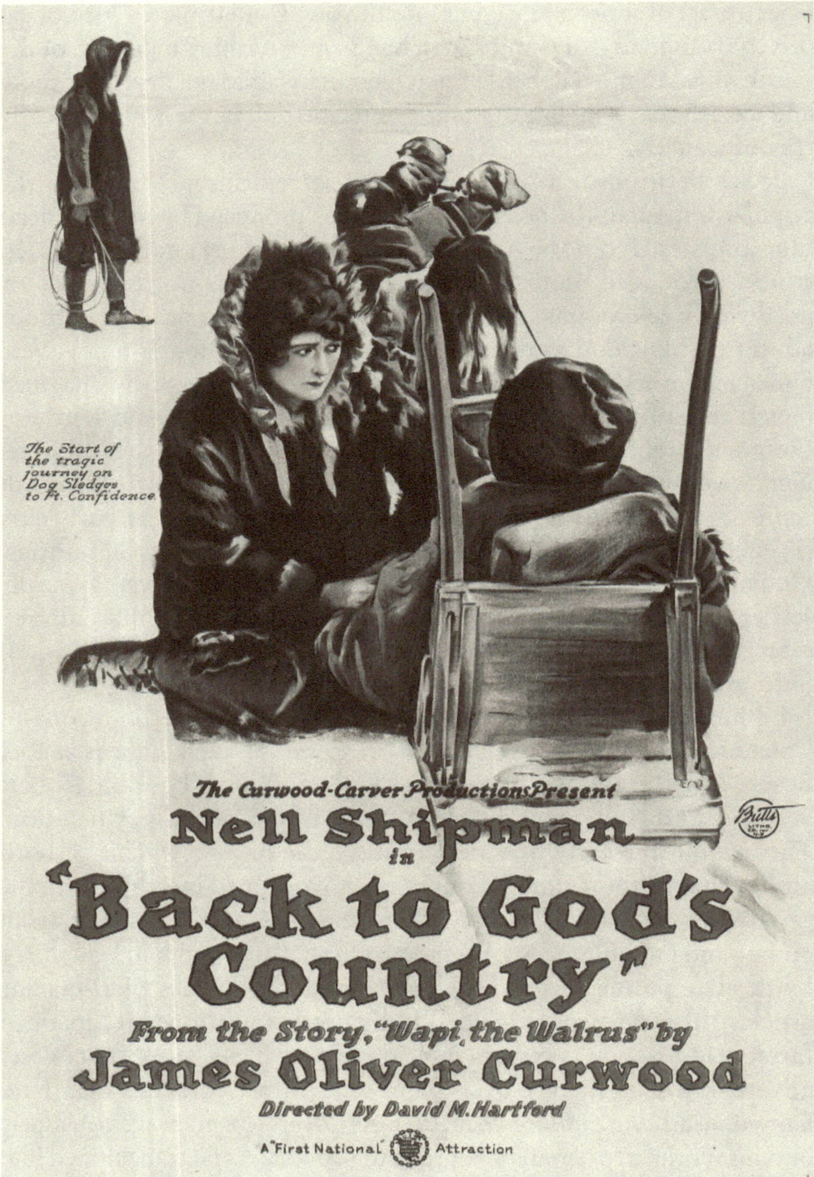

2.8 Advertisement for *Back to God's Country*, *Motion Picture News*, 27 September 1919

Although Peck never named the author, he expressed his concern that sensational depictions of Canada in Curwood-type northwest melodramas could result in "unfavourable publicity." Fortunately, his CGMPB productions offered a necessary antidote by "illustrating graphically" the Dominion's "natural attractions, agreeable climate, historical associations, up-to-date cities, big-game hunting possibilities, unrivaled fishing resorts and unsurpassed scenery." For Peck, Seeing Canada's representations were responsible "for correcting false impressions," held particularly by "our closest neighbor and friend, the United States," as disseminated by Hollywood melodramas.[120] Yet, as the *Globe* points out, this appeared to be a Sisyphean task. "In view of the fact" that the CGMPB "has been operating since 1918 and that the films which it sends out represent views from every section of Canada, from Halifax to Vancouver and from Windsor to Baffin's Land, it is hard to explain the presence of tourists who come to Southern Ontario in July equipped with snowshoes and toboggans and those who think Canada has nothing to offer but bush, bears, and booze."[121]

Peck believed that rectifying such misleading images needed more than government-sponsored scenics. To ensure the success of cinematographic advertising on tourism, he advocated for the Bureau's cooperation with private American interests in pictures related to the Dominion. Beyond simply welcoming American producers who would "cross the line" to harness Canada's "wonderful advantages" for producing motion pictures, he favoured government support.[122] He hoped that such backing would help his agency influence or shape Hollywood's depictions of Canada.

This was evident in First National's *The Knockout* (dir. by Lambert Hillyer, 1926), a starring vehicle for Milton Sills, "the concentrated essence of He-Manhood."[123] During the summer of 1925, Lambert Hillyer shot exteriors in a lumber camp located 150 miles (240 kilometres) north of Ottawa in northwest Quebec and included scenes of log drives and jams filmed on the Ottawa, Gatineau, and Beauchêne rivers. Peck was "actively engaged with First National officials in laying plans for the shooting" and ensured the CGMPB's full participation by turning over its laboratories and resources to Earl Hudson's eastern production unit.[124] The Bureau's hope that this Hollywood production could indirectly play up the allure of Canada's north woods ended when several members of Parliament (MPs) and Ottawa-based exhibitors ascertained that advance advertising referred to *The Knockout* as "a story of the Maine woods." E.A. Eschmann, First National's distribution manager, called the film "the story of a prize fighter in the Maine lumber camps." An irate T.L. Church, a former Toronto mayor and MP, clamoured for banning pictures that had been taken in the Dominion, but represented other nations.[125]

To avoid further contretemps, Fred Stanley, location manager for Earl Hudson's unit, affirmed that "full screen credit for all exterior scenes will be given to Canada," as well as to the CGMPB for its assistance. Ads appearing in the autumn stated that the film's "gorgeous atmospheric scenes of the north" were "secured through the cooperation of the Canadian government." Stanley speculated that more American producers would use the Dominion's scenic locales.[126] During the summer of 1926, the Board offered its full cooperation to Metro-Goldwyn-Mayer (MGM) for its Klondike Gold Rush epic, *Trail of '98* (dir. by Clarence Brown, 1928), based on a Robert W. Service story. Likewise, Peck, RCMP officials, and representatives of the Dominion's Forestry Branch assisted an MGM representative who was scouting outdoor locations near Ottawa for *The Flaming Forest* (dir. by Reginald Barker, 1926), a Mountie melodrama adapted from a Curwood novel. Neither production, however, appears to have been filmed in Canada (figure 2.9).[127]

Believing that Hollywood's status and the popularity of the Western could draw tourists, the Dominion also cooperated with Universal's *The Calgary Stampede* (dir. by Herbert Blaché, 1925). The six-reeler stars Hoot Gibson as an American who goes to Canada for adventure and competes in the Calgary Stampede's rodeo as a Roman rider – a trick in which the rider stands upon a pair of horses with a foot astride each animal's back.[128] Guy Weadick, a Rochester-born performer from the vaudeville and Wild West Show circuits, founded Calgary's Canadian Exhibition and Stampede in 1912. In the lead-up to the July 1925 iteration of "The Greatest Outdoor Show on Earth," he courted show-business celebrities to drum up publicity. The festivities honoured the fiftieth anniversary of the arrival of the North-West Mounted Police at Fort Calgary. Steeped in anglophone settler-colonial narratives and celebrating technology, the jubilee included a midway, rodeo competitions (with both settler and Indigenous riders), and a parade featuring local First Nations, cowboys/cowgirls, dignitaries, and a historical pageant.[129]

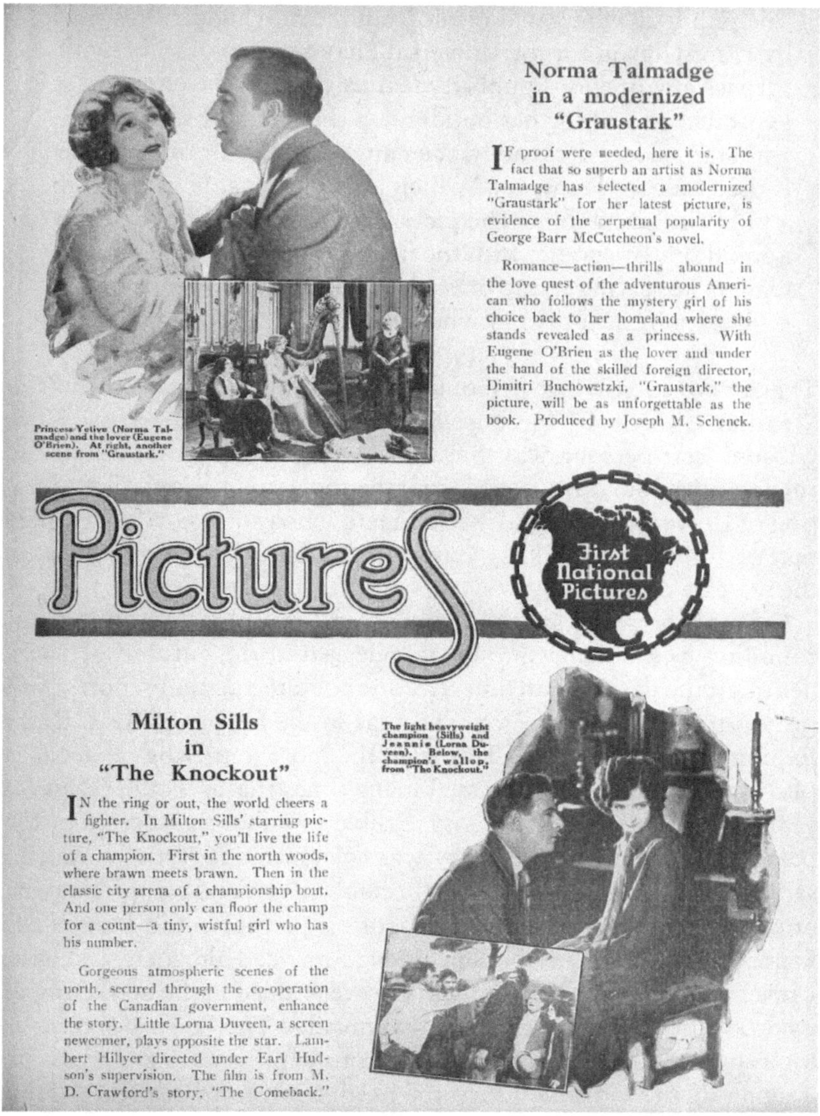

2.9 Advertisement for *The Knockout*, *Picture-Play Magazine*, October 1925

Weadick persuaded Universal's sagebrush star to not only attend the 1925 Stampede, but also to use it as the backdrop for a Gibson vehicle.[130] The annual report predicted:

> The publicity which will result from the moving pictures made by Hoot Gibson for the Universal Pictures Corporation, will surpass any previous publicity feature and will be of great assistance in still further building up the annual Exhibition and Stampede. Fortunately, the name selected for this picture is the "Calgary Stampede" which is of inestimable value from a publicity standpoint. The picture will likely be shown to 30 or 40 millions of people, with the necessary advertisements and readers appearing in the press and illustrated billboard paper appearing in each district where shown.[131]

The American cowboy personality was a logical choice to bolster Weadick's vision of the occasion. Throughout the 1920s, Hoot Gibson's star persona was that of an award-winning horseman and rope spinner who transitioned from the rodeo to filmdom. The adoration of Universal's straight-shooting and wholesome cowboy rivalled that of Tom Mix and Harry Carey among fans of virile stories set in the western outdoors.[132]

Gibson's presence at the stampede and resulting promotion surrounding *The Calgary Stampede*, released in the autumn of 1925, delivered the desired outcome. According to the annual report, 1926 proved to be "the most successful year in the history of the Calgary Exhibition and Stampede. This is all the more gratifying on account of the general opinion expressed many times that it would be an off year, as it was thought to be impossible to equal the success of the previous year in which Calgary was celebrating its fiftieth anniversary."[133] The correlation between the film's release and record-breaking attendance demonstrated that a motion picture could launch the Stampede as a destination brand among American filmgoers. Likewise, Universal's exclusive rights to film the event aided in the marketing of its production. Trade periodicals commended *The Calgary Stampede* for its use of footage from the rodeo events, which appear at the climax, arguing that this distinguished the production from other Westerns. "Shots of the various contestants and the different events," wrote one critic, "offer unusually realistic thrills that cannot be mistaken for 'staged' thrills. They are the real thing."[134]

The optimistic rhetoric surrounding such American productions seemed to support the Dominion's potential as a "strategic production zone" for Hollywood film interests, which would ultimately advertise the country and boost tourism. "Canada has much to offer the American film producer in the way of outstanding scenic locations," wrote F.C.T. O'Hara in his annual report of 1926, "and the Bureau is closely in touch with the leading American film producers and is encouraging them to make use of Canadian locations from time to time."[135] Confidentially, however, O'Hara wrote to the joint secretary of the Office of the High Commissioner of Canada in Washington, DC, that "the sentiment in Canada is strongly in favour of British films, for the Canadian public are pretty well fed up on United States vapouries."[136]

Certainly, most members of the Canadian and British elite bemoaned the domination of American-made films in their countries for both cultural and economic reasons. In the aftermath of the war, the US film industry had increased its exports to Europe and beyond exponentially, saturating the global market. This generated calls for protectionist measures to support filmmaking within the British Empire. Peck saw this as an opportunity to establish a subsidiary film industry in Canada, parallel to the automobile branch-plants. He believed that "legitimate American producers" would flock north to qualify their pictures under Britain's proposed "Kontingent Plan," referring to Germany's 1925 legislation that limited the proportion of foreign films exhibited in its domestic market. More than a dozen countries were pressing for quotas to challenge US films' global domination. Canadian Liberal Prime Minister William Lyon Mackenzie King conjectured that such a scheme would diminish "the initial advantage of the United States" over time.[137]

At the Imperial Conference of 1926 in London, delegates maintained that since film was a powerful publicity medium, the constant showing of foreign – read American – films was a concern but could be rectified with limits and an increase in empire film production. British protectionism would culminate with the Cinematograph Films Act in 1927, effective April 1928, requiring that exhibitors show a quota of British films (initially 5 per cent and rising to 20 per cent over ten years). To qualify, a film must be made by a British subject and a registered British company, filmed within the empire, and have at least 75 per cent of its cast and crew be British subjects.[138] While Canada did not adopt similar legislation, it did make a case for increasing domestic production "principally directed to the United States with its 110,000,000 of prospective tourists." The Dominion's Chief Government Trade Commissioner pointed to the success of Seeing Canada as evidence that government film investment played "an important part in stimulating the immense increase in the visits of United States tourists to Canada." He added that "atmospheric ... conditions favourable to the production of film equal to those existing in the United States" meant that Canada too could manufacture feature-length fictional motion pictures in addition to its scenic films.[139]

Hence, in March 1927, Peck travelled to Los Angeles to meet with film executives to discuss producing possibilities within the Dominion. James Malcolm, minister at Trade and Commerce (1926–30), anticipated revenue from Peck's "return from Hollywood with certain contracts in his pocket."[140] Roughly two months after his trip, however, Peck died suddenly at the age of forty-two. His successor was Captain Frank C. Badgley. Wounded in France during the First World War, Badgley handled still and moving images for British propaganda in the United States. Metro Pictures had hired him after the war, and he also worked for various film companies as an actor, scenarist, and/or technician before joining the Bureau in 1922.[141]

Although he did not live to witness it, Peck's branch-plant film industry materialized under Badgley. Between 1928 and 1938, Canadian-based, US-financed companies produced twenty-two "quota quickies" – cheap, rushed feature films for American distributors who needed British Empire product.[142] While Canadian (British-)quota films potentially displayed local colour, the desired injection of Hollywood expertise and capital to stimulate a domestic industry was a pipe dream; the American colossus was consolidating its own interests as opposed to mentoring Canadian filmmakers or generating product to publicize Canadian tourism. For roughly the next decade and a half, the CGMPB under Badgley (served 1927–41) would produce non-theatrical tourism films to advertise Canada abroad. Yet it was not the only Dominion agency making films to promote tourism; the Parks Branch was equally active.

According to Paul Rotha, all film "is a means of propaganda, either in a fictional way, or as a specifically designed piece of advertisement. It is a medium which offers to any creative mind a wealth of experiment in its peculiar technical devices for appealing to the human beings of this world."[143] During the 1910s and 1920s in Canada, government agencies and private filmmaking interests adopted a variety of propaganda strategies to promote tourism through film. Between 1911 and 1914, domestic productions surged during a wave of nationalism that formulated a positive destination image. Such films might well influence the behavioural intentions of American tourists. As nationalism intensified during the war, the Dominion, alongside private organizations, held that cinema's massive reach across a diverse population and its ability to engage audiences emotionally indicated its value for promotion. Film's role in wartime propaganda encouraged the postwar production of useful pictures for both education and advertising. Armed with psychological studies on spectators' apparent receptivity through the "eye gate," government agencies embraced theatrical and non-theatrical film production that straddled visual education and cinematographic advertising. Couching offerings as educational, the OMPB and the Exhibits and Publicity Bureau/CGMPB could advertise a particular destination(s) without an overtly commercial plug that could "turn off" audiences.

Seeing Canada particularly indicated film's potential as a subtle advertising medium to sell Canada to American tourists. Concurrently, Peck believed that Hollywood's pervasive northwest melodramas, which often depicted Canada as a frozen and dangerous wasteland, could undermine his agency's goal of depicting a tourist-friendly destination. While it was unlikely that the CGMPB could sway or restyle Canada's on-screen presence in Hollywood productions, Peck hoped to tap into their global influence by encouraging on-location filming and offering government assistance. Later the CGMPB adopted a bifurcated strategy of collaborative government film production and active cooperation with US commercial film interests to promote tourism.

3

Settler-Colonial Tourism Films

W.J. Oliver and Publicizing the National Parks during the 1920s and 1930s

W.J. Oliver is the most modest of men, yet few men have so effectively made Canada known the world over.

Canada Weekly, 29 March 1946[1]

During the interwar period, Calgary-based William (Bill) J. Oliver was the primary filmmaker for Canada's National Parks. Released in both theatrical and non-theatrical circuits, his one- and two-reel non-fiction films conveyed the institutional priorities of Commissioner James B. Harkin and the Parks Branch, emphasizing scenic vistas accessible by automobiles, year-round recreation, and wildlife preservation. Oliver also filmed several productions featuring Grey Owl, the fraudulent "Indian" identity of the English-born immigrant Archibald Belaney. Together these motion pictures carry the complex legacy of elimination and appropriation of settler-colonial states. While most of Oliver's films expunge Indigenous peoples and perspectives, helping to reframe wilderness landscapes as accessible tourist spaces, the Grey Owl films demonstrate that appropriation is equally central to transnational settler-colonial tourist narratives.[2]

Canada's National Parks had since war's end marketed their destinations through films, most of them produced by the Exhibits and Publicity Bureau for its Seeing Canada series. Although these Dominion agencies seemingly collaborated towards a common goal, tension rather than cooperation characterized their relationship. Parks Commissioner James B. Harkin expected that his branch would create narrative and visual representations through its Publicity and Information Division, established in 1921 under J.C. Campbell. It would produce or sponsor its own films and lend them at no charge to "conservation societies, universities, schools, writers, lecturers," which touted "the many attractions of Canada's national playgrounds."[3] Between the late 1920s and the Second World War, Oliver had become the Parks Branch's main filmmaker. His motion pictures constructed myths of settler-colonial nationhood – erasing and creating spaces by deleting, appropriating, and re-inscribing Indigenous cultures – that the parks in turn used to sell themselves to American tourists. By the end of 1938, the publicity arm boasted that it had 84 subjects in 35-mm (for theatrical circulation) and 87 subjects in 16-mm (non-theatrical), "comprising a total of 1,817 prints descriptive of the scenic, recreational, and wild life aspects of Canada."[4] On the eve of the Second World War, this tourism film library represented a substantial investment of governmental funds for publicity.

JAMES B. HARKIN AND PARKS PUBLICITY

Under the pretext of conservation and recreation, the establishment of the Dominion's first National Parks – Banff, in 1885; Glacier, in 1886; Yoho, in 1886; Waterton, in 1895; and Jasper, in 1906 – involved the removal and exclusion of the First Nations that had resided on those lands. "Indians" would later be restored as spectacles or guides for settler-colonial tourists. The method of setting aside so-called empty lands as protected areas, regulating resources, excluding Indigenous communities, and encouraging visitors was not unique to Canada. Settler-colonial governments in the United States, New Zealand, and Australia engineered similar processes. "Imperialism, internationalism, and nationalism," as Bernhard Gissibl, Sabine Höhler, and Patrick Kupper argue, "all provide frameworks and opportunity structures for the global transfer and local appropriation of the national park idea."[5]

In 1911, the Dominion Forest Reserves and Parks Act designated the parks as "pleasure grounds for the benefit, advantage and enjoyment of the people of Canada." Believing that modern industrial and urban society had stultified the play instinct necessary for well-being, Commissioner Harkin maintained that the "pure, wholesome, healthful recreation of the great out-doors" available in the various parks could revitalize those so affected. He also recognized that tourists, especially from the United States, provided substantial revenue for the Dominion, and therefore advocated government's exploiting the parks' "commercial side." The Branch also worked to counteract the active "See America First" campaign in the United States. In his report for fiscal 1914, Harkin noted that Canada's slogan should be "See America's Best" due to its "outstanding advantages in the way of natural scenic and other attractions."[5] He used these therapeutic, nation-building, and business rationales to justify requests for more funds to develop the parks, especially to construct first-rate roads and expand promotional activities.

The interwar period was opportune for the Parks Branch to expand its brand presence in the United States. In January 1920, that country's Volstead Act came into effect, enforcing the 18th Amendment to the constitution, which prohibited the manufacture, sale, importation, or transportation of alcoholic beverages. Canada, particularly communities along the border, became a temporary "wet" refuge for those fleeing these "dry" strictures and expanding its tourism infrastructure.[6] Thirsty Americans typically trekked across the border by automobile, reflecting the growth of car ownership and improving roads. Beginning in the 1910s, provincial governments had recognized that the new automobile culture necessitated modern highways linking cities on both sides of the border to attract American motorists. Canada's interprovincial highways, by contrast, lagged by decades.[6] Moreover, a more tolerant view of leisure and the postwar rise in paid vacations made tourist-related activities more accessible to a greater number of working-class Americans. While socioeconomic and racial barriers continued to limit vacation experiences for wage earners, the tourism industry expanded and diversified.[7]

A former journalist, Harkin appreciated publicity's power to unlock the National Parks' potential as an economic generator. "The ultimate in scenery," he declared, is "the raw material for tourists," which needed to be cultivated through publicity.[8] M.B. (Mabel) Williams, a Department of the Interior file clerk and de facto publicist 1911–30 for the Parks Branch, was equally eager to advocate for increasing tourism. She helped articulate and disseminate the branch's philosophy through promotional literature.[9] Much to Harkin's dismay, during the Parks Branch's first decade the railways had handled the bulk of the efforts to attract tourists, specifically elite travellers.[10] Although he undoubtedly relished the free advertising, he reasoned that this was an inadequate and ineffective tactic. Expressing his frustration at the National Parks Conference in 1917, he stated that railways targeted "the people who travel largely in order that they may boast to their less fortunate friends that they have seen Banff." Conversely, in-house publicity would give the branch more control over its public image and allow it to target "the rest of the people who do not get the sort of recreation the parks afford."[11]

Therefore, when Harkin reorganized the branch in 1921, renaming it the Canadian National Parks Branch (eventually dropping "Canadian" in 1930), he set up a publicity division under J.C. Campbell.[12] The branch began ardent promotion that included coloured slides, still photography, and printed materials. M.B. Williams, for example, wrote a series of mass-market travel guides, which framed the parks as ideal venues for automobile tourism, particularly after the Banff-Windermere Highway opened in 1923 and the Kicking Horse Trail in 1927.[13]

Buoyed by the success of the Seeing Canada series, in which Raymond S. Peck and the Parks Branch shared costs on securing material, Harkin surmised that film offered "the most valuable publicity."[14] Seeing it as an ideal medium for both education and marketing, his annual reports emphasized that motion pictures of the parks were in high demand throughout the United States and Canada. He reported that in 1923 films were screened in several theatres in the US Pacific coast region with the cooperation of the California Audubon Society and the Universities of California and Southern California.[15] The following year, the Parks Branch expanded its illustrated lecture tours, targeting automobile clubs, boards of trade, Kiwanis Clubs, and Rotary clubs. J.C. Campbell, accompanied by a lecturer and a projectionist, travelled to 14 midwestern, western, and Pacific coast states, reaching 74,375 Americans in 1923–24 alone, as well as going to Quebec, Ontario, Alberta, and British Columbia. While ostensibly educational, as Harkin reported for fiscal 1923–24, "the lectures in the United States were for the purpose of promoting tourist travel to Canada's National Parks during the year."[16]

The use of film as a publicity device to visually articulate and disseminate a destination brand for the National Parks expanded throughout the decade. This would result in tensions with Peck. From the outset, the Exhibits and Publicity Bureau/CGMPB prided itself on building bonds with other government agencies in pursuit of a shared goal, that is, promoting Canada through motion pictures. According to Peck, the Bureau's "outstanding feature" "is the co-operative work which has been and is being performed for the various Federal Departments, and the Canadian National Railway System." He noted that the Parks Branch employed a lecturer who screened the Bureau's motion pictures to over 23,000 people. Moreover, exploitation and distribution through Bray Productions reached an estimated four to five million Americans. "These lectures and films," Peck added, "have been the means of increasing the number of visitors to the National Parks of Canada."[17]

Animosity between Peck and the Parks Branch, however, permeated this seemingly cozy relationship as early as 1922. Writing to Deputy Minister of Trade and Commerce F.C.T. O'Hara, Peck remarked that, although his agency was doing "more free publicity work for the Dominion Parks Branch than for any other branch of the Federal Government," the National Parks desired "a film plant of their own." He warned O'Hara that it might "make statements concerning our Bureau to further their own film plant schemes." According to Peck, Campbell was trying to create the impression that the Bureau was uncooperative, and he wanted to prove the contrary. He specified that Campbell had contacted him about making a film featuring the well-known American outdoor author Rex Beach on a hunting and fishing trip to Gatineau, in Quebec near Ottawa. Peck agreed, foreseeing a good instalment for the Seeing Canada series, but denied Campbell's request for a special $2,000 camera. Concerned that the latter would characterize his handling of the situation as proof of the Bureau's contrariness, he assured O'Hara: "We have not refused to co-operate with any governmental department when the request was reasonable and justified."[18] He wrote again, suggesting "something clean-cut and definite must be done with the Parks Branch people, as we are always running foul of them in our work."[19] Although the CGMPB claimed that its original order-in-council of 1918 was intended to centralize the nation's film activities, the Parks Branch increasingly circumvented this directive, as Campbell advocated enlarging its motion-picture interests as a method of direct publicity.[20]

WILLIAM J. OLIVER AND *THE LAST FRONTIER*

Between the wars, the Parks Branch relied on photographer and cinematographer William J. Oliver to oversee film production. Perhaps inspired by the CPR's campaign to encourage tourism and settlement in the western interior, Oliver immigrated from England to southern Alberta as a young man in April 1910. His interest in photography as a pastime developed into a career. Employed as a camera assistant at a Calgary studio, he worked briefly as a photographer for the *Morning Albertan* (1911–12) before joining the *Calgary Herald*, the city's largest newspaper, and opening his own studio in 1912. Over the next decade, he honed his skills as an outdoor still photographer and, beginning in 1917, established himself as a freelance motion-picture operator. As early as 1919, Oliver sold a film of his camping trip to Waterton Lakes National Park in Alberta to the Parks Branch. He also shot *Jasper of the Lakes* (1921), a picturization of a poem by T.P. O'Connor, a local schoolteacher, for the Seeing Canada series, which features wildlife views (beaver, bear, squirrel), as well as mountain scenery.[21]

In 1921, the Matador Land and Cattle Company hired Oliver to film the moving of 6,000 head of cattle from Swift Current, Saskatchewan, to South Dakota after it closed its Canadian operations.[22] With his newfound proficiency in filming large herds, in the autumn of 1923 Oliver was hired as a spare cameraman for *The Last Frontier*, an epic Western about the building of the transcontinental railway in the United States. On 10 April 1923, producer Thomas H. Ince had contracted author Courtney Ryley Cooper to write a story that incorporated scenes of the round-up and stampede of buffalo at Buffalo National Park, south of Wainwright, Alberta. He somehow knew that the Dominion was preparing to cull a portion of its Wainwright herd.[23]

Established in 1908, following the Dominion government's purchase of a free-ranging bison herd from Montana ranchers Charles Allard and Michel Pablo, Buffalo National Park was a 160-square-mile reserve for the nearly extinct species, which co-existed with several specimens of antelope, elk, deer, and moose. Materially and symbolically central to the First Nations of the North American Great Plains, pemmican (dried buffalo meat mixed with fat and other ingredients) became a key energy source for the fur trade, resulting in the near-extermination of these animals by the 1880s. By the turn of the twentieth century, a preservation movement emerged, stemming from a desire to save this living relic of the imagined, masculine frontier past, as well as from the urging of ranchers keen to preserve the animals for meat or sport tourism.[24]

The commercial value of the Pablo-Allard herd was not lost on the Parks Branch. Howard Douglas, superintendent of Rocky Mountains Park, wrote to Deputy Minister of the Interior W.W. Cory that the unique acquisition would be a "great advertisement" for

Canada, which could boast the largest bison herd in the world.[25] Boosters similarly projected that these monarchs of the plains would transform Wainwright into a "famous tourist resort." A.E. Duff, chief passenger agent for the Grand Trunk Railway, declared that the buffalo "would become one of the greatest attractions for tourists along their line and an attraction which the company would make it a point to keep before the travelling public." By 1911 the *Wainwright Star* proclaimed, "Thousands of strangers visit this famous park every year, many coming to the town for no other purpose."[26] Six years later, recreational facilities were developed at Mott Lake, within the park, where visitors could swim and picnic on its sandy beaches.[27]

The promise of flourishing tourism built around the buffalo preserve did not materialize. Visitors numbered about 6,000 each year in the mid-1920s, far below the average at the other parks.[28] Meanwhile, the original bison herd quickly proliferated, reaching approximately 6,600 head by 1923. Too many buffalo now grazed a rapidly degrading, drought-ridden range. Harkin authorized the culling of approximately 2,000 excess bulls during the annual round-up to reduce overpopulation, which threatened to spread disease, particularly tuberculosis. The hides and meat would then be sold to generate revenue.[29]

Harkin reached an agreement with Ince to film the cull with a view to earning additional income and generating publicity for the test-marketing of buffalo pemmican, steaks, robes, and mounted heads. The Parks Branch expected this collaboration with a renowned Hollywood figure to generate free advertising for Buffalo National Park's lagging tourism business. The National Parks would receive the surplus cuttings from the thousands of feet of film, with which "an educational and scenic film picture" could be made by "the Dominion government." Moreover, Ince and Harkin agreed that the main title of the completed film would acknowledge the government's cooperation for the use of the herd.[30] In a prepared statement, Harkin remarked: "The outstanding fact is that the Wainwright buffalo herd has had the most wonderful advertising which can be capitalized not only in regard to our forthcoming sale of buffalo products but also in regard to tourist business next year for Buffalo Park. Years of ordinary publicity work would not have served to educate the public of this continent on Buffalo Park and buffalo products as this has done in a few weeks; and the educational work will be increased when the film is put into circulation and all the advertising of the film by the Ince people carried out."[31]

Rehearsals and filming took place 17–22 October 1923 under directors John Ince (Thomas Ince's older brother) and Reeves Eason. A.G. Smith, park superintendent, supervised the round-up of several thousand buffalo. In this scene, the "hostile Indians, short of ammunition," stampede a herd of wild bison directly over the frontier settlement. One hundred Cree and twenty-five "squaws" from the nearby Hobbemma Reservation were hired, "through the courtesy of the government," at a dollar and a half per day, and provided with food.[32] Oliver was one of nine cameramen placed in hidden pits in the very centre of the stampede. Camouflaged sharpshooters opened fire as the animals came in range of the cameras, resulting in the death of twenty-four.[33] According to the *Wainwright Star*, the buffalo killing was "purely for historical detail and dramatic interest"; the planned slaughter of excess bulls took place in early 1924 and was not filmed "for the reason that such scenes would not be educational or entertaining" (figure 3.1).[34]

Impressed with Oliver's work on shooting this harrowing sequence, Thomas Ince apparently offered him a position at his southern California studio. As M.B. Williams communicated to Oliver, "I thought when they saw your coolness and willingness and the kind of work you could do, they were almost certain to make you an offer." She also suggested that Oliver encourage "the Ince people to come to Waterton" and film the national park.[35] Oliver's involvement on *The Last Frontier* equally excited J.C. Campbell, who believed the film would result in "wonderful publicity."[36] The town of Wainwright also assumed that once audiences learned that the American film pioneer shot this "great historical Western drama" on location, the park would be "made famous."[37] A letter to the editor of the *Wainwright Star* proposed that the town leverage the resulting publicity from the film to justify modernizing automobile routes for the predicted onslaught of tourists.[38]

While local and national boosters hoped that the hype would raise the profile of the Parks Branch's buffalo products and tourism, it did the opposite. Public criticism emerged over the slaughter of buffalo seemingly so that a Hollywood producer could generate "a movie thrill for American audiences."[39] Animal-welfare groups were particularly vocal in their protests. Emerging from Progressive-era reform initiatives, the humane movement had been criticizing the film industry's callous treatment or depictions of cruelty towards animals since the 1910s – especially in its epic Westerns.[40] Fannie Thompson

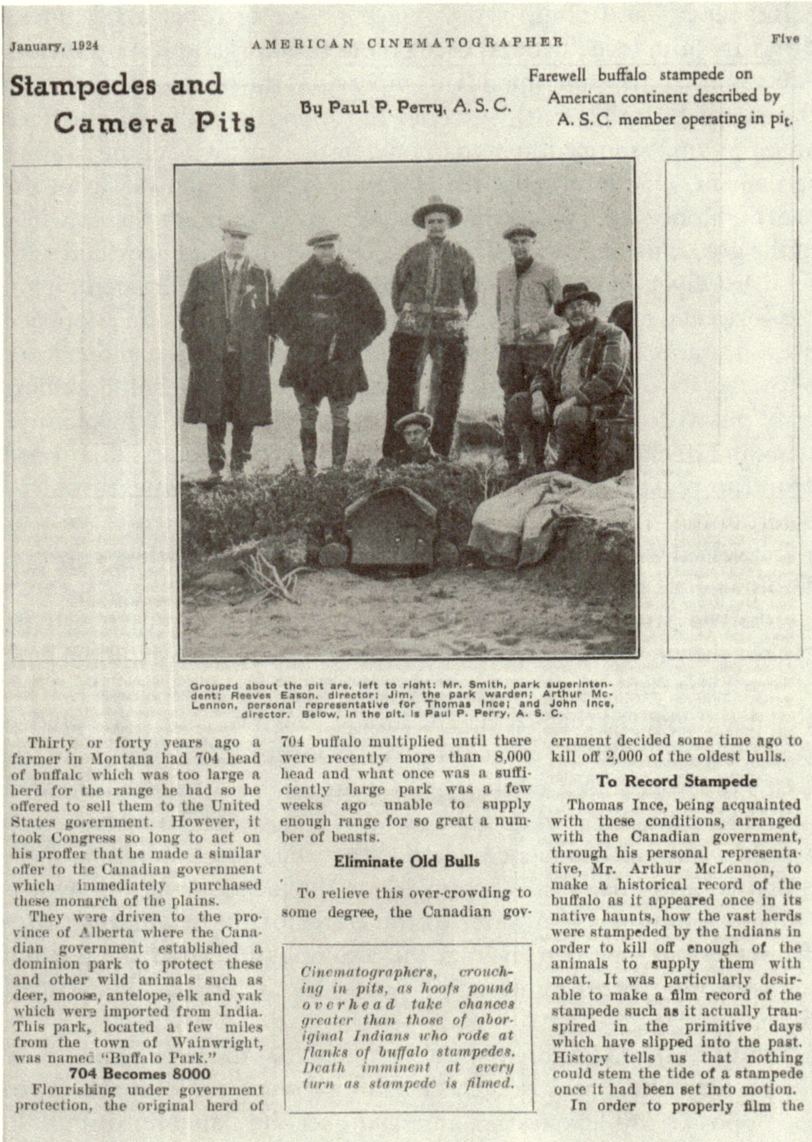

January, 1924 AMERICAN CINEMATOGRAPHER Five

Stampedes and Camera Pits

By Paul P. Perry, A. S. C.

Farewell buffalo stampede on American continent described by A. S. C. member operating in pit.

Grouped about the pit are, left to right: Mr. Smith, park superintendent; Reeves Eason, director; Jim, the park warden; Arthur McLennon, personal representative for Thomas Ince; and John Ince, director. Below, in the pit, is Paul P. Perry, A. S. C.

Thirty or forty years ago a farmer in Montana had 704 head of buffalo which was too large a herd for the range he had so he offered to sell them to the United States government. However, it took Congress so long to act on his proffer that he made a similar offer to the Canadian government which immediately purchased these monarch of the plains.

They were driven to the province of Alberta where the Canadian government established a dominion park to protect these and other wild animals such as deer, moose, antelope, elk and yak which were imported from India. This park, located a few miles from the town of Wainwright, was named "Buffalo Park."

704 Becomes 8000

Flourishing under government protection, the original herd of 704 buffalo multiplied until there were recently more than 8,000 head and what once was a sufficiently large park was a few weeks ago unable to supply enough range for so great a number of beasts.

Eliminate Old Bulls

To relieve this over-crowding to some degree, the Canadian government decided some time ago to kill off 2,000 of the oldest bulls.

Cinematographers, crouching in pits, as hoofs pound overhead take chances greater than those of aboriginal Indians who rode at flanks of buffalo stampedes. Death imminent at every turn as stampede is filmed.

To Record Stampede

Thomas Ince, being acquainted with these conditions, arranged with the Canadian government, through his personal representative, Mr. Arthur McLennon, to make a historical record of the buffalo as it appeared once in its native haunts, how the vast herds were stampeded by the Indians in order to kill off enough of the animals to supply them with meat. It was particularly desirable to make a film record of the stampede such as it actually transpired in the primitive days which have slipped into the past. History tells us that nothing could stem the tide of a stampede once it had been set into motion.

In order to properly film the

3.1 Article about Thomas H. Ince's *The Last Frontier*, *American Cinematographer*, January 1924

Kessler, president of the Los Angeles–based American Animal Defense League (AADL), lobbied a formal protest to Alberta's lieutenant-governor on the grounds that filming the stampede represented "needless cruelty of a demoralizing spectacle unworthy of the great human[e] Province of Alberta." AADL Vice President Rosemonde Rae Wright explained that *The Last Frontier* would harm "impressionable children" and the humane movement's goal of kindness towards animals, which it deemed necessary to a moral and just citizenry. "The sight of such suffering, and the knowledge which the youngest spectator is sure to have," Wright argues, "that the whole thing was deliberately planned and executed by men to make money, will cause either sorrowful pity or the feeling that it is not wrong to make animals suffer."[41]

Arthur MacLennan, director of advertising and publicity for the studio, countered these criticisms. He denied that Ince had organized "the wanton slaughter of buffalo," referring to the scheduled government cull of 2,000 buffalo, to add "realism to certain scenes" in the picture.[42] Defending his film, Ince stressed that the killing of "a *few* buffalo" was essential "to truthfully and historically depict the actual concurrences in the early American western history." These animals, he continued, "were despatched summarily and humanely by an expert rifleman, employed by the Canadian government," and immediately butchered and "fed to the populace in that section."[43] In an interview with the *Calgary Daily Herald*, Oliver corroborated these statements, claiming use of "the most humane methods."[44]

Later obstacles further impeded *The Last Frontier*'s potential as a pseudo-advertisement for the Parks Branch. Although the film was slated as the pinnacle of his 1924–25 schedule, Ince died suddenly (and under mysterious circumstances) on 19 November 1924 at the age of forty-two. Hunt Stromberg took over the production after buying the Buffalo National Park footage from the Ince estate. He sold the producing rights in September 1925 to Metropolitan Pictures. Director George B. Seitz ultimately completed the picture, which Metropolitan released in 1926.[45] In the meantime, the Parks Branch had been erased from the discourse appearing in the trade periodicals. For example, *Motion Picture News* claimed that Seitz filmed "the buffalo stampede scenes in Northern Arizona, where the largest existing herd of buffalo have been rounded up for use in this picture." It is unclear whether Seitz incorporated the original Buffalo National Park scenes in the final production, or whether Harkin ever received any of the promised negatives.[46]

While Harkin could perhaps not have predicted the public's reaction to the buffalo round-up and stampede, the lesson gleaned was that trans-border agreements with powerful motion-picture concerns stymied the Parks Branch's control of its destination image. As a result, the Branch worked on managing its own filmic interpretations by overseeing the production of scenics, most of them shot by Oliver. Although *The Last Frontier* was a debacle for Harkin and the Parks Branch, it had made Oliver a sought-after outdoor cinematographer. For instance, Universal hired him to work as a cameraman on the Hoot Gibson vehicle *The Calgary Stampede* (dir. by Herbert Blaché, 1925).[47] Ultimately, Oliver did not move to Inceville, the filmmaker's studio/ranch in the Santa Ynez Canyon outside of Los Angeles, and instead stayed in Alberta, where he shifted between the private and public spheres of the film industry.

In 1924, Oliver became the western field cameraman for the Canadian edition of the Fox Film Corporation's expanding newsreel service. He routinely won bonuses for his enterprising subjects and technical filming skills, which typically featured scenery and recreational activities in western Canada's National Parks.[48] Fox also awarded a yearly prize to the best work produced by one of its Canadian cameramen, which Oliver attained two years out of his six at the company. His proficiency at producing scenic newsreels made him an asset to Fox News. As its Canadian news editor, George Mitford, told him: "I look upon you as an expert whereas most of my field men are amateurs ... I know that you understand your work thoroughly so that I have come to depend on you ... Scenics in the mountains ought to be very good just now and in fact if you will send me as many as three subjects all at once ... I feel sure I could use them almost immediately."[49]

Meanwhile, Oliver continued to submit photographs and moving pictures to the Parks Branch, largely promoting southern Alberta. According to Dan E.C. Campbell, city editor of the *Calgary Herald* and later director of publicity for Alberta's Tourism Bureau:

> If you have ever seen the word stampede in print the chances are that you have seen some of W.J. Oliver's incomparable action pictures somewhere near it. If the calendar on your kitchen wall is illustrated ... by a picture of snowy peaks and singing pines, it's wholly likely to be from Oliver's camera. If your folks back in Shepherd's Bush, or Kans' City are arrested by immigration

> literature depicting big game in the Rockies, again you've come across Oliver's trail. In fact, southern Alberta is the best advertised corner of Canada, and the mainspring of that advertising appeal is the photographic contribution made by Canada's best outdoor camera artist, W.J. Oliver.[50]

PROMOTING SCENERY, RECREATION, AND WILDLIFE IN THE NATIONAL PARKS

By the late 1920s, W.J. Oliver had left Fox and devoted his energies to producing still and moving pictures for the Parks Branch. This visual imagery effaced the settler-colonial past, transforming a seemingly pristine wilderness into accessible tourist playgrounds. Oliver's filmic opus combined sublime landscapes *and* the modern machines that enabled more visitors to connect with primeval nature.[51] His work was thus in step with the Parks Branch's efforts to rebrand its locations as destinations for a new class of auto tourists. Harkin's report for fiscal 1921–22 had credited the interwar increase in tourist traffic to the "democratization" of road-based travel, noting that anyone who "owns a car may now enjoy the delights and benefits of a holiday among the mountains at a slight expenditure of both time and money."[52] While this category of recreational motorists was far from inclusive in terms of race or class, Harkin's vision of motor-age "people's parks" contrasted with the elite train travellers previously targeted by railway promotion.

One of Oliver's earlier projects, *Motoring through the Canadian Rockies* (192?), allowed audiences to experience the parks via new roadways, which would ideally incentivize travel. The film centres on "the grandeur of scenery" along the Banff-Windermere Highway, signalling that the auto road had superseded rail for engaging with nature. A fleet of Brewster Studebaker passenger trucks departs Banff and travels through the Yoho Valley past Moraine Lake and Takakkaw Falls. One critic relishes the vicarious experience of watching from the vantage point of these vehicles: "Up hills, down grades and along a picturesque winding road, the Studebakers roll smoothly onward, and one feels, in viewing the film, something of the glorious experience of the ride." Yet beyond a form of visceral film entertainment, which recalls the early "phantom ride" railway pictures, the scenic advertises "Alberta's great scenic highway," sure to pique tourist interest.[53]

In other films, Oliver frames the parklands as attractive recreation areas for American motoring vacationists. Automobile ownership had become a powerful symbol of a more modern, secular culture, marked by pleasure, leisure, and consumption. Moreover, Oliver's auto films noticeably include male and female tourists: Harkin surmised that the woman of the household was primarily responsible for making travel decisions.[54] Although we cannot be sure whether these films were made with the female spectator in mind, the hope was for women to identify with the content, which could then influence their travel plans.

For instance, in *Sunshine Trails* (1929), a young husband and wife from Great Falls, Montana, drive north into Alberta – the tourism film cuts to a road map with an animated, superimposed car that situates the viewer and reinforces the geographies of mobility. At the border, they face a few courteous formalities from a Canadian official before they go on to Waterton Lakes National Park, where visitors boat, fish, golf, hike, swim, and play tennis. The young people motor towards Banff, stopping to take in forests, lakes, and waterfalls. They also visit the Alberta Motor Association and the Calgary Automobile Club for maps and information. Rather than picturing an isolated wilderness, the film emphasizes accessibility, flexibility, and movement. *Sunshine Trails* depicts Alberta as an easy drive from the United States, a restorative northern getaway from urban life but with modern amenities.[55]

Holidaying among the Peaks (1930?) similarly emphasizes ease of access. A friend invites a brother and his two sisters from Great Falls, Montana, to join him at Waterton Lakes for two weeks. The Montanans pack the car and enjoy motoring and assorted outdoor pursuits.[56] Like *Sunshine Trails*, the film combines *looking* at the scenic beauties and *doing* open-air physical activities. In *Holidaying*, as in other films, Oliver reinforces Harkin's park ethos: "Recreation in the out-of-doors is essential for the physical, mental, moral health of the people."[57] A parallel belief in the "therapeutic promise" of outdoor recreation had swept the United States. In 1924 and 1926, President Calvin Coolidge convened the National Conference on Outdoor Recreation to develop a federal policy on outdoor recreation.[58]

Meanwhile, in *Through Mountain Gateways* (1930), a couple from Spokane, Washington, drives to the Kootenay National Park and Banff. An intertitle reads: "For fifty miles we travel – by still lakes, through green aisles of silence, and around breathless hair-pin curves." More than transportation from A to B, the automobile here, as in Oliver's other films about motoring tourism, is steeped in settler-colonial cultural meaning: mobility, technology, and tourism, signifying freedom and independence for the white middle class. Oliver thus uses film to reconcile the machine with the natural world; the automobile allows access to nature while its destructive impact (noise, pollution, spatial reorganization, speed) is erased.

Indeed, association, ingenuity, intensity, and repetition, according to psychologist Walter Dill Scott, were essential for successful advertising. The frequent reappearance of diverse key themes "becomes fixed in the [consumer's] memory."[59] Oliver produced other tourism films for the Parks Branch, including *Banff* (1929), *The Trail to Jasper* (1934), and *Through the Heart of the Rockies* (1935), with attractive and traversable roadways, visitor accommodation and services, and ample opportunities for outdoor recreation. Ideally, the prolonged repetition of these representations would forge mental images of these destinations and influence spectators' minds.

To that end, many of Oliver's productions focused on the National Parks as centres for sport tourism, ranging from fishing and riding to mountaineering and skiing, in keeping with Harkin's belief in outdoor recreation for moral and physical well-being. In *Goodbye to All That* (1930), *Trails to the Wilderness* (1930), and *Border Trails* (1932), Oliver conveys the majestic scenery and adventures available in wilderness pack trips and trail riding. For the Parks Branch, he also made tourism films centred on various forms of recreational fishing throughout Canada. *Fishin' in the High Spots* (1932) features the noted American humourist Irvin S. Cobb and Courtney Ryley Cooper, the freelance writer and avid fly fisher who wrote Ince's *The Last Frontier*, fishing for speckled trout in the Maligne-Medicine Lakes of Jasper National Park. Other comparable films include *With Lure and Line in Jasper* (1932), *Fishing for Tyee* (1933), *Where Fighting Beauties Rise* (1935), *Angling in the Infinite* (1936), and *Where Cohoes Play* (1938). Oliver also filmed New York City retailer-turned-big-game-angler Michael Lerner deep-sea fishing off Nova Scotia in *Warriors of the Deep* (1936) and *Battling the Tuna* (1937). The Nova Scotia government, in conjunction with the American Museum of Natural History, sponsored the Lerner-Oliver expedition to develop interest in deep-sea sport fishing as tourism.[60]

Not all productions were filmed during the peak summer tourist season. Oliver also shot winter scenes of snow-covered mountains designed to beckon more adventurous tourists, particularly Alpine skiers, and boost burgeoning off-peak tourism. Skiing, which Scandinavian settlers introduced to North America in the mid-nineteenth century, initially served as transportation in snowy regions and gradually became an organized sport. By the 1920s, the rise in popularity of winter sports – outdoor curling, skating, skiing (cross-country and downhill), snowmobiling, snowshoeing, and tobogganing – were transforming places like Banff, Jasper, and Mt Revelstoke into year-round tourism destinations. Chambers of commerce, civic boosters, and recreational associations encouraged the growth of outdoor winter recreation to boost local economies. Hence Oliver learned to ski, and used his skills to film *Skiing in Cloudland* (1930), *Skiing at Lake Louise* (1933), *Sunshine and Powder Snow* (1935), and *Winter Wonderland* (1936), featuring athletic men and women whooshing down the slopes.[61] For the more intrepid alpinists, he featured mountaineering in the Canadian Rockies in such productions as *New Skyscrapers for Old* (1931), *She Climbs to Conquer* (1933), *Climbing Mount Tupper* (1934), and *In the Shadow of Assiniboine* (1936).[62]

As well, Oliver filmed *Island of Enchantment* (1930) and *Canada's Evergreen Playground* (1934) about Vancouver Island. The Parks Branch sponsored these travelogues, cooperative ventures by J.C. Campbell and the Victoria and Island Publicity Bureau (VIPB). George I. Warren, VIPB commissioner 1922–60, had been branding his city as not only an evergreen playground, but also a community steeped in "British-ness."[63] The films, with scenic views of Butchart Gardens, the Inner Harbour, the Empress Hotel, and golf courses, and Indigenous canoers braving the Cowichan Rapids, were intended to "provide a more alluring way to advertise" the island.[64]

Oliver's Parks Branch films were not limited to the west, as seen in the Lerner-Oliver Atlantic fishing collaboration. Furthermore, to advertise Nova Scotia's Cape Breton Highlands National Park (established in 1936), Oliver filmed *The Highlands of Cape Breton* (1937), showcasing the dramatic, rugged coastline along the Cabot Trail, the motor road that crosses the park. Unlike the mountainous west, Cape Breton boasted what Alan MacEachern dubs "the coastal sublime," which Oliver aimed to convey through his films. Atlantic Canada's first National Park was the outcome of provincial demands to nationalize the parks system. Cross-country support likewise came from government officials who recognized that tourism's economic benefits from such a park could help alleviate the Depression.[65]

Oliver produced wildlife films as well for the Parks Branch. Saving native non-human animals in their natural habitat had been one of the factors that spurred establishment of the parks. As Harkin explains, "National parks exist to preserve not only as much as possible of the natural scenic beauty of the country, but also the fauna and flora, and other wild life, for the pleasure and benefit of the generations that are to come." Accordingly, he implemented protection for fur-bearing animals and set up sanctuaries for wild fowl and migratory birds. Other conservation measures were put in place to allow tourists to observe wildlife in the great outdoors.[66] Harkin deemed the system successful, as evidenced by the increase in non-domesticated animals and birds, which "are losing practically all fear of man." From "the recreational point of view," the widespread presence of bears, beavers, ducks, elk, geese, grouse, moose, mountain goats and sheep, and ptarmigans "constitutes one of the most important features of the parks. It is of no less consequence than the scenery itself, in fact it is almost said to be a part of the scenery."[67]

Unlike the hunting-related scenics of the early 1900s, Oliver's films promoted shooting animals with cameras, not guns, as part of an ostensibly more humane form of tourism. As *Forest and Outdoors* remarks, "We look to the dawn of a new day when the camera will replace the gun, and the hunting instinct – a hang-over from pre-historic times – will be succeeded by friendship and the earnest desire to protect."[68] These wildlife films fostered appreciation for the creatures within the parks' mountains and forests. *Sanctuary* (1930), for example, depicts wildlife in an area protected from hunters. Additionally, Oliver filmed *Hunting without a Gun* (1930) while on a trail trip in Jasper with the noted guide and outfitter Jack Brewster. The film is notable for Oliver's close-up views of a grizzly bear. Similarly, he filmed Brewster and Dan Byck, a prominent businessman from Louisville, Kentucky, in *Stalking Big Game* (1934). Armed with only cameras, Oliver filmed them as they photographed black bears, caribou, and Rocky Mountain goats and sheep.[69]

Oliver's films encouraged the new "wildlife tourism," which emphasized experience over product, and also positioned non-human animal subjects so as to elicit an emotional response, potentially conditioning attitudes towards non-human animals.[70] Researchers would later term these interactions, "wherein the focal organism is not purposefully removed or permanently affected," "non-consumptive wildlife-oriented recreation."[71] The Parks Branch positioned seeing wildlife as integral to *experiencing* Canada. During his lecture tours throughout Canada and the United States, publicity director J.C. Campbell presented bears, birds, buffalo, caribou, mountain goats, and other denizens of the forests and mountains as "screen stars" – a sort of National Parks trademark to draw in filmgoers and tourists/nature lovers.[72]

THE BEAVER FILMS AND GREY OWL

W.J. Oliver's late-1920s' films about the interactions between beavers and Grey Owl, the imagined "Indian" identity of Archibald Stansfeld Belaney, epitomized Harkin's pledge to protect wildlife and treat non-human animals compassionately. The beaver films were equally intended to generate tourist interest in Canada's scenic playgrounds. Like Oliver, Belaney was born in England and immigrated to Canada as a teenager. He worked as a trapper and tourist guide for wealthy, mostly American vacationers in the Lake Temagami region during the early 1900s. There, he immersed himself in First Nations cultures, particularly the Ojibwe (Teme-Augama Anishnabai) of Bear Island.[73] Refuting his Victorian British upbringing and the perceived over-civilization of modern society, Belaney cloaked himself in Indian-ness, and gradually adopted a new persona, that of Grey Owl (Wa-sha-quon-asin), the son of a Scots frontiersman and an Apache mother. Attired in buckskins and moccasins and wearing his hair long, Belaney exploited the non-Indigenous trope of the "Noble Savage" or the "ecological Indian" by presenting himself as a trapper turned naturalist, who also advocated for Indigenous rights.[74] By the mid-1930s, Grey Owl had become one of the most famous "Canadians" and was credited for saving the beaver from extinction. It was only after his death on 13 April 1938 that the truth about his racial impersonation became public.

By tapping into the longstanding practice of "playing Indian," Grey Owl seemingly spoke from a position of authority and authenticity, centring his broader conservationist message on the beaver – a national signifier – whose population had declined across the north due to over-hunting.[75] According to Anahareo (Gertrude Bernard), his Mohawk/Algonquin common-law wife, she rescued a pair of kitten beavers after one of their traps killed their mother and convinced Belaney to keep them as pets, curiously naming them McGinnis and McGinty. In the autumn of 1928, the foursome moved to Cabano, Quebec, near the New Brunswick border, to start a beaver colony.[76] Belaney subsequently published articles in *Country Life*, a British magazine, and *Forest and Outdoors*, a publication by the Canadian Forestry Association, championing the beaver as intelligent, industrious, possessive of a distinct language, and capable of human-like emotions. For Grey Owl, the key to wildlife conservation, as Tina Loo notes, "was to see animals as human."[77]

Gordon M. Dallyn, associate editor of *Forest and Outdoors*, suggested to J.C. Campbell that Grey Owl would be an ideal spokesperson for Harkin's philosophy of wildlife protection.[78] Sometime between 1928 and 1930, Oliver filmed Grey Owl, Anahareo, and their domesticated beavers in the Quebec wilderness for the Parks Branch. *The Beaver People* displays the assiduousness of the beaver and the bond between human and non-human animals and bemoans the "ruthless greed and slaughter" of the historic fur trade. The beaver, however, is apparently a forgiving creature. As one of the intertitles explains, the former trapper "and his young wife have become conservationists" who have befriended "the Beaver so that they will come at call, sharing food, friendship and even play."[79] Patrick Wolfe's "logic of elimination" – colonial policies on Indigenous peoples – here applies to the film's broader history of the decimation and restoration of the beaver.[80] Grey Owl and Anahareo embody a teleological narrative of Canada's evolution from a resource-based economy to a supposedly more enlightened and conservation-minded nation.

In January 1931, Grey Owl travelled to Montreal to lecture and screen *The Beaver People* to the Canadian Forestry Association. The enthusiastic response further convinced Harkin that Grey Owl and his beavers would be a tourism draw and a symbol of the Parks Branch's conservationist ideals.[81] On the verge of publishing the first of Grey Owl's four books, *The Men of his Last Frontier*, replete with lively tales of wilderness adventures, the Parks Branch wagered that the author's beaver experiment would secure favourable publicity and entice visitors. Consequently, Grey Owl began work as the caretaker of animals in Riding Mountain National Park, Manitoba. A few months later he requested a transfer to Saskatchewan's Prince Albert National Park, which opened in 1928 and catered largely to automobile tourists.[82] Park Superintendent James A. Wood welcomed Grey Owl, not necessarily to encourage the beaver population, but rather hoping that this increasingly renowned writer and lecturer would stimulate tourism.[83] Grey Owl and his tame beavers relocated in the autumn of 1931 to Ajawaan Lake in Prince Albert National Park, where he remained until his death in 1938.

Motion pictures provided a means to broadcast Great Owl and the beaver experiment to encourage park tourism. According to the Parks Branch annual report of 1931, "Motion pictures of merit were taken in the parks of beavers" that both showed the "results of the Government's policy of wild life protection" and directed "the attention of recreation seekers throughout the world to the great advantages of a holiday spent in Canada's national playgrounds."[84] Oliver filmed *The Beaver Family* (1931?) in Riding Mountain National Park and *Strange Doings in Beaverland* (1932) in Prince Albert National Park.[85] Like *The Beaver People*, they upheld Grey Owl's nature writings on the acumen of the beaver, offering numerous close-ups of his pet beavers (Jelly Roll and Rawhide) eating, grooming, and building a dam. Moreover, scenes focused on Grey Owl communicating with his beavers, emphasizing interspecies kinship, and indirectly importuning audiences to heed his missive of protecting wildlife. Later, Oliver filmed *Grey Owl's Neighbours* (1933?) featuring Grey Owl "and his furred and feathered neighbours in Prince Albert National Park, Saskatchewan." His *Pilgrims of the Wild* (1935) is similar, sharing a title with Grey Owl's most widely read book.[86]

Associated Screen News (ASN), the Montreal-based commercial film producer and distributor, re-edited together *The Beaver People* and *The Beaver Family*, releasing the result theatrically as *Grey Owl's Little Brother* (1932) – the film was nominated for an Academy Award. Likewise, ASN released *Grey Owl's Strange Guest* (1934), a sound version of *Strange Doings in Beaverland*. Corey Thompson, a Montreal radio announcer, provided the recorded narration, and composer Howard Fogg supervised the music for both films. Gordon Sparling, head of ASN's commercial production, later recalled that the deal with Parks Branch was informal and mutually beneficial, arranged by J.C. Campbell and B.E. Norrish, ASN's managing director and former director of the Exhibits and Publicity Bureau. In exchange for processing the original negatives, ASN received a print for making sound pictures for theatrical release, giving the Parks Branch free access to a wider audience while retaining the silent versions for non-theatrical distribution. Campbell reserved the right to approve or amend the narration prior to release (figure 3.2).[87]

Sparling, a former film editor at the Ontario Government Motion Picture Bureau and its Dominion counterpart (CGMPB), supervised these theatrical sound shorts released under his Canadian Cameo series

(1932–54). The ASN releases recount the legend of Grey Owl as an Indigenous backwoodsman living in harmony with nature (i.e., "ecological Indian"), who becomes the beaver's friend and protector in the National Parks. Prefiguring the anthropomorphized non-human animals and "synthetic reconstruction of nature" in the Walt Disney Corporation's *True-to-Life Adventures* series of short and full-length wildlife films between 1948 and 1960, ASN's beaver films were light-hearted, privileged feeling over fact, and encouraged audiences to invest emotionally in the survival of the species.[88]

T.D.A. Cockerell, professor of zoology at the University of Colorado, cited the Grey Owl beaver films as a "a major factor in determining the Canadian policy with reference to the beaver" because of their "appeal both to the intellect and the emotions." He explained that his wife, "thanks to the courtesy of the Canadian Park Service," screened the films "to many thousands in Colorado, California, and Wyoming, always meeting with enthusiastic appreciation and requests to have them repeated." He noticed that such public showings created "lively interest and sympathy" that might "democratiz[e] conservation."[89] He thus articulates the unique ability of motion pictures to engage spectators and foster a connection between humans and marginalized non-human animals, resulting in concrete policies.

In Oliver's films, the beaver functions as the axis for both a declentionist narrative – a story of loss and degradation – and a more progressive paradigm in which Indigenous (albeit ersatz) knowledge and government-led management could stop or even reverse that decline. In practice, the beaver films provided the parks with public exposure that promoted tourism while preaching conservation. "There is not the slightest doubt," Harkin stated, "that we have secured for our Parks ... countless thousands of dollars worth of publicity through Grey Owl, his beaver, his books, his magazine articles and the motion pictures which we have secured of him and his beaver."[90] For example, a delegation from Alberta travelled to Great Falls, Montana, for the annual meeting of the Sunshine Trail Association, which promoted an all-weather road from "the famous wheat fields of Sunny Alberta to the orange groves of Sunny California." They took with them several Parks Branch films "very attractive to those interested in highways and tourist traffic," including a "Grey Owl beaver film."[91]

J.C. Campbell similarly reported that the beaver films drew large crowds during his 1935 lecture tour of such cities as Cleveland,

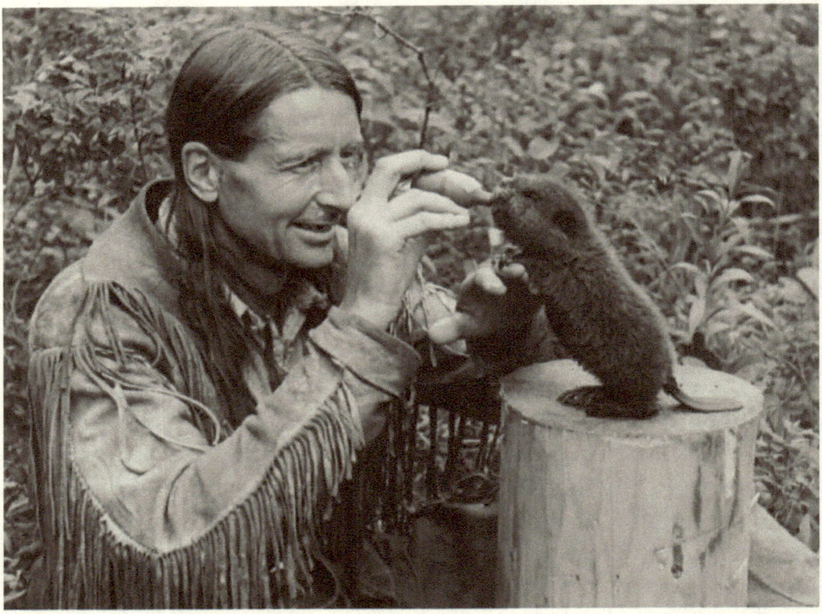

3.2 Associated Screen News, *Grey Owl's Little Brother*, 1932.

Dayton, Seattle, and Spokane. He predicted a resulting increase in American tourists visiting Prince Albert National Park: "If we are to judge the enthusiasm with which our programs depicting Canada's National Parks on the screen were received as any criterion of the interest of prospective tourists we may look for a splendid year in the parks."[92] By the end of the year, Campbell claimed that the Parks Branch was shipping upwards of 1,500 films to the United States, "which means quite a lot of publicity in that country."[93]

Recognizing the profile-raising value of motion pictures, Grey Owl and his promoter, the publisher and writer Lovat Dickson, who had organized his 1935–36 lecture tour of England, toyed with producing a feature film to showcase his expertise as a backwoodsman. In a series of letters to M.B. Williams, Campbell expressed his lack of enthusiasm. Despite the writer's international celebrity, he believed a feature film would not attract tourists: "I have been getting more materialistic for the simple reason that all anybody seems to be concerned is to get the tourist in ... and I feel quite certain that a picture such as he has in mind ... would not be a big success." Beyond Grey Owl's lack of experience in directing, Campbell saw the proposal as purely a product of his mounting egotism and feared that his drinking and philandering were making him a growing liability.[94] This prompted Harkin to remind the now-famous writer that "employees of the Dominion Government must, at all times, be discreet in their personal conduct. You will realize if you conduct yourself in a manner which arouses criticism it reflects not only on yourself but also on the Department."[95] Grey Owl apparently ignored the warning. A year later, Roy A. Gibson, director of the re-organized and renamed Lands, Parks and Forests Branch, as of 1936 under the new Department of Mines and Resources, also fretted that their star's hubris could tarnish the parks' reputation. Grey Owl "has capitalized to the limit his connection with the Department and used our films to create a back-ground for himself … Unfortunately [his] personal conduct on certain occasions has not reflected much credit upon this Department and there is a certain amount of criticism."[96]

In 1937, Grey Owl took a leave of absence without pay from the Parks Branch to produce and direct two films for his planned British lecture tour (including a royal command performance at Buckingham Palace). Financed by his Canadian publisher, Macmillan, and filmed in Quebec, the "winter picture" documented "the camping and travelling activities and winter wild life in the Canadian North," including sleighing and snowshoeing.[97] The "summer picture," which Grey Owl funded, featured 250 miles (400 kilometres) of canoeing – "a sentimental tribute" to his "boyhood haunts."[98] It is unclear whether these films were ever distributed or shown publicly. According to Frank C. Badgley, who had become CGMPB director following Raymond S. Peck's death in 1927, "the films were valueless."[99]

Regardless, during his only US lecture tour in early 1938, Grey Owl screened Oliver's ever-popular beaver films. According to a representative from Macmillan, which had organized the event, "His propaganda as regards the Parks is subtle because it is indirect, but apparently it is very effective. This was shown by the fact that many of those at the lecture expressed their firm intention of visiting Beaver Lodge next summer … I am satisfied that it will mean that it will mean a very considerable influx of visitors from the United States to see the thing at first hand."[100] Yet for the Parks Branch, the risk of continuing a relationship with such an unpredictable character outweighed the potential advertising benefits. Roy A. Gibson (director of the Lands, Parks and Forests Branch), F.H.H. Williamson (controller of the Parks Bureau), and James Wood (superintendent of Prince

Albert National Park) debated on what to do. Grey Owl's unexpected death on 13 April 1938, following his gruelling British and North American lecture tours, would untangle the Parks Branch from this predicament.

For at least a decade, conservation groups, schools, and other organizations kept requesting Grey Owl's beaver films, despite the revelation of his fraudulent Indigeneity. Robert J.C. Stead, superintendent of Publicity and Information, who replaced the retired J.C. Campbell following the re-organization of the Parks Branch under Mines and Resources in 1936, reported: "We do continue to make use of him in our films, as the films in which he appears have very great interest ... they are in constant demand and in constant use."[101] Moreover, M.U. Bates, associate editor of *Hunting and Fishing in Canada*, claimed that the man's legend continued to attract tourists to Canada. Bates's lectures to sportsmen's and conservation groups, in which he screened the beaver films, garnered a "unanamous [*sic*] response," which convinced him that "the whole Grey Owl incident was a means of drawing American outdoor lovers to those particular sections of Canada which were the locale of [his] activities," specifically Prince Albert National Park.[102]

Under Harkin and Campbell, the Parks Branch expanded publicity in the early 1920s and invested in the production and distribution of theatrical and non-theatrical motion pictures. It had placed its faith in film's incomparable ability to appeal to the senses, stimulate emotion, and nurture mental imagery stimulating the desire to travel. This in turn reinforced its insistence on creative direction of those film narratives and visual representations, as we can see in Harkin and Peck's disagreements over which agency – the Parks Branch or the CGMPB – should film Canada's national playgrounds and consequently shape the Dominion's image. Moreover, the fiasco over the killing of buffalo in Thomas Ince's *The Last Frontier*, which resulted in negative publicity, together with Grey Owl's unpredictability, further cemented the need for control of destination branding through film.

Ultimately, Oliver's films expressed Harkin's vision of the National Parks as simultaneously playgrounds for tourists and wildlife preserves affirming settler-colonial constructions of place. Whether screened at a movie theatre or to illustrate a lecture in a non-theatrical venue, they mediated the Parks Branch's conceptions of nature, conservation, non-human animals, and human activities in protected areas. Their repetition of images and themes (accessibility, amenities, recreation, scenery, and wildlife) would foster positive associations towards the various parks. Ideally, these feelings would morph into a visit. The onset of the Second World War in 1939, however, required that the Parks Branch put its publicity endeavours largely on hold. The responsibility of promoting tourism through film would gradually fall to two centralized government agencies – the Canadian Travel Bureau (chapter 4) and the National Film Board (chapter 5).

4

The Canadian Travel Bureau, Talking Colourful Travelogues, and 16-mm

Promoting Canada as a Vacationland during the Depression

Canada is rated as the first country to make substantial use of motion picture films for propaganda and trade advertising.

Motion Picture Herald, 22 April 1933[1]

In the years following the First World War, Canada had developed an enviable reputation as a trendsetter in the use of motion pictures to promote tourism, yet it would eventually face increasing competition from other countries. The Dominion's tourism industry throughout the 1920s broadly benefited from a variety of interrelated factors and changes in North American leisure and recreation patterns, namely US prohibition, the rise in automobile ownership, and an increase in paid vacations. Following the stock-market crash of 1929, US tourist expenditures in Canada receded as millions of Americans lost their jobs or had their wages reduced. The Dominion Bureau of Statistics estimated that foreign (mostly American) tourists had spent only $117,124,000 in Canada in 1933, compared with $212,448,000 in 1932 and $309,379,000 in the peak year of 1929.[2] By the mid-1930s, various US New Deal initiatives to stimulate tourism, as well as the extension of vacation leave to more industrial workers, revived the holiday spending of American labourers as a percentage of US national income.[3]

Canada vied with other nations for coveted American tourists as governments surmised that tourism could help them rebuild their beleaguered economies hit by both the Depression and the lingering fallout from the Great War. According to British economist Frederick W. Ogilvie, they recognized that "the great moving markets of tourists" had become "an important factor in many of the balances of payments in international trade." Tourist traffic became a valued invisible export that enabled countries to pay interest on external loans or for goods and services. In other words, tourism could generate wealth with only minimal expenditure.[4] Dominion Statistician R.H. Coats was familiar with Ogilvie's study and cited it to support his argument for tourism's economic significance as "the largest single export fact – in keeping our international balances in sound condition."[5]

As early as 1917, James B. Harkin, Parks Branch commissioner 1911–36, recognized that the war was making such nations as France, Italy, and Switzerland "realize fully for the first time the amount of money which had been brought into their countries by foreign visitors." Several countries set up national tourism bureaux and/or invested more in tourism. Harkin argued that the Dominion should follow suit with a national tourism bureau that cooperated with provinces, municipalities, motor associations, and transportation interests. Only a centralized body could fully exploit Canada's "incomparable scenic areas" and keep it competitive in postwar tourism.[6]

Certainly, according to the US Bureau of Foreign and Domestic Commerce, private interests (such as hotels, transportation companies, and chambers of commerce) and government-sponsored tourist offices or information bureaux of nations ranging from Australia to Sweden advertised in US newspapers and magazines and distributed guidebooks, maps, pamphlets, and posters. As well, about "90 per cent of the more important countries" were using films "to stimulate foreign interest."[7] Within this spirited international market, the Dominion wagered that increased film production would be an ideal method to market Canada as an attractive destination and counteract other foreign solicitation of American tourists.

In 1934, the Canadian Senate's Special Committee on Tourist Traffic articulated the need for increased tourism promotion. Several witnesses underscored film's value in that role. The Dominion resolved that tourism's immense value required a centralized agency, which led to the creation of the Canadian Travel Bureau (CTB). Under director D. Leo Dolan, the CTB coordinated the activities of public and private tourist agencies throughout the provinces. Initially, it lacked funds to produce tourism films, which remained with Dominion, provincial, and local agencies. Meanwhile, the advent of synchronized sound and colour technologies, the financial constraints of the Depression, and Hollywood's drive to stimulate the

Depression-era film industry invigorated short subjects, including 35-mm sound and Technicolor travelogues. Unable to compete with theatrically released travel talkies, the Canadian Government Motion Picture Bureau (CGMPB) focused on making 16-mm films and turned to the expanding US non-theatrical circuits, which offered a viable market for promoting tourism.

THE 1934 SPECIAL COMMITTEE ON TOURIST TRAFFIC

On 25 April 1934, William H. Dennis, publisher of the *Halifax Herald*, addressed his fellow senators on the importance of the US tourist trade to the Canadian economy. He urged that the Dominion consider more "intensive efforts" to develop the industry in collaboration with the provinces. The following day Senator Arthur Meighen, a former Conservative prime minister, moved for a special Senate committee to "consider the immense possibilities of the tourist traffic" and "to inquire as to the means adopted by the Government looking to its encouragement and expansion."[8] The eight senators, with Dennis as chair, on the Special Committee on Tourist Traffic started work on 2 May 1934.[9] Over the next two weeks, government officials and witnesses representing provincial tourist groups, transportation and hotel companies, and newspaper associations brought forth suggestions, such as a centralized tourism bureau and financing film production to encourage American tourism.

J.B. Harkin was the first witness. He informed members about the Parks Branch's "active publicity and propaganda campaign," which included filming subjects depicting scenery both inside and "outside the park areas."[10] J.C. Campbell, director of publicity, likewise emphasized film's paramount role in attracting American tourists. When Senator Dennis asked Campbell to describe his agency's promotional work, he listed "the motion picture business, both sound and silent" first. To illustrate, Campbell singled out the success of William J. Oliver's beaver films as a tourist draw to Prince Albert National Park.[11] "Considering the value of motion picture publicity intelligently directed," John Murray Gibbon, the CPR's general publicity agent 1913–45, recommended that the Dominion allot the Parks Branch an additional $20,000 to produce more films promoting tourism.[12]

To maximize his agency's publicity work, Harkin argued for a "definite plan of [national] co-operation and co-ordination." He added,

"A tourist coming into British Columbia is of great value to Nova Scotia and every other province. We must have a national outlook."[13] John Murray Gibbon also called for an interdepartmental committee to "smooth out any troubles arising in connection with the tourist business." He referred specifically to a missed opportunity when "prohibitive customs regulations regarding moving picture apparatus" barred an "outstanding American lecturer, whose moving picture travelogues have an immense circulation in the United States" from "sending his cameramen to Canada." Senator W.A. Buchanan saw this as "an argument in favour of a national tourist bureau in Ottawa – to deal with matters of that kind."[14]

H.E.M. Chisholm, director of publicity for the Department of Trade and Commerce, also called for a "central co-ordinating effort of a national character" to foster tourism. Since motion pictures constituted "one of the best forms of advertising one country to another country, and to thereby stimulate a desire for travel," he lobbied for increased funding for the CGMPB so it could better "sell Canada" to the world.[15] The CGMPB's 1933 catalogue had similarly emphasized this national vision of useful film for both advertising and education:

> The motion picture, because it is the closest approximation to actual visualization and because its appeal is universal and its influence far-reaching, is today recognized as the most valuable existing medium for the world-wide dissemination of national information, publicity and advertising. The motion picture, too, has become a great force in education and is being more and more utilized in this field, while as a factor in creating and encouraging increased development, trade, tourist travel, settlement, etc., its scope is almost limitless and its value immeasurably great.[16]

CGMPB Director Frank C. Badgley elaborated on the tangible effects of his agency's "tourism encouragement films." In keeping with advertising theories that focused on appeals to emotion and experience, he asserted that "one of the first principles of advertising is to create desire." Therefore, rather than working towards "direct sales," his Bureau's films "make people Canada-conscious." He added that it did not put the government's name on films exhibited in the United States, for fear that it would be considered propaganda or direct advertising. "If a picture of the Rocky Mountains makes people want to go there," he claimed, "it has done its job whether or not the Government's name is on it or not." It would then be up to the Parks Branch or provincial bureaux to follow through with direct publicity. A central bureau, he urged, would streamline this process and enable his agency to spread "the gospel of Canada" through film.[17]

Stressing tourism's value to the nation's economy, D. Leo Dolan, a former journalist and since 1931 director of New Brunswick's Bureau of Information and Tourist Travel, similarly challenged the existing, scattered approach. He advocated for a centralized, state-run tourism agency to "sell Canada" as a "vacation land" to Americans.[18] Such action was urgent, given the decline in US tourists since 1929. To make his point, Dolan listed the bodies advancing tourism, including the Parks Branch, the provincial governments, the railway companies (i.e., the CNR and CPR), and the Canadian Association of Tourist and Publicity Bureaus (CATPB).[19] Additionally, regional and municipal tourist associations, such as chambers of commerce and motor clubs, were also active. Despite their good intentions, Dolan contended, these sectional organizations lacked the time and resources "to make a proper study of the tourist psychology." Moreover, without the "guidance of a central body," there was unnecessary overlap resulting in wasteful efforts and the ineffective use of limited funds. Canada thus could not compete with "the centralized promotional stream" from such countries as Britain, France, Italy, Japan, Sweden, and the Soviet Union directed towards American tourists.[20]

On 22 May 1934, after hearing from nearly thirty witnesses and receiving briefs, memoranda, and reports, the Special Committee submitted its unanimous final report. It reiterated tourism's value to the economy and acknowledged that the precipitous decline since 1929 had created an emergency. The committee called for an immediate and aggressive national program to induce visitors to Canada. Impressed "with the possibilities of motion and sound pictures as a medium of travel publicity," the report proposed inducing US theatre owners to screen Canadian tourism films, which would present "an opportunity for extensive and valuable tourist publicity at a minimum of cost." It also encouraged the filming "of motion pictures within Canada by agencies located outside Canada."[21] These recommendations aligned with the Dominion's focus on producing non-fiction tourism films while cooperating with and/or encouraging Hollywood producers to shoot narrative motion pictures in Canada.

The committee concluded that Ottawa should establish a central organization to harmonize (i.e., supplement but not supplant) the activities of public (Dominion and provincial) and private tourist agencies. It anticipated that a coordinated effort would reduce duplication, saving energy, money, and time.[22] Ottawa's 1935 formation of the Canadian Travel Bureau (CTB), which Alisa Apostle explores, reveals the state's recognition of tourism as an essential component of nation-building, as well as the importance of centralized bureaucratic administration, or governmentality.[23] According to media scholar Michael Dorland, Michel Foucault's concept of governmentality "has been enormously productive in un-thinking the state and seeing in its stead not only a fundamentally discontinuous historical as opposed to coherently conceptual entity, but also a complex, contested, and changing articulation of the practices of the techniques of governance in interaction with new fields of knowledge."[24]

D. LEO DOLAN AND CANADIAN TRAVEL BUREAU

In July 1934, Minister of Railways and Canals R.J. Manion, whose department included the new Canadian Travel Bureau (CTB), named D. Leo Dolan from New Brunswick its director, a position he held until 1957. Dolan had pushed fervently for a centralized tourist agency similar to the Canadian Radio Broadcasting Commission (CRBC). He was also the only witness who testified at length twice before the Special Committee.[25] The CTB was launched the first week of August 1934 with a $100,000 budget for the remainder of the year and a twofold mandate: to coordinate Canada's public and private tourist agencies and to disseminate information on the nation's attractions. Dolan's goal was to "develop Canada as a Vacation-land" primarily to American tourists, from whom he estimated the country derived 90 per cent of its tourist revenue.[26]

With its modest budget, the CTB concentrated on advertising in US print media, such as newspapers ranging from Boston to San Francisco and periodicals encompassing general (such as *Collier's* and *Saturday Evening Post*), sporting (*Field and Stream* and *Outdoor Life*), women's (*Harper's Bazaar* and *Ladies Home Journal*), and so-called class (*Literary Digest* and *National Geographic*) readerships. The Canadian-based McConnell, Eastman and Company handled the Bureau's account. "Tourist advertising is a specialized form of advertising,"

Dolan informed new Liberal Minister of Transport C.D. Howe, whose department included the CTB as of 1935, "In view that our contact is mostly with United States periodicals it is essential from our standpoint that the agency entrusted with our account should have sufficient prestige to secure … the type of service which we, of necessity, must demand." This campaign seemed fruitful, as Dolan boasted that the response "far exceeded" his expectations, judging by "the tremendous number of inquiries" the CTB received.[27]

In 1936, Howe reported Canada's best tourism year since 1929 and credited the CTB's publicity; he was also hopeful about the future.[28] Figures from the Dominion Bureau of Statistics supported this outlook: foreign tourists spent about $257,000,000 in 1936 and $274,771,000 in 1939.[29] The birth on 28 May 1934 of Ontario's Dionne Quintuplets, the world's first-ever surviving quints, and their relocation to a state-of-the-art hospital/nursery, Quintupletland, near present-day North Bay, further stimulated the province's and Canada's tourism industries.

Following the success of Twentieth Century–Fox's *The Country Doctor* (dir. by Henry King, 1936) and *Reunion* (dir. by Norman Taurog, 1936), two feature-length productions shot partially on location and featuring the Dionne Quintuplets, Ontario tourism broke records.[30] The CTB hoped to capitalize on the cachet of Hollywood's newest child stars by marketing their home and environs to tourists. Its first promotional booklet, "Canada Your Friendly Neighbor Invites You," which circulated 1936–38, featured the five identical sisters and encouraged tourists to "include the 'Quints' in their vacation itinerary."[31] Dolan had requested $20,000 to produce the booklet, arguing that it would provide "all the essential data and information on Canada" and was thus "one of the most important steps … taken to co-ordinate our tourist services."[32]

Beyond promoting the Dionnes, the booklet demonstrated the new Bureau's destination branding of Canada as a "friendly land." This was a reference to US President Franklin Delano Roosevelt's recent mention of "Canada, the friendly neighbor," during 1936 negotiations for a reciprocal trade agreement.[33] Neighbourliness and courtesy henceforth became key tenets of the Bureau's promotion strategy, particularly after a series of US newspaper articles outlined American tourists' difficulties at the border. One woman, for example, insisted: "Never have we been treated with less courtesy than this year. We were searched, not examined, by a very zealous young man."[34] The "Canada

Your Friendly Neighbor Invites You" campaign aimed to ease concerns by emphasizing that tourists would face "a minimum of border regulations" due to "relaxed customs and immigration regulations" and "will receive every courtesy."[35]

Additionally, the glossy booklet emphasized good roads and "beautiful cities, modern and well planned," along with many year-round outdoor recreational activities. In particular, hunting and fishing were touted, reflecting Dolan's belief that these were "a leading factor" in attracting tourists.[36] To boost Canada's standing as the premier recreation destination, the CTB depicted famous outdoorsmen, such as Rex Beach, the prolific adventure novelist, avid sportsman, and erstwhile film producer, with his catch of rainbow trout in Kamloops, British Columbia: "Ask Zane Grey – or Irvin Cobb or Rex Beach or Corey Ford – ask any one of them where the big fellows are biting. 'Canada' will trip off their tongue before they know it."[37]

Initially, the CTB did not have a still- or moving-image branch due to insufficient funding, but Dolan recognized film's potential. In 1934, he had told the Special Committee about the impact of motion pictures made during President Roosevelt's visit to his summer home on Campobello Island, New Brunswick, in 1933: "Sound pictures were taken, and New Brunswick secured on that occasion alone a publicity the like of which I doubt was ever given to any one Canadian province at any time in the history of this country."[38] Moreover, Dolan believed that the Fox newsreel *Canada Calling Tourists*, filmed in Ottawa during a conference of the Canadian Association of Tourist and Publicity Bureaus, would "arouse interest in the tourist industry throughout the country."[39] His Bureau reproduced images obtained from private and public agencies, such as the railway and steamship companies, the Parks Branch, and the CGMPB, which had functioning still- and moving-picture departments. These bodies would do most of Canada's encouraging of tourism through film until the NFB's founding in 1939.

Under Badgley's leadership (1927–41), the CGMPB had strived to perpetuate its Seeing Canada series – what British film critic and documentarian Paul Rotha called "propaganda films of Canadian scenery."[40] Badgley also continued to encourage Hollywood to make films using identifiable Canadian locations, "placing resources at their disposal, undertaking research work, finding locations, arranging transport, equipment, &c." The Bureau's support of outside commercial producers, together with its producing of non-fiction short subjects, generated publicity for the nation's tourism.[41] Writing in the 1929 *Film Daily Yearbook*, Badgley states: "The Canadian Government is interested in the general development of the Dominion as a tourist's holiday-land. In this field of endeavor, the films produced by the Bureau are doing a work of far-reaching national influence. Canada's tourist trade in recent years has had a tremendous development and is now classed as an important industry of the Dominion."[42]

By 1929, the CGMPB was circulating about 1,500 films, distributed theatrically and non-theatrically by more than forty US agencies, including the YMCA, the Izaak Walton League (promoting anglers' interests), the extension divisions of fifteen colleges and universities, and other educational, religious, and sporting, travel, and welfare bodies. On average, about 250,000 Americans a day, "expecting to find only Mounties, Indians, and bears," saw films that "depict the outstanding features of every Canadian city, as well as highways, waterways, scenic beauty spots, natural resources, and other attractions."[43] The Bureau's productions presented a modern tourist destination to counteract filmic representations of a pre-industrial hinterland – an image perpetuated by Hollywood's popular northwest melodramas, which the Bureau itself indirectly encouraged.[44]

Having outgrown its original facilities, in 1930 the CGMPB moved from downtown Ottawa into a new, larger film plant (still within the nation's capital), anticipating the installation of a Western Electric film and disc system to produce sound films.[45] The rapid, late-1920s' advent of synchronized sound technology, according to Dana Benelli, "created dynamic textual enrichment" in travelogues that had heretofore "been hindered by the necessity of alternating written intertitles with passages of recorded images."[46] Within the American film industry, recorded narration and diegetic sounds enhanced the images on screen and ushered in a new era of travelogues. For example, in 1930 veteran travelogue filmmaker Burton Holmes released his series of twelve single-reel Around the World Travel-Talkies under contract to MGM. The following year, James A. FitzPatrick began a series of one-reel TravelTalks for MGM release – the studio would distribute his travelogues until 1955. The self-styled "Voice of the Globe," FitzPatrick aimed "to present in as concise and striking form as possible salient facts and intimate glimpses of the world's most interesting spots."[47] These "spots" would include scenics shot in Canada and distributed in theatres through MGM.

JAMES A. FITZPATRICK AND THE RESURGENCE OF THE THEATRICAL TRAVELOGUE

James A. FitzPatrick began writing and directing TravelTalks, "combining the advantages of sound with the roving eye of the camera," in 1928.[48] The independent travelogue producer developed off-screen narration by recording his voice on disc and synchronizing the narration with the silent on-location footage. "The advantage of synchronized sound," he notes, "is that through a custom arrangement of the songs and music peculiar to each locality, we are better able to portray the atmosphere of each locality we visit. The audience actually is made to feel that it is touring along with our party."[49] *Film Daily* praised him for bringing "something brand new" to the travelogue, which "makes you feel that you are right there with him."[50] His light-hearted intonation, cadence, and inflection functioned as a distinct mode of address – he had experimented with the technical complications of synchronized sound recording while borrowing from the first-person narrative vocal strategies used by travelling illustrated lecturers.[51]

FitzPatrick's distinctive voice-over narration, combined with sound effects and synchronized orchestral music peculiar to each locality, would trademark his TravelTalks and became the gold standard for travelogues of the 1930s and 1940s. Each TravelTalk had a similar structure: a crude map and brief historical background to situate the viewer spatially and temporally; an idiosyncratic collection of architectural and/or natural sites (typically panoramic views); pseudo-ethnographic observations regarding the inhabitants, who are themselves without a voice; and a picturesque farewell scene. FitzPatrick's tone is upbeat, conversational, and informed. According to Burnet Hershey, a writer at the Warner Vitaphone studio, audible descriptions in travelogues "should be served up 'sugar-coated' ... The talk should be light, serving to point up the various facts rather than launch[ing] into a detailed account of what is pictured on the screen."[52] In an interview with the *Los Angeles Daily News*, FitzPatrick later admitted that his objective was "to romanticize travel, to present its more glamorous aspects, and to stay away from the 'grim realities.'"[53]

For his 1934–35 season, FitzPatrick innovated again: a three-strip (red, green, and blue) Technicolor process. Hollywood reserved this complex, labour-intensive, and expensive system for high-budget feature films or prestige short subjects, such as the MGM TravelTalks.[54] The trade journals lauded FitzPatrick's adoption of Technicolor's bold aesthetics, which justified the cost of colour for future ventures. In the words of *Motion Picture Daily*, he had made "ground that has been gone over many times before" novel and breathtaking again.[55] MGM employed his early adoption of Technicolor to publicize the overall quality of its short subjects and to market itself as the industry leader. "The selection of a short subject on your program," advised one full-page ad, "is often the factor that sells your show against competition. A FitzPatrick Traveltalk [*sic*] in Technicolor with exquisite music is a breathing-spell of beauty and fascination on a well-balanced program."[56]

Confident that Technicolor represented the travelogue's future, in 1935 FitzPatrick sent a colour unit to Canada under Benjamin D. Sharpe. He obtained 10,000 feet of "colorful material," including a panorama of the Royal Canadian Mounted Police (RCMP) musical ride.[57] These scenes were included in *Beautiful Banff and Lake Louise* (1935) and, opined *Film Daily*, "would make a nice morsel for any program." Reviewers concurred that Technicolor enhanced the scenery. Colour "strikingly brings out the natural beauties of this famous Canadian resort," including "glimpses of the beautiful glass-enclosed swimming pool built on the shore of the lake."[58] *Box Office Check-up of 1935* selected the film as a high point of the year and a masterpiece of pictorial composition.[59] Other Canadian-themed Technicolor TravelTalks soon followed, including *Quaint Quebec* (1936) and *Victoria and Vancouver: Gateways to Canada* (1936). The use of three-tone process, together with FitzPatrick's narration and orchestral accompaniment, highlighted historic monuments, scenic landscapes, skylines, and cultural activities in these locations.

FitzPatrick also featured New Brunswick in one of his Technicolor travelogues, which he presented as "a tribute" to Louis B. Mayer. The production head of MGM had spent his boyhood in Saint John, and FitzPatrick featured "the red brick schoolhouse" that Mayer attended.[60] Moreover, *Glimpses of New Brunswick* (1938) presented "the scenic beauties of the countryside" alongside the province's industrial and agricultural activities.[61] The following year, Mayer travelled to Fredericton to receive an honorary doctorate from the University of New Brunswick "in view of the contribution he has made to public education through films."[62] University President C.C. Jones conferred the accolade in gratitude for *Glimpses*' marketing of the province as a tourist destination. Mayer's "interest in New Brunswick is evidenced by the fact that he was instrumental in having a [FitzPatrick] travelogue of the province prepared recently and distributed throughout the world."[63] Fredericton and its Board of Trade hosted a luncheon to honour two most prominent "native sons," Louis B. Mayer and D. Leo Dolan.[64] Dolan's Hollywood connections would later support the postwar Canadian Cooperation Project (1948–58) (figure 4.1).

Glimpses was not the only colourful vignette of the province to be released in 1938, but was part of a trend in Maritimes travelogues produced by Hollywood.[65] Universal showcased New Brunswick as "a land of picturesque beauty with an interesting historical background" in number fifty-one of its Going Places travelogue series narrated by Lowell Thomas, a well-known and respected radio personality.[66] Provincial tourist officials were "highly elated by the fact that more than a million theatregoers have seen Universal's travelogue," which had been shown recently at New York's Radio City Music Hall. The province surmised that this production, together with FitzPatrick's, "will give a great impetus to motor travel up this way."[67] Likewise, Minister of Lands and Mines Frederick William Pirie (served 1930–45) informed the legislature that these two travelogues promised extensive publicity for the province.[68] The convention manager of Kiwanis International further observed that the MGM and Universal tourism films "doubtless would be a strong factor in bringing many Kiwanian families on tours of the Maritimes at the close of the convention" held in Boston.[69]

Not everyone was pleased with these American productions. Saint John journalist Ian Sclanders wrote that the "inaccuracies" around New Brunswickers "eating blueberry pie" and "picking flowers" in the Going Places travelogue outweighed tourism promotion. Despite the film's depiction of wildlife, outdoor recreation, and scenery, the expense "to the tune of several thousand dollars" would ultimately prove wasteful.[70] Regardless, the government's investment of funds demonstrated its confidence in the tourism film for advertising, while Hollywood studios' involvement indicated the travelogue genre's renaissance.

Nova Scotia too had begun in the mid-1930s to bankroll extensive tourism publicity. While cooperating with both the CTB and the CGMPB, the province did not want to rely on Dominion bureaux for promoting tourism. In February 1935, the Department of Highways hired the New York–based Mandeville Press Bureau to publicize the province through print advertising, as well as radio and motion pictures. Ernest W. Mandeville's office emerged in the 1930s as part

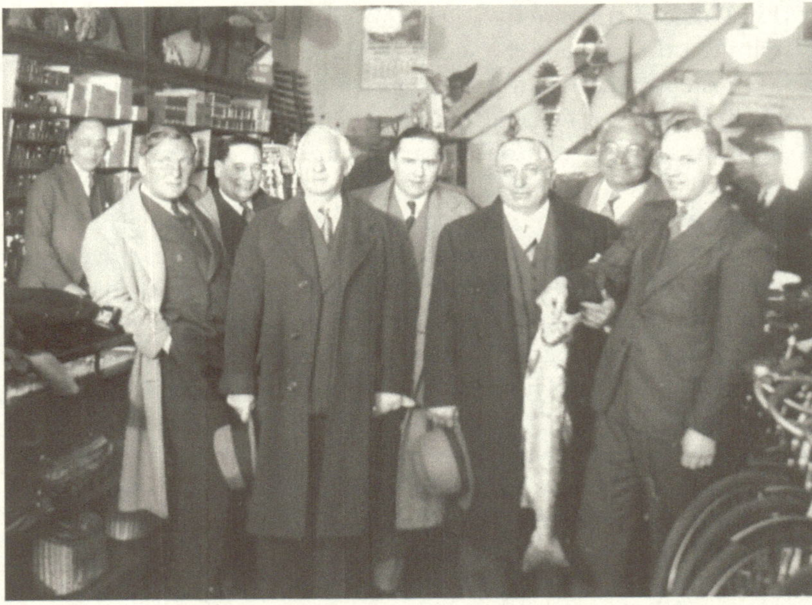

4.1 D. Leo Dolan and Louis B. Mayer at a sporting-goods store in Fredericton, New Brunswick, 1939

of a wave of publicity agencies masquerading as "news services."[71] He arranged to produce *Land of Evangeline* (1935), a travelogue produced by the Van Beuren Corporation and released through RKO Pictures as part of its World on Parade travel series. Helmed by the explorer/big-game hunter Harold McCracken and narrated by the celebrated radio announcer Alois Havrilla, the ten-minute black-and-white film depicts "the beautiful landscapes that abound everywhere."[72] The following year, through the efforts of the Mandeville Press Bureau, Universal also released a one-reel travelogue depicting "comprehensive scenes of the land of the Acadians" as part of Lowell Thomas's Going Places series.[73]

By the 1930s, the addition of sound and/or colour had elevated theatrical travelogues within the film industry. As early as 1931, *Film Daily* reported that "travel numbers have not only held their own but actually show a numerical increase."[74] In addition to FitzPatrick's TravelTalks, RKO's World on Parade, and Universal's Going Places, other sound travel series included Tom Terriss's Vagabond Adventure Series (RKO-Pathé), Newman Travel Pictures (Educational Films), E.M. Newman Travel-Talks (Warner Bros.), Walter Futter's TravelLaughs

(Columbia), and Along the Road to Romance on the Magic Carpet of Movietone (Fox). Although travelogues had been a mainstay of the American cinema since its start, the genre experienced a renewed sense of importance within Hollywood's new, balanced program of entertainment – a feature presentation alongside short subjects: cartoons, comedies, newsreels, and so forth – that reflected shifting economic and industry-wide circumstances.

With the rise of feature-length film production in the mid-1910s, the short subject had emerged, distinguishing one- and two-reel films from multi-reel productions. The promotion of features as being of higher quality – the main attraction – diminished shorter films as less prestigious, or fillers.[75] This balance began to shift after the Depression's onset in autumn 1929. The financial crisis rendered pre-show live performances no longer feasible, making the relatively quick and cheaply produced shorts a viable alternative. Further, as Rob King explains, Hollywood's growing involvement in short subjects helped to secure its oligopoly over film production by freezing out independently produced shorts.[76] Block booking or full-line forcing required theatres to buy both prestige "A" and lower-budget "B" features, together with an assortment of shorts in bundles, as opposed to case by case. Though buying packages, exhibitors could mix and match features and shorts to suit specific audience demographics. They had more flexibility with selecting short subjects than with features.[77]

Producing companies tried to persuade exhibitors that a variety of high-quality sound shorts, including cartoons, comedies, musicals, newsreels, and travelogues, would stimulate box office, and not as mere padding.[78] MGM was a case in point. Beginning in the late 1920s, the studio ramped up its short-subject release schedule by distributing – in addition to FitzPatrick's TravelTalks – Dogville Comedies, Flip the Frog cartoons, and Hal Roach's short comedies.[79] Under Fred Quimby, general manager of the studio's short features, MGM in 1930–31 increased its shorts by 25 per cent, up to 60 from 48 the previous year. The studio also dedicated more money, time, and energy to producing and publicizing its first-rate short features. "To thousands of people who lay down their money at the box-office," argued Quimby, "the most interesting part of the program is the short subjects ... The smart exhibitor knows this and buys and books accordingly ... and his patrons show their enthusiasm for his choice by spending their money at the box office."[80]

In Canada, Associated Screen News (ASN), the Montreal-based private film company, managed to insert a "wedge into that almost impregnable American domination of short-subject features."[81] In 1931, ASN's managing director, B.E. Norrish, placed Gordon Sparling, who had been working at Paramount's Astoria Studios in New York City, in charge of direction and editing of commercial film production. At ASN, Sparling launched a series of sound-synchronized theatrical short subjects called Canadian Cameos (1932–54). Under his direction, ASN astutely recognized the industry-wide revitalization of the theatrical short subject in its marketing efforts: "IT'S A RISING MARKET SELL SHORTS! Audiences everywhere are paying more attention to shorts than they have for several years. During the depression it was quantity that counted. Now it's variety. The zip and dash of good shorts add zest to the whole programme. It's a wise showman who gives the public what it likes" (figure 4.2).[82]

According to an ASN brochure, Canadian Cameos aimed to be "Canadian in atmosphere, but international in entertainment interest."[83] These "little gems" carved in high relief are "sparkling with variety," covering a range of topics, including history, music, recreation, and scenery. The series enjoyed wide distribution in Canada, the United States, and throughout the British Empire/Commonwealth.[84] Referencing its success, Roly Young of Toronto's *Globe and Mail* observed that, while making feature-length films was "impractical" in Canada, short subjects were "big business."[85] Sparling used that format, which ASN dubbed "featurettes," as a discursive strategy to denote their quality, to experiment with imaginative editing and filming techniques. This was evidenced in probably the best-known Cameo, *Rhapsody in Two Languages* (1934) – a visually creative look at Montreal as a city of contrasts – "It's modern! It's old! It's gay! It's pensive!" – that underscores its seemingly harmonious linguistic and cultural binaries – "It's French! It's English! It's Montreal!"

As the title suggests, *Rhapsody* was part of a cycle of "city symphonies" from the 1920s and 1930s. These non-fiction shorts imagined a day in the life of "the modern city in ways that could be abstract, poetic, metaphorical, and rhythmic."[86] Writing in the *Lethbridge Herald*, Donald W. Buchanan states that *Rhapsody* was produced "in the manner of those travel series on cities of the world that have been done for so many years and so well by American camera-men."[87] Buchanan is comparing *Rhapsody* probably not to such avant-garde city symphonies as Paul Strand and Charles Sheeler's *Manhattan*

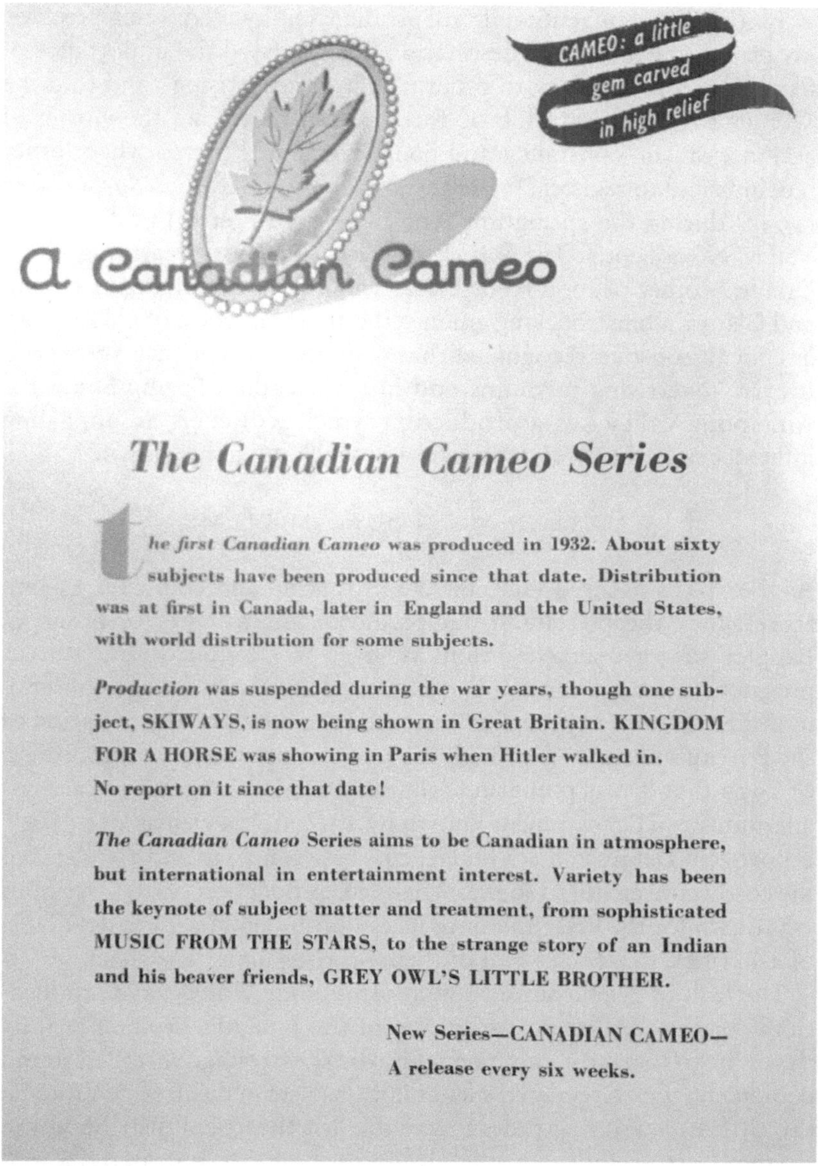

4.2 Canadian Cameos

(1921) or Jay Leyda's *A Bronx Morning* (1931), but rather to sound travelogues distributed by major Hollywood studios, such as MGM's FitzPatrick TravelTalks.

Sparling's unconventional "rhapsodic technique" did not preclude his promoting a tourism destination. He "stressed the importance of films as complementary to other media of advertising" and told the Women's Advertising Club of Toronto that they "had the virtues of action, realism, constancy and could be carried places where other mediums fail to register."[88] For instance, he shot *Acadian Spring Song* (1935) during the springtime Apple Blossom Festival in Annapolis Valley, Nova Scotia. The featurette was a love story, featuring Philip Donat, brother of soon-to-be-Oscar-winning film star Robert Donat, and Gladys White frolicking among "the apple blossoms of old Acadia." Yet local boosters recognized that "sound pictures" are "powerful tourist advertising mediums and in the 'Acadian Spring Song' the Annapolis Valley has a production which will exert an appealing influence over the three continents on which it will be shown."[89]

SIXTEEN-MM TOURISM FILMS

As the 1930s ushered in a new era of talking and colourful 35-mm travelogues, the CGMPB struggled. According to Director Frank C. Badgley, such general conditions as "over-production, double-feature programs, quotas, and tariff barriers raised in various foreign countries militated against any marked increase in the theatrical circulation of the Bureau's films."[90] Although the Bureau announced in the autumn of 1929 that it was preparing talkies to "make Canada's attractions and industrial development known by 'ear-gate' as well as 'eye-gate,'" 40-per-cent Depression-era budget cuts between 1930 and 1934 stalled the costly conversion to sound.[91] In 1932, production of CGMPB films was down for the first time since its establishment. Its 1933 catalogue of 166 titles, more than half of them tourism films, was silent.

The lack of synchronized sound technology would have ramifications for the theatrical distribution of the Bureau's productions. By the early 1930s, most commercial movie theatres had installed sound equipment, which rendered silent films obsolete in theatres.[92] Although the CGMPB kept its product available for theatrical distribution in 35-mm (nitro-cellulose prints), it increasingly concentrated on non-theatrical circulation, where 16-mm films for education, community enterprise, and entertainment enabled tourism promotion.

Although films had circulated non-theatrically since the early days of motion pictures, the standardization of 16-mm equipment enabled their expansion. In 1923, the Eastman Kodak Company introduced the Cine-Kodak process, a combination camera and projector that used 16-mm safety reversal film (standard narrow gauge on cellulose-acetate stock), which was an alternative to the highly flammable 35-mm nitrate base used in theatrical circulation.[93] This cheaper, more accessible 16-mm gauge soon became the standard for amateur cinematography and home use, replacing the 28-mm gauge previously employed in non-commercial settings. Portable 16-mm projectors also expedited distribution and non-commercial exhibition. While 16-mm was initially black and white and silent, the introduction of Kodacolor in 1928 facilitated the addition of colour (it was replaced by Kodachrome in 1935), while synchronized sound had become available, albeit in limited fashion, by the early 1930s.[94] By this time, the small-gauge format had amply demonstrated its value to industrial, governmental, and educational sectors. Film libraries and other lending institutions proliferated, increasing access to 16-mm motion pictures.[95] As early as 1924, Canada's Department of Trade and Commerce confirmed that its Seeing Canada films were available to schools and other organizations on the new safety-standard film.[96] Non-theatrical distribution of 16-mm films through US-based extension services and other community circuits would eventually supersede theatrical distribution for Canada's filmic tourism promotion in the United States.

During the 1934 hearings of the Senate's Special Committee on Tourist Traffic, several witnesses or briefs outlined the specific advantages of 16-mm motion pictures for advertising Canadian tourism in the United States. According to Gordon Smith, director of British Columbia's Bureau of Information and Publicity, the 16-mm film is of "inestimable value for the purpose of publicity." This is due to inexpensive prints and ease of distribution: "The film is sent to borrower 'A' to be passed on to 'B', by 'B' to 'C' and so on. A card goes to 'A', requesting him to pass the film along to a kindred organization ... The same routine is followed with 'B' and 'C' until finally the film finds its way back to the point of origin, having in the meantime been shown to several thousand people – and paid for much more than its original cost."[97]

C.K. Howard, manager of CNR's Tourist and Convention Bureau, similarly stated that the ease of 16-mm film made it the most effective mechanism to direct American tourist traffic to Canada. He explained that the CNR offices in the United States were stocked with 16-mm motion pictures. These could be easily screened in the home or before such groups as the Knights of Columbus, the Knights Templars, and the Shriners, "who may be contemplating a trip and want to see what the place looks like before they go." They could be "put on and shown right in the office" to anyone interested "in a trip to Jasper Park, or Minaki, or the Maritimes" (figure 4.3).[98]

Badgley similarly stressed to the Special Committee the value of postsecondary extension divisions, museums, and the YMCA, which in turn distributed CGMPB product to camps, fish and game associations, motor clubs, and sportsmen's clubs throughout the United States.[99] As an example, he discussed the powerful impact that the Bureau's fishing films had on a group of American outdoor enthusiasts. After the CGMPB, in cooperation with the CNR, filmed at Vermillion Lake in present-day Sudbury, Ontario, "a party of fifteen people from the Chicago district, among whom were the presidents of two large fishing tackle concerns," arrived in "a special car" and spent "in the neighborhood of $3,000 or more on a ten-day trip." The Vermillion Lake Lodge now "has so many people coming there that he canot [*sic*] take care of them. He has a huge lodge, almost as big as the Minaki Inn, but he has difficulty in accommodating all the people who want to come there. That gives an idea of what films can do."[100]

By acknowledging the need to develop tourism to boost the Depression-era economy and by recognizing the important role of film (particularly 16-mm) in tourist advertising, the Special Committee indirectly re-energized the CGMPB. In 1934, the Dominion increased the Bureau's budget for the first time since 1929, allowing it to finally install sound equipment and improve its laboratories.[101] The re-invigorated Bureau would focus on non-theatrical distribution in the United States and created a separate division to meet the increasing demand. Badgley had told the committee:

> While you reach far more people when you get a film in the theatres than you can reach in any other way, I think you get a larger percentage of reaction from smaller gatherings … When a film is shown before a small gathering, as at a school or a fishing club, it constitutes the bulk of the program. The people are in a receptive frame of mind and undoubtedly the majority of them come away with more knowledge than they had before of the story that we want to tell them. I think my opinion in this respect is supported by the fact that most of the commercial advertisers who use films restrict them to the non-theatrical field.[102]

France and the bounding countries. The camera is set up and centered so that the map fills the entire frame. Run off one or two feet to allow the map to be scanned. The route is to be shown by means of a progressive dotted line. Start at the extreme left to take this line across the ocean (every one knows where the Atlantic

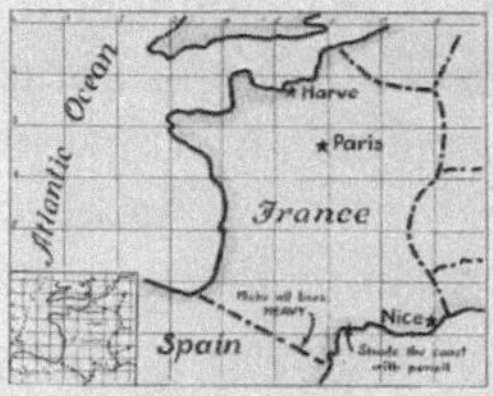

An example of the type of map recommended for titling travelogs intelligently

Ocean is located) and advance to the port of entry, perhaps to Le Havre. Now, the mental picture of the exact location of this port may be vague to the average person but the progressive dotted line locates it definitely. To do the animation, make each dash of the line a quarter of an inch wide and half an inch long. With the first dash, photograph six or eight frames. Without changing the location of either camera or map, put in the next dash, photograph and repeat until the path of the line has been traced out. On arriving at a port, letter in the name and photograph long enough to permit this shot to be used for arrival and first flash of departure.

It may be found that this method is tedious and also that, with some cameras, considerable splicing will have to be done as there will be a light frame at the beginning of each shot. Here is a faster method. First letter in all the necessary locations. Cut a simple silhouette from a piece of thin tin and paint it black. For water voyages, a ship silhouette may be used, and for land a 'plane (top view) or automobile (side view). Hold a strong magnet at the back of the card which will attract and hold the tin model to the front. Start the camera and move the magnet so that the model moves through its prearranged path. For stiffening, the card may be tacked to a skeleton picture frame so that it is easily accessible from the back.

After the introductory shot of the complete map, the camera may be brought closer (if the lens is in a focusing mount) to include only the section which is required to illustrate the shift from one location to another. Follow the map insertion with a close-up of the name of the new location taken either from the map or from station signs if these are available. With maps in your travelog, the audience knows definitely, when they leave one location for another, where they are bound.—*R. P. Ewing.*

Sound ahoy!

[Continued from page 75]

type of pickup and connections for use through the radio or a separate amplifying system. With the Pathé 9.5 mm. Projector in a separate case, it will sell at $135.

Each of these models can be adapted for 16mm. projectors. The difference in cost for either model without 9.5mm. projector, it is said, will be approximately $57 less.

So much for the showing equipment for home talkies.

There follows a listing of the sound or talkie releases already announced by various companies, collected under the names of the sponsoring firms.

Bell & Howell 16mm. sound offerings are: *Alabama Snow, Laundry Act, Love Is King; Ruby Darby Blues, Vagabond, Tramp, Tramp; Lonely Troubadour, Months And Months, Harmonica Harry; Song And Dance, Ed Mahoney, Song Of The Island; Tango Dance, Old Aunt Dinah, At The End Of The Lane; Two Guitars, Hobo Jubilee, St. Louis Blues; When The Curtain Comes Down, Ken And Duke, Slim And Slender; Shawl Dance, Maiden's Prayer, Whispering; La Paloma, The Ramblers, Yah Yah; Some Day Sweetheart, Four Covans, Hot Pepper; Collegiana, The Juggling Jester, Steamboat Bill; Violin Solo, Skating Act, When The Bloom Is On The Sage; Open Fireplace, I'll Be With You, Japanese Dance; Dixie Wait For Me, Don't Gyp Me Little Gypsy, Modern Minstrels; Roll Dem Bones, Sailor Dance, You Left Me In The Rain; Trail Of The Lonesome Pine, Novelty Skating Act, Gypsy Love; Carolina Moon, Violin Solo, Adagio Dancers; Out On The Open Road, I Love You Truly, Tap Dance; That's Funny; The Happy Ranch Boys; The Dizzy Four; Bum Business; The Lion's Roar; The Cuckoo Nuts; The Wise Crackers; The Royal Flush; Irish Romance; Gypsy Troubadors; Gypsy Melodies; Down in Dixie.* The Ufa educational sound subjects are also contained in the Filmo Library and are listed below under Ufa.

Cine Art 16mm. sound pictures offered by the Hollywood Film Enterprises include: *The Lion's Roar; The Happy Ranch Boys; The Wise Crackers; The Cuckoo Nuts; Bum Business; The Dizzy Four; The Royal Flush; That's Funny; Gypsy Melodies; Down*

4.3 Canadian National Railways, *Movie Makers Magazine*, February 1931

To supply these "smaller gatherings," the Bureau organized a 16-mm film-rental library from which prints could be borrowed for a small service charge. It advertised its Seeing Canada productions in, among other publications, H.H. Wilson Company's *Educational Film Catalog* of 1936, which informed visual-education departments and other buyers of available instructional films. Classified according to the Dewey Decimal system, the catalogue itemized nearly 1,200 non-theatrical film titles, providing details about each regarding sources, distributors, forms of the film, and suggested uses and adding short synopses. According to one trade publication, the directory was "the *sine qua non* of all film listings in the school-club-church film field."[103]

In 1938, the CGMPB issued its own forty-page catalogue providing titles with descriptions and a supplementary list of twenty-one sound films (most of them tourism films) available for non-theatrical distribution. In his report for that fiscal year, Badgley observed that the production and distribution of 16-mm sound films was "an outstanding development," which has "opened up new and valuable fields for publicity." Detailing the marked increase in circulation, he noted that about 6,500 one-reel subjects were flowing through over 30 countries, with 3,579 films in US use. He estimated that 200,000 people had seen these films that year and added that supply could not keep up with demand.[104]

In Canada, the growth of 16-mm coincided with a rise in nationalism that encouraged cultural authorities to consider film's possibilities as a mechanism of national culture and public education. In 1935, Donald W. Buchanan, son of Senator W.A. Buchanan, publisher of the *Lethbridge Herald* and member of the 1934 Select Committee, established the National Film Society (NFS) to promote "the study, appreciation, and use" of film as "educational and cultural factors in the life of the Dominion."[105] The NFS received funding from such American philanthropic organizations as the Carnegie Corporation and the Rockefeller Foundation, which had developed an interest in 16-mm film for educational purposes.[106] Loosely modelled after the British Film Institute (BFI), the NFS was a voluntary organization, without formal government support. It maintained branches in such major cities as Montreal, Ottawa, Toronto, and Vancouver that planned screenings, advocated for visual instruction in schools, and acted as a clearing house for information on educational and art films. As Charles Acland indicates, the NFS quickly became the most active proponent of non-theatrical applications of film and "an important institutional embodiment of particular discourses about nationhood and film culture" within Canada.[107]

The cultivation of cultural standards through visual instruction was aligned with Canada's adult-education movement. After US universities and colleges began to offer extension programs, adult education in Canada commenced with the University of Alberta's Extension Department, founded 1912 under A.E. Ottewell. In 1917, the university would establish the Dominion's first library of educational films. The department's job, according to E.A. "Ned" Corbett, assistant to the director, "was to bring to the remote places of the Province whatever cultural and entertainment values the University could offer as a means of encouraging community solidarity, strengthening morale, awakening the civic conscience in regard to better home and school conditions; to bring colour and some kindliness to the hard and lonely lives of frontier people."[108]

As Zoë Druick demonstrates, the Extension Department's film work was intended to instill middle-class Anglo-Saxon Protestant values in a largely rural and immigrant (primarily from eastern and central Europe) population.[109] This paralleled the ways in which the growth of visual instruction in the United States aligned with the broader processes of Americanization, through language and civics, that followed the postwar Red Scare and the subsequent passage of the restrictive Emergency Quota Act (1921) and the Immigration Act of 1924. According to Herbert Kaufman, assistant secretary under US Secretary of the Interior Franklin K. Lane, the distribution of film through public schools and extension programs taught "Americanism" to those who "live in America but America does not live in them."[110]

In 1927, Ned Corbett succeeded A.E. Ottewell as director of extension at the University of Alberta. That same year, he helped set up the university's radio station (CKUA) and organized the Banff School of Fine Arts (renamed the Banff Centre for Continuing Education in 1933), serving as its founding director. Two years later, Corbett left Alberta to become the first director of the Canadian Association for Adult Education (CAEE). Supported by a Carnegie Corporation grant, the CAEE was primarily an advisory and planning body and "a forum for the discussion of common problems."[111] As head of this educational lobby and a board member of the new NFS, Corbett would become a driving force behind creation of the NFB, which would replace the CGMPB as the national agency producing films.[112]

Corbett, along with other influential Anglo-Canadians such as Frank C. Badgley and Donald Buchanan, saw themselves as protecting the national interest and uniquely qualified to both assess cultural products and inculcate these standards of good taste into the public. In 1936, Buchanan wrote "Educational and Cultural Films in Canada," a survey report that called for a national centre for information on film in education and encouraged the medium's use as a "cultural instrument." Two years later, he and D.S. McMullan, director of visual education of the Provincial Association of Protestant Teachers of Quebec, prepared a twelve-page document – the so-called Buchanan-McMullan report – suggesting more cooperation with Britain, France, and the United States in producing "quality" non-commercial educational films. The writers also proposed that Canada produce educational films and nationally coordinate related activities.[113]

While they were preparing their report, John Grierson, the pioneering force behind the British documentary movement, arrived in Ottawa in May 1938, invited by the Canadian government and the Imperial Relations Trust (IRT). The IRT, set up in 1937 to reinforce ties between Britain, Canada, Australia, and New Zealand, also supported the NFS as part of its drive to encourage sharing of film information around the empire. Grierson's mandate was to conduct a survey of film development in the Dominion and of film activities within government, particularly the CGMPB. Whereas the NFS promoted distribution of non-theatrical productions, especially educational and international art films, Grierson encouraged the making and distribution of national documentary films as techniques for encouraging social change, citizenship, and modernization.[114]

Hence, the NFS and the adult-education movement laid the groundwork for a restructured film agency in Canada, which paralleled the centralized tourism bureau. The fragmented nature of film production invited systematization, rationalization, and governmentality. In May 1939, the National Film Act established the National Film Commission, with Grierson appointed as its inaugural commissioner (1939–45). Corbett was initially offered the position, but declined.[115] Grierson was "to advise upon the making and distribution of national films designed to help Canadians in all parts of Canada to understand the ways of living and the problems of Canadians in other parts." Initially, the CGMPB continued to produce films, but with the outbreak of war in September 1939, the renamed National Film Board oversaw wartime filmic propaganda and information, and in 1941 it absorbed the CGMPB. The NFB worked to shape Canadians' filmic vision of their country as a modern democratic society, while still crafting a destination brand aimed at the American tourist market.[116]

The interwar period was volatile for tourism in Canada, as tourist traffic from the United States rose steeply in the 1920s, crashed early in the Depression, and regained ground in the mid-1930s. With the establishment in 1935 of the CTB under D. Leo Dolan, the Dominion committed itself to bolstering tourism by promoting itself as the Americans' friendly neighbour to the (mostly) north. The final report of the Senate's Select Committee on Tourist Traffic of 1934, which led to the Bureau, depicted film as the most effective means of travel publicity in the United States and encouraged filming in Canada by American producers as a cost-effective measure. Indeed, the Senate hearings coincided with a new era of theatrical travelogues. More and better short subjects, for instance the FitzPatrick TravelTalks or ASN's Canadian Cameos, allowed US filmgoers to experience Canadian tourist destinations on film through the addition of sound and colour.

Meanwhile, a cash-strapped CGMPB focused on distributing 16-mm films via US non-theatrical circuits, including public schools, college and university extension programs, and other community organizations. The expansion of the visual-instruction movement permitted the Bureau to circulate its tourism films as education. Within Canada, a powerful group of imperial-minded cultural nationalists and adult-education specialists advocated for a new kind of documentary attentive to the everyday lives of Canadians. They perceived the CGMPB to be primarily outward looking, promoting and exporting depictions of Canadian scenery, as well as agricultural, industrial, and manufacturing activities. The same centralizing impulse that generated the CTB would by the late 1930s lead to the NFB. Under Grierson, the NFB produced film for social use – specifically to promote modern citizenship and democracy. Nevertheless, the NFB was not entirely opposed to film for tourism promotion, nor would the Second World War signal a moratorium on tourism promotion in Canada.

5

Documentarians, Amateurs, and Diplomacy

The National Film Board and Tourism during the Second World War

Just over the border, Canada, with its vast wilderness and its beehives of modern activity amid quaint settings, has always beckoned to the American cameraman.

American Cinematographer, January 1941[1]

On the eve of the Second World War for Canada, Hollywood-produced Canadian tourism films circulated in theatres as part of the American film industry's balanced program of shorts and feature-length motion pictures reaching a mass, undifferentiated audience of filmgoers. Conversely, tourism boosters within Canada increasingly sponsored or produced 16-mm films targeted to such intimate venues as US clubs and community organizations. Non-theatrical distribution concentrated on specific groups of potential American tourists, such as those interested in camping, fishing, or sightseeing. This strategy indicates a rudimentary form of market segmentation at a time when the promotion of tourism and the production of film in Canada were becoming centralized and bureaucratized within the Canadian Travel Bureau (CTB) and the National Film Board (NFB). At the same time, the country's tourism destinations would entice non-professional filmmakers from the United States to produce amateur tourism films, often with encouragement from the NFB.

The NFB quickly expanded in scope and size with Canada's entry into the war in September 1939. Staffed originally by Commissioner John Grierson, filmmakers Stuart Legg and Ross McLean, and secretaries Jean McIntyre and Janet Scellen, it swelled to nearly eight hundred personnel by 1945. Its production of both theatrical and non-theatrical releases also increased exponentially; from some forty in various stages of production in 1940 to an annual release of two hundred by fiscal 1943–44. Following its absorption of the CGMPB in 1941 to consolidate government film activities, Grierson organized a system of travelling projectionists who took NFB films to trade-union workers and rural communities. The NFB evolved largely in response to the Dominion government's need to disseminate information and propaganda to mobilize Canadians for the war effort. Beyond promoting national unity on the home front, the film board also positioned the nation's wartime role on a global scale for an international audience.[2]

Grierson wanted to recast Canada's national film project. He was determined it should no longer be defined as a struggle "with subtitles dealing with moose and goose," so he worked to imbue the NFB's oeuvre with his social conscience and vision of public engagement – a *documentary* approach.[3] Under Grierson's stewardship, it seemed that tourism's role in Canada's institutional film program would be anathema to the transformative potential of realist filmmaking. This understanding of the tourism film and the documentary movement as incompatible in wartime Canada, however, obscures the linkages in practice. From its inception, the NFB cooperated with the CTB and the Parks Branch. Although war drastically cut back the travel bureau's staff and budget, it continued to promote tourism. Prior to the US entry into the conflict after Pearl Harbor, in December 1941, Canadian tourist interests declared their country open for business, hoping American tourists would bring much-needed US currency into the nation's war chest.

At the same time, the documentary-film movement inspired novel – even radical – approaches to Canadian tourism films, in terms of their photo-realism, non-traditional narrative structure, and techniques of persuasion. Amateur filmmakers had been experimenting with the travelogue format, which bridged the nation-state and the individual. The NFB supported non-professionals as they imaginatively reconstructed the tourism film by offering a personalized vision of the citizen-subject as tourist, whose journey was informed by government-produced promotional literature. Alongside these non-commercial efforts, Hollywood studios produced Canadian-themed, 35-mm travelogues, often encouraged by Dominion or provincial agencies, stressing neighbourly friendship and goodwill. In the war against fascism, tourism more broadly served intercultural diplomacy, urging hemispheric defence. After December 1941, US and Canadian propaganda agencies deepened ties, enabling the NFB to expand its non-theatrical distribution into the United States in anticipation of a postwar travel boom.

JOHN GRIERSON AND DOCUMENTARY FILM

In 1938, the Imperial Relations Trust (IRT) commissioned Grierson to travel to Canada, as well as New Zealand and Australia, to strengthen links with those dominions in the event of war. The film producer had already made hundreds of government-sponsored films in Britain while he oversaw film units for the Empire Marketing Board (EMB) 1927–33 and, after it disbanded, for the General Post Office (GPO) 1933–37. The state-run EMB film unit emerged out of the Imperial Conference of 1926, which recognized cinema as an instrument of education capable of influencing public opinion. Delegates also lamented the preponderance of Hollywood film product throughout the British Empire, which resulted in quota legislation. The following year, the head of the EMB, Sir Stephen Tallents (chair of the IRT beginning in 1937) hired Grierson, recently returned from the United States, to put "into practice the theories about cinema which he had formed as a Rockefeller research student of psychology in Hollywood and elsewhere in the United States."[4]

Born in Scotland and educated at Glasgow University, Grierson in 1924 received a Laura Spelman Rockefeller Memorial fellowship for postgraduate study at the University of Chicago, which was known for research innovations in social psychology and pioneering statistical methods. Although he never received a degree there, his biographer Forsyth Hardy notes that he developed an interest in film "not as an art form, but as a medium for reaching public opinion."[5] In addition to this training in empirical research, the writings of American journalist Walter Lippmann, mostly his theories on the relationship between the media and public opinion in modern democracies, showed Grierson the possibilities of film for informing a mass citizenry. Grierson additionally spent time in New York, delivering lectures and writing articles for newspapers and periodicals. He also travelled to Los Angeles to meet with several filmmakers and observe film production under Hollywood's studio system. When he returned to Britain in 1927, as Jack Ellis states, it was with the belief that "citizenship education was the broad necessity, film the chosen medium, documentary its special form."[6]

While employed at the EMB and GPO, Grierson advocated for the production and distribution of documentary film, which he later defined as "the creative treatment of actuality."[7] Addressing the Society of Motion Picture Engineers in 1927, Grierson argued for the "obligations of cinema as a public and popular institution." Film's "creative possibilities as a guiding force among the needs, desires, and ambitions of emergent democracy," he added, "are obviously enormous."[8] Grierson sought to develop a socially useful cinema by dramatizing aspects of contemporary life and focusing on vital issues that affected common people. According to him, documentaries contrasted with other short subjects, including travelogues, advertising, and industrial films, due to their storytelling approach and aesthetic qualities. The documentarian sought to depict sociological problems on screen, to arouse the public conscience, and to stimulate problem-solving. Grierson's experimental approach combined propaganda, education, and citizenship, helping to launch the documentary-film movement, which influenced filmmaking throughout the British Empire and beyond.[9]

Grierson and other progenitors of the documentary movement cautioned against confusing their genre with commercial advertising films. As his compatriot Paul Rotha writes, "The documentary film was the outcome of a public relations movement and came about as a result of a desire on the part of the Government, Industry, and other Public Bodies to create a deeper sympathy between the activities and public understanding in Great Britain."[10] Canada had arguably been one of the first nations to engage in government films with its Exhibits and Publicity Bureau, founded 1917–18, and was intrigued by this new move to dramatize everyday life, which had worked well in Britain. Prime Minister William Lyon Mackenzie King and other officials ventured that this new film form would not only advertise Canada to the world in novel ways, but could also help citizens understand themselves.[11] Hence, while Grierson was in Canada under the auspices of the IRT, which was funding transnational educational and cultural film activities throughout the empire, Minister of Trade and Commerce W.D. Euler asked him to conduct a fact-finding survey of Canada's film scene.

In 1931, the EMB had sent Grierson to Ottawa on a trade mission. He visited the CGMPB and commended its film labs, observing that the Bureau produced films of the "'uplift' type" mostly for non-theatrical audiences and stressing "the advantages of Canada from a tourist point of view, and an enormous tourist business has developed as a result."[12] Yet when he returned in 1938, he publicly disparaged the tourism promotion that had dominated government film production. He told the Canadian Manufacturers Association that documentary film could provide "a picture of an up and coming continent of great achievements, great industries and even greater possibilities. Instead of that, they are getting for the most part a tourist picture of Canada." While he praised Director Frank C. Badgley for developing government-sponsored motion pictures, he intimated that these had become banal and clichéd. Quoting an educational expert, he added that if Canada desired to "build up a reputation for its modern industrial developments," it should not present solely "fishing, golf and the observation of wild animals." Since Canada could not compete with Hollywood in making entertainment films, it should focus on prestige-building documentaries.[13] He did not wholeheartedly oppose use of film to advertise tourism but proposed a new kind of tourism film using documentary techniques.

During the summer of 1938, as Grierson crisscrossed the country at the behest of the Dominion, he recognized the challenges posed by the nation's vastness and regional diversity. Still, he confidently touted realist film to "integrate the country mentally" by educating Canadians in one region about their counterparts elsewhere.[14] He called for imaginative and dramatic "propaganda which would have its roots in everyday life of the people," that is, showing the "big drama behind the routine things which looked dull at first appearance." Grierson and tourism boosters thus both saw motion pictures as instruments to promote Canada as a modern nation yet had contrasting views on "the type of creative work that film could do in advancing national interests. Grierson believed that film should predominantly promote citizenship and democracy."[15]

When Grierson delivered his report on Canada's film needs, he recommended ways to increase what Zoë Druick calls "empire communication" through film. Given US dominance of the commercial market, he argued that existing non-theatrical circuits could best distribute cultural and educational films at home and with the rest of the empire. His report also proposed a central body to bring together government film activities. This culminated in the NFB, which he helmed until 1945.[16] Despite cries from opposition parties that a centralized board would duplicate government services and waste money, Bill 35, received royal assent as the National Film Act on 2 May 1939, and the National Film Board (initially Commission) came into existence on 31 August 1939.

W.D. Euler, along with most supporters of the legislation, maintained that it would coordinate the film business of government branches, thereby eliminating redundancies and ensuring efficiency and savings. Euler asserted that a central production and distribution service would not reproduce the CGMPB's work or interfere with commercial film organizations. Housed within the Department of Trade and Commerce, the CGMPB produced films that came from "various departments" but "has nothing to do with their initiation."[17] Conversely, a centralized board could produce "national films" – those "which might be of an educational nature intended for all the people of the whole country, and which would not touch the particular interests of any one department." In other words, it would produce and distribute Grierson-style documentaries for information and publicity.[18]

Showing Canadians in their "working clothes" did not prevent the NFB from advertising the country's scenic attributes to potential tourists.[19] During the Senate debates, defenders of Bill 35 emphasized the film board's potential for promoting tourism. Quebec-born Ontario Senator Joseph-Henri-Gustave Lacasse argued that, in addition to stimulating national consciousness by developing citizens' love and knowledge of their country, "the proposed National Film Board will be of great educational value in making known to Americans and others the tourist attractions and industrial advantages of the Dominion." Senator Creelman MacArthur, known for developing his home province of Prince Edward Island as a tourist destination, reminded opponents that they had "voted a considerable sum for a tourist bureau," which "is a great asset to this country." The board, he continued, would achieve similar results as a "publicity organization."[20]

Hence, to ensure that the new body promoted tourism, the CTB's D. Leo Dolan was appointed to the interdepartmental committee advising it. Euler was the chair, and other members included such tourism boosters as Deputy Minister of Trade and Commerce J.G. Parmelee, who had supervised the CGMPB; Deputy Minister of Transport Colonel V.I. Smart, who also oversaw operation of the CTB; and Minister of Mines and Resources T.A. Crerar, whose department "also makes scenic films" of the National Parks.[21]

THE NEW YORK WORLD'S FAIR

By the end of 1939, Trade and Commerce posited that the New York World's Fair, which had opened on 30 April 1939 in Flushing Meadows, Queens, would provide an auspicious non-theatrical venue to exhibit "the new films of Canada" produced by the new NFB.[22] Since their emergence, motion pictures have been vital to the world's-fair movement, in keeping with its "dreams of empire and consumerism." Economic elites backed by government sponsorship financed these spectacles to celebrate technology, scientific achievements, and consumer goods, as well as to present a worldview rooted in imperialism and material progress. Universal expositions reinforced dominant class, colonial, gendered, national, and racial relations of power.[23] Imagined as places to visually structure and organize knowledge, international expositions were also spaces of leisure and recreation. Normally lasting between six months and a year, they were ephemeral tourist magnets at a time of increased mobility, each attracting between 10 and 25 million people before being mostly dismantled. National and local governments, along with economic interests (particularly railways and other transportation companies), recognized that these transient global stages proffered long-lasting promotional value. Through architecture, exhibit design, motion pictures, and static dioramas, Canada would display its resources and scenic attributes, thereby defining its national brand to a target audience of fairgoers who were marked as an ideal market of tourists and consumers.

After an underwhelming showing at the 1937 exposition in Paris, wherein critics deemed Canada's exhibit "dull and old-fashioned," New York provided an occasion to show the world a "young and virile country full of opportunities and prospects."[24] This jibed with the fair's "world of tomorrow" theme, propounding utopian visions of efficiency, innovation, and prosperity, as well as expanded, experimental, and immersive cinema exhibition. Despite the easing Depression and the onset of world war, the exposition was utopian, celebratory, and looked to a prosperous future. Companies and nations displayed images of themselves that emphasized consumer abundance and technological innovation. The Dominion recognized that world's fairs were no longer "places of business and barter and sale"; rather fairgoers would be attracted to Canada "as a place *to play* in rather that *to work in*." The targeted demographic was thus the "tired businessman" seeking recreation, as opposed to "lumbermen ... interested in forest exploitation and wood-using industries."[25]

In keeping with the fair's overarching design aesthetic, the Canadian Pavilion was "modern in every respect." A streamlined, L-shaped, white stucco building that incorporated elements of Indigenous art, it displayed the era's tendency towards primitivism in settler-colonial art.[26] This contrasted with Canada's more rustic exhibits and agricultural-design aesthetic at the Paris Expo of 1937, which evoked grain silos. According to Trade and Commerce, which handled the nation's participation in New York, during its first year of operation over 20,000 people daily visited the pavilion, and a very large percentage of those expressed a desire to travel to the Dominion. Nevertheless, after visiting in November 1939, J.R. Dickson of the Dominion Forestry Service observed that other national exhibitions maintained small moving-picture theatres, where special "propaganda films were run." He concluded: "There is little doubt that a good-sized auditorium, with comfortable seats, is a most useful and valuable medium of securing desired advertising through selected films." He suggested, for example, that films featuring the Dionne Quintuplets would attract visitors to Canada.[27]

To further encourage tourism, for the fair's second season Trade and Commerce added motion pictures that highlighted Canada's scenic attractions and recreational offerings, emphasizing easy access for US visitors.[28] The new film theatre at the Canadian Pavilion was part of a diversified, consumer-driven exhibition environment. As Haidee Wasson demonstrates, a sizable number of corporate and government bodies were using film technology in novel ways at the fair. Over six hundred films were exhibited throughout thirty-four auditoriums – most in sound, some in colour, and even a few in three dimensions. Motion pictures at the fair, noted *Business Screen Magazine*, had one important task: attract "the largest possible percentage" of fairgoers and then hold "their attentive interest for the longest possible time." This would pay off in "more sales or an improvement in the public's attitude toward" the product or service.[29]

Daily between 2 and 8 p.m., the Canadian Pavilion screened about two dozen sound short subjects produced by ASN/CPR, the CGMPB/NFB, the CNR, and the Parks Branch. After each program, a recorded invitation urged patrons to visit the CTB booth and plan their trips. Far from Grierson's vision of film as creative actuality, these were mostly tourism films, about half in colour, emphasizing scenic vistas from coast to coast along with images of camping, fishing, and trail riding. Films also emphasized modern transportation. For example, ASN's *The Banff-Jasper Highway* (1939) celebrated the new mountain route linking two of Canada's most popular National Parks, while *The Swift Family Robinson* (1940), sponsored by the newly minted Trans-Canada Air Lines (the precursor to Air Canada), showcased the freshest way to experience the vast landscape – by air.[30] Although the government planned to present films produced by its newfangled film board, missing were Canada's first documentary films, such as *The Case of Charlie Gordon* (dir. by Stuart Legg, 1939), which focused on training activities for unemployed youth for the Department of Labour; or *Heritage* (dir. by J. Booth Scott, 1939), sponsored by the Department of Agriculture, documenting the activities of its Prairie Farm Rehabilitation Administration, which emulated the prestige US government documentary, *The Plow That Broke the Plains* (dir. by Pare Lorentz, 1936).[31] The NFB's other early productions covering wartime mobilization and economic activities were apparently also not on the program.[32]

After visiting the World's Fair for a second time in September 1940, J.R. Dickson of the Forestry Service praised Canada's new and improved pavilion. He commended in particular "our splendid Cinema," calling it "a fine tourist lure" to encourage visitors to "spend their play-time with us in search of fun, beauty, sport and good health."[33] Between May and October 1940, nearly 300,000 fairgoers visited the cinema, which planted the seeds for a postwar cross-border tourism boom.[34] Of course, the fair took place against the backdrop of the European crisis that led to war (but not in the United States) in September 1939. At a time of reduced staff and minimal funding, promoting Canada's destination brand in New York showed visitors a fully functioning tourist destination despite its involvement in the war overseas.

The 1939 fair provided a venue to persuade tourists that war was not harming Canada's tourism infrastructure nor complicating entry at the border. Motion pictures focused on the country's tourist appeal, highlighting the mobility that complemented the surrounding physical exhibits promoting industry and manufacturing, sublime landscapes, and state-of-the art tourism infrastructure. The CPR's diorama showed model trains travelling through the Banff area, with miniatures of the main hotel and points of interest. The CTB exhibit featured a neon tube spread across a road map, on which the main US highways leading to

Canada were indicated with red neon flashers, and another illuminated conduit showed the Trans-Canada Air Lines routes. A conspicuously large sign read "American Tourists Require NO PASSPORTS," to counteract a popular misconception about wartime border exigencies.[35]

Likewise, the Canadian Pavilion's communication platform emphasized British-Canadian-US ties in ideological opposition to totalitarianism. According to Trade and Commerce, "the paramount consideration" was to show the country "as a member of the Empire taking her place with the other Dominions in the war" and "to strengthen the goodwill and mutual understanding" between the vast neighbours.[36] These themes were palpable when King George VI and Queen Elizabeth explored the pavilion on 10 June 1939 when they spent five days in the United States as a side trip late in their cross-country Canadian tour between 17 May and 15 June. According to Frank C. Badgley, "Canada is securing a tremendous amount of valuable advertising through the royal visit."[37] The CGMPB accordingly produced the feature-length film *The Royal Visit* (1939), covering the entire tour, which underscored solidarity against the fascist regimes of Europe. This display of international cultural diplomacy came at the invitation of US President Franklin Roosevelt. Wanting to avoid the ire of domestic isolationists, the president arranged this first official visit of a reigning monarch to the United States as a brief and subtle form of psychological propaganda to influence American opinion towards Britain and its dominions.[38]

The tourism framework of the Canadian Pavilion also emphasized friendship and goodwill vis-à-vis the United States in the context of the war that already engaged Canada. Unrestricted travel across the border exemplified democracy in action and flew in the face of fascism. By promoting the country's "tourist appeal," according to Deputy Minister of Trade and Commerce J.G. Parmelee, Canada was demonstrating its "unshaken faith in the future" by providing fairgoers with "an opportunity to investigate at first hand the many attractive interests to be found in a young and progressive country, while enjoying to the fullest extent the kind of vacation he can best afford to take and appreciate."[39] For Parmelee, tourism thus functioned as a form of "soft power" that, as Joseph S. Nye, Jr, explains, can help obtain certain foreign-policy outcomes via persuasion as opposed to coercion. In other words, through enticement, tourism promotion at the fair could strengthen cultural bonds and build relationships that were essential early in the war and even more so later.[40]

WARTIME TOURISM AND FILM IN CANADA

The onset of war precipitated a general downturn in Canada's tourism industry. As the nation girded itself for the struggle, the CTB gradually curtailed its activities and by 1942 operated with a skeleton staff.[41] The government nevertheless understood that American tourists provided much-needed US dollars for its wartime economy. In June 1941, the CTB, together with the Bureau of Public Information (Canada's propaganda agency), the Canadian Broadcasting Corporation (CBC), and the NFB, were transferred to the reorganized Department of National War Services under minister J. (Joe) T. Thorson. When challenged in the House of Commons on the logic of attaching the tourism bureau to a war department, Thorson argued that "grouping together" all these information and publicity agencies would streamline cooperative promotion of tourism, which would supply crucial US currency for the war effort.[42]

As in the First World War, tourism boosters initially promoted Canada to those thousands of Americans blocked by war from their annual travel abroad. Yet Axis propaganda sought to deter them. Schuyler B. Terry observed in *Hygeia* – an educational health magazine published by the American Medical Association – that Canadians "have made every effort to acquaint our [US] public with the beauties and pleasures of travel in Canada." Yet, he warned, enemy propaganda reportedly circulating in his country discouraged such travel. Although tourist traffic generated well-being and wealth, Terry contended that "others of opposite purpose" have discouraged "our happy and healthful visiting with our time-honored neighbor" by spreading malicious and false rumours regarding conditions there and about the "difficulties that United States citizens might encounter."[43]

The CTB's D. Leo Dolan was aware of such foreign sabotage. He was notified that a group of Americans with reservations for a fishing trip to Quebec's Anticosti Island during the summer of 1940 each received letters advising them not to go. These notes were traced back to a Bund (a German-American pro-Nazi organization).[44] Dolan also learned from a Canadian tourist agent based in Seattle that the North German Lloyd steamship company "appointed various pro-axis travel agents throughout the US." These operatives deterred potential travellers by falsely informing them that food was scarce in Canada, that the hotels were crowded with soldiers, that "every place of interest is used for a barracks," and that American tourists would have difficulty leaving the country.[45] Dolan informed the Dominion's wartime Economic Advisory Committee – deputy ministers and other senior civil servants advising the prime minister – about possible countermeasures against such enemy propaganda. Since maintaining and/or increasing tourism "represented the easiest way of expanding our receipts of United States dollars," the CTB launched a promotional campaign: magazine ads, news stories, and a pamphlet "on wartime conditions in Canada as they affect the tourist" to convince Americans that they were welcome.[46]

Lacking both the financial means and film-production capabilities, Dolan also reached out to John Grierson about joint wartime "motion pictures as tourist promotional work."[47] At an October 1940 conference of Dominion and provincial transportation officials in Ottawa called by the Advisory Committee on Travel and Tourist Industry, NFB Director of Distribution Philéas Côté (the only francophone on the committee) recommended that Canada "should be publicized to a greater extent in the United States by means of motion pictures" and "that steps should be taken to modernize all films" in government libraries. As well, each province "should endeavour to make a short film with the assistance and co-operation of the National Film Board."[48]

Despite this expressed commitment, Grierson initially aimed most of the NFB's resources to producing two prestige short-subject documentary series comparable to Time, Inc.'s, monthly screen magazine *The March of Time* (1935–51). Theatrically distributed by Columbia Pictures in both English and French for largely domestic audiences, *Canada Carries On* examined wartime activities on the home front and covered international events as they affected Canadians. Beyond providing "information," the series, Grierson argued, was "primarily helping the people to a simple pattern of thought and feeling."[49] The NFB also introduced an outward-looking companion series, *World in Action*, which placed Canada in relation to the war from a global perspective. United Artists distributed these films to approximately 5,000 theatres throughout the United States, as well as in Latin America (with Spanish and Portuguese soundtracks), Britain, and its dominions.[50]

After their commercial theatrical run, the NFB circulated its *Canada Carries On* and *World in Action* films to non-theatrical audiences. "In the documentary world," according to *Business Screen Magazine*, "the theatres constitute the holding line, and the main advance is made in the non-theatrical field."[51] The NFB concurrently produced more

16-mm films on topics such as agriculture, labour, shipping, and Canada's ethnic communities. Beginning in January 1942, the NFB expanded its non-theatrical circuits to convey, as Donald Buchanan states, "the full story of Canada at war to isolated rural areas by means of films" and "stimulate community discussion regarding the objectives of war." Armed with a projector, soundbox, 16-mm films, and a screen, field workers crisscrossed the country, serving approximately 1,600 rural and remote communities while the industrial circuits reached more than 1,000 factories. Serving "Canada's wide spaces and scattered population" via automobile, train, and even by sleigh, NFB films appeared each month in factories, farmers' cooperatives, schools, town halls, and trade unions. Following each film program, tailored for the community in question, the itinerant NFB representative mediated a forum discussion with the audience on related issues.[52]

The NFB targeted the US market as well for its 16-mm productions, specifically those encouraging tourism, given its copacetic relationship with the CTB. Discussing his early years at the NFB, scriptwriter–turned–Information Editor Graham McInnes observed that, while non-theatrical production was "supposed to embody all the passionate educational zeal for which the medium was famous, it lacked glamour." Yet Grierson "cast his eyes covetously at the enormous 16mm USA market," which would provide "Canada a window on the world" through American "schools, colleges, universities, museums, adult education groups, service clubs and just about every potential specialist audience you could think of."[53] In the autumn of 1941, Grierson appointed the Chicago-based Wesley H. Greene to oversee US distribution of 16-mm films. Greene, a onetime high-school social-sciences instructor and prominent figure in the visual-instruction movement, was the director of the College Film Center at Northwestern University and founder of the International Film Bureau, which imported and exported educational films.[54]

In November 1940, Grierson composed an eight-page memorandum to Dolan detailing the pros and cons of wartime theatrical and non-theatrical distribution of Canadian tourism films. He made clear that he favoured the more direct approach of specialized distribution via non-theatrical circulation to educational facilities, sporting clubs, and women's groups in the United States. He recommended building a circulating library of 16-mm colour films on such subjects as the cities and communities of Canada, expeditions by rivers and lakes, flora and fauna, and recreational sports (fishing, golf, hockey, and hunting). He also advocated a coordinated approach to producing and disseminating tourism films. "Small, piecemeal and disorderly approaches are a waste of money," he stressed. With a "national plan" in place, as opposed to "presenting a series of films of relatively parochial interest," Canada could once again lead in using film to advance publicity.[55] The NFB therefore endeavoured to produce a distinct type of Canadian tourism film rooted in *documentary* principles and creative intention.

In early 1941, Britain's *Documentary News Letter*, dedicated to the goals of the documentary movement, speculated that tourism's important role in Canada would be reflected in "the coming policy of close cooperation between the Tourist [*sic*] Bureau and the National Film Board. Travel pictures in colour for US distribution will probably be the result." To that end, Grierson contracted small, independent commercial producers throughout Canada to capitalize on the "new US public interest in Canadian life and government" and to "promote knowledge among the American people of their Northern neighbour who is now a vital part of the New World defense system."[56]

Most notably, Grierson commissioned the Ottawa-based husband-and-wife filmmaking team of Radford "Budge" and Judith Crawley (née Sparks) to shoot in 16-mm Kodachrome during the autumn in Quebec's nearby Gatineau Hills, at the foothills of the Laurentian Mountains, which Prime Minister Mackenzie King had begun to develop – around his country home, "Kingsmere" – as a protected park, for "tourist purposes."[57] The Crawleys, known as the NFB's "Ottawa Unit," incorporated these scenes into *Ottawa on the River* (1941). The seventeen-minute film shows tourists from across Canada and the United States photographing themselves in and around Parliament Hill. Additionally, it highlights the recreational opportunities in and around the nation's capital and offers a visual sketch of its diverse citizens – no hint of the wartime backdrop that could discourage tourists.[58]

Later that year, the Crawleys made *Canadian Landscape* (1941), centring on A.Y. Jackson. The well-known painter was a founding member of the Group of Seven, a collection of artists whose modernist landscapes of Canada's pristine wilderness established a distinctive (and problematic) nationalist aesthetic that also demarcated a settler-colonial tourist gaze. As Lynda Jessup writes, "Landscape in paintings by the Group of Seven was not a place of productive labour, nor a permanent home, but rather a place of recreation – of scenic value and spiritual renewal."[59] Likewise, Crawley's camera fetishizes the dense forests and craggy hills of Canada's "frontier land," documenting Jackson as he canoes, camps, paints, and sketches. Graham McInnes, who wrote the script, recalled that the film was "to show the artist at work and through his work in the North Country which had a powerful, indeed an almost mystical, appeal to Canadians."[60] The film's documentary impulse, however, did not negate the tourist appeal of Ontario's blazing autumn colours and sparkling blue lakes, combined with the quaint, snow-covered Quebec countryside, complete with a visit to a "folksy" French-Canadian family. While exploring the beauty of nature through the eyes of an artist, *Canadian Landscape* reinforces a tourist perspective rooted in a settler-colonial fantasy of a virginal wilderness devoid of Indigenous peoples.

Prior to establishing their private production company, Crawley Films, Limited, which made primarily non-theatrical films for corporate, educational, government, and industrial sponsors, the Crawleys had cut their teeth making amateur films.[61] Given their success, the NFB in its early years encouraged other Canadian and US amateurs to produce documentary-style Canadian tourism films – harnessing the expanding amateur-film movement to promote Canadian tourism creatively. Amateurism offered non-professionals the discursive and aesthetic space to experiment, often incorporating avant-garde techniques. Unlike casual point-and-shoot home or family movies, amateur films involve pre- and post-production work and often invoke recognizable (largely non-fiction) genres, such as ethnographic pictures, industrial, nature studies, sporting events, and travelogues. As Charles Tepperman establishes, amateur film culture "created an alternative world of small-scale movie production and circulation."[62]

In 1926, the wealthy inventor Hiram Percy Maxim, a ham-radio and cinema enthusiast, established the Amateur Cinema League (ACL) in New York City. Amateur movie clubs were proliferating, providing a diverse international population (though mostly American or Canadian, white, and middle class) of non-professional filmmakers with lectures, technical assistance, and workshops; holding participatory, non-theatrical screenings; and supporting amateur-film culture through exchange and distribution ("swaps"). These groups, as well as such film periodicals as *American Cinematographer*, *Movie Makers Magazine* (an ACL publication), and *Photoplay*, in turn sponsored contests and competitive screenings, indicating "a nationalization of aesthetic norms … and the concentration of amateur film technology and discourse within major institutions."[63] Most notably, beginning in December 1930, *Movie Makers Magazine* began selecting its ten best amateur films submitted for the year. Motion pictures of travel, including various Canadian locations, frequently populated its lists.[64]

Budge Crawley, who had been an accountant in his father's Ottawa firm, won awards for his amateur holiday films, which favoured social experiences over landscapes. *Movie Makers Magazine* praised his silent, one-reel *Glimpses of a Canoe Trip* (1937), which documented a summertime excursion on the nearby Gatineau River: "Fundamentally, it's the inherent human interest of his treatment, which concentrates throughout on the chaps making the trip rather than on the vast (and to us slightly monotonous scenery) ... When the final sunset fades off the screen, believe me, you know mighty well the deep feeling of enjoyment which the four chaps had in their trip."[65] The magazine awarded the film, which employed attention-grabbing colour techniques, honourable mention vis-à-vis its ten best for that year. As Crawley and his three male companions paddle, portage, and camp, *Glimpses* points to a new type of tourism film – the vacation record or cine travel, communicating human interest rather than scenery. He accomplishes this through presenting "the natural sequence of events" and close-ups of the mundane: "bacon and eggs sizzling, flames licking around the frying pan, golden toast crisping beside glowing wood coals."[66] Crawley selected and arranged the scenes in a thoughtful and deliberate way, belying the naturalistic appearance. By finding beauty in the everyday and through his creative shaping of the material, Crawley had assimilated the principles of documentary filmmaking (figure 5.1).

Two years later, *Movie Makers Magazine* awarded Budge and Judith the coveted Hiram Percy Maxim Memorial Award (i.e., top achievement in amateur filmmaking) for their *L'Île d'Orléans* (1939). The Crawleys filmed this picture on their honeymoon after falling "under the spell of this secluded backwater of the Old World [*sic*]" near Quebec City.[67] This seemingly spontaneous decision belies their preparatory planning and research. Shot in 16-mm Kodachrome, *L'Île d'Orléans* begins with shots of the suspension bridge (Pont de l'Île) spanning the St Lawrence River – a figurative gateway taking both filmmakers and spectators across space and time to an ostensibly different epoch. The camera then captures what the Crawleys found fascinating about the area, namely its distinctive Norman architecture and peaceful parishes. To maintain the illusion of a pre-industrial countryside, Budge confessed that "we were cautious not to include any evidences of modern speed and ugliness. In several cases, our camera had to be set up with extreme care, to eliminate

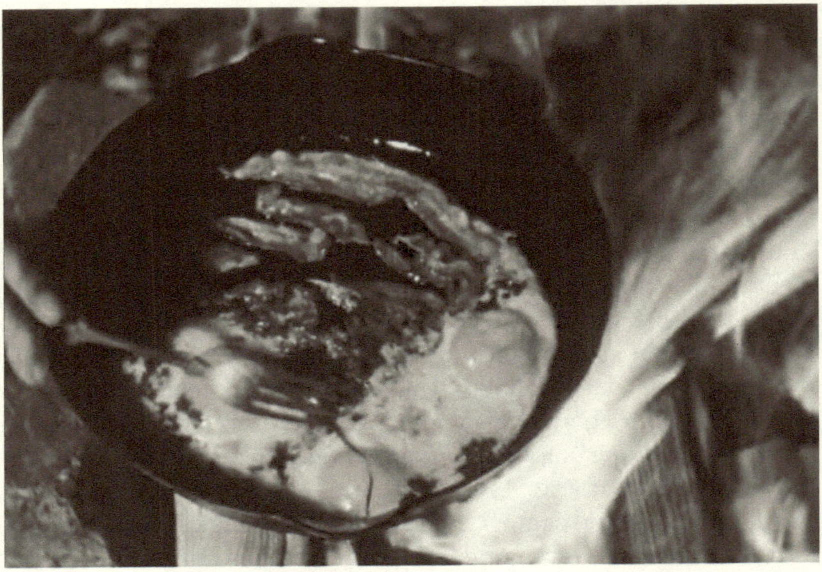

5.1 Radford Crawley, *Glimpses of a Canoe Trip*, 1937

telephone poles which are a recent addition to the picturesque roadways of the island."[68]

The Crawleys wanted to convey as well "the simple dignity of the French Canadian habitant," a sequence that *Canadian Landscape* would echo two years later. On their honeymoon, Budge and Judith lodged with a local family, the Aubins. Over three days, these "subjects were filmed at their usual tasks," such as traditional home cheese-making (*fromage raffiné*) and ploughing with oxen. As "a general rule," Budge notes, the locals "were apparently quite *unconscious* of the camera."[69] This observational style accords with the era's ethnographic filming, "record[ing] the meeting between a filmmaker and that society" as if "the camera were not there."[70] In *L'Île d'Orléans*, the filmmakers' seeming invisibility and passive role belied their authorial presence and subjectivity. Ultimately, they framed the shots, edited and ordered the material, and established what they deemed significant for the viewer. In making these decisions, they were perhaps influenced by their friend Marius Barbeau, the pioneering Québécois anthropologist, ethnologist, and folklorist, who had suggested they honeymoon in this location. Barbeau had helped popularize ethnographic film between the wars and promoted tourism for his province.[71]

According to *Movie Makers Magazine*, *L'Île d'Orléans* was "personal filming at its best," demonstrating a polished combination of spontaneous shooting and planned sequences, contemplative title cards, and honest pictures of "everyday life," albeit to the modern observer ones laden with clichéd romanticism and ethnographic hubris.[72] Through public non-theatrical screenings of the film, accompanied by music via a double turntable system, the seemingly self-reflexive experience of the Crawley honeymoon allowed viewers not only to participate in their cine travel but also to imagine a similar excursion. In other words, these amateur filmmakers brought a level of enthusiasm and subjective voice to their vacation pictures, which encouraged a tourism sensibility. As the editors explain in their rationale for awarding the Crawleys the Maxim Award, beyond recognizing "technical brilliance" of cinematography, it is "for that almost indefinable, but easily recognizable, thing which manages, if it is present, to identify and unite the emotions of the audience with those of the makers and participants in the picture."[73]

The CNR had already recognized the advertising possibilities within the personal connections between amateur motion pictures and audiences. In 1937, Hamilton Jones of Buffalo, New York, won the first Maxim Award for *Western Holiday* (1937), a Kodachrome four-reeler sponsored by the railway, which promoted travel to the Canadian Rockies, as well as to Vancouver and Victoria. Since the CNR did not compensate Jones, who paid all expenses, *Western Holiday* was eligible for the prize, which generated free publicity for the railway company. Jones employed the film as part of his work as an itinerant lecturer "on the vacation advantages of the Dominion of Canada." Yet in the spirit of a documentary-style travelogue, he wanted to do more than "just scenery" and intermingle "the glorious natural settings" with "as much humour and human interest as I could find."[74] Regardless, the heart of *Western Holiday* was its railway sequences, shot *from* and *of* the train, which seem to be a (probably unconscious) homage to the English *Night Mail* (dir. by Harry Watt and Basil Wright, 1936). These included scenes of arriving passengers, "the giant engine breathing," and "atmosphere shots" of the Continental Limited passing over bridges, "rushed into snowsheds and out of tunnels."[75]

Jones had previously made other train-related Canadian subjects. *Canadian Capers* (1932), "a beautiful scenic study" of the country that "contains one of the best railroad film studies ever made," landed on *Movie Makers Magazine*'s top ten. It was screened for Ontario government officials, who subsequently adopted it in their tourism publicity. The following year, Jones re-edited and partially re-filmed this work, adding new scenes to extend it to four reels and renaming it *Under the Maple Leaf* (1933).[76] Discussing his approach, Jones professed, "If there is one subject I thoroughly enjoy filming more than anything else it is railroad trains ... I have never made a picture of any proportions that did not include a railroad sequence in some form." Using the industry's rhetoric, he also urged his fellow amateurs to follow his practice: "You will enjoy the modern luxury of travel that only the railroads of the United States and Canada can provide, and you can film in comfort a picture that, properly edited, will make your reputation as a movie maker. You will be surprised at the number of requests you will receive to screen 'those films with the railroad shots.'"[77]

Hence only a fine line separated the worlds of amateur film and tourism promotion in Canada. In preparation for cine travel, amateurs consulted promotional literature, typically issued by Dominion, provincial, and local tourism boards. For instance, to help him devise a "plan of action" for *Hail, British Columbia!* (1941), which won the 1941 Maxim Award, Leo J. Heffernan of New York City consulted guidebooks and visited the British Columbia Travel Bureau in Victoria. He advised other amateurs to also "save time and energy by using travel literature as a guide to movie subjects" and to seek the guidance of an official travel consultant or service. For his film, Heffernan structured a loose narrative framework connecting the various scenes based on his research and the travel bureau's suggestions.[78] It would all be seen through the perspective of a female tourist, who asks a Mountie about what BC sights to see. The scarlet-clad Mountie, a symbol of nationalism and settler colonialism, functions as a tour guide. For every point of interest that this "tall chap in a bright red coat" suggests, the scene dissolves to footage of that locality and its recreational activities, which Heffernan and his wife visited during their three-week cine vacation, as laid out by the BC tourism board.

After departing Victoria, Heffernan hoped to encounter a Mountie and a "young lady traveller" who would agree to be filmed. This would not be a problem, he later mused, as he found it "easy to induce strangers to join one's movie work."[79] The amateur filmmaker found willing participants in Banff, Alberta. He persuaded a female staff member of the Banff Springs Hotel and Constable William Neff, neither with film experience, to act as tourist and Mountie, respectively.[80]

His fortunate encounter with an RCMP officer in this legendary destination was not an anomaly. In 1937, D. Leo Dolan wrote to RCMP Commissioner Major-General Sir James Howden MacBrien, DSO, regarding use of members of his force as tourist attractions. He asked if officers in scarlet tunics could serve at border entry points and other tourist sites. MacBrien replied that they did not wear the red serge in summer because it was too warm, but he would instruct all divisions to have some officers so apparelled "during the tourist season, so that our friends from the South may get more glimpses of them in what has now become their historic uniform" (figure 5.2).[81]

As Heffernan's cine travel indicates, amateur films could serve as a win-win for both filmmakers and tourism boosters. Perhaps in the hopes of finding the next *L'Île d'Orléans*, *Western Holiday*, or *Hail, British Columbia!*, the NFB cast a wide net in the world of amateur film so that its distinctive aesthetic might inexpensively revitalize sponsored tourism films. In March 1942, it launched a "Come to Canada" contest, inviting American non-professional filmmakers to "turn their cameras on Canada's north woods, its fishing streams, its beautiful old world cities, its lands in Quebec, where peaceful farmers follow the traditions of their French ancestors." The goal was "to discover the best films by United States tourists who visit" any of the four cooperating provinces of British Columbia, Quebec, New Brunswick, or Prince Edward Island during the coming vacation season. Entries were to be in 16-mm and silent and could be either black and white or colour. The NFB reserved the right to distribute copies of all prize-winning films "in any manner that it sees fit." In addition to an NFB grand prize of $500 cash for the best film, each of the four provinces would grant an all-expense tour for the filmmaker and his/her companion in 1943 for the best film made within its borders (figure 5.3).[82]

The NFB hoped that the competition would bring in US currency, because the nation "needs all the American dollars possible to help carry on its magnificent war effort."[83] Moreover, it pitched the movie contest in terms of world events, particularly the developing wartime relationship with the United States, as evinced by the public camaraderie between Franklin Roosevelt and W.L. Mackenzie King. This was a politically expedient friendship, in which Canada saw itself as a linchpin between Britain and the United States. For its part, the Roosevelt administration reasoned that a coordinated approach to defence and economic planning would shore up hemispheric security,

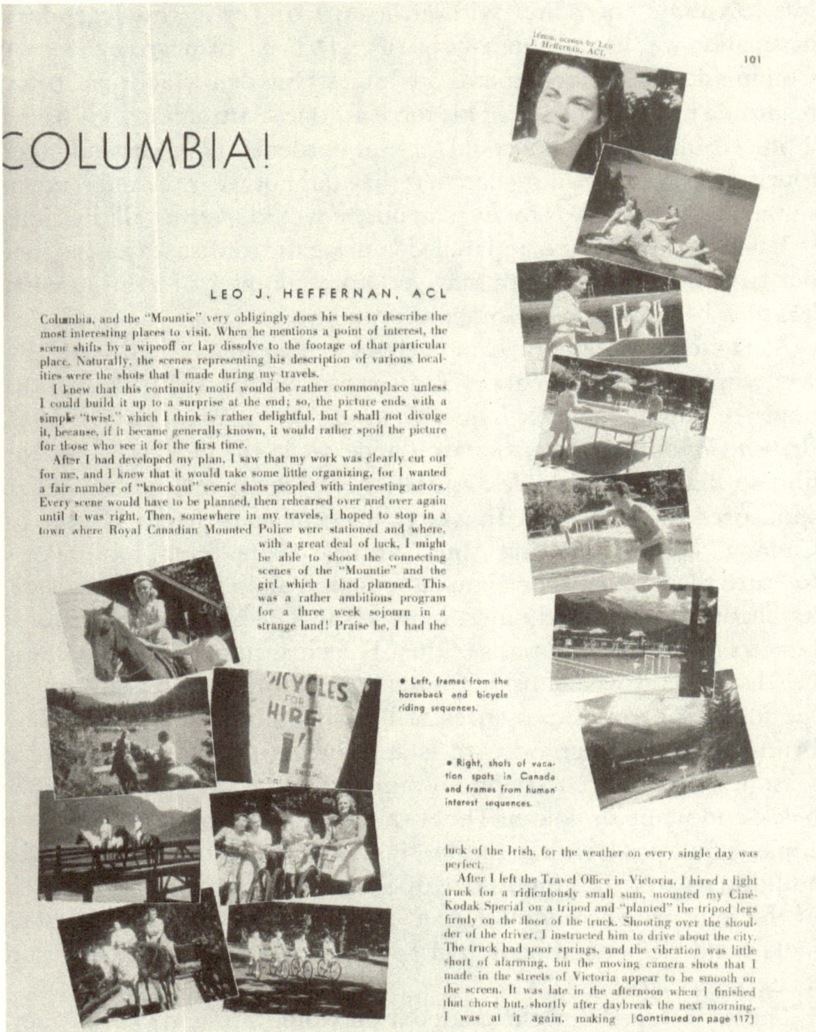

101

COLUMBIA!

16mm. scenes by Leo J. Heffernan, ACL

LEO J. HEFFERNAN, ACL

Columbia, and the "Mountie" very obligingly does his best to describe the most interesting places to visit. When he mentions a point of interest, the scene shifts by a wipeoff or lap dissolve to the footage of that particular place. Naturally, the scenes representing his description of various localities were the shots that I made during my travels.

I knew that this continuity motif would be rather commonplace unless I could build it up to a surprise at the end; so, the picture ends with a simple "twist," which I think is rather delightful, but I shall not divulge it, because, if it became generally known, it would rather spoil the picture for those who see it for the first time.

After I had developed my plan, I saw that my work was clearly cut out for me, and I knew that it would take some little organizing, for I wanted a fair number of "knockout" scenic shots peopled with interesting actors. Every scene would have to be planned, then rehearsed over and over again until it was right. Then, somewhere in my travels, I hoped to stop in a town where Royal Canadian Mounted Police were stationed and where, with a great deal of luck, I might be able to shoot the connecting scenes of the "Mountie" and the girl which I had planned. This was a rather ambitious program for a three week sojourn in a strange land! Praise be, I had the luck of the Irish, for the weather on every single day was perfect.

After I left the Travel Office in Victoria, I hired a light truck for a ridiculously small sum, mounted my Ciné-Kodak Special on a tripod and "planted" the tripod legs firmly on the floor of the truck. Shooting over the shoulder of the driver, I instructed him to drive about the city. The truck had poor springs, and the vibration was little short of alarming, but the moving camera shots that I made in the streets of Victoria appear to be smooth on the screen. It was late in the afternoon when I finished that chore but, shortly after daybreak the next morning, I was at it again, making [Continued on page 117]

• Left, frames from the horseback and bicycle riding sequences.

• Right, shots of vacation spots in Canada and frames from human interest sequences.

5.2 Leo J. Heffernan, *Hail, British Columbia!*, *Movie Makers Magazine*, March 1942

given the two countries' lengthy undefended border. Such bilateral measures as the Ogdensburg Agreement (1940), establishing the Permanent Joint Board on Defence, and the Hyde Park Declaration (1941), for cooperation on defence production, laid the groundwork for a closer bond. Additionally, in early 1942, construction began on

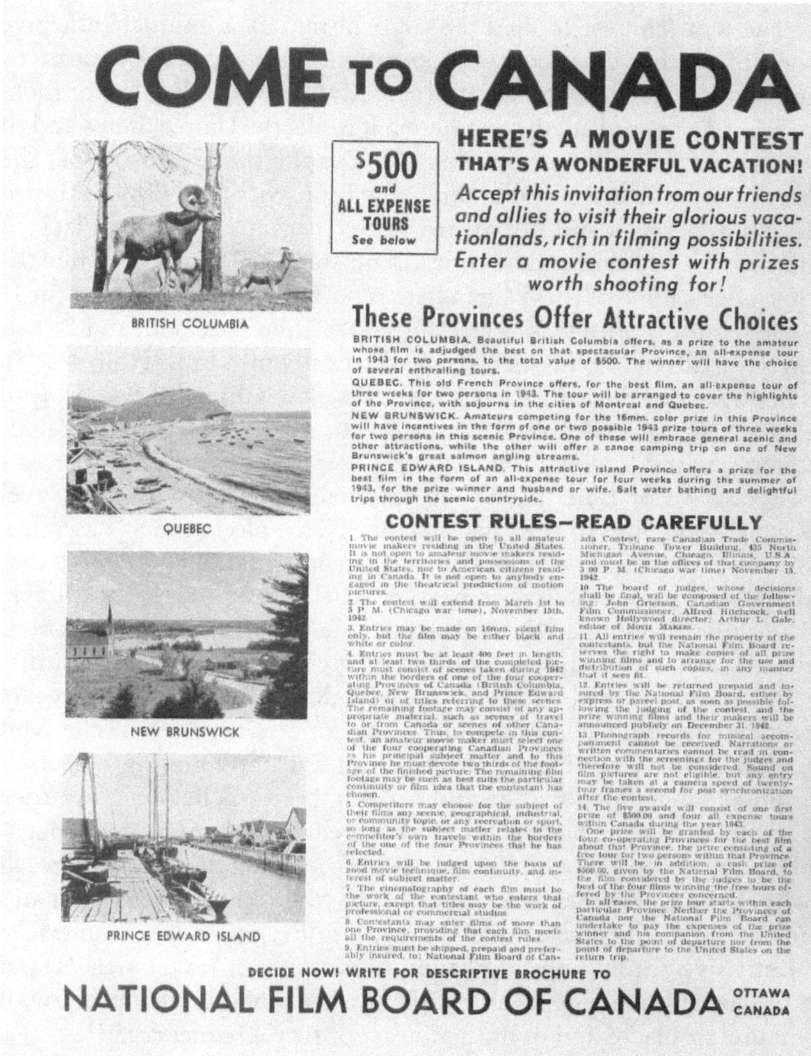

5.3 Come to Canada Contest, *Movie Makers Magazine*, March 1942

the Alaska Highway (initially called the Alcan) from Dawson Creek, British Columbia, to Fairbanks, Alaska. More than just a road, the project "was a reaffirmation of the United States' commitment to the defense of North America, and a pledge that the far Northwest would be defended against invasion."[84]

The NFB contest framed the tourism film as a uniquely effective form of wartime cross-border cooperation. "One way for Americans to understand Canada," asserted *Movie Makers Magazine*, "is for them to see it on the screen, to see wherein it is like the United States and to see where in it differs from them."[85] Despite the "hands across the border" appeal, British Columbia, New Brunswick, and Prince Edward Island apparently did not award prizes, perhaps because of lack of film entries or other extenuating circumstances. The panel of illustrious judges, none of them Canadian, reportedly consisted of Arthur L. Gale (editor of *Movie Makers Magazine*), John Grierson, and British director Alfred Hitchcock (who had recently moved to Hollywood). They awarded the top, $500 prize to Frank E. Gunnell's *Baie St. Paul* (1943); he also received a three-week, all-expenses-paid tour of Quebec with his wife, Alberta.

Evocative of *L'Île d'Orléans*, Gunnell's picture was a two-reel Kodachrome film of the Quebec countryside along the St Lawrence River that looks at "the daily life of the habitant, who believes that the simple way of living is best."[86] The editors of *Movie Makers Magazine* also named the travelogue one of the year's ten best non-theatrical films because of its "human interest," as in scenes featuring "an intent, sharp[-]featured little woodcarver, a housewife coolly competent about her embroidery and an aloof mademoiselle who presides with dazzling beauty over an ancient spinning wheel."[87] Gunnell later stated that he and Alberta, both teachers in New York City, selected Baie Saint-Paul after searching "through travel magazines, folders and geographic articles for a location that we could reach within the wartime restrictions then in force." Echoing Heffernan's advice, Gunnell cited advanced preparation using tourism materials: "Extensive reading and the study of pictures in travel articles and advertising folders make an excellent way of obtaining a preview of unfamiliar places and of noting ideas for travel sequences."[88]

GOOD NEIGHBOURS MAKE GOOD TOURISTS

Beyond encouraging cine enthusiasts to film in Canada, the NFB also made overtures to Hollywood to produce 35-mm tourism films. In his 1940 memo to the Economic Advisory Committee, Grierson recognized that first-class theatrical showings could create a general disposition favouring Canada. Commercial showings attracted large audiences and provided an "impressive atmosphere" to showcase the nation's tourism destinations. To achieve this goal in a cost-effective manner, Grierson suggested that the NFB work with the American film industry. He recommended considering only major studios capable of "first-class production quality" to fit in with "the big time atmosphere." This approach, he declared, could succeed only through "personal acquaintance with those in the major film companies in a position to influence production."[89]

Given wartime difficulties filming overseas, and in keeping with evolving cross-border relations, the US film industry was amenable to producing tourism films of destinations in Canada and throughout the western hemisphere. James A. FitzPatrick was an early proponent of using travelogues as an instrument of intercultural diplomacy. As early as the summer of 1939, he announced a new policy: he would exclude "European themes" and produce TravelTalks covering Latin America, various US states and cities, and Canada, "in line with the United States' current and growing interest in the sister republics [*sic*] of the hemisphere." These items would not only be "worthy propaganda, but also enlightening, because I think people know less about the neighboring countries than they do about Europe.[90] To that end, in 1942 MGM released FitzPatrick's *Land of the Quintuplets* in which "the former globe-trotting, now western hemisphere–trotting" host filmed the Dionne sisters, Dr Dafoe, and tourists visiting their northern Ontario surroundings.[91] This was soon followed by two "hands across the border" subjects: *Glacier Park and Waterton Lakes* (1942), featuring the national parks straddling the Montana-Alberta border, and *Mighty Niagara* (1943), filmed from both nations' sides.

In the spirit of trans-border amity, other major US studios produced Canadian-themed travelogues, often invited or induced by the Dominion or provinces. "Understanding the needs of American producers," wrote veteran American cinematographer Charles W. Herbert, "the National Film Board of Canada has opened the way for closer cooperation," which promised "the greatest production activity of shorts to date in Canada." This flurry of documentaries, newsreels, and travelogues, Herbert astutely observed, "ties in closely with the United War Effort Plan of Canada to not only acquaint the Empire with what Canada is doing for its part, but also to make a large bid for the American Tourist Trade."[92] For example, Grierson arranged with RKO-Pathé to produce a film short on the Dionne Quintuplets, called *Growing Up* (1941).[93]

The film commissioner also prevailed on Universal to include films about Canada among its short subjects. In 1941, Universal's Going Places with Lowell Thomas covered the recreational and scenic delights found in Banff and the Canadian Rockies (*Mountain Summer*), as well as Victoria and Vancouver Island (*Garden Spot of the North*). Charles Herbert shot the latter film and praised Grierson for expediting arrangements. He noted that the BC Travel Bureau and the Victoria Tourist Information Office ensured "the best possible subject-matter was put in front of the camera," so he could focus on technical details. "Such an arrangement," he added, "is naturally ideal for all concerned. It gives assurance to the government that a first class reel will be made which meets with its approval. And it also makes it possible for the producer to turn out a worthy job efficiently at minimum expense and trouble."[94]

Likewise, Universal's Variety Views, a series of one-reel pictures narrated by radio announcer Graham McNamee, released *Northern Neighbors* (1941). "With interest in our Canadian neighbors stronger than ever," the film "seeks to acquaint audiences of the States with aspects of Canadian life, including pilots training for the Royal Air Force, Niagara Falls, and the Dionne Quintuplets." Similarly, *Peaceful Quebec – At War* "touches only lightly on the war effort" and instead appeals "to US folks to visit the Province, wherein there are no fettering tourist regulations."[95] Twentieth Century–Fox's *Call of Canada* (1941), part of the studio's Magic Carpet of Movietone series, was another timely short subject combining the travelogue and war-actuality genres in its display of Canada's war activities and tourist sites.[96] Moreover, Columbia Pictures produced *Pleasurebound in Canada* (1940) and *Beautiful Ontario* (1941), both in colour, which offered "tie-ups with travel bureaus."[97] These were part of the Columbia Tours series of one-reel travel films, which began in 1936.

Hollywood's Canadian-themed travelogues underscored the themes of wartime bilateral democracy and friendship and were adjacent to the Roosevelt administration's Good Neighbor Policy designed to increase goodwill towards the United States in Latin America.[98] Eschewing earlier heavy-handed, interventionist diplomacy, Washington now advocated mutual respect and supported cultural exchanges and economic endeavours through the Office of the Coordinator of Inter-American Affairs (OCIAA), headed by Nelson Rockefeller (1940–45). As Europe and Asia teetered on the brink of full-scale war and wielded modern weapons that threatened to penetrate Fortress America, Roosevelt encouraged Pan-American networks and associations to shore up hemispheric defences, secure Latin American resources, and combat pro-Axis propaganda.[99]

Rooted in this concept of cooperation, the US administration encouraged inter-American tourism as central to projecting hemispheric neighbourliness and solidarity. Tourism as cultural diplomacy was evident during the first Inter-American Travel Congress (IATC) in San Francisco in 1939, which included the governments and private organizations of twenty Latin American republics, the United States, and Canada. Opening on Pan American Day on 14 April 1939, under the joint auspices of San Francisco's Golden Gate Exposition and the Travel Division of the Pan American Union, the meeting encouraged "international good will through the medium of tourist traffic."[100] Accepting an invitation to the meeting, US Secretary of State Cordell Hull replied: "Travel in this hemisphere has definite recreational, cultural, and economic values and contributes to the stimulation of the spirit of genuine understanding and goodwill among the peoples of the Americas."[101]

The IATC and Pan American Union were components of the Inter-American system, founded in 1889 and linking all the hemisphere's sovereign states except Canada (which, though participating in various capacities, opted out of the Pan American Union). The system consisted of piecemeal policies – resolutions and declarations – as well as permanent and ad-hoc agencies of mutual interest.[102] Although Canada had no pavilion at the Exposition, it accepted the IATC's invitation and sent D. Leo Dolan as its envoy. Delegates discussed simplifying passport requirements, improving transportation, establishing adequate standards for lodging, and increasing the promotion of tourist travel within the hemisphere. Tourism's proper development, according to José Tercero, chief of the Pan American Union's Travel Division, required "cooperation instead of rivalry, coordination instead of scattered efforts, and combined resources instead of expensive duplication."[103] After a rousing speech urging all of the Americas, "from the bottom of South America to the ancient stamping ground of the Hudson Bay Company, to stand solidly together against unwarranted aggression," Dolan was unanimously elected IATC chair.[104]

The IATC meeting also hastened the creation of a US agency to encourage domestic tourism and develop travel throughout the Americas. An Act of Congress established the US Travel Bureau (USTB) on 19 July 1940 within the Department of the Interior to develop, encourage, and promote tourism, as well as conduct research concerning tourism's value. With headquarters in Washington, DC, the USTB also maintained offices in New York and San Francisco. These were information-clearing houses staffed by (New Deal) Works Progress Administration personnel who collected and distributed literature on historical, recreational, and scenic attractions. They worked to publicize and promote travel through radio programs, advertising, and participation in conferences and exhibitions.[105] The USTB represented unprecedented federal involvement in travel promotion and synergy with the commercial travel industry, as well as exemplifying New Deal–era legislation "to provide Americans with a sense of communal identity and common heritage."[106]

Recognizing that the "exigencies of international conflict may be expected to deter travel," President Roosevelt had already in January 1940 designated the ensuing twelve months as Travel America Year. During much of the near-decade of Depression, his administration promoted tourism as a vital economic and social force to rebuild national health and morale. The USTB slogan, "Travel Strengthens America. It Builds the Nation's Health, Wealth, and Unity," testified to this objective.[107] Unlike the earlier "See America First" campaign, which centred on domestic tourism as nationalistic, Roosevelt framed travel as intercultural diplomacy. He invited US citizens, together with "friends from other lands," to join in "a great travel movement so that our peoples may be drawn even more closely together in sympathy and understanding."[108]

Canada and the Latin American republics rightly interpreted "Travel America" to mean "the American continent rather than the United States itself."[109] In this spirit of hemispheric unity, the USTB worked closely with both the Pan American Union and the Dominion to cultivate cross-cultural relationships based on democracy, goodwill, and understanding. As American involvement in the war approached, hemispheric solidarity through recreational travel became even more pressing. For example, at the first annual convention of the International Association of Tourist Officials in Detroit in the autumn of 1940, W. Bruce Macnamee, chief of the USTB, met with D. Leo Dolan and various representatives from Latin America and agreed that inter-American travel was central to hemispheric defence.[110]

After US entry into the war in December 1941, appropriations for the USTB ceased, and the New York and San Francisco offices closed. The needs of wartime industry and the military meant the limiting of pleasure travel because the government rationed fuel and rubber. Yet before the USTB was discontinued in 1943, it continued to endorse "the utilization of available recreational travel facilities to keep war workers and the public fit for their patriotic duties."[111] Tourism boosters argued that recreational travel was aligned with the war effort due to its economic and morale-boosting benefits. With Americans "working longer hours, and harder" because of the conflict, "the need for vacations will be more obvious than ever. The therapeutic value of a change of scene, of relaxation, of a week or two at the seashore, the mountains, the North Woods, is recognized under normal conditions. Under the strain of war-times, vacation travel may cease to be a luxury; it may become a necessity."[112] This situation did not preclude cross-border travel. As one newspaper urged, "Every American dollar spent in Canada helps Canada's war effort, which is now our war effort, too."[113]

Following Pearl Harbor, officials in both countries networked about producing wartime film propaganda, which was informed partly by a commercial strategy that promoted Canadian tourism. Established in 1939, Canada's Bureau of Public Information (BPI) informed citizens about the war effort via radio, newspapers, and motion pictures, notably the NFB's *Canada Carries On* series. Director of Public Information Walter Thompson and his successor, G. Herbert Lash, had both worked in CNR publicity and brought expertise in advertising (particularly selling scenery through visual media) to the BPI.[114] In 1942, the Wartime Information Board (WIB), which combined both domestic and foreign information activities, replaced the BPI under chair Charles Vining. After he resigned in 1943 due to ill-health, Grierson, who remained NFB commissioner, was appointed general manager of the WIB, so as to facilitate the flow of information among wartime agencies and departments.[115]

The formation of the WIB, as Evan H. Potter recognizes, was "a direct acknowledgement of the growing importance that external audiences were beginning to play in the formation of public policy." The board maintained external offices in London, Paris, Canberra, and around Latin America.[116] Grierson also expanded Canada's publicity presence in the United States by establishing two offices. Harry Sedgwick, president and managing director of independent Toronto radio station CFRB, who had a background in theatre and moving pictures, headed the New York office, while J. Hugh Campbell, a CPR publicity representative, ran the one in Washington, DC. Sedgwick and Campbell liaised with the US Office of War Information

(OWI), established on 13 June 1942 as the central agency for morale-building and propaganda both at home and abroad.[117]

Headed by news-radio commentator Elmer Davis, the US OWI was to carry out, through press, radio, and motion pictures, information programs to create an "informed and intelligent" public understanding of the war effort and government aims at home and abroad.[118] Lowell Mellett, a former newspaper editor and executive assistant to President Roosevelt, with no film-industry experience, was appointed director of the OWI's Bureau of Motion Pictures (BMP).[119] In the summer of 1942, Dana Doten was named chief of the OWI's Canadian section, and he travelled to Ottawa to facilitate the reciprocal coordination of publicity. During his four-week stay, he met with both Lash and Vining, studied Canada's propaganda operations (including press, radio, and branches of government), and spent considerable time with Grierson. Doten later observed that the Scotsman "has developed an almost personal philosophy of Canadian nationalism" in which he strongly opposed the "British colonial concept of Canada" and was "apprehensive at the growing influence of the US in Canada." He thus advised the OWI to be cognizant of this.[120]

Following his visit, Doten concluded that the United States did "not face a dissemination problem in Canada which has any resemblance to the problem of disseminating Canadian news in the United States." He observed that most Canadians read, listened to, and watched American periodicals, radio, and motion pictures, respectively. Therefore, to expand American content for them would surely provoke a negative reaction and cries of cultural imperialism. The OWI's vital function in Ottawa was accordingly to help place Canada's story before the US public. Doten noted further that Grierson believed that an American liaison stationed in Ottawa would be helpful to expanding the NFB's US activity. Grierson had already established "direct operating relations with Mr. Lowell Mellett and also with the various officials in Hollywood."[121]

With this in mind, Wesley H. Greene, supervisor of NFB distribution, wrote to C.R. Reagan, in charge of the BMP's non-theatrical division, proposing an extension of 16-mm prints into the United States as "an opportunity of exploring possible fields of Canadian–American cooperation."[122] The following year, Canada's acting trade commissioner in Chicago perceived that his nation's "war effort, industrial and *scenic* life" were shown regularly in American theatres and via non-theatrical circuits to "large plants and factories, clubs and organizations."[123] That is, in addition to war-related NFB releases, the OWI received 16-mm prints of *Four New Apple Dishes* (1940), *Canadian Landscape* (1941), *Iceland on the Prairies* (1941), and *Ottawa on the River* (1941), all produced by Crawley Films, as well as *Hot Ice* (dir. by Irving Jacoby, 1940), *Great Lakes* (1941), and *Peace River* (1942). Though not directly related to the conflict, these tourism films offered "valuable background material for the study of democracy in war and have a place in the program promoted in the United States whose objective is a better understanding between peoples of the western hemisphere."[124]

Additionally, Irving Jacoby, an American independent writer-producer who had worked for Britain's GPO film unit before joining the NFB in early 1940, produced *High over the Borders* (1942) in cooperation with the New York Zoological Society and Nelson Rockefeller's OCIAA. Directed by pioneering British documentarian Raymond Spottiswoode, the two-reeler is ostensibly about the migratory north–south journey of birds in the Americas but is intended, according to, Minister of National War Services J.T. Thorson, as "a parable of unity in the Americas, with emphasis upon the importance of free movement across international borders ... It is a comment on the deep natural forces making for mutual understanding between peoples, and contributes to an appreciation of the common interest of the countries of the western hemisphere in wartime defence."[125]

Meanwhile, J. Margaret Carter, who since early 1943 had handled the non-theatrical distribution of the NFB's films to US educational outlets via its Chicago office, cooperated with the OWI to make them available for rental through US educational-film libraries. For example, in its 1942–43 catalogue, Audio-Film Libraries of Bloomfield, New Jersey, offered films "designed to give Americans more intimate acquaintanceship with our ally and neighbor, Canada. Some of the subjects are scenic and some deal with the war efforts of Canada with which we are very much concerned." In addition to NFB titles, American non-theatrical distributors included older films produced by the CGMPB or the Parks Branch, including *Canoe Trails through Mooseland* (1927), *Grey Owl's Little Brother* (1932), *Victoria, City of Sunshine* (1928), and *The Banff-Jasper Highway* (1939).[126] Carter recognized that tourism films could advance intercultural diplomacy. At a meeting of the Visual Education Institute at the University of Wisconsin in July 1944, she delivered an NFB paper entitled "Building Understandings of our Neighbors to the North." She combined her lecture with a screening of *The Maritimes* (year unknown), a travelogue sponsored by the CPR "covering places of historic interest and scenic beauty in New Brunswick and Nova Scotia."[127]

Ultimately, the ties forged during wartime set the stage for further, postwar Canadian-US cooperation in tourism and film. During the war, the CTB's personnel and budget had shrunk precipitously, while the NFB's workforce and production output expanded rapidly. With minimal resources, D. Leo Dolan positioned Canada as a key component in hemispheric travel. Committed to encouraging tourist traffic from the United States, he reached out to Grierson, hoping he would promote tourism – either directly or indirectly – through documentary productions. In addition to commissioning private, non-theatrical films, the NFB encouraged amateur filmmakers' cine travel as a creative and cost-effective way to promote tourism to Canada.

The country needed thriving tourism to earn US dollars during the war – a constant postwar theme as well. Prior to Pearl Harbor, American tourists supplied their currency, which helped fuel Canada's industry and military. After US entry into the war, rationing and shortages on both sides slowed cross-border tourist traffic. Yet in both countries, officials acknowledged that modest tourism could boost morale. Moreover, the concept of hemispheric travel symbolized goodwill and intercultural friendship, in contrast to fascist regimes overseas. Canada's Department of National War Services thus continued to promote tourism moderately, if only to keep "the name of Canada" before American eyes, anticipating a peacetime resurgence of recreational travel. To that end, in 1942 War Services Minister Thorson requested $50,000 for the NFB to produce films for the CTB intended for US distribution when peace came.[128]

Even during the depths of the war, officials recognized the tourism film as a means to advertise Canada to its neighbours but also to ease the transition back to a peacetime economy and society. As Allied victory in Europe approached, J. Margaret Carter conjectured that the NFB's "films of tomorrow" would be built around "themes of fundamental significance ... The life of people in other lands, for example, is not adequately seen through travel films of public buildings." She hoped that Canadian-themed travelogues would "cut to the core of realism in clean sharp strokes," as they appealed to returning American GIs and their families planning for a Victory Vacation.[129] Tourism and film would indeed become central to reconstruction, yet not in the ways that Carter had imagined.

6

From Victory Vacations to the Canadian Cooperation Project

The Golden Age of the Postwar Tourism Film

"You've Earned a Vacation – Now Take It!"
Slogan of the [US] National Association of Travel Officials, 1946–47

In 1943, the National Association of Travel Officials met in Chicago to discuss how best to revive the tourism industry after the war. Members decided to make the first twelve months of peace a "Victory Vacation Year."[1] Representatives of travel-related businesses and government officials predicted that after years of sacrifice and scarcity, US citizens would embrace self-indulgence and act on their innate wanderlust. "Thousands of Americans have worked thru the past four years with little vacation time spent away from home [*sic*]," suggested one magazine in September 1945, "and it is felt that many plan on hitting the road now that gas is back in the tank and there is a promise of 500,000 new automobiles by the end of the year."[2] With the unconditional surrender of the Axis powers in 1945, this "Victory Vacation Year" would take place between June 1946 and June 1947 under the slogan: "You've Earned a Vacation – Now Take It!"

This euphoric edict positioned leisured mobility not as a luxury, but as an essential component of national identity and global harmony by fostering freedom, prosperity, and material comfort. As Canadian Minister of Trade and Commerce James A. MacKinnon told the Hotel and Restaurant Suppliers Association in Montreal, "I believe that the tourist trade is one of the greatest agencies in promoting world peace ... We will never properly understand each other by staying at home."[3] In Canada as well, tourism promised to demonstrate the primacy of capitalism and democracy over repressive, Soviet-style state apparatuses. As D. Leo Dolan, director of the Canadian Travel Bureau (CTB), informed the American Automobile Association, "I think the most potent weapon to make Communism a forgotten thing among the people of this nation, and of my own, would be an encouragement of travel among one another ... We will probably have border crossings approaching a figure of 26 million. That is, more people who travel across our frontier, or the boundary which unites us, than cross any international frontier in the world."[4]

Here, Dolan underscores the symbolic power of the shared "longest undefended border" as evidence of bilateral friendship, unfettered movement, and the superiority of a prosperous tourist economy over authoritarian communist regimes. Non-fiction films also celebrated that demarcation line. For example, Larry O'Reilly's short subject *Border without Bayonets* (1947), part of RKO's This Is America series (1942–51), showed that it "should serve as a model for world understanding." Two years later, ASN devoted the similar *Borderline Cases* (dir. by Gordon Sparling) to that "3000 miles of undefended frontier."[5] The hyperbolic praise of trans-border tourism as a bulwark against communism speaks to the era's broader sociopolitical concerns and economic challenges. Fears surrounding the expansion of communism overseas intensified in step with anxieties regarding communist infiltration at home. At the same time, cultural elites in Canada bemoaned the Americanization that threatened to subsume their nation's cultural identity. Nevertheless, tourist greenbacks seemed to offer an economic panacea to the country's ongoing shortage of US currency just as government officials applauded tourism as a progressive cultural force both within Canada and beyond.

Tourism and film were front and centre amid these contradictory impulses of trepidation and optimism, as well as vis-à-vis the tension between nationalism and internationalism, which marked the decade following war's end. Even before then, Dominion and provincial officials were preparing for all-out promotion directed at Americans, particularly white and middle-class families. For these efforts to thrive, Minister MacKinnon called for a joint, cooperative effort between the provinces and the renamed Canadian Government Travel Bureau (CGTB).[6] Hence, beginning in 1946, the Dominion-Provincial Tourist Conference would provide an annual occasion to share ideas and collaborate on ways to promote tourism. These postwar meetings increased Dominion investment in the production of tourism films and expanded 16-mm distribution networks into the United States at a time when the NFB faced intense scrutiny. Several provinces also turned aggressively to making non-theatrical films, adopting a regional strategy to attract American tourist dollars. To prepare for the anticipated flood of visitors, an educational campaign informed Canadians about the value of tourism to the economy and encouraged courtesy towards tourists.

Mass tourism exploded after 1945 as Americans with increased leisure time and discretionary income travelled abroad, spending their coveted US cash and spreading tenets of liberal individualism. In the summer of 1947, the Dominion enjoyed one of its biggest tourist seasons as "wartime jeeps and shiny silver-trimmed roadsters from Providence and Pasadena" crossed the border to enjoy Canada's vacationlands.[7] Despite this windfall, US currency remained scarce, prompting austerity measures on a variety of imported consumer goods. Concerned that these restrictions could harm the film industry, Eric Johnston, president of the Motion Picture Association of America (MPAA), made an explicit commitment to encourage tourism to Canada to stimulate the flow of US dollars into the economy – an arrangement known as the Canadian Cooperation Project.[8]

THE ROLE OF TOURISM AND FILM DURING POSTWAR RECONSTRUCTION

According to L.B. Kuffert, planning was a crucial element in the nation's "culture of reconstruction" as it prepared for "the further modernization of Canadian society."[9] Government-industry tactics sought to expand tourism, which required more investment in film production. Recognizing that a successful first peacetime tourist season for American visitors was essential to establishing a robust postwar tourist trade and economy, government representatives organized carefully. One could not simply count on pent-up tourist demand in the face of possible rising inflation, unemployment, housing shortages, and a return to a Depression-style economy. For example, P.J. Jennings, superintendent of Banff National Park, feared that immediately "after the war people will be so busy getting re-established and re-settled in their new locations that they will not have time to travel and many will not wish to expend the money for luxury and travel until they know a little more about their future."[10] Well before wartime travel restrictions were lifted, tourism-related businesses and government agencies prepared for tourism in the short term (i.e., the anticipated surge during the Victory Vacation summer of 1946) yet set long-term goals (i.e., strategies for future growth and development) by undertaking research, creating preparation boards, and developing advertising campaigns that included producing tourism films.

As early as 1943, Dominion officials prepared reconstruction plans to keep Canada the pre-eminent destination for its good neighbours to the south as many countries competed for US tourist dollars. Major-General L.R. LaFlèche, who took over the Department of National War Services in the autumn of 1942, called a meeting in Quebec City of business interests involved in the tourist trade. Anticipating a brisk tourism bump in Canada following the inevitable victory, he pushed for coordination and planning to forestall any potential problems within the industry's infrastructure.[11] As a result, his department's new National Tourist Advisory Committee, made up of representatives from the provincial governments and private interests, convened in Windsor, Ontario, 25–27 September 1944 to formulate a national tourist policy. It recommended increased funding for the CTB, renamed the Canadian Government Travel Bureau (CGTB), and emphasized the need for good roads, high-quality accommodations, and trained personnel to meet the anticipated demand.[12]

Proponents of developing recreational travel in Canada after the war cited its ability to pull in US currency, needed to balance the nation's trade deficit with the United States. American tourists were "good spenders," Joseph Warner Murphy (PC MP, Lambton West) proclaimed in Parliament. They purchased an array of goods and services, including food, lodging, transportation, and souvenirs, which provided a direct benefit to farmers, retailers, and other businesses, as well as furnishing jobs for returning veterans. Furthermore, Murphy argued that a hardy tourism industry would "pay dividends in international relationships."[13] For policy-makers, it would deepen ties with the United States. Informal interactions between hosts (Canadians) and guests (Americans) would undergird more formal state-to-state relations in the first years of peace and amid looming Cold War tensions.[14]

D. Leo Dolan similarly recognized cross-border tourism as a driver of peace and stability, telling the annual meeting of the [US] National Association of Travel Officials in 1946:

> I believe we have formed this alliance of ideals which inspire our hearts and minds, not because your President or my Prime Minister have affixed their signatures to a treaty, or a pact,

> or an alliance. We have created this great friendship and respect for one another – the greatest example known in the history of the world – because, year after year, millions of American citizens come to Canada to relax and enjoy our country and hundreds of thousands of Canadians go south of the border to meet and mingle with you in this great Republic.[15]

To bolster economic links and neighbourliness through travel, the CGTB named full-time representatives at the Consulates General at New York and Chicago in the summer of 1948 to ensure "as much interest as possible in Canadian tourist travel."[16]

The short-lived Canadian Information Service (CIS), which had replaced the WIB in 1945, also denoted the vaunted place of tourism and film in peacetime.[17] With the cooperation of the CBC, the NFB, and Trade and Commerce, the CIS was to broadcast globally the nation's cultural, economic, political, and social stake in world peace, stability, and understanding. Justifying its existence, Acting Prime Minister J.L. Isley stated: "Those with whom we trade must know our country and its possibilities; those with whom we are associated for the maintenance of world security must know with whom they are co-operating and what may be expected of our co-operation. In short, both trade and diplomacy, to be carried out successfully, need a background of understanding based on factual information, objectively presented."[18]

The CIS's immediate task was to coordinate and circulate Canadian material into the United States, given "the tremendous importance" of attracting tourist dollars. During a meeting at New York's Biltmore Hotel, the CIS outlined "basic Canadian themes," anxious that "too many American[s]" imagine "merely a country of farms, forests and snow." These talking points included the nation's "physical story," comprising its industrial sector, natural resources, and transportation networks; its "political position" in international affairs; its "international outlook"; its "distinctive Canadian culture"; and "the relative efficiency of our form of democratic organization."[19]

The CIS stressed the need to control the national narrative amid the climate of postwar internationalism and to attract American revenue by circulating government-produced or -sponsored tourism films. Envisioned "as a clearing house for private and government groups interested in disseminating Canadian information abroad," the CIS devised a catalogue of material and services, including booklets, films, and radio programs with potential to promote tourism. The collection included such 16-mm tourism films as *Atlantic Salmon* (1947), *Great Northern Tackle-Busters* (1947), and *Speckled Trout across Canada* (1947). Produced in conjunction with the American magazine *Field and Stream*, which also ran special stories about each motion picture, these were the first releases from a novel NFB-CGTB initiative to produce films encouraging tourism.[20]

This inter-bureau film collaboration stemmed from the first annual Dominion-Provincial Tourist Conference, held in Ottawa 21–3 October 1946 and hosting representatives from the nation's larger transportation interests, as well as Dominion and provincial officials. Before peace came, most provinces had already formed reconstruction committees or bureaux to coordinate postwar activities and rehabilitation, with the understanding that vigorous tourism would boost the economy. A case in point is Alberta, which contended that a robust tourist trade was, according to Minister of Trade and Industry (and Premier) E.C. Manning in March 1942, "most important to the general welfare" of the province.[21] Government officials were preparing the groundwork to expand the province's already successful tourism industry after the end of hostilities. In March 1942, an order-in-council established a Tourist Advisory Board under Dan E.C. Campbell, director of Alberta's Publicity and Travel Bureau. At its first meeting, Manning declared that "while it was necessary to curtail somewhat the government's promotion effort" due to wartime conditions, "the government was fully aware of the importance of laying plans for the future."[22]

Dan Campbell maintained that the revival of Alberta's "tourist traffic publicity program" after the war necessitated new 16-mm films in colour and sound. The new Tourist Advisory Board recommended that, since "motion pictures made by the Federal Government are mostly old and in black and white rather than in color, films of hunting, fishing, motoring etc. in color and set to sound should be made as soon as possible for distribution in the United States and other countries."[23] At war's end, staff numbers and funding for the renamed Alberta Travel Bureau increased dramatically, along with Campbell's commitment to tourism films as the ideal form of publicity.[24]

As part of a general retooling of its Department of Economic Affairs, in April 1948 Alberta organized a Film and Photographic Branch to ensure self-sufficiency in both still and motion pictures. A provincial film library was also established. In 1949, Film Commissioner Kenneth Hutchinson began production on seven scripts, including such tourism films as *Autumn in Alberta* (1950), a multi-coloured exploration of autumnal scenery, along with scenes of boating, golfing, and riding. Moreover, *Alberta Vacation* (1950) follows a party of American vacationers after they visit a tourism-information bureau at McLeod, one hour's drive north of the Montana border.[25] Hutchinson claimed that within the first nine months of its release, over 700,000 people in Canada, the United States, and Britain saw the film.[26]

Likewise, British Columbia had been "actively planning for the greatly augmented volume" of US tourists after the war.[27] The province was promoting tourism through film before the conflict. The British Columbia Government Travel Bureau (BCGTB) was formed in 1937 within the new Department of Trade and Industry. Two years later, Clarence Ferris, a long-time civil servant and self-taught filmmaker, initiated a one-person still- and moving-picture branch.[28] Ferris "worked day, night and Sundays" taking care of "shooting, editing, processing, and printing."[29] Following the war, the photographic branch expanded its personnel and added 16-mm colour pictures to its "already important library of films that is proving of inestimable value in publicizing British Columbia to the rest of the world."[30] In the autumn of 1947, Deputy Minister of Trade and Industry E.G. Rowebottom boasted at the second Dominion-Provincial Tourist Conference in Ottawa that the photographic branch was functioning in "a highly effective manner. Six persons are employed ... doing an excellent job in advertising and publicizing British Columbia through the medium of 16 m. m. films. The Bureau has a library of more than 100 films which are constantly in circulation and are giving an immense amount of publicity to British Columbia."[31]

Also anticipating Americans keen for their Victory Vacation, in 1946 Ontario set up the Department of Travel and Publicity, with Arthur Welsh as minister. One of its earliest initiatives, in conjunction with the Canadian Weekly Newspaper Association and the Hotel Association of the Province of Ontario, was an eight-day, 1,500-mile (2,400-kilometre) "Goodwill Tour" of the province for 21 US-based editors and publishers, which became an annual event. A colour motion picture of the excursion depicted "Ontario's natural attractions" and circulated widely among lodges, outdoor organizations, and service clubs. The following year, Deputy Minister Tom C. McCall announced that Travel and Publicity "was meeting the steadily growing demand for motion pictures" and assembling a library of 16-mm films. "Recognition of the important part that motion pictures play in influencing prospective visitors in their selection of a vacation region" resulted in such tourism films as *Algonquin Adventure* (1947), *Land of Niagara* (1947), *Manitoulin Holiday* (1947), and *Northern Autumn* (1947). To "meet the steadily growing demand for motion pictures," the department invested in additional 16-mm productions in colour and sound dealing with the Lakehead, Lake of the Woods, and Nipigon areas.[32] By 1952, it reported that about 200 prints of Ontario tourism films were in circulation in the United States, "where National Film Board distribution services are utilized very satisfactorily."[33]

Nova Scotia was the Atlantic province most actively producing tourism films as part of its postwar reconstruction strategy. Understanding that the medium "undoubtedly lends itself more than any other to an attractive, quick and convincing method of introducing Nova Scotia and its vacation attractions," the province, which had operated a tourism-information bureau since 1923, created the Nova Scotia Film Bureau to produce motion pictures in 1945. Its "primary purpose" was making films "designed to attract tourist visitors to the Province."[34] T.J. (Tom) Courtney, provincial director of publicity 1947–53, championed the film bureau's expansion. Formerly the supervisor for Odeon's Maritime theatres, Courtney was also an avid amateur filmmaker.[35] In addition to circulating its 16-mm productions through NFB and CGTB distribution outlets, Nova Scotia's growing library of tourism films was accessible through two full-time information bureaux, which Courtney established in New York and Boston.

Under Margaret L. Perry, who had worked under John Grierson at the NFB, the Nova Scotia Film Bureau in 1948 produced and released seven films and planned to release four more.[36] Perry's "film program" aimed "to tell the pictorial story of Nova Scotia." For instance, *Battling 'Blue-Fins'* (1947) gave viewers a ringside seat to watch tourists and their local guides fishing for tuna off the shores of Wedgeport. In her annual report, Perry stated that "the film will have great tourist appeal," and distinguished it from earlier sport-fishing films. It is, she clarified, "a film for sportsmen, yet the style is *documentary*."[37] While she acknowledged that her role meant "selling" the province through film, she approached tourism films with Grierson-style documentary principles.

The NFB *"Sells" Canada in the Postwar Period*

At the first annual Dominion-Provincial Tourist Conference in October 1946, CGTB Director D. Leo Dolan announced that he was in talks with the NFB "to plan an over-all program of motion pictures for Canada" with an emphasis on 16-mm colour productions distributed to schools, sporting associations, and so forth. "People go to the theatre to be amused," he argued, "and usually go to a club meeting, lecture, etc. to see a series of travel films." Addressing the delegates, Dolan emphasized their duty to "sell Canada as a travel nation ... to make the people, first in the United States, and later in the rest of the world, 'Canada-Conscious' in their travel view."[38] The NFB also recognized that selling Canada to American tourists through film was a major part of its mission because of the Cold War and the need for US currency (figure 6.1).

Janet Scellen, with the NFB since 1939 and head of its New York office since 1945, stated that her immediate priority was the free US distribution of its 16-mm films.[39] Liaison Officer Walter Bowker made the NFB's commitment to promoting tourism even more explicit: "No one was more aware of the importance to this country of the tourist industry than the National Film Board." In keeping with the Dominion's longstanding practice of "throwing everything at the wall to see what sticks," in terms of its film production agenda, he added "that any film about our country that is distributed abroad is basically a tourist film."[40] Consequently, the NFB produced an eclectic collection of 16-mm films promoting the nation's recreational and scenic advantages. In addition to the sport-fishing films produced with the CGTB for *Field and Stream* in 1947–48, it released *Bronco Busters* (dir. by Laurence Hyde, 1946), which features Alberta's wild horses and highlights from the Calgary Stampede. Moreover, *Montreal by Night* (dir. by Jean Palardy and Arthur Burrows, 1947) showcases the bilingual metropolis's nightlife.

The NFB also kept commissioning non-theatrical films from private Canadian firms, most notably Crawley Films. For example, *Holiday Island* (dir. by Judith Crawley, 1948) presents vacation opportunities on Beausoleil Island in Ontario's Georgian Bay. By the late 1940s, Budge and Judith Crawley had turned their "honeymoon hobby to a business with a turnover of over half a million dollars a year," becoming the country's largest independent producer of sponsored films. In 14 years, they produced about 400 films, numerous trailers,

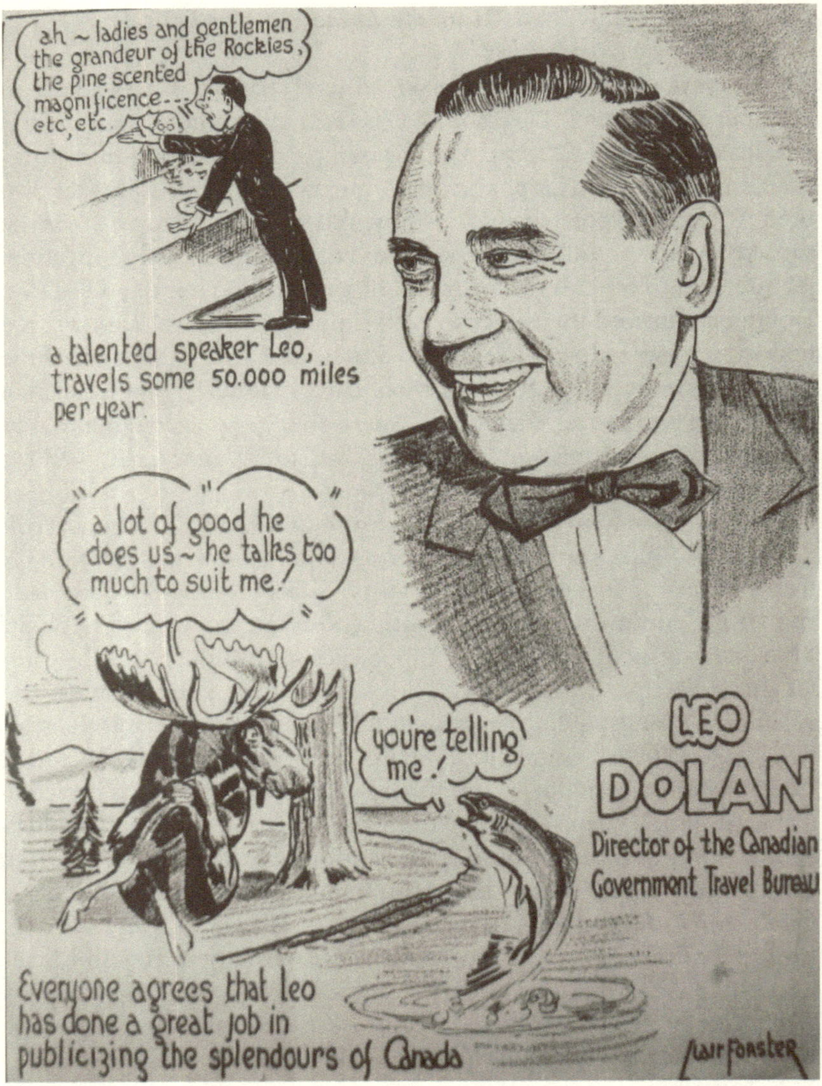

6.1 Cartoon of D. Leo Dolan

editing jobs, and shooting assignments for education, government, and industry.[41] Headquartered in a 30,000-square-foot (2,787-square-metre) studio in Ottawa, with a sound stage and two recording studios, Crawley Films opened branches in Montreal and Toronto. According to Vice President Graeme Fraser, "We offer integrated service," controlling "everything from research to release printing," as well as maintaining an animation department and a staff music director/composer, William McCauley. The company promised that each film was tailor-made to the needs of its sponsor.[42]

The NFB's catholic postwar approach drew criticism from *Documentary Film News*, which advocated more grandiose – or, as Paul Rotha later scoffed, "deadly dull" – documentary filmmaking.[43] In its January 1947 review of the new NFB releases, it characterized *Bronco Busters* as "a pretty ordinary piece of film-making" that "merits no more than the term 'programme fill-up.'" Grierson, one of the journal's founders, defended the film, as well as the board. Canada's reportage approach, he wrote, demonstrated "a profound element of common sense and good taste ... Its style is based on a policy of doing a large number of jobs with the money it has ... and they are all practical jobs fitted to a particular need and a particular audience."[44]

After Grierson resigned from the NFB in 1945, his successor, Ross McLean, whom the *Canadian Motion Picture Digest* described as having "the stocky, powerful build of a professional wrestler, the affable charm of a skilled diplomat, a broad wealth of scholarship and the grass-roots origin of a Manitoba small town," upheld this pragmatic strategy.[45] McLean saw the NFB's post-1945 mandate as providing a public service to Canadians through films on such wide-ranging issues as agricultural conditions, health, housing, industrial safety, and psychiatry. It equally sought to address international audiences. In this new era, the documentary movement no longer needed to grind "the axe of a particular national attitude," wrote an NFB educational specialist, and could instead promote global understanding, community-building, and the preservation of peace. McLean envisaged film as a modern, universal means of communication to promote "closer relations between nations" to advance peace and prosperity.[46] Exemplifying this trend were such NFB films as *Food: Secret of the Peace* (dir. by Stuart Legg, 1945), *Now – the Peace* (dir. by Stuart Legg, 1945), and *Suffer Little Children* (dir. by Sydney Newman, 1945), which supported the ethos of the United Nations and UNESCO, its cultural, economic, and social arm.[47]

The NFB applied its internationalist bent to useful films closer to home, specifically for American tourists. Rather than emphasizing foreignness and difference, tourism films functioned as sites of cultural exchange, shared perspectives, and common interests. McLean, however, had initially shared Grierson's ambivalence towards travelogues.

While acting as the personal secretary to Vincent Massey, the Canadian high commissioner in London between 1935 and 1946, he criticized the CGMPB for "picturing Canada not as a country where Canadians live and work, but as one where wealthy Americans play."[48] Still, he apparently believed that the documentary mode could rejuvenate tourism films, as when the NFB collaborated with the National Parks. As Superintendent of Publicity and Information Robert J.C. Stead stated, the "circulation of these films, particularly in the United States ... is an important factor in promoting information and goodwill towards Canada" in that country.[49]

In 1947, about 1,400 prints of films distributed by the Parks Branch were transferred to the NFB for its travel-film program in the United States.[50] Dolan feared that these pre-1939 productions were antiquated, not portraying a modern nation. In 1949, addressing the Senate Standing Committee on Tourist Traffic (set up in 1946), Dolan stressed the production of up-to-date colour films so as to remain competitive in an increasingly crowded tourism market. "Most of our travel films in the United States at the present are outdated. They were taken years ago and they show old cars and dresses that are obviously far out of style." He continued, "As soon as Americans see a picture showing old-fashioned styles they say 'Phooey, that's no good.'"[51] Heeding these concerns, McLean and the NFB worked closely with the Parks Branch to update its tourism films in the documentary style. As Branch Director Roy A. Gibson explained, his agency paid for new 16-mm motion pictures in sound and colour with the "expert advice" of the NFB. Productions promoting the scenic and recreational features of individual parks were then "put in the National Film Board mould, and brought up to the standard that has been so acceptable to our people" before being distributed throughout Canada, the United States, and beyond.[52]

In 1949–50, the Parks Branch sponsored four new NFB shorts: *Historic Highway – Lower Canada* (1950), highlighting historical sites and parks along the St Lawrence River waterway; *Canada's Historic Highway – Upper Canada* (1950); *Holiday at Waskesiu* (dir. by Jack Olsen, 1950), featuring the scenery and recreational activities of Prince Albert National Park, Saskatchewan; and *Holiday in Manitoba* (dir. by Jack Olsen, 1950), about a summer vacation at Riding Mountain National Park. With its growing collection of parks-related motion pictures, the NFB issued a string of *Canadian Travel and Wildlife Films* pamphlets listing its 16-mm productions available on a free-loan basis for "the family planning a leisurely tour, fishing and hunting films for the sportsman, and summer and winter playground films for recreation enthusiasts. Whatever your interest, all the films show the scenic grandeur of the country and the neighborly friendliness of the people of Canada – your vacation-land to the north" (figure 6.2).[53]

The NFB's conspicuous embrace of film as a medium to promote Canada as a friendly vacationland, in conjunction with the CGTB and the Parks Branch, was based on political, cultural, and economic reasons. During wartime, the film board mushroomed and peaked in terms of personnel, production releases, and distribution. Peace brought retrenchment. The board scaled back staff numbers, reduced newsreel production, and abandoned the trade-union circuit, partly in response to a wave of criticisms of extravagant and wasteful use of public funds. Conservatives called it an expensive, state-run agency that propagated socialist and/or communistic propaganda.[54] Canada's postwar Red Scare intensified after revelations of a Soviet spy ring following the defection of Igor Gouzenko, a cipher clerk in the Soviet embassy in Ottawa, in September 1945. Grierson had been implicated through his onetime secretary, Freda Linton, who was named as a conspirator. McLean also came under fire, particularly after he refused to purge employees whom the RCMP had deemed security risks – a stance that would force his resignation in late 1949.[55]

In 1950, Minister of Resources and Development Robert Winters appointed W. Arthur Irwin, editor of *Maclean's* magazine, as the new NFB commissioner. Under Irwin's tenure, a new National Film Act took effect in October 1950. The act followed the recommendations of the business-management consultant J.D. Woods and Gordon, Ltd, and restructured the NFB's bureaucracy to increase its efficiency and distance it from government.[56] Most notably, the act's section 9a both reaffirmed its nationalist mandate and enshrined an internationalist directive. The NFB was to "initiate and promote the production and distribution of films in the national interest and, in particular, to produce and distribute films designed to interpret Canada to Canadians and to *other nations*."[57] During the Commons debates on section 9a, Joseph Warner Murphy (PC, Lambton West) strongly suggested that the NFB should develop tourism through its films. "We can tell the Hollywood moguls that if they want to show pictures in Canada they will have to show pictures of Canada" in the United States, so that Canadians could host its "vacation-minded people."[58]

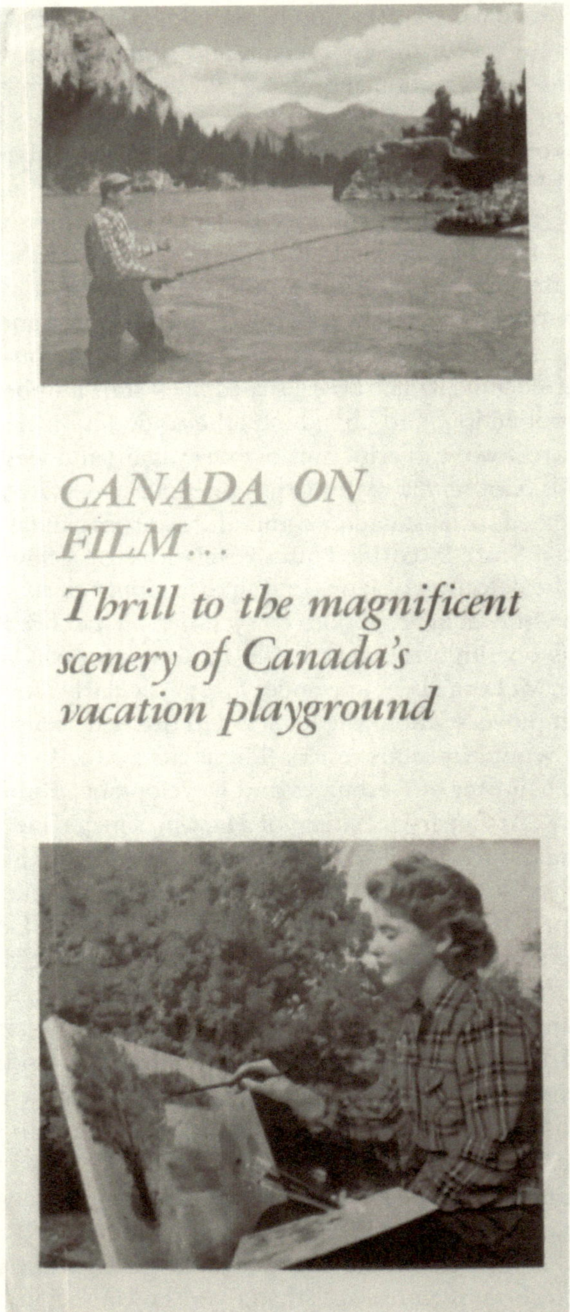

6.2 NFB, *Canadian Travel and Wildlife Films*, 1950

Murphy's reference to "Hollywood moguls" speaks to the larger concerns in Canada surrounding commercial US films' influence as a form of cultural imperialism. The revising of the film act overlapped with the Royal Commission on National Development in the Arts, Letters and Sciences, chaired by Vincent Massey. Prime Minister Louis St Laurent appointed the Massey Commission in April 1949 to assess the state of Canadian arts and letters and the influence of American mass culture. After two years of hearings and submitted briefs, the substantial Massey Report of 1951 recommended expanding Dominion involvement in the nation's cultural life via such state-sponsored agencies as the NFB: "Nearly all Canadians go to the movies; and most movies come from Hollywood," making the cinema "the most potent but also the most alien of the influences shaping our Canadian life." Nevertheless, the NFB's experiments in documentary filmmaking exacted a counter-hegemonic weight on the Canadian public.[59]

This observation is an example of what Zoë Druick terms the commissioners' "double cultural logic"; in the report's "attempt to return to a less mediated form of culture," it "calls both for increased mediation and for its erasure."[60] Concerned about the negative impact of Hollywood film (a highly mediated form of popular culture) on national life, the document promoted a state-sponsored cultural institution while glossing over the NFB's actively selling Canada to American tourists through its films. As NFB Secretary Alan Field proclaimed in Ottawa at the Third Dominion-Provincial Tourist Conference (October 1948), "We endeavor in making films to keep in mind their possible use for tourist promotion."[61] While the Massey Report acknowledged that "the promotion abroad of a knowledge of Canada is not a luxury but an obligation" to stimulate immigration, tourism, and trade, its authors were concerned more with "exchanges with other nations" that "will help us to make our reasonable contribution to civilized life."[62]

The sense of anxiety surrounding the growing impact of American popular culture among domestic cultural critics, embedded in the Massey Report, contrasted with the enthusiastic rhetoric surrounding tourism and the urgent need for American dollars. As Michael Dawson argues, Dolan and other tourism boosters "presented tourism as a positive and dynamic force that was expected to achieve many of the same ends that the cultural critics were pursuing."[63] Against this backdrop of Cold War intrigue, bureaucratic scrutiny, and hand-wringing over cultural policy, the increased production of films advertising Canada's scenic and recreational highlights allowed the

NFB to maintain its relevance among the cultural and intellectual elites while ideologically representing itself in support of free enterprise and amiable relations with the United States.

Tourism advocates worried that anxiety over the perception of Canadian culture under siege could lead to general resentment towards American tourists. Such antipathy, if outwardly expressed, could tarnish the country's carefully constructed reputation as a friendly destination. A two-pronged education campaign explained the value of American tourists to the economy and stressed hospitality and customer service. According to Trade and Commerce Minister MacKinnon, the key was to make citizens "individually realize the importance of this tourist business, so that when people come to Canada they may be taken care of properly and courteously."[64] Alberta was more blunt, telling farmers: when you see "a tourist car go whizzing by," do "not be envious or hostile," but rather think, "There goes more bacon, eggs, etc."[65]

In 1945, the CGTB inaugurated a campaign to teach fellow citizens how to be good hosts. The following year, the Canadian Association of Tourist and Publicity Bureaus (CATPB) held the first Tourist Service Education Week. The annual event advised people outside tourism of its role and educated those within it – such as managers and employees of hotels, information booths, restaurants, and service stations – how to be more welcoming and attentive to American guests.[66] The CATPB encouraged the cooperation of chambers of commerce, Dominion and provincial travel bureaux, the NFB, press, and radio (figure 6.3).

To that end, delegates at the second Dominion-Provincial Tourist Conference, held in Ottawa in autumn 1947, recommended that the NFB, working with the CGTB and provincial tourist officials, produce a short subject for domestic distribution depicting "the economic value of the tourist industry to the whole people of the country," in addition to stressing such themes as courtesy and service.[67] *Welcome, Neighbour!* (dir. by Leslie MacFarlane, 1949) informed audiences: "The job of entertaining millions of guests has become one of Canada's biggest peacetime industries ... When millions of guests enjoy Canadian hospitality, the friendship between two countries is made stronger."[68] As part of this education initiative, Crawley Films also produced a follow-up for the CGTB. *Travellers' Cheques* (1952) told "the story of Canada's tourist industry as explained by a teacher to a group of students" and displayed the country's "wealth of tourist attractions from coast-to-coast."[69]

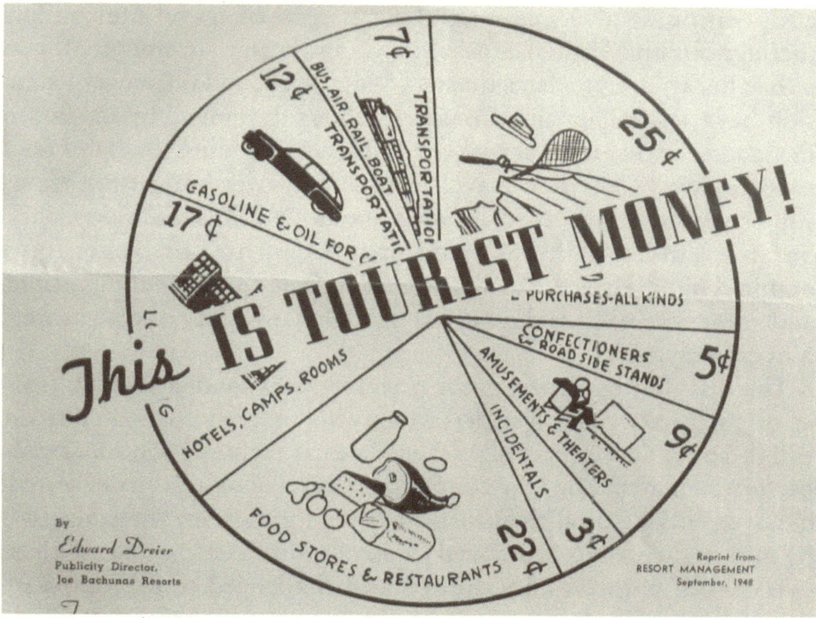

6.3 This is Tourist Money, 1948

EXPANDING NON-THEATRICAL DISTRIBUTION AND DOMINION-PROVINCIAL COOPERATION

The NFB recognized that collaborative film endeavours to promote tourism would be effective only with wide US distribution. During the war, Grierson maintained that disseminating 16-mm tourism films to specific groups through non-theatrical circuits was preferable to theatrical release.[70] McLean continued this practice and oversaw the peacetime expansion of non-theatrical distribution, often through innovative means. Speaking before the Senate Standing Committee on Tourist Traffic in 1948, he termed the non-theatrical film "the most effective way of presenting whatever there may be in Canada which is of interest to people in the United States or in any other country." To further develop tourist traffic, he added that the NFB had been working jointly with the CGTB and the Parks Branch and was ramping up the delivery of the Dominion's 16-mm film product in the United States.[71]

In 1947, the NFB established the Travel Film Library, initially at its Washington, DC, office, and transferred it to Chicago the next year, with a second major library in New York. With the CGTB's cooperation, it also maintained a network of travel-film outlets throughout the United States: in Canadian-government offices, public libraries, state departments of education, and university extension libraries.[72] The "distribution methods developed by the board in Canada and carried across the border," according to a later NFB report, gave "Canadian travel films a lead over competing travel subjects promoting other vacation lands."[73] Films were deposited on an extended-loan basis and in turn lent to borrowers for a nominal handling fee. Details, including a summary, running time, and colour or black and white, appeared in a variety of educational film catalogues.

The distribution program for travel films expanded steadily from its original sixty-two US outlets to sixty-six in thirty-five states by the end of 1951. They reportedly reached nearly eight million Americans per year, not including "the continuous casual bookings" from several hundred private, non-theatrical libraries throughout the country.[74] By mid-decade, the NFB moved to decentralize distribution. With its two central libraries understaffed and challenged to keep up with demand, "the Board intensified its efforts to provide alternative sources of Canadian travel films in the US" by supplying more state and municipal libraries "to seek out new and particularly important audiences such as travel and sportsmen's clubs, and to develop new and more efficient methods of distributing travel films."[75]

In keeping with this policy "of attempting to show Canadian travel films wherever potential tourists gather for showings," the NFB inventively arranged to provide large US industries with tourism-film programs. According to T.V. (Vic) Adams, chief of the NFB's International Distribution Division, its products reached "the various divisions of each company on a schedule and are shown at noon hour" to make the most efficient use of each film, which "may be shown thirty times in a month on such a circuit."[76] An ad promoting the circuit appeared in *Business Screen Magazine*: "Plant program directors and recreation executives seeking material for weekly employe [*sic*] showings will be interested in this extensive library of Canadian travel films." The list of available colour and sound films included *Canadian Cruise* (1950), *Canoe Country* (1950), *North to Hudson's* [*sic*] *Bay* (1950), *Road to Gaspé* (1950), *Sailing in Canada* (1950), *Silks and Sulkies* (1950), and *Winter Carnival* (1950), all sponsored by the CGTB; and *Rocky Mountain Trout* (1947), *Highland Holiday* (1948), and *Ski Holiday* (1948), sponsored by the Parks Branch.[77]

In addition to the two main Travel Film libraries, their satellites, and the industrial-film circuit, the NFB accelerated distribution via expanding US educational distribution networks. J. Margaret Carter, who had handled the wartime non-theatrical distribution of NFB prints for US educational-film libraries, had conjectured that after the conflict educational films would help in "building a mutual understanding" and in stimulating "a deep and sympathetic understanding of the similarities and diversities" among the youth of the neighbouring countries.[78] Notwithstanding her idealistic vision, business-minded tourism boosters envisioned American students as the next generation of holiday-makers, and the classroom as a venue to encourage profits.

During the Third Dominion-Provincial Tourist Conference in 1948, delegates acknowledged that "school children can be an important factor in making Canada more attractive to tourists."[79] Children, adolescents, and teachers could influence family decision-making regarding travel at various stages of the planning process. As Marie L. Kerkmann, assistant advertising manager for Scholastic Magazines, professed to Dan E.C. Campbell, "Two key groups to *inform* and *sell* on travel are high school students and high school teachers," representing the future and present tourist markets, respectively. To reach this new demographic, Scholastic Magazines began publishing a travel annual in April 1946 geared towards US junior- and high-school teachers. *Your Vacation* provided "travel-conscious" teachers "excellent classroom material" and guidance for vacation preparation "such as where-to-go suggestions, mean temperatures of all places accessible this summer, suggested wardrobe for various climates, currency exchange values, and the latest information on new types of equipment and facilities for land, sea and air travel."[80]

The *Instructor*, which reached 350,000 "Travel-Minded Teachers" in American elementary schools, similarly positioned educators as a key link in children's ability to influence their parents' choice of destination. "The way of least resistance to parents and the home market is the child," proclaimed the advertising manager, "for he can get what every advertiser wants – the undivided attention of an adult audience." The strategy was to sell to the teachers first, as they exerted "a powerful influence" on their students through daily instruction. Pitching tourism as "a part of education," the Chicago-based magazine regularly published articles of "the actual travel experiences of teachers who took these trips, described in school-teacher language."[81]

In Canada's overall program of promotion, the long-term value of distributing tourism films to schools under the pretext of education functioned alongside the circulation of film product to such targeted groups as angling clubs, fraternal lodges, and women's groups. A film certified as "educational" by the NFB paid no sales taxes on either production or prints.

The NFB also developed a way to reach American tourists already *in* Canada to encourage them to plan *return* trips to other parts of the country. According to J.D. Ralph, the director of distribution, "We have found it is a most important supplement to our distribution in the United States ... The American visitor, once he is in Canada, is very much interested in learning something about other parts of the country ... He may often begin to plan his holiday for the following year on the basis of what he learns about other places and the film provides the most effective medium for arousing his interest."[82]

In the summer of 1948, the NFB launched the Summer Tourist Program through its regional field offices, together with the cooperation of the CGTB, the Parks Branch, provincial authorities, and railways. It offered free screenings of 16-mm colour motion pictures on Canadian subjects (usually four or five at a time, about four times a week, from June through September) at nearly fifty major tourist points across the country, including exhibitions, fairs, ferries, hotels, lodges, museums, National Parks, passenger ships, and resorts. The NFB loaned prints and equipment, including projectors, screens, and speakers, for the films shown in indoor theatres and at campgrounds. Its representatives also provided training on the use of its equipment.

The Summer Tourist Program, which by 1959 averaged 12,000 shows annually to an audience of a million, appeared to hit the mark.[83] A questionnaire found that these screenings encouraged the US visitor to revisit Canada and explore other regions. For example, the Minnesota Film Council replied that the "type of films shown arouse interest in other aspects of Canadian life and in many cases create a desire to see these things first hand." A resort owner in Gull Lake, Ontario, remarked, "The numerous comments from our guests have only been favourable and we are certain that the pictures have done a good job of selling future vacations to our American guests." Another resort owner in Muskoka commented, "Very few miss the shows despite the other attractions here and at Bracebridge close by. The Americans eat it up."[84]

The success of the Summer Tourist Program was contingent on Dominion-provincial coordination. According to a 1953 report, "It is equally clear that early co-operation between the National Film Board and provincial travel bureaus enables a far more effective campaign."[85] Consequently, provincial bureaux added their 16-mm films for the program. Despite the possibility of interprovincial rivalries, participation denoted a spirit of teamwork. Active Dominion-provincial-private collaborations demonstrated that post-1945 tourism was not a "zero-sum game." Joint efforts to promote the nation as a whole and/or a province or region were not necessarily self-defeating but might unlock new markets.

Hence, the CGTB worked closely with provincial motion-picture and/or tourism boards. Such Dominion-provincial cooperation was intended to "prevent overlapping in the production of films" and optimize tourism promotion.[86] Moreover, Dolan argued that fostering such partnerships would result in the "right" kind of tourism film. At the ninth Dominion-Provincial Tourist Conference, held in Ottawa in autumn 1954, he advised the provinces to produce films "dealing only with travel. Composite films, using industrial and agriculture material in detail, are not suitable for these outlets. Travel is such an important part of our economy, we should get films devoted exclusively to travel. We're up against the best film-makers in the world and we must have a good product to secure new audiences."[87]

Regardless, provinces, to limit costs, routinely made more general motion pictures that promoted agriculture, industry, and manufacturing alongside tourism as an "all-in-one" marketing tool. For example, Nova Scotia's Film Bureau produced an overall picture of the province highlighting its tourist attractions that could double for school use. *This Is Nova Scotia* (1948) underlined the province's agriculture, historic sites, industry, peoples – "its daily work and holiday pleasures. To the carefree tourist, the province offers salmon fishing, golfing, yachting and most exciting of all the thrill of a battle with such deep-sea giants as the tuna."[88] Moreover, the New Brunswick Bureau of Travel and Tourist Promotion availed itself of Crawley Films' services in 1951, resulting in *Let's Look at New Brunswick* (1951). Employing existing 16-mm Kodachrome footage, the film provided an overview of the province's agricultural sector, fishing and timber industries, and tourist attractions, particularly its beaches and sport fishing, conveying its "natural beauty and historical interest."[89]

In the summer of 1954, Crawley Films proposed to R.A. (Robert) Tweedie, director of the New Brunswick Travel Bureau since 1951, that the company make a new tourism film aimed at the American travel market. The film, Crawley insisted, ought to be "planned to achieve some definite purpose" – not "merely interesting, entertaining, or provid[ing] a good 'documentary' treatment" of the region. "It should create in the minds of the audience a definite desire to go there and enjoy the recreation facilities portrayed." A tourism film ideally proffers practical information, such as "the various types of accommodation, and the conveniences and quality of food services." Above all, the "guiding factor" should not necessarily be "a 'nice' film" but "subject-matter that will motivate audiences in far-off Timbuctu (*sic*) or Bull's Bay [to] decide to go and visit the area."[90]

Indeed, Crawley, together with government officials and tourism stakeholders, believed that they had a formula for persuasive tourism-promotion films. This contrasted with the NFB's seemingly ad-hoc approach, whereby possessing "some interest for people who wish to come to Canada or are planning to visit this country" made a tourism film.[91] Prior to the sixth Dominion-Provincial Tourist Conference in 1951, a Select Committee on Canadian Travel Films had been formed to review "the use of motion pictures as a medium of promoting travel." Committee members, T.J. Courtney of Nova Scotia, Budge Crawley, W.A. Macdonald of British Columbia, and Homer S. Robinson, assistant director of the CGTB, concluded that a "good travel film" "will influence audiences to visit the areas portrayed." It "convey[s] ideas to groups of people in a manner that will create a desire in them to see these places for themselves."[92]

To that end, committee members' report concluded that effective tourism films should be

- in colour with sound and only one reel in length;
- feature "the unique or special vacation attractions of the area depicted" while and avoiding industrial activities, which "would spoil the effectiveness"; and
- be "entertaining and interesting," with "a definite theme," as opposed to "hodge-podge footage."

The document emphasized such practical considerations as the intended audience and insisted on pre-payment for the costs of production, an adequate number of prints, and distribution. It further recommended that the sponsoring agency appoint a liaison officer to work with an experienced producer to help prepare a story outline, but then "*leave the producer alone*" to make the film. The report concluded, "It is like a three-legged milking stool. Properly planned, the film will sit comfortably, but if even one of these factors is not levelled up, it will fall."[93]

The committee also circulated a questionnaire to provincial representatives asking, among other queries: "To what extent have you used travel films in your promotion activities?" and "How can we improve the effectiveness of Canadian travel films in promoting tourist travel to Canada?" To achieve a satisfactory return on an investment, the report suggested location targeting. Provinces should distribute their films in contiguous areas, because one can "hardly expect that a film featuring Prince Edward Island as a vacation spot would draw many travellers all the way across the continent, say, from Seattle or San Diego."[94] Unlike Dominion efforts to propagate tourism films widely, provinces had tended to adopt a *regional* approach, believing that travellers from California and Arizona, for instance, were more likely to visit western Canada, just as Americans from the northeast were more prone to travel to the Maritimes. Distribution of province-specific tourism films should thus focus on salient regions.

Alberta, for one, had recognized that its postwar campaign needed a coordinated, transnational effort that zeroed in on its surroundings. In early 1944, provincial publicity director Dan Campbell argued that "the Pacific Northwest Tourist Association [PNWTA] is our most immediate and important ally." He suggested harmonizing efforts with it through direct contact and tie-ups with local travel bureaux and resorts and encouraged the hiring of winter lecturers equipped with scenic motion pictures. Instead of covering the entire United States, Alberta worked with the PNWTA and distributed its films and other advertising materials in California, Colorado, Idaho, Montana, Oregon, Washington, Wyoming, and Utah.[95] Campbell urged member provinces and states to invest in the production of "interesting motion pictures for exhibition purposes" and for the PNWTA to organize and maintain a library of films contributed by each member jurisdiction for use at travel shows and made available to university libraries and private distributors.[96]

THE CANADIAN COOPERATION PROJECT: CURRENCY AND CINEMASCOPE

In the immediate years after 1945, tourism stakeholders within the provincial and Dominion governments that sponsored, produced, and/or distributed 16-mm films promoting Canadian travel also worked with the American film industry to produce tourism films that directly and indirectly encouraged holidaying in Canada. This transnational arrangement was known as the Canadian Cooperation Project (CCP). In effect between 1948 and 1958, the CCP has been largely vilified as a "devil's bargain" with Hollywood that undermined Canada's ability to foster a domestic feature-film industry.[97] Apart from the issue of cultural imperialism, the CCP stemmed from more pragmatic considerations: namely, Canada's shrinking reserve of US currency and Hollywood's desire to maintain its films' unrestricted access to Canadian theatres (considered a key domestic market, though outside the United States). Canada, in particular Alberta, would also offer Hollywood fresh vistas for its novel widescreen processes, most notably, CinemaScope.

The main impetus for Canada's focus on the American tourist market had been the troubling balance of payments. As Ontario's Deputy Minister of Travel and Publicity Tom McCall remarked candidly, "The cold hard fact is we are after US dollars."[98] By 1947 a full-blown balance-of-payments crisis had emerged, caused partly by domestic demand for US goods after wartime constraints were lifted. This eventually drained the nation's supply of US dollars, prompting Dominion import restrictions to conserve it.[99] The shortage of greenbacks boosted the need for US tourists in Canada, as well as throughout western Europe, as its tourism infrastructure rebounded, with observers hoping that their purchasing power would close the dollar gap.[100]

To address the crisis, in November 1947 Ottawa announced widespread import restrictions and taxes on a variety of non-essential US consumer goods, including motion-picture projection and sound equipment. American film interests feared eventual quotas, particularly following Britain's imposition in August 1947 of a 75 per cent tax (the Dalton Duty) on films from abroad (most were from the United States). Hollywood recognized that similar austerity measures in Canada would hit revenues at a time of growing uncertainty. Following record-high audiences in 1946, box-office receipts began a precipitous decline and in fact would not recover for decades. Moreover, US anti-trust action against Hollywood's monopolistic practices culminated in 1948 with the Supreme Court's decision in *United States* v. *Paramount*, which compelled the vertically integrated major studios to divest their exhibition holdings. Meanwhile, the rise in popularity of television and other home/community-based leisure pursuits, combined with the negative publicity surrounding the House Un-American Activities Committee's investigation of alleged Communist influence, threatened Hollywood's economic, political, and cultural dominance.

The Motion Picture Association of America (MPAA) and Canadian Minister of Reconstruction and Supply C.D. Howe, who admitted to rarely going to the movies, commenced negotiations in late 1947 to devise a "quid pro quo" to alleviate the currency crisis while avoiding regulations against Hollywood productions. Howe, transferred to Trade and Commerce in November 1948, believed that the stimulation of greater production within Canada could halt the yearly outflow of an estimated $12 million to the United States.[101] The Connecticut-born J.J. (John) Fitzgibbons, president of Famous Players Canadian Corp., and Francis Harmon, MPAA vice president, were largely responsible for hammering out a reciprocal plan with Canadian government officials.

On 21 January 1948, MPAA President Eric Johnston outlined what would become the CCP in a letter to Fitzgibbons, which was circulated to the heads of the film studios. Fitzgibbons and Francis Harmon also conferred with D. Leo Dolan, Ross McLean, E. (Ernie) L. Bushnell of the CBC, Lester B. Pearson and Saul Rae from the Department of External Affairs, and Donald Gordon and Herbert Richardson from the Bank of Canada.[102] The agreement was formalized during a series of meetings in Ottawa on 5–6 April 1948. During a luncheon at the Château Laurier Hotel, Harmon informed prominent Canadian officials that the CCP's main objective was "to see whether, through the application of Hollywood showmanship, Canada's tourist business from the United States" could increase to "an amount equivalent to the dollars Canada spends annually for Hollywood films." Shortly thereafter, the Executive Committee of the MPAA voted to appropriate $20,000 for expenses related to the project.[103]

The goal of increasing the US dollar supply by stimulating the tourist trade into Canada would require a triangulated set-up between Los Angeles, New York, and Toronto/Ottawa to make "possible immediate service to producers of motion picture shorts and features incorporating Canadian background material."[104] Working under Harmon's direction and supervision, Taylor Mills of the MPAA's international division in New York handled newsreel sequences, short subjects, and the overall coordination of the CCP. Mills, who had been the assistant director of the OWI Motion Picture Bureau and headed the agency's domestic-film division September 1944–August 1945, would bring his experience as a government administrator to the project. The English-born Welshman Blake Warwick-Owensmith, formerly in the public-relations department at Twentieth Century-Fox, joined the MPAA's Los Angeles office in early 1948. He was put in charge of features and acted as the main contact between Hollywood producers and Canadian officials. Nicknamed "Mr Canada," during the war Owensmith had served in the Canadian army and thus claimed to have knowledge of both the American film industry and Canadians alike.[105]

Donald Henshaw, a senior executive at the Toronto-based MacLaren Advertising Company, Ltd, which maintained offices in Ottawa, Montreal, Winnipeg, and Vancouver "staffed by former working newspaper men," represented the MPAA in Canada. The agency coordinated all phases of the CCP's implementation, such as expediting customs and immigration passage for production crews, stars, and technicians, as well as arranging for housing and transportation required by location units.[106] In July 1948, C.D. Howe appointed A. (Archibald) H. Newman as the film liaison officer between Ottawa and the MPAA to whom the film industry could turn to quickly to cut through bureaucratic red tape. Newman, formerly the public-relations manager at Polymer Corporation (a crown corporation established in 1942 to produce artificial rubber), had most recently served as the director general of the Publicity Branch of C.D. Howe's wartime departments.[107]

The CCP consisted of a combination of short-term and long-range objectives. The first point in Johnston's letter of 21 January 1948 concerned the MPAA's immediate sponsorship of a short subject on Canada's dollar crisis. Paramount's *Neighbor to the North* (dir. by Gene Martel, 1948) used live action and animation to spotlight "the need for us to come to the aid of our cousins across the border." The NFB's Stuart Legg wrote the treatment. In addition to explaining Canada's economic predicament to Americans, the thirteen-minute film encouraged tourism by pictorially highlighting the country's "magnificent scenery" through the eyes of an American (Walter Abel) and a Canadian (Ralph Forbes) driving through fishing country. The film screened in approximately 12,000 theatres across the United States.[108]

Following the dissemination of the Johnston letter, US newsreels ramped up their coverage of Canadian content. During February and March 1948, thirty-one US newsreels included Canadian topics, compared to ten during the same months in the previous year. Moreover, as per the MPAA's encouragement, fourteen Hollywood luminaries, including Cary Grant, Gregory Peck, and Barbara Stanwyck, plugged Canadian attractions over approximately five hundred US radio stations, in a series of broadcasts produced by the CBC. As part of the CCP plan, Hollywood studios also obtained stock footage and purchased NFB prints for release in US theatres. For example, Columbia acquired *Rhapsody on Ice* (1947), produced by the Toronto-based Audio Pictures, and *Champions in the Making* (1948), which both feature the Ottawa-born figure-skating phenom and (as of 6 February 1948) Olympic gold medallist Barbara Ann Scott.[109]

The last two elements outlined in the Johnston letter – the production of 35-mm Canadian-themed travelogues and on-location shooting of feature films in whole or in part in the Dominion – formed the bulk of the CPP's long-range outlook. Johnston pledged that the American film industry would escalate its production of films focusing on Canadian "beauty spots which should increasingly become a magnet for American vacationists."[110] To assist Hollywood filmmakers, Donald Henshaw at MacLaren prepared a portfolio entitled "Ideas for Canadian Short Subjects" that circulated to CCP department heads in New York and Hollywood, and later produced a bibliography of Canadian fiction and non-fiction books for possible story ideas for feature films.[111] Moreover, the MacLaren agency compiled a "Canadian Talent Roster" for Hollywood producers for casting on location, while the MPAA's Hollywood office prepared a detailed survey of facilities in Canada for film production.[112]

Most studios responded ardently to Johnston's urging to produce Canadian tourism films. In the summer of 1948, Universal released *Snow Capers* (dir. by Arthur Cohen, 1948), a two-reeler featuring winter sports near Banff in the Canadian Rockies. Although *Capers* was already complete, the studio rewrote the commentary to highlight "Canada's glorious vacation land" as "Seven Switzerlands in One." Meanwhile, Gordon Hollingshead produced *Calgary Stampede* (dir. by Richard Bare, 1948) for Warner Bros. This Technicolor two-reeler was nominated for an Academy Award for best live-action short film. After receiving Johnston's letter, Warner Bros. had sped up the film's exhibition, hoping it would spur American audiences "to visit the Calgary

Stampede this year." Paramount, which had already released *Neighbor to the North*, produced two additional CCP films for its Sportlight unit: *Iced Lightning* (1948), highlighting Canadian hockey, and *Big Game Angling* (1948), about tuna fishing off Wedgeport, Nova Scotia, narrated by famed American sportswriter Grantland Rice. Moreover, as proof of his studio's eagerness, Twentieth Century–Fox President Spyros P. Skouras noted that producer Edmund Reek was putting together a one-reel subject on Quebec in hopes that "thousands of Americans who see this subject ... will plan vacations in Canada during the next twelve to eighteen months." The studio permitted the NFB's Stuart Legg to revise the commentary to convey the province's vacation opportunities more effectively. The result was *Quaint Quebec* (1948), a Technicolor tour along the St Lawrence narrated by Lowell Thomas.[113]

With the encouragement of MGM's president, Nicholas Schenck, and Eddie Mannix, its infamous fixer/vice president in charge of production, the prestigious studio similarly produced short subjects "showing the scenery and opportunities for vacationists in Canada." James FitzPatrick began filming two 35-mm TravelTalks in Canada during the summer of 1948: *Ontario, Land of Lakes* (1949) and *Quebec in Summertime* (1949).[114] FitzPatrick, for whom Canada had "been one of his deepest loves," had already released a trio of Technicolor one-reel scenics – *Glimpses of New Scotland* (1947), *On the Shores of Nova Scotia* (1947), and *Cape Breton Island* (1948) – to portray the picturesque province and its great fishing.[115] Prior to his filming tour of Quebec and Ontario, FitzPatrick visited Ottawa and met with Dolan, who put him in touch with tourist officials and transportation companies to expedite filming. FitzPatrick was delighted with the cooperation extended by governmental officials. "Just as an example," he mentioned, "I asked for a speedboat at 2:30 this afternoon and 10 minutes later I was informed it was waiting for me."[116] As evidence of quid pro quo, Dolan informed the Third Dominion-Provincial Tourist Conference in 1948 that FitzPatrick allowed the CGTB to edit the films before their release.[117]

Dolan welcomed the CCP as part of an "aggressive policy for the future development" of Canada's tourism industry. For example, the CGTB sent its posters to dress movie sets with a view to advertising Canada – for example, in the Warner Bros. musical *Romance on the High Seas* (dir. by Michael Curtiz, 1948), featuring Doris Day – Curtiz had won the Oscar for directing *Casablanca*.[118] Dolan also assembled and compiled a survey of locales and facilities "adaptable to the requirements" of the studios.[119] Throughout the spring of 1948, his office arranged meetings with Hollywood executives to stimulate the production of Canadian-themed feature films with an eye to tourism promotion. For the next decade or so, Dolan would continue to leverage his personal connections with Hollywood's elite to keep Canada relevant to the US film industry. Among his friends, he could count on fellow New Brunswick "native" Louis B. Mayer, head of MGM, with whom "each year he spends a holiday in Hollywood" as his guest. His other "friends in the movie capital – many of whom have fished and hunted with him in Canada," included Don Ameche (Oscar winner, 1986), Clark Gable (1934), Frank Morgan, Walter Pidgeon, Mickey Rooney, and Spencer Tracy (1937, 1938). Dolan was "not unaware of the importance to the Canadian tourist industry of this contact which he maintains with American celebrities. When a well-known figure catches a mess of fish or bags the limit of game, Dolan sees to it that the information gets back to the press."[120]

With the combined efforts of Dolan and other CCP adherents, American producers began to deliberately incorporate Canadian location shots in their feature films. This was an early indication of the shift towards "runaway" productions that had begun in the late 1940s, wherein Hollywood studios increasingly shot on location in western Europe and beyond. As *Motion Picture Herald* exclaimed, "Hollywood is packing its cameras, donning its traveling clothes, and moving outside US borders to find new locales for production." Contributing factors included lower production costs abroad, the need to use revenues frozen overseas by restrictions on remittances to the United States, and the desire for novel and/or authentic visuals, particularly with the advent of widescreen technology.[121] Although the American film industry had occasionally shot Canadian-themed fictional stories on location to convey authenticity and realism in promoting their film product, which maintained residual tourism-promotion effects, the CCP-era productions filmed wholly or partially in Canada expressly marketed a destination brand.

Paramount's *The Emperor Waltz* (dir. by Billy Wilder, 1948) was one of the earliest feature-length CCP tourism films and the first Technicolor effort for the Academy Award–winning team (for *The Lost Weekend*, 1945) of producer (and writer) Charles Brackett (who won eventually three Oscars) and director Billy Wilder (six). Set in 1906 Vienna, it stars Academy Award–winner (in 1944) Bing Crosby as a "corn-fed American salesman" at Emperor "Franz Joseph's

(Richard Haydn) court, peddling a newfangled phonograph and wooing a countess (Joan Fontaine [Oscar in 1941]) on the side." Brackett and Wilder set the story partly in the Tyrolean Alps, with Jasper National Park standing in for the mountain scenes.[122] The Austrian-born Billy Wilder, cast, and crew headed north in the spring of 1946. Filming was completed in September 1946, well before the CCP was put into play. When the film was screened for Paramount executives, they were underwhelmed and decided to postpone its release until the marketing department could devise a suitable advertising campaign (figure 6.4).[123]

In the meantime, the public announcement of the CCP permitted Paramount to revamp its publicity for the film, which premiered in May 1948, to emphasize that the Alpine scenes were shot in Canada. Advance stories in the pressbook – a studio-produced publication outlining a film's sales and publicity campaign through suggestions for exploitation, prepared reviews, production stories, and visual materials – underscored "the scenic magnificence" of the Canadian Rockies. It states that Wilder chose the "Canadian vacation paradise … as the best to simulate the Austrian Alpine background" of his childhood. For this "lyrical romantic comedy," the director believed that "Jasper's high peaks, forests, rivers and lakes made the Canadian park a perfect setting in which to reproduce the Tyrolean countryside."[124]

Anita Colby, a former model and erstwhile actress nicknamed The Face, was in charge of the press junket, touring more than thirty key US cities. Colby also travelled to Toronto, where she outlined the studio's exploitation plans vis-à-vis Jasper. This pleased government officials, who anticipated that the Canadian locations would stimulate tourism, resulting in US dollars.[125] To that end, the CNR devised a campaign around *The Emperor Waltz* stressing that shooting took place partly at Jasper. The railway company owned and operated the Jasper Park Lodge, located within the park boundaries, where many members from the Paramount movie party stayed during shooting. Seeking a boost in the tourist trade from the cachet of Bing Crosby and Joan Fontaine, the CNR placed ads in such mass-circulated magazines as *Life*, declaring that Hollywood chose Jasper to shoot the film's Alpine sequences.[126]

Aside from the scenery, the Jasper resort was recognized for its world-class fairway, designed by renowned golf-course architect Stanley Thompson. Cross-promotion surrounding *The Emperor Waltz* marketed the region as a premier destination for golfing, as well as

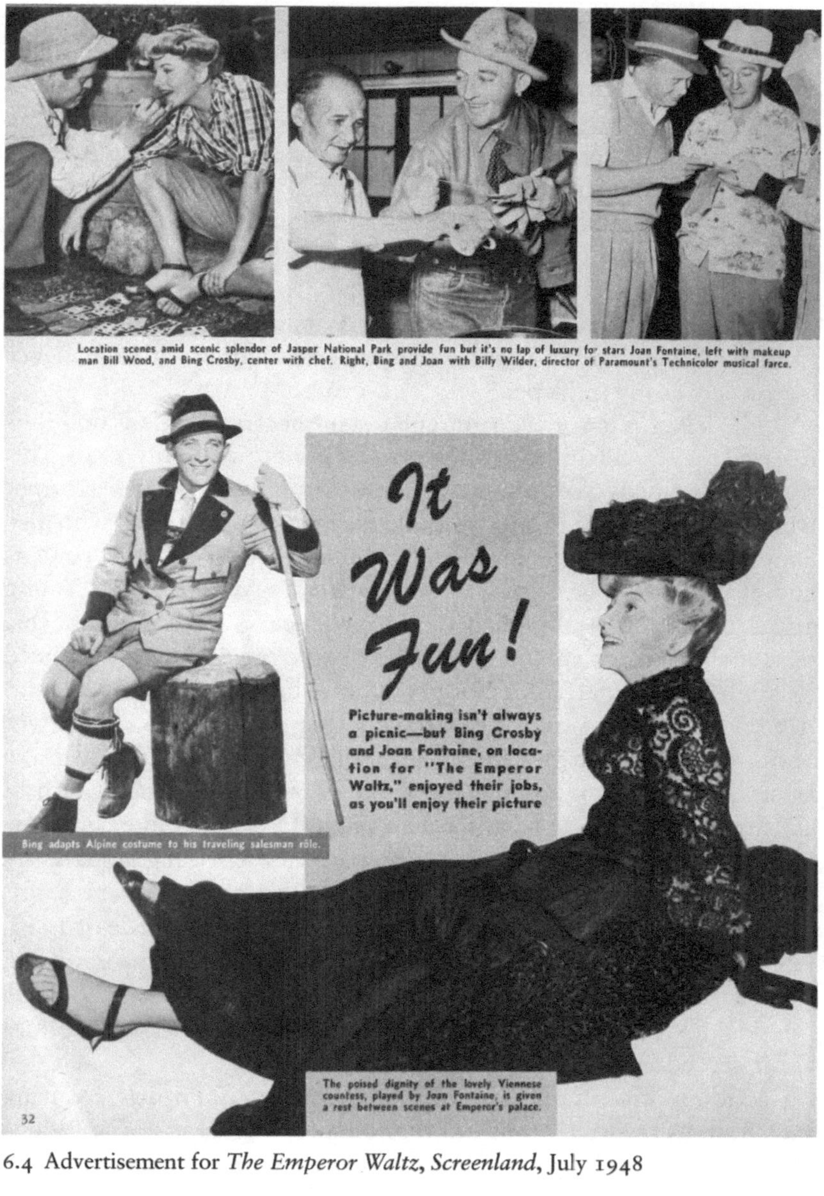

6.4 Advertisement for *The Emperor Waltz*, *Screenland*, July 1948

other recreational pursuits. An avid sportsman, Bing Crosby later became an "ambassador of goodwill" and a de-facto tourism booster for the park. Stories appearing in trade journals and fan magazines reported that this was his first visit "to that part of Canada, and he fell in love with it. Each day, when shooting was finished, he whipped off to the golf course, the tennis courts, or went fishing." Wilder reputedly had to post guards at all strategic outlets to ensure the star did not wander off the set to pursue his favourite hobbies. After filming was complete, Crosby returned to Jasper Park Lodge, winning its eighteenth annual amateur Totem Pole Golf Tournament, which generated even more publicity.[127] To further capitalize on Crosby's passion for golf to promote Canadian tourism, the CGTB sponsored the NFB's *From Tee to Green* (dir. by Grant Crabtree, 1950). The 16-mm colour single reeler provided a visual tour of Canada's finest golf courses, from Newfoundland to Vancouver Island, concluding with a sequence featuring Crosby in Jasper.[128]

While *The Emperor Waltz* circulated in theatres, Eagle-Lion Films released the Canadian-themed *Northwest Stampede* in July 1948. This romantic comedy/Western stars James Craig as a rodeo performer who inherits a ranch run by a female foreman (Joan Leslie), who also happens to be a championship rodeo personality. Realized in 1946 as a joint venture between the American railway tycoon Robert Young and British industrialist-turned–film producer J. Arthur Rank, this outdoor Cinecolor spectacle was the most expensive film produced by Eagle-Lion to date. Director-producer Albert S. Rogell travelled to Alberta in the summer of 1947 to shoot on location for about two-and-a-half months. In addition to scenes shot in Banff and Lake Louise, filming took place at the Duke of Windsor's ranch south of Calgary, in the Alberta foothills near High River. The duke, who was friends with the company's co-founder, Robert R. Young, apparently spent $30,000 of his own money to make his ranch camera-ready. Much of the action was also filmed at the Calgary Stampede of 1947. Recalling the buzz surrounding Hoot Gibson's participation during *The Calgary Stampede* (1925), comedic actor Jack Oakie, who plays the sidekick, rode in a chuck wagon during the parade, while James Craig served as its honorary grand marshal.[129]

Canadian officials anticipated that *Northwest Stampede*, by using such famous resort areas as Banff and Lake Louise, would "produce tourist trade as well as intensify interest in Canada as a film centre."[130] Prior to the MPAA's proposal for the CCP, Calgary and environs were already aspiring "to become the Hollywood of western Canada." Director-producer Albert Rogell informed residents, "I am sure this community will benefit by the future influx of motion picture companies who will further exploit the city and its surrounding scenery, which was beyond our wildest dreams."[131] With the CCP in force in early 1948, this aspiration appeared to be within reach. Government officials and the local Chamber of Commerce who had cooperated during the filming requested that Rogell's horse opera open in the city. In June 1948, Bryan Foy, vice president in charge of production at Eagle-Lion, travelled to Toronto and met with David Griesdorf, president and general manager of International Film Distributors, which represented Eagle-Lion in Canada, to arrange for the opening. Held on 15 July 1948, the première was accompanied by all the glitz and glamour of Hollywood, complete with stars hobnobbing with Canadian political and business leaders.[132]

While in Canada, Foy also conferred with such government officials as Dolan on how to promote the film effectively, given the CCP. The pressbook urged exhibitors to "sell the rodeo" and "sell the scenery" by arranging tie-ins with local CPR offices. It also suggested contacting travel agencies "to set up window displays using stills from 'Northwest Stampede' showing the scenic splendor of the Canadian Rockies, with copy reading: 'See Canada's vacation wonderland in Eagle Lion's Cinecolor spectacle, "Northwest Stampede." Why not let us plan a trip there for you?'"[133] To tie the film in with the CCP, Eagle-Lion President Arthur J. Krim addressed American filmgoers as would-be tourists: "The picture you are about to see was photographed in the Canadian Rockies. Eagle-Lion (Hollywood) Films is deeply grateful to the Government of Canada and to the people of Lake Louise, Banff and Calgary for their co-operation in making this picture against the background of this glorious vacation land."[134] At least one critic wrote that, while the story was plodding, the "stunning countryside" and "the famed Calgary Stampede" provided "this saga with its sole excitements." He or she concluded: "The spectacular backdrop of 'Northwest Stampede' leaves one with a strong desire for a vacation to say nothing of a vacation from such yarns."[135]

Meanwhile, exhibitor-turned–independent producer Nat Holt began filming *Canadian Pacific* (dir. by Edwin L. Marin, 1949) for Twentieth Century–Fox in Alberta during the summer of 1948. In February, Holt had written to J.J. Fitzgibbons outlining his plans for the Cinecolor feature, which dramatizes the CPR's 1880 push across the prairies, through the foothills, and into the Rockies. Holt also planned an opening sequence "of the beautiful resorts extending across Canada from Chateau Frontenac to Vancouver" (a scene not in the film). Nat Holt requested Fitzgibbons's assistance to obtain a "firm commitment of cooperation" from CPR officers, as well as the Canadian government.[136] Both agreed, hoping for a film on a par with Cecil B. DeMille's 1939 railway epic, *Union Pacific*. By harnessing western Canada's beauty, officials hoped to bring in US dollars and "reflect favourably on Canada" in the long term. Fitzgibbons informed Spyros Skouras that *Canadian Pacific* would represent "the cornerstone of the Canadian Cooperation Project."[137] Twentieth Century–Fox's commitment to the CCP was demonstrated when Skouras decided to hold the company's annual sales convention in Toronto – "the first time that a major American film company crossed the border to hold such an important meeting."[138]

After communicating with Blake Owensmith, Hollywood contact for the CCP, the film company engaged in a scouting trip and "found working conditions in Canada of the finest type."[139] With Randolph Scott playing the railway's chief surveyor, location filming took place in both Alberta (Banff, Lake Louise, and the Stoney-Nakoda Reservation in Morley) and British Columbia (the Fraser River gorge, Kicking Horse Pass, and the Yoho Valley). John Rhodes Sturdy, a public-relations officer for the CPR, provided technical assistance to ensure "documentary authenticity," such as arranging for the use of period railway equipment. The book *Steel of Empire* (1935), a romanticized narrative of the building of the CPR by John Murray Gibbon, its general publicity agent 1913–45, provided the historical background to this fictional tale of derring-do.[140] Meanwhile, Owensmith and Trade and Commerce's new film liaison, A.H. Newman, handled customs clearances and arranged for the location crew's use of the National Parks.[141] As further evidence of the cooperation among government, the CPR, and the studio, the Canadian consul general and a CPR representative attended the San Francisco première in March 1949.[142] Although Herbert Whittaker excoriated the railway yarn in Toronto's *Globe and Mail*, reviewers in American periodicals praised the "camera craftsmanship" that recorded the "towering beauty of the Canadian Rockies and the lush wilderness."[143]

Reflecting on the first year or so of the CCP, those involved in its realization were apparently pleased. Eric Johnston boasted that, although the CCP was in its infancy, it resulted in an all-time tourist high in Canada, up about ten per cent over 1947, which would ease the dollar shortage.[144] C.D. Howe pronounced that the US film industry was "faithfully keeping its promise of quid pro quo ... [and] increasing its spending for the production of films in Canada. It is boosting its use of Canadian films and film subjects in the United States. And it is performing an invaluable service in publicizing Canada."[145]

In October 1948, film liaison A.H. Newman informed the Third Dominion-Provincial Tourist Conference that the CCP had brought in US dollars and given Canada widespread publicity in the United States. At no cost to the Dominion, an estimated 241,200,000 theatregoers were exposed to American studios' tourism films about Canada, destined for non-theatrical circuits.[146] The following year, he credited the CCP with "making Hollywood so Canada-conscious that inaccuracies or unfavourable impressions about Canada are no longer likely to find their way into theatrical films."[147] The Massey Commission also weighed in on the "policy of encouraging companies from the United States to produce commercial feature films in Canada on Canadian themes." The CCP scheme "seems to us highly desirable so long as every care is taken that the films, though fictional in character, do not grossly falsify Canadian life or Canadian history." The report recommended that, whenever official assistance was provided to a commercial film, "proper measures be taken to prevent injurious distortion of Canadian institutions or of Canadian history."[148]

NFB Commissioner Ross McLean similarly anticipated encouraging outcomes. He informed a film festival staged by the Hamilton Film Council at McMaster University, "What has been accomplished to date is an indication of the willingness on the part of United States film producers to make a closer study of Canadian backgrounds." It was also evidence "of a greater concern for public enlightenment in the film industry and a desire to share in community life as well as to draw revenues from it."[149] In private, however, McLean was less enthusiastic. Writing to Francis S. Harmon at the MPAA, he complained that the US distribution of Canadian pictures lagged. He was also disappointed that many CCP features dealt with crime or "other forms of the 'cops and robbers' motif," potentially counterproductive to tourism. He did not "mean to say that a limited number of pictures on the work and tradition of the Royal Canadian Mounted Police would not be useful and interesting[,] but surely there is to be found by digging, a great many other stories springing from the development of Canada's national life during the last three centuries."[150]

The Montreal-based journalist Charles J. Lazarus was also critical of the CCP, writing in the *Motion Picture Herald* that it "has met with partial success only." Canadian producers, anticipating a great increase of US production in Canada, were complaining that Hollywood had "not lived up to its pledges." Hollywood location units had "failed to recruit either Canadian studio facilities or personnel."[151] A.H. Newman in confidence assured Harmon that Lazarus's article was "not inspired by the Canadian Government, and that the Canadian Government does not endorse it." He wanted to reassure the MPAA that government officials understood that the use of Canadian production facilities by Hollywood "could only be a by-product of the Project." Harmon surmised that the negative publicity emanated from "people owning studios in Montreal and Quebec who wanted more business from us than they were getting." He emphasized that the MPAA never promised "that any specified number of feature pictures will be made in Canada or any specified amount of production will be transferred from Hollywood to Canada." The main reasons for this lack of such a promise were its economic unfeasibility and fear that other countries would want a similar deal.[152]

Variety later quoted Eric Johnston as stating, "We never committed ourselves for making any pictures in Canada." Rather, the "MPAA merely offers producers every facility for shooting in Canada and we try to be of assistance to the Canadian Film Board [*sic*] here in its handling of Canadian shorts." Concerned about possible pressure for similar arrangements with other countries, the US film industry walked a fine line between advertising Canada in its films and not widely publicizing the CCP. "American film companies are spreading the word abroad that they are no longer willing to turn their pix into illustrated travel folders and make shorts advertising other countries' scenic attractions in order to gain economic advantages from foreign governments," announced *Variety*. Yet an exception was made for Canada, "which has very smooth working relations with the US industry."[153]

Certainly, by the early 1950s, the CCP had shifted away from being a device to save/earn US dollars towards "bringing Canada to the attention of American tourists."[154] As Owensmith once articulated, "Rather than using the broad canvas utilized by your Federal, Provincial and other Canadian public relations agencies, we [Hollywood] are more the little brother specializing in presenting to the US public in particular and the world in general the magnificent attractions of Canada through the medium of motion pictures."[155] Following a lull 1950–52 in feature pictures concerning Canada, in the summer of 1952 producer/director Alfred Hitchcock took a cast and crew to Quebec for location work on *I Confess* (1953), while Twentieth Century–Fox began shooting *Niagara* (dir. by Henry Hathaway, 1953) in Niagara Falls, Ontario. Although these two feature films dealt with such dark subjects as adultery, homicide, trauma from war, and suicide, the marketing of their Canadian locations as tourist destinations served the CCP's goals.

In *I Confess*, a Catholic priest (played by Montgomery Clift) hears a murder confession. Refusing to break church law, he refuses to reveal the killer's identity, even when he is himself accused of the crime. In addition to shots on Quebec City's narrow and cobblestoned streets, scenes included such tourist landmarks as the CPR's Château Frontenac Hotel, the Église Saint Zéphirin-de-Stadacona. the Parliament Building, and the St Lawrence River. Hitchcock selected the city because "of its quaint Old World quality and its architecture of medieval flavor."[156] Raised Catholic, Hitchcock affirmed that "there is no other town on the North American continent, at least to my knowledge, where priests walk around wearing their cassocks (a key plot point), so Quebec is the only suitable city in which to start the plot this way."[157] Here, the director reinforces a common belief that the province's distinctiveness was rooted in its traditional Catholic beliefs. Quebec Premier Maurice Duplessis (in power 1936–39, 1944–59) ran it essentially as a fiefdom, consolidating his power through both church and state, and promoting a society based on Catholicism, a separate French-Canadian culture, and a pastoral way of life.[158]

Given the sensitive nature of this psychological drama, Hitchcock obtained the cooperation of the Catholic church, which assigned Father Paul La Couline as a technical adviser to ensure the script would not offend religious authorities. Recognizing that the arrival of the Hollywood company would generate publicity that would likely benefit the province's tourist trade, government officials extended their support as well. Warner Bros. organized a series of flights to transport newspaper, syndicate, and national-magazine representatives to document filming and generate advance press for the thriller. This also would raise the public profile of its filming location.[159] Despite the dark storyline and noirish aesthetics, in keeping with the CCP the studio promoted the authentic milieu of "colorful" Quebec to encourage tourism (figure 6.5).[160]

Producer Charles Brackett considered Anne Baxter, who performed opposite Clift in *I Confess*, for his upcoming project, *Niagara*. The film ultimately featured Twentieth Century–Fox's rising "blowtorch blonde," Marilyn Monroe, as the *femme fatale* Rose Loomis. Yet for Brackett, the true fulcrum of this Technicolor thriller was the cataract itself. "The object of this film," he wrote, "is to take full advantage of

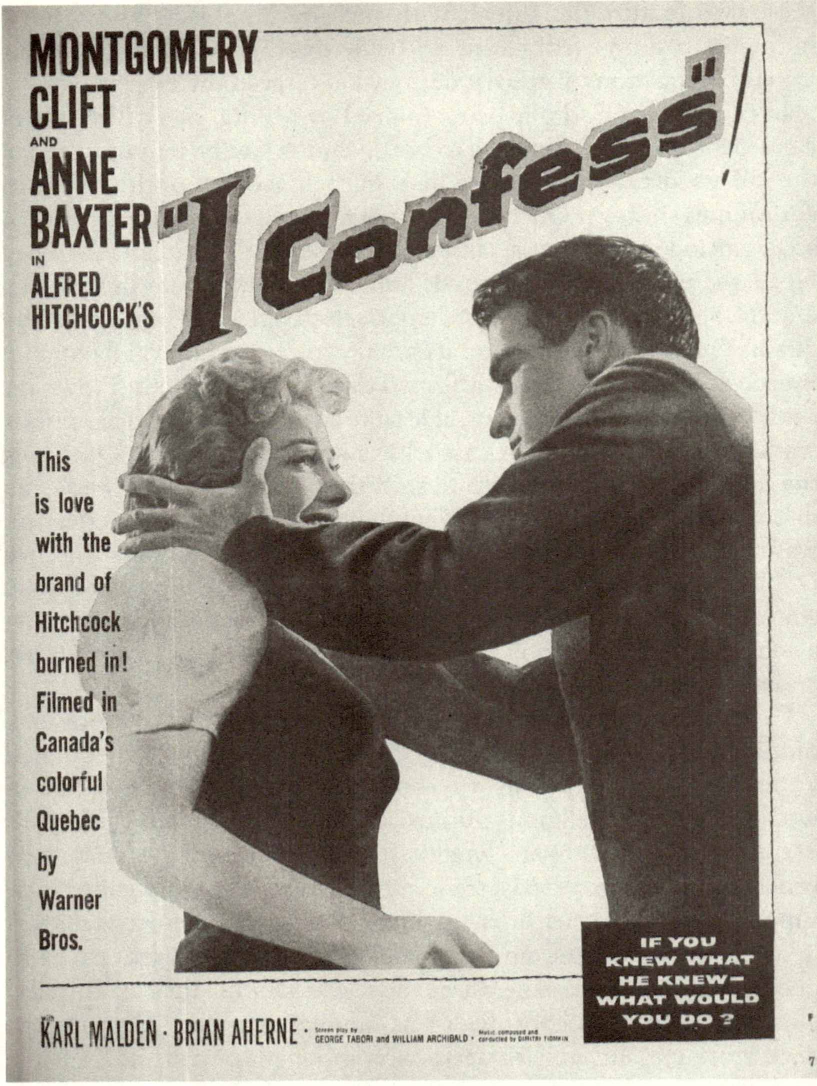

6.5 Advertisement for *I Confess*, *Photoplay*, April 1952

its overpowering, often terrifying beauty – a beauty which brings it more visitors per year than any wonder of nature in the world."[161] On the Canadian side of the falls, Rose and her paramour (Richard Allan) plot to murder her neurotic husband (Joseph Cotten), a battle-weary veteran of the Korean War, while making it appear a suicide.

Meanwhile, Polly and Ray Cutler (Jean Peters and Casey Adams, respectively), an American couple spending a belated honeymoon at the same tourist cabins, are drawn into the unfolding intrigue. Just as tourist-friendly Quebec City served as the setting for Hitchcock's moody parable, the "spectacular scenic beauty" of this postnuptial resort was used as "a locale for murder and infidelity."[162]

In April 1952, a provincial liaison was assigned to work with the studio to ensure maximum tourist-drawing potential under the CCP. Filming over three weeks in June incorporated such attractions as the Carillon Tower, the Cave of the Winds, the Journey behind the Falls, and the *Maid of the Mist*. The resulting sequences emulated a lush travelogue. Regardless, William L. Houck, former mayor of the city and an MLA, decried the film, contending that its morbid plot would turn away visitors. We "do not want to convey the impression that murders are on the rampage here," Houck insisted. He even reportedly wanted the discovery of a corpse in the film to occur on the American side, since locating it in Canada would "be bad for the tourist business."[163]

Conversely, most merchants and local officials believed that this big-budget melodrama would generate tourist dollars and spur economic growth. They were correct; *Niagara* was not only a top earner for the studio that year, but boosted tourism. In the months following simultaneous premières in both border cities on 28 January 1953, the region enjoyed a record-breaking number of visitors, many likely disappointed to learn that the Rainbow Cabins, where the two couples stayed, were a constructed set (costing $26,000). The realistic-looking motel, in Queen Victoria Park and facing the falls, was torn down shortly after location filming wrapped.[164]

Beyond the releases of *I Confess* and *Niagara*, 1953 marked a "new high in Canadian-made 'Hollywood' features. Entire production crews with full equipment were transported to Western Canada and hundreds of thousands of dollars of production money was spent in Canada during this past year."[165] Four multi-million-dollar Technicolor productions – *River of No Return* (dir. by Otto Preminger, 1954), *Rose Marie* (dir. by Mervyn LeRoy, 1954), *Saskatchewan* (dir. by Raoul Walsh, 1954), and *The Far Country* (dir. by Anthony Mann, 1955) – were shot wholly or in part in Alberta between June and September 1953. Together with the tireless efforts of CCP representatives who encouraged producers to go on location, the advent of widescreen technology, which aimed to lure viewers away from their small black-and-white television sets, had sparked "a demand for the big pictorial epic, necessitating as it does the filling in of the background with scenic splendor such as the Rockies can provide."[166]

During his annual Ottawa visit to report on the CCP in June 1953, the MPAA's Taylor Mills met with officials from the CGTB, External Affairs, and Trade and Commerce. According to CBC broadcaster John Fisher, Mills spoke "the language of stars and projects and projectors." Name-dropping such icons as Alan Ladd, Marilyn Monroe, and Jimmy Stewart, he dazzled the stuffy civil servants with "daring new words in the Hollywood lexicon," namely CinemaScope, Cinerama, Stereophonic Sound, Technicolor, and 3D. These new tricks of the screen, he maintained, would give Hollywood a new lease on life, in which Alberta, as "keeper of the Rocky Mountains," would become "the chosen land."[167]

For *River of No Return*, set during the 1870s Gold Rush, Twentieth Century–Fox shot mostly in Banff and Jasper, where the "striking beauties of the Canadian Rockies co-star with the blonde charms of Marilyn Monroe and the masculine muscles of Robert Mitchum in … a fairly diverting western actioner."[168] Using CinemaScope, the new widescreen-motion-picture technology, producer Stanley Rubin and director Otto Preminger captured the river sequences in panoramic pictures and stereophonic sound during the summer of 1953. Although the fictional action of the Technicolor revenge drama unfolds in the American northwest frontier, in keeping with the CCP the studio ensured that audiences were aware that the production was photographed in Alberta. At the conclusion of the film, a title card announces in all caps: "THE TWENTIETH CENTURY-FOX FILM CORPORATION THANKS THE CANADIAN GOVERNMENT FOR ITS COOPERATION IN THE PRODUCTION OF THIS MOTION PICTURE" (figure 6.6).[169]

In a similar fashion, MGM expressed its gratitude to the Canadian government for the making of *Rose Marie*, starring Ann Blyth in the title role, Fernando Lamas as a French-Canadian trapper, and Howard Keel as a scarlet-clad Mountie. This was the third film adaptation of the popular 1924 operetta set in the Canadian Rockies, but the first photographed (at least partially) in Canada, specifically Banff and Jasper.[170] *Rose Marie* was the studio's second use of the novel anamorphic CinemaScope process. As one reviewer noted, "The breathtaking scenic backgrounds of the Canadian Rockies … are alone worth the price of admission" in spite of the film's "rather weak and slow-moving" story.[171] The CGTB capitalized on its tourist possibilities

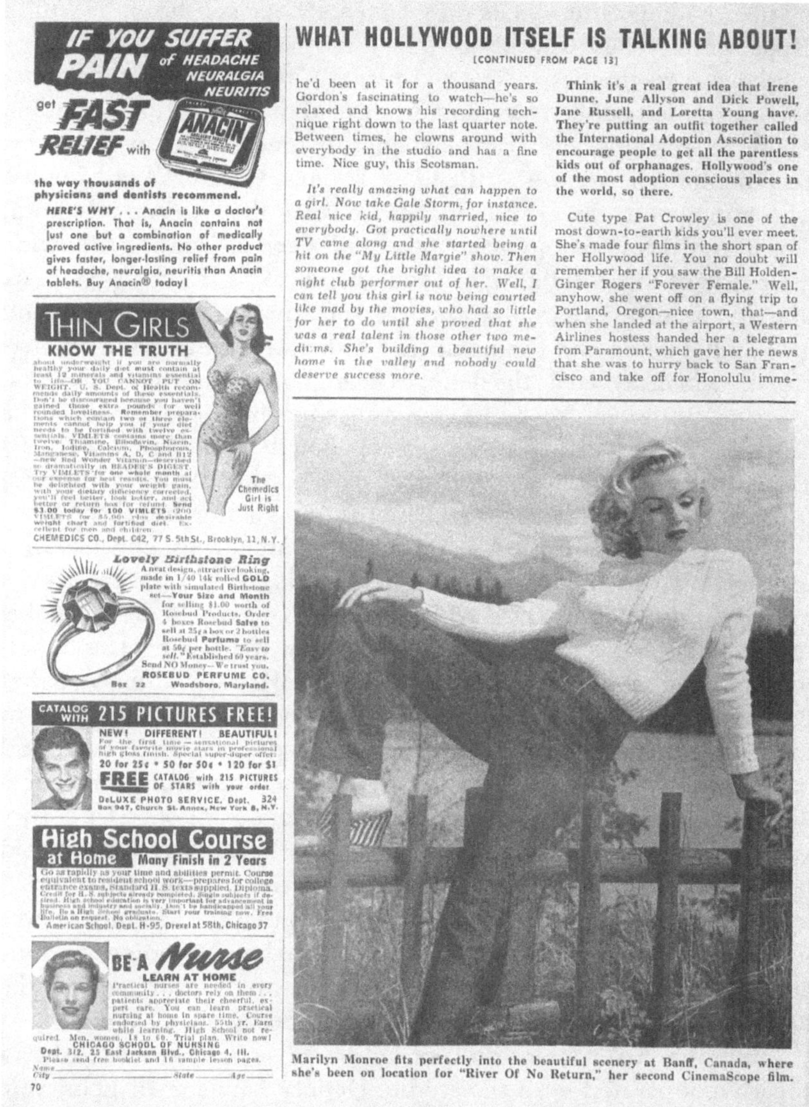

IF YOU SUFFER PAIN of HEADACHE NEURALGIA NEURITIS get FAST RELIEF with ANACIN

the way thousands of physicians and dentists recommend.

HERE'S WHY . . . Anacin is like a doctor's prescription. That is, Anacin contains not just one but a combination of medically proved active ingredients. No other product gives faster, longer-lasting relief from pain of headache, neuralgia, neuritis than Anacin tablets. Buy Anacin® today!

THIN GIRLS KNOW THE TRUTH

The Chemedics Girl is Just Right

CHEMEDICS CO., Dept. C42, 77 S. 5th St., Brooklyn, 11, N.Y.

Lovely Birthstone Ring

A neat design, attractive looking, made in 1/40 14k rolled GOLD plate with simulated Birthstone set—Your Size and Month for selling $1.00 worth of Rosebud Products. Order 4 boxes Rosebud Salve to sell at 25¢ a box or 2 bottles Rosebud Perfume to sell at 50¢ per bottle. "Easy to sell." Established 60 years. Send NO Money—We trust you.

ROSEBUD PERFUME CO. Box 22 Woodsboro, Maryland.

CATALOG WITH 215 PICTURES FREE!

NEW! DIFFERENT! BEAUTIFUL! For the first time—sensational pictures of your favorite movie stars in professional high gloss finish. Special super-duper offer: 20 for 25¢ • 50 for 50¢ • 120 for $1

FREE CATALOG with 215 PICTURES OF STARS with your order

DeLUXE PHOTO SERVICE, Dept. 324 Box 947, Church St. Annex, New York 8, N.Y.

High School Course at Home Many Finish in 2 Years

Go as rapidly as your time and abilities permit. Course equivalent to resident school work—prepares for college entrance exams. Standard H. S. texts supplied. Diploma.

American School, Dept. H-95, Drexel at 58th, Chicago 37

BE A Nurse

LEARN AT HOME

Practical nurses are needed in every community . . . doctors rely on them . . . patients appreciate their cheerful, expert care. You can learn practical nursing at home in spare time. Course endorsed by physicians. 55th yr. Earn while learning. High School not required. Men, women, 18 to 60. Trial plan. Write now!

CHICAGO SCHOOL OF NURSING

Dept. 312, 25 East Jackson Blvd., Chicago 4, Ill.

Please send free booklet and 16 sample lesson pages.

Name

City State Age

70

WHAT HOLLYWOOD ITSELF IS TALKING ABOUT!

[CONTINUED FROM PAGE 13]

he'd been at it for a thousand years. Gordon's fascinating to watch—he's so relaxed and knows his recording technique right down to the last quarter note. Between times, he clowns around with everybody in the studio and has a fine time. Nice guy, this Scotsman.

It's really amazing what can happen to a girl. Now take Gale Storm, for instance. Real nice kid, happily married, nice to everybody. Got practically nowhere until TV came along and she started being a hit on the "My Little Margie" show. Then someone got the bright idea to make a night club performer out of her. Well, I can tell you this girl is now being courted like mad by the movies, who had so little for her to do until she proved that she was a real talent in those other two mediums. She's building a beautiful new home in the valley and nobody could deserve success more.

Think it's a real great idea that Irene Dunne, June Allyson and Dick Powell, Jane Russell, and Loretta Young have. They're putting an outfit together called the International Adoption Association to encourage people to get all the parentless kids out of orphanages. Hollywood's one of the most adoption conscious places in the world, so there.

Cute type Pat Crowley is one of the most down-to-earth kids you'll ever meet. She's made four films in the short span of her Hollywood life. You no doubt will remember her if you saw the Bill Holden-Ginger Rogers "Forever Female." Well, anyhow, she went off on a flying trip to Portland, Oregon—nice town, that—and when she landed at the airport, a Western Airlines hostess handed her a telegram from Paramount, which gave her the news that she was to hurry back to San Francisco and take off for Honolulu imme-

Marilyn Monroe fits perfectly into the beautiful scenery at Banff, Canada, where she's been on location for "River Of No Return," her second CinemaScope film.

6.6 Article about *River of No Return*, *Screenland*, December 1953

by offering free 18" x 24" colour travel posters for department-store displays, combined with film stills stressing the Canadian locations, or for local tourism bureaux, with the following sign: "Plan your vacation trip to breath-taking Canada here now; see the beauty of the great Canadian outdoors as only CinemaScope can bring to you in 'Rose Marie'" (figure 6.7).[172]

Likewise, to emphasize *Saskatchewan*'s Canadian setting, its pressbook proposed publicity around displays of the CNR, CPR, Canadian Pacific Steamships, and Trans-Canada Air Lines.[173] Set in 1877, this Technicolor epic stars Alan Ladd as Thomas O'Rourke, a Mountie who attempts to thwart an alliance between the "hostile" (Lakota) Sioux from Montana and the "peaceful" Cree of Canada following the Battle of Little Bighorn, in Montana, in 1876. To cross-promote tourism, a puff piece in *Modern Screen* featured a rugged Ladd and his family golfing and fishing at the "lush and famous Banff Springs Hotel," which served as the de-facto headquarters for the Hollywood invasion. Referring to Banff, the fan magazine proclaimed: "The Canadian mountains are advertisement enough for *Saskatchewan*."[174] The national park, however, is located over 500 kilometres (311 miles) from the Cypress Hills region where the film's action unfolds.

Cypress Hills, in both Alberta and Saskatchewan, consists of a forested plateau rising above the grassy plains, as opposed to the towering Canadian Rockies, which the studio deemed more amenable to the wide-angle screen. In a press story written by Universal-International's publicity department, director Raoul Walsh stated that Banff was "extremely suitable for the new wide screen processes. In the USA. we have literally used up every spectacular background location and people ... Canada offers us new territories and new dimensions."[175] The film's inaccuracies did not go unnoticed. BC Tory MP Major-General George R. Pearkes, a former RCMP officer, told Parliament that *Saskatchewan* was a "travesty of the true facts." Ignoring settler-colonial violence, he asserted that the Mounties never killed large numbers of "natives" nor engaged with "Indians in murderous battle." He was concerned that public funds resulting from the CCP "were expended in the production of this atrocious film."[176]

While the government did not subsidize *Saskatchewan*, Alberta eagerly cooperated with the studio. Deputy Minister of Economic Affairs Ralph Moore, the province's executive contact for the US-based filmmakers, defended the film and his department's involvement: "People go to the movies to be entertained, not to receive a history lesson," he asserted, adding that Hollywood routinely takes liberties in adapting factual history to a fictional tale: "As it stands, 'Saskatchewan' is a fine movie which shows to the credit of western Canada the beautiful scenery of the Rocky Mountains."[177] Further, the

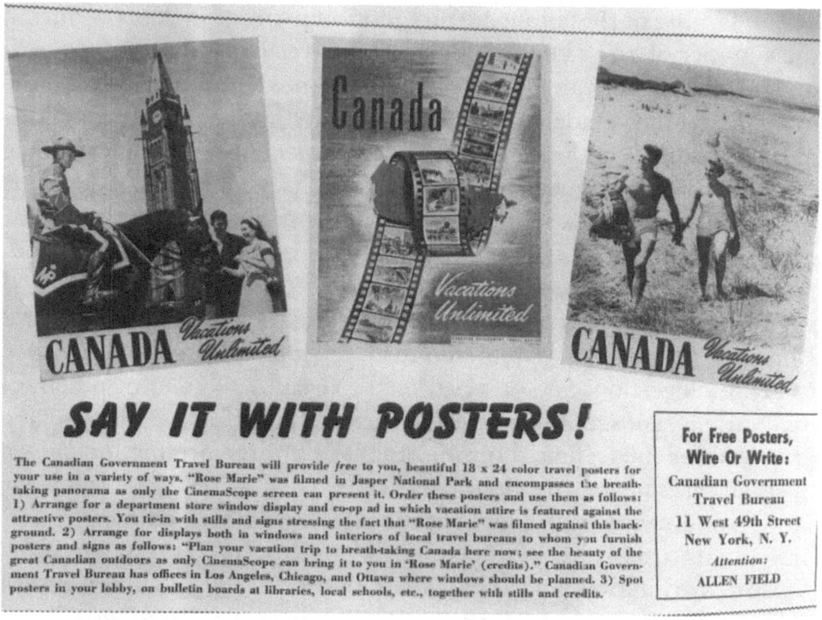

6.7 Advertisement for *Rose Marie*, 1954

studio employed more than three hundred local Canadians. According to Alberta's Film and Photographic Branch, "Local people and industry in Alberta were benefitted by about two million dollars."[178]

Lastly, during the summer of 1953, Universal-International filmed *The Far Country* in and around Jasper, including the Athabasca Glacier and the Columbia Icefield, with Dominion and provincial assistance. In this psychological Western, Jeff Webster (Jimmy Stewart [Oscar winner, 1940]) and his partner, Ben Tatum (Walter Brennan [1936, 1938, 1940]), drive a herd of cattle up north to Skagway, Alaska, to sell. In the Klondike, Jeff confronts the elements and the lawlessness and greed of the goldfields. Publicity centred on Canada's beautiful backgrounds and included suggestions for tie-ins with the Canadian railways, the CGTB, and travel agencies. A suggested window ad announced: "Trips to THE FAR COUNTRY ... that place you have always planned to visit." The publicity department also recommended playing up the ski angle by approaching local department stores about "a tie-up in which title and scenes from 'THE FAR COUNTRY' are utilized as copy angles for newspaper ads and as a theme for a special window on ski clothes and equipment."[179]

The filming of these four feature motion pictures in Alberta during the summer of 1953 kept CCP representatives busy fulfilling requests and helping to facilitate production and the movement of cast and crew into and out of Canada. The CCP arranged for road permits, reductions in customs duties or duty-free entry of equipment, the customs clearance of railway baggage cars, and permission to charter aircraft loaded with film equipment and personnel for location filming. Furthermore, Henshaw, Mills, and Owensmith provided research material on subjects related to the settings and screened Canadian 16-mm tourism films to show shootable types of scenery. MGM, Twentieth Century–Fox, and Universal-International submitted early versions of the shooting scripts to invite suggestions and observations "to ensure maximum authenticity." Studios sent scouting parties to inspect filming sites, while the CCP arranged for the feeding, housing, and work of the production crews, in some cases nearly one hundred people. The CCP delegates also put Hollywood people in contact with local government and commercial individuals to assist them in planning.[180]

After working with various directors, producers, and stars associated with *River of No Return*, *Rose Marie*, *Saskatchewan*, and *The Far Country*, Ralph Moore informed Owensmith that "all of the people I met appeared very satisfied with the cooperation from here." He personally thanked the CCP representative for "helping to bring these people here," which would publicize Alberta as both a destination for future feature-film production and for tourism.[181] In reality, Universal-International was disgruntled with its experience shooting *Saskatchewan* and *The Far Country* on location. Owensmith informed Henshaw that the studio claimed that the Banff-based Brewster Transportation Company committed "one of the most blatant cases of bare-faced blackmail known in the industry. They had the Company over a barrel and there was nothing they could do but pay or pull out of Canada." Commercial companies similarly "gouged" Twentieth Century–Fox with "overcharges of between $125,000 and $200,000, after firm prices had been quoted; deliberate threats of 'pulling' men, machines and cattle off locations unless higher prices were paid." Owensmith feared that Alberta would be put on a Hollywood "blacklist." "As you know, Ralph Moore is one of our most ardent supporters," he added, "and personally I feel it is a great shame that the word has now got around the industry that although all departments of the Canadian Government, both Federal and Provincial, bent over backwards to help in every way possible, Alberta should be shunned like the plague unless something can be done to ameliorate the situations found this summer in certain sections of this Province by the Companies in their business dealings with certain individual contractors."[182]

Despite the negative feedback, in the Cold War context of enhanced cultural, defence, and economic relationships across the border, the MPAA in 1954 voted to extend the CCP "as a living example of the mutual benefits derived from cooperation rather than retaliation in international trade."[183] In its 1955 report, the MPAA continued to tout the program's success. Since its implementation in 1948, the CCP had resulted in 1,179 US newsreel items about Canada and its people, 123 short subjects, and 153 feature films either made in Canada or containing Canadian sequences, characters, or references. Due to the efforts of the CCP representatives, "Canada has become a by-word to studio heads, producers, writers, story department heads, location departments and library and research departments."[184] Yet although the CCP officially continued through 1958, the quid-pro-quo scheme petered out after 1955, especially following the retirement of Owensmith – the most visible and ardent champion of the project. In July 1955, Alfred Corwin, with the press-relations staff at the MPAA's New York office, succeeded him as Hollywood contact for the CCP.

Described by Canadian nationalist and popular historian Pierre Berton as "a public relation man's boondoggle," the MPAA never intended that the CCP – this "gentleman's agreement" – would commit the US film industry to making feature pictures in Canada, as it feared other countries would want to broker a similar arrangement.[185] As Owensmith stated, for the MPAA, any full-length production filmed north of the border "is pure gravy" for Canada – "purely a little extra premium which we have been able to arrange."[186] The CCP, however, was more than window dressing, but rather reflected enduring Canadian efforts to use film to sell the country as a northern getaway to American tourists.

The CCP materialized out of Canada's ongoing wartime and later need for US currency via tourism development and consumer diplomacy. Attracting middle-brow American tourists by cooperating with the US film industry was not a novel approach for Canada in 1948. Beyond economic exchange, however, the free movement of tourists across the border served to promote western values and alliance-building within the intensifying Cold War and the emergence of global mass tourism. Wagering that defeat of the fascist Axis was inevitable, Canadian officials at the Dominion and provincial levels planned for what would become the Victory Vacation year of 1946–47. To stymie any latent anti-Americanism or resentment of American cultural imperialism, officials developed a campaign to encourage Canadians to treat these guests with courtesy and kindness.

Building on wartime reconstruction plans, the CGTB, the NFB, the Parks Branch, and several provincial film-publicity bureaux produced, sponsored, and distributed 16-mm films, most notably through the Canadian Travel Film Library and Summer Tourist Program, to entice the coveted American tourist. These productions balanced the familiar themes of an accessible paradise for anglers, golfers, outdoor enthusiasts, and skiers with images of vibrant cities and communities rife with Old World charm. Despite the record-breaking tourist season of 1947–48, the currency crisis deepened, which motivated coordinated efforts to further expand tourism. Stakeholders also supported cooperation with Hollywood, which faced unprecedented postwar challenges, to bring in more US dollars, enhance bilateral commercial, cultural, and political relations, and more generally publicize Canada through feature films, newsreel content, and short subjects. Ultimately, the CCP was short-lived, and the lionized place of the tourism film in Canadian culture would give way to the primacy of television advertising by mid-century.

Conclusion

Did the Tourism Film Pay Off?

Following approximately five decades of trial and error, from fleeting glimpses of Canadian tourist attractions in actualities to the anamorphic widescreen processes of the early 1950s, the tourism film within Canada had come of age. Yet the question remained: "Does the Travel Film Pay Off?" This was the title of a Canadian Government Travel Bureau (CGTB) report presented to the Eleventh Dominion-Provincial Tourist Conference in 1956, which determined that tourism films generated a significant return on their investment. Within the postwar culture of bureaucratic rationality, the CGTB used applied research, data, statistics, and surveys to gauge film's effectiveness as promotion. For example, a 1955 survey of American visitors confirmed that "the cumulative effect of Canadian Travel Films is becoming more evident each year." When asked, "WHAT MOSTLY INFLUENCED YOU TO COME TO CANADA FOR YOUR VACATION?" of the 33,000 replies, "6.1% credited 'FILMS' as the reason, and 3.5% credited 'TELEVISION.'" Films in this case included not only government-sponsored tourism films, but also references to Canada in Hollywood motion pictures and non-travel films produced by the NFB, which held that "any type of material which brings the name of Canada before the peoples of other countries is, in a sense, travel promotion." This included NFB newsreels distributed to the United States, "any of which are of tourist value." According to the 1955 report, visitors lured to Canada "through this medium of promotion" represented "a sizeable group – 420,470 according to statistics – and they spent about $22,000,000 while up here."[1]

To illustrate, the CGTB cited figures related to *Rocky Mountain Trout* (dir. by Grant Crabtree, 1947). Produced by Crawley Films and filmed in Jasper, it portrayed "the grandeur of the Canadian Rockies and the enjoyment of fishermen." The 15-minute, 16-mm production (in colour and sound) along with prints cost $29,707. It proved a recurring asset; since its release, it had "promoted Canada's Tourist Industry pictorially to audiences totalling nearly thirteen millions … which figures out at less than ¼ of a cent per impression." Distributed through Canadian Travel Film Library outlets, it would have "many future years of usefulness, especially when colour TV becomes more universal, and the resulting costs 'per minute of impression' will be even lower."[2] In addition to direct screenings in the United States, the film had already been telecast in 106 cities in 36 states and viewed by "a minimum television audience of 10,100,00."[3]

Certainly, television had become increasingly crucial for mid-century tourism. As early as 1948, delegates at the Third Dominion-Provincial Tourist Conference discussed for the first time the prospects of this relatively new medium. "Conservative estimates show that some television sets will be installed in the United States by the end of the year," so NFB Secretary Alan Field reported that the film board was preparing a program of five tourism films for the CGTB expressly for TV distribution to thirteen US stations via its New York office.[4] Shot in 16-mm Kodachrome, and processed into black-and-white prints for television, *Canoeing and Camping*, *Cruising to Canada*, *Sports Fishing across Canada*, *Winter Carnival*, and *Youth Hostelling* display the nation "as a haven for vacationers."[5] NFB Director of Distribution J.D. Ralph also announced that 60 films, "the great majority of tourist interest," were televised in the United States to an estimated 7 million viewers.[6]

While producers of feature-length motion pictures struggled to meet competition from such home-based leisure activities as television viewing by offering, according to J.J. Fitzgibbons, "more expensive and higher quality product," television broadcasts provided Canadian tourism films with additional audiences.[7] As part of the drive to develop television use, in September 1954 the CGTB opened a free Travel Film Television Library in its New York office. Boasting some two dozen titles at its start, it expanded to 38 over two years. By the end of September 1956, "Canadian travel films had been telecast a total of 3,613 times by 215 US television stations. Altogether, the films have been telecast in 178 cities in 44 states."[8] In 1959, the CGTB wound down its film program to focus on TV advertising to an open-ended mass market.[9]

By the close of the 1950s, the tourism and film nexus had undergone a sea change, marked by the waning of the Canadian Cooperation Project (CCP), the transition towards television production, and the resignation of D. Leo Dolan – the "Barnum of the tourist business" – from the CGTB in 1957. Alan Field, who took over the travel bureau's New York office after resigning as NFB secretary when it reorganized in 1950, succeeded Dolan, demonstrating the continuing close links between these two Dominion agencies. As a testament to his decades-long relationship with Hollywood insiders, Dolan was appointed Canada's consul general at Los Angeles. He hoped to continue hyping "Canadian scenery to film makers, looking for Canadian stories for the films, plugging Canadian talent."[10] He served there until 1960, but it is unclear whether his role there helped continue Canadian tourism promotion in Hollywood.

Perhaps unintentionally marking these shifts, at decade's end the NFB produced for the Canadian Tourist Association (CTA) *Tourist Go Home* (dir. by Stanley Jackson and Ronald Weyman, 1959). This 25-minute production introduces the fictitious Canadian Anti-Tourist League, which criticizes the government for using "our taxes to sell our birthright" by producing tourism films. The tongue-in-cheek effort also features a smuggled, uncut film-within-a-film, complete with an insipid symphonic soundtrack, which shows an average Michigan family vacationing in Ontario's Muskoka region and Algonquin Park. Its less-than-flattering portrayal of the foursome hints at Canadian society's latent anti-Americanism. The whining tourists encounter surly customer service, Japanese-made "Indian" souvenirs, substandard facilities, and unappetizing meals. While the CTA intended the film to educate tourist operators and employees on how *not* to handle visitors, in a similar vein to *Welcome, Neighbour!* released a decade earlier, its "provocative title" hinted at worries about over-tourism[11] (figure 7.1).

Films such as *Tourist Go Home* produced in institutional settings and with institutional funding, as Heide Solbrig states, support and reproduce "the ideological frameworks of the state."[12] The sponsored production insinuated, in satirical fashion, that Canada had become a victim of its own success; the strategy of using film (Canadian/American and/or public/private) as a marketing tool during the first half of the twentieth century unquestionably resulted in an influx of visitors. At the same time, tourism films furthered a settler-colonial destination brand in which Canada functioned as a northern getaway for restless and demanding American tourists. As the fictitious members of the

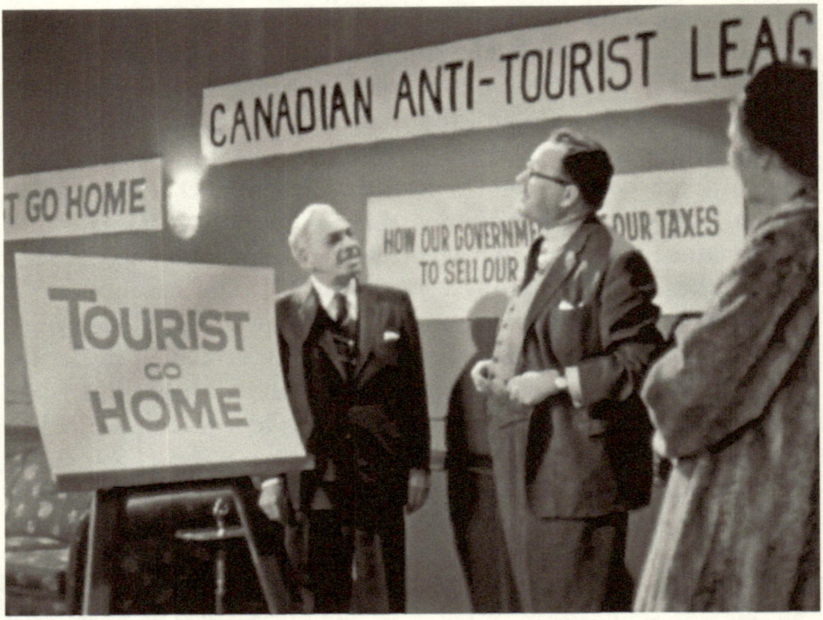

7.1 NFB, *Tourist Go Home*, 1959

Anti-Tourist League observe, US visitors flock in every summer like "locusts" and proceed to "destroy our peace and quiet," cause traffic jams, over-fish the country's rivers and lakes, breathe our "fresh air," and eat our "own fried egg sandwiches." Obliquely addressing US cultural imperialism, *Tourist Go Home* suggested that, despite the temporary inconveniences, tourism was "everybody's business" – the sponsoring CTA's mantra. That is, tourist spending on goods and services in any part of the nation provided economic growth and jobs that benefitted all citizens.[13]

Tourism's role in economic development was one of the key pillars upholding policies related to marketing by sponsoring or producing public and private films. As author T. Morris Longstreth once observed, "The tourist is God's gift to a producing country, because he consumes without producing."[14] For the first half of the twentieth century, Canada hankered specifically for "His Majesty, the American Tourist," and his/her coveted US dollars.[15] The prospect of economic gains motivated governments to invest in tourism films or to encourage and/or collaborate with private commercial studios or filmmakers from both countries.

Since the first actualities c. 1900 through Edison's CPR melodramas of 1910, as we saw in chapter 1, boosters recognized early on that motion pictures delivered ample returns on invested capital to local and national economies. Beyond "armchair tourism," these first tourism films not only presented novel ways of seeing Canada, but also were intended to influence travel-making decisions. Whether fiction or non-fiction, the intense filmic impressions animated spectators to *see themselves* as consumers of tourism services, such as railways and hotels, and guided their expectations of the destination. As psychologist Walter Dill Scott wrote about the power of advertising, observing passengers in a railway tourism film would "stimulate me to imitate their action, i.e., to get aboard the train and enjoy its luxuries."[16] Motion pictures encouraged non-conscious mimicry, with on-screen tourists functioning as exemplars of consumer behaviour.

With the groundswell of nationalism brought about by the First World War, direct provincial and Dominion involvement in film production increased to solicit trade and tourism. As chapter 2 revealed, the Exhibits and Publicity Bureau/Canadian Government Motion Picture Bureau (CGMPB) recognized the advertising potential of "useful pictures" to bolster the Dominion's growing tourism industry during the 1920s through its Seeing Canada series. "Where Hollywood films are tinsel and show," wrote Kenneth S. Edey of the *Ottawa Journal*, "Bureau subjects are leaping waterfalls, stately mountains or the beautiful public buildings and hurrying crowds of the larger Canadian cities." Yet this did not prevent the Dominion from cooperating with American film producers to encourage Hollywood's inclusion of Canadian tourist destinations in their productions. As Edey continued, "The advertising force of the fictional film background is quite imponderable, but without doubt enormous ... The assurance that the more subtle and possibly more powerful appeal of the background of fictional film shall be authenticated as Canadian, when it is such, is evidence that the Motion Picture Bureau is steadily penetrating into the larger field, and for doing so the Bureau deserves full credit."[17]

As a greater number of "dry" Americans with more discretionary income and leisure time crossed their border into their largely "wet" neighbour during prohibition, the CGMPB maintained that its impressive film program helped cause the country's record-breaking tourism numbers. The onset of the Depression stymied this boom. Government officials again contended that boosting tourism would stimulate overall economic growth. A case in point is the appeal of tourism films concerning the Dionne Quintuplets and Quintupletland, which produced a spike in tourist traffic by the mid-1930s far beyond northern Ontario. Recognizing the monetary value of a thriving tourist trade, the Dominion established the Canadian (Government) Travel Bureau (CTB/CGTB) – the topic of chapter 4 – to centralize its tourism promotion.

Lacking the means to make their own films, these two Dominion agencies – for tourism and for motion pictures, respectively – fostered unofficial ties with Hollywood studios and filmmakers, such as James FitzPatrick at MGM, which had increased its production of talking travelogues and other short subjects within the consolidating US film industry. The CGMPB, however, struggled due to Depression-era budgetary constraints, which had prevented its conversion to sound technology. Cognizant of film's centrality in the development of the tourism industry, it moved away from 35-mm theatrical productions and concentrated on 16-mm films directed at market-segmented non-theatrical audiences in the United States.

For its part, the Parks Branch (chapter 3) distanced itself from the CGMPB and instead financed in its own film productions between the wars. As Commissioner James Harkin told the Senate's Select Committee on Tourist Traffic in 1934, "The main purpose of the National Parks organization is the preservation and development of what I might call the raw material for tourists." To that end, W.J. Oliver made tourism films that presented the parks, particularly in the Rockies, as *terra nullius* (nobody's land) for the American auto-tourist, fashioning through film a vision of the landscape and wildlife that communicated the ongoing legacy of settler-colonial elimination and appropriation of First Nations. For the parks commissioner, the overarching goal was to attract the "foreign tourist trade," specifically Americans, whose dollars helped ease the balance of trade.[18]

Canada's wartime economy likewise relied heavily on US trade, its largest source of outside capital. Seeking an infusion of greenbacks, the CGTB and the new National Film Board (NFB) cooperated to convey to their then-neutral neighbours that tourism was "business as usual" and to counteract Axis propaganda against border-crossing. Although Commissioner John Grierson and his successor, Ross McLean, at times disparaged travelogues for portraying a land solely for "fishing, golf and the observation of wild animals," the NFB's commitment to documentary film sparked unconventional approaches to tourism films (see chapter 5).[19] This included nurturing amateur filmmakers, most notably the Crawleys, buoyed by expanding networks for US non-theatrical distribution.

As Eric Barnouw notes in his history of the documentary film, "The 16mm film had grown up in war" and would advance after 1945.[20] Wartime cross-border collaboration through such agencies as the [US] Office of War Information (OWI) and Canada's Bureau of Public Information–turned–Wartime Information Board (BPI/WIB) set the stage for widening the NFB's free distribution of its non-theatrical tourism films when peace came. This is evident in the NFB's launch of its travel-film libraries (in conjunction with the CGTB) in the United States and its Summer Tourist Program of film showings aimed at US tourists vacationing in Canada. The Dominion government had turned energetically to producing or sponsoring and distributing 16-mm tourism films in the hopes of enticing Victory Vacationers (and their greenbacks). During post-1945 reconstruction, the dire need for US currency led in 1948 to creation of the Canadian Cooperation Project (CCP), whereby Hollywood would produce feature films and travelogues aimed at stimulating Canada's tourist trade and easing the dollar crisis (see chapter 6). CCP proponents remarked that, since its inception, US tourists in Canada had been spending about $2 million a year more than in 1947.[21] Moreover, nearly every province "at some time had films specially produced on behalf of some branch or department," with Alberta, British Columbia, Ontario, and Nova Scotia coordinating film-tourism activities.[22] Provinces typically adopted a regional approach, targeting adjacent areas of the United States, while the Dominion continued national marketing of tourism through film. By and large, the relationship within and between the Dominion and provincial governments in this field was more collaborative than competitive.

Beyond aiding economic development, the tourism film served sociocultural functions. As Rick Prelinger observes, ephemeral productions are "not simply documents of how things looked or how people behaved, but they're documentation of how it was wished that people would behave."[23] Tourism films curated ideal tourism experiences – highlighting certain destinations and activities while omitting others, essentially teaching spectators how to be good tourists. Emergent film technology at the turn of the twentieth century, part of a broader shift towards mass consumerism and modernity, offered novel ways of experiencing spaces and places through the production and circulation of moving images, thus creating unique visual settler-colonial iconographies of tourist destinations in Canada. Films dealing with railways and later automobiles particularly fashioned these modern, mobile forms of tourist perception.

Likewise, educators glommed onto the pedagogical possibilities of tourism films. Progressive-era moral reformers held that moving pictures of differing lands and peoples could serve as "an educational instrument of great service and a source of wholesome recreation" for diverse audiences.[24] Furthermore, the visual-instruction movement, which intensified after 16-mm technology emerged in 1923, heralded the educational use of motion pictures, arguing that the "eye gate" outpaced the "ear gate" for learning and retention. This is also in keeping with the period's psychology of film and advertising, which contended that moving images perpetuated a consumerist mentality.

Purveyors of 16-mm tourism films within educational contexts (colleges, extension programs, public schools, universities), often under the subject heading of geography, counted on them to inspire hundreds of thousands of viewers to visit the places they saw on screen. Classrooms were largely unaware of the travelogue as a discreet form of manipulation, which caused some visual educators to worry that these free so-called educational films were indeed ads for tourism. Although evidence that viewing tourism films resulted directly in actual travel was largely anecdotal, government officials continually pointed to rising tourist numbers as proof that film campaigns worked. In contrast to Canadian-themed feature films, believed to stir emotional reactions that could influence travel decisions, non-theatrical tourism films were a form of indirect advertising that appealed to the intellect. Government officials also anticipated that sponsored/produced travelogues could remedy incorrect impressions produced by the popular northwest melodramas of the 1910s and 1920s.

Whether fiction or non-fiction, film functioned as a form of propaganda to promote tourism. John Grierson enthusiastically embraced film as an instrument of propaganda, whether to foster democratic citizenship, bolster the war effort, or encourage tourism. As his British documentary colleague Paul Rotha writes, "In one form or another, directly or indirectly, all films are propagandist, negative or positive, for their place of origin." Regardless of whether or not audiences are aware of this fact, they will be swayed by this "most influential medium" to "believe this or do that."[25] The Dominion's use of film to promote tourism stemmed from propaganda techniques developed during the First World War. Buoyed by a wave of patriotism and a distaste for American jingoism, it saw the war stimulate a modest, homegrown film industry that in peacetime would become a forerunner in the production of state-sponsored "useful pictures," which it directed at the US tourist market. Film propaganda would later educate Canadians on the economic value of American tourism and/or instruct them to be courteous and friendly hosts.

During the Second World War and its aftermath, the tourism film also served as a tool of intercultural diplomacy between the two nations – initially to bolster hemispheric defence against the Axis powers and subsequently to contain communism. Tourism, defined by the largely unfettered movement of individuals across national borders, was a vibrant example of democracy in action in contrast to totalitarianism. Recreational travel equally boosted morale or offered therapy for a war-weary populace. Moreover, Canada recognized that robust tourism could generate (albeit-limited) "soft power"; fortifying sociocultural bonds through tourism might even influence geopolitical relationships. Hollywood film studios highlighted Canada in their pre-1941 travelogues that emphasized bilateral friendship, while through such wartime agencies as the United States' OWI and Canada's BPI/WIB, the two nations liaised over their film propaganda to communicate an appreciation of neighbourliness and cooperation. "Nations fighting on the battlefields for their existence," wrote an American correspondent, "must not fight each other for screen space."[26]

Following the war, government officials and tourism boosters argued that the tourist trade would not only aid economic recovery, but also deepen cross-border ties forged during the conflict. According to Parks Branch Director Roy A. Gibson, "This is a business which will be most advantageous to us, not only for the tourist dollars, but for the better understanding which we will have with our neighbours."[27] Tourism films figured as evidence of freedom and prosperity and a persuasive weapon in the fight against communism. The besieged NFB, for example, ramped up its production and/or distribution of tourism films – emblems of free enterprise – to stave off accusations of communist infiltration during the early Cold War's climate of paranoia. This denoted a contradictory blend of state-supported elite culture (16-mm documentary film) and mass culture (tourism), as well as a combination of nationalist and internationalist methods. Yet while the NFB routinely considered *any* film with Canadian content potential propaganda for tourism, the CGTB aimed to specify or standardize the elements of an effective tourism-encouragement film that other agencies could emulate.

Finally, tourism films must be viewed as settler-colonial narratives that Canada used to sell itself to another settler state. Steeped in the trappings of national mythmaking, scenic pictures depict landscapes, non-consumptive wildlife, and recreational activities in ways that erased the violent displacement of First Nations from the land and pushed Indigenous peoples to the periphery, typically under the pretext of development and progress. When made visible, "Indians," to paraphrase Natalie J.K. Baloy, appear as spectacles and/or spectres.[28] Manifesting the unfinished business of colonialism, they haunt tourist spaces as guides, cultural performances and visual art as conservationists, or Hollywood productions as background extras. Even when Indigenous peoples are rendered invisible or marginalized, tourism films legitimize white entitlement to the land for the temporary and transitory enjoyment of the American tourist.

Notes

COMMONLY CITED PERIODICALS AND NEWSPAPERS (WITH ABBREVIATIONS)

American Cinematographer (AC)
The Billboard
Boxoffice (BO)
Business Screen Magazine (BSM)
Canadian Moving Picture Digest (CMPD)
The Daily Colonist (TDC)
Documentary Film News (DFN)
Documentary News Letter (DNL)
Educational Film Magazine (EFM)
Educational Screen (ES)
Exhibitors Herald (EH)
Exhibitors Herald-World (EHW)
Exhibitors Weekly (EW)
Film Daily (FD)
Film News (FN)
The Globe
The Globe and Mail (GAM)
Home Movies
The Lethbridge Herald (LH)
Maclean's
Modern Screen (MS)
Motion Picture Daily (MPD)
Motion Picture Herald (MPH)
Motion Picture News (MPD)
Motography
Movie Makers Magazine (MMM)
Moving Picture Age (MPA)
Moving Picture Weekly
Moving Picture World (MPW)
New York Clipper
New York Dramatic Mirror (NYDM)
New York Times (NYT)
The Nickelodeon
The Optical Lantern and Cinematograph Journal (OLCJ)
Photoplay
Picture Play Magazine (PPM)
Reel and Slide (RAS)
See and Hear (SAH)
Showmen's Trade Review (STR)
Toronto Daily Star (TDS)
The Toronto World
Transactions of the Society of Motion Picture Engineers (TSMPE)
Variety
Visual Education (VE)
Wainwright Star (WS)

INTRODUCTION

1 Aydelotte, "Your Vacation in Hollywood – and the Cost," 12.
2 Research into destination or place branding started in the 1990s, and the literature expanded rapidly. See Anholt, "Nation-Brands of the Twenty-first Century"; Gnoth, "Branding Tourism Destinations"; Kotler, Haider, and Rein, *Marketing Places.*
3 See, for example, Beeton, *Film-Induced Tourism*; Buchmann, "Planning and Development in Film Tourism"; Croy, "Film Tourism"; Heitmann, "Film Tourism Planning and Development"; Hudson and Ritchie, "Promoting Destinations via Film Tourism."
4 *Report of Proceedings, Third Dominion-Provincial Tourist Conference*, 9.
5 "Travelogue" is a neologism attributed to the American illustrated-travel lecturer Burton Holmes in 1903, which has become the standard expression (Barber, "The Roots of Travel Cinema," 82). According to Jennifer Peterson, the travelogue "began to take shape as a film genre with specific formal and stylistic conventions around 1907" (Peterson, *Education in the School of Dreams*, 3).
6 Francis, *Selling Canada*, 170, 176.
7 *Destination Canada*, "Brand Identity," accessed 31 March 2021, https://brand.destinationcanada.com/en/brand-identity.
8 Hulette, "An Interview with Thomas A. Edison," 104. Benedict Anderson coined the term "imagined communities" in his 1983 study of nationalism and national identity (Anderson, *Imagined Communities*).
9 *MPN*, 14 October 1922, cover; *VE*, February 1923, 57.
10 Hearon, "New Film Sources and How to Get Information about Them," 196. Fanning Hearon was the executive director of the Association of School Film Libraries.
11 Morgan and Pritchard, *Tourism Promotion and Power*, 72–7.
12 See, for example, Czach, "A Thrill Every Minute!"
13 "HoMer Network," accessed 23 July 2020, http://homernetwork.org/about; Maltby, "New Cinema Histories," 3. See also Biltereyst, Maltby, and Meers, *The Routledge Companion to New Cinema History*; Chapman, *Film and History*; Chapman, Glancy, and Harper, *The New Film History.*
14 Solbrig, "Orphans No More," 100.
15 "Prelinger Archives," accessed 22 July 2020, https://archive.org/details/prelinger?&sort=titleSorter&page=2. The National Film Preservation Archive (NFPA), which the US Congress formed in 1997 as a non-profit organization to save the country's film heritage, has also helped archives, museums, universities, and other cultural and historical societies to

salvage and preserve motion pictures that would not likely survive without public funding and support. It publishes award-winning DVD sets and guides, most notably the series *Treasures from American Film Archives*, which gives "new life to culturally significant films that, for one reason or another, had dropped from public memory" (https://www.filmpreservation.org/dvds-and-books/dvds-and-books, accessed 23 July 2020).

16 "What is an orphan film?," accessed 22 July 2020, http://www.sc.edu/filmsymposium/orphanfilm.html. In 2007, together with Martina Roepke and Anke Mebold, Dan Streible edited a special issue of *Film History* (vol. 19, no. 4) dedicated to non-theatrical films.

17 Acland and Wasson, *Useful Cinema*, 3. Key works on non-theatrical film include Cammaer and Druick, *Cinephemera*; Florin, De Klerk, and Vondereau, *Films That Sell*; Hediger and Vonderau, *Films That Work*; Orgeron, Orgeron, and Streible, *Learning with the Lights Off*.

18 Kirby, *Parallel Tracks*. See also Schivelbusch, "Railroad Space and Railroad Time"; Whissel, *Picturing American Modernity*.

19 Ruoff, *Virtual Voyages*.

20 Peterson, *Education in the School of Dreams*, 208.

21 Friedberg, *Window Shopping*, 2.

22 Bruno, *Atlas of Emotion*; Bruno, "Site-Seeing"; Strain, *Public Places, Private Journeys*. See also Mazierska and Walton, "Tourism and the Moving Image."

23 The terms "modern," "modernity," and "modernism" are complex and contentious, and cinema's relationship to modernity has been debated in film studies over the past two decades. I use "modern" and its variants as shorthand for the sensory and aesthetic shifts (at their most extreme, shock) in response to industrialization and urbanization; intensifying circuits of virtual/actual mobility of images, goods, and individuals; novel forms of mass culture and commodification; societal secularization; and the rise of bureaucracy and governmentality.

24 Butler, "The Influence of the Media in Shaping International Tourist Patterns"; Cohen, "Promotion of Overseas Tourism through Media Fiction."

25 Riley and Van Doren, "Movies as Tourism Promotion." See also Busby and Klug, "Movie-Induced Tourism"; Tooke and Baker, "Seeing Is Believing."

26 A second edition of *Film-Induced Tourism*, with a new introduction, was published in 2016. Beeton, *Film-Induced Tourism*; Beeton, "Tourism and the Moving Image"; Beeton, *Travel, Tourism and the Moving Image*; Beeton, "Understanding Film-Induced Tourism." See also Croy and Walker, "Rural Tourism and Film"; Heitmann, "Film Tourism Planning and Development."

27 For an excellent overview of this literature, see Connell, "Film Tourism – Evolution, Progress and Prospects."

28 Bolan, Boyd, and Bell, "We've Seen It in the Movies, Let's See If It's True"; Butler, "It's Only Make Believe"; Karpovich, "Theoretical Approaches to Film-Motivated Tourism"; Rittchainuwat et al., "Authenticity in Screen Tourism."

29 Tzanelli, *The Cinematic Tourist.*

30 Lefebvre, "On Landscape in Narrative Cinema," 63. See also Lefebvre, "Between Setting and Landscape in the Cinema." Other studies of landscape and film include Brereton, "Nature Tourism and Irish Film"; Corbin, *Cinematic Geographies*; Harper and Rayner, *Cinema and Landscape*; Jewell and McKinnon, "Movie Tourism"; Lefebvre, *Landscape and Film;* Roberts, *Film, Mobility and Urban Space.*

31 Connell, "Film Tourism," 1021; "Britain's Hollywood Movie Hotspots!," accessed 6 August 2020, https://www.visitbritain.com/ca/en/britains-hollywood-movie-hotspots.

32 Bolan and Kerney, "Exploring Film Tourism Potential in Ireland"; Edensor, "Mediating William Wallace"; Edensor, "Performing Tourism, Staging Tourism"; Edensor, "Reading Braveheart"; O'Boyle, "Place, Peripherality, and Play."

33 Buchmann, "Planning and Development in Film Tourism"; Carl, Kindon, and Smith, "Tourists' Experiences of Film Locations"; Jones and Smith, "Middle-Earth Meets New Zealand"; Tzanelli, "Constructing the 'Cinematic Tourist.'"

34 Chan, "Film-Induced Tourism in Asia"; Kim, "A Cross-Cultural Study of On-Site Film-Tourism Experiences"; Kim, "Audience Involvement and Film Tourism Experiences"; Kim and Reijnders, *Film Tourism in Asia*; Rattanaphinanchai and Rittchainuwat, "Film-Induced Tourism in Thailand."

35 Karpovich, "Theoretical Approaches to Film-Motivated Tourism," 9.

36 Morris, *Embattled Shadows*. See, for example, Gittings, *Canadian National Cinema*. On the challenges of writing Canadian film history, see Dorland, *So Close to the State/s*, 3–18.

37 Lester, "Cultural Continuity and Technological Indeterminacy"; P.S. Moore, *Now Playing*.

38 Gaudreault, Lacasse, and Sirois-Trahan, *Au pays des ennemis du cinéma*; Lacasse and Véronneau, *Histoires de scopes*; Pelletier, "The Fellows Who Dress the Pictures." See also the website *Filmographie des "vues" tournées au Québec au temps du muet (1897–1930)*, accessed 15 September 2020, http://cri.histart.umontreal.ca/grafics/fr/filmo/default.asp.

39 Armatage, *The Girl from God's Country*; Armatage, Banning, and Longfellow, *Gendering the Nation*; Whitehead, Pelletier, and Moore, "The Girl Friend in Canada."

40 See Druick, *Projecting Canada*; G. Evans, *In the National Interest*; G. Evans, *John Grierson and the National Film Board*; Khouri, *Filming Politics*; Low, *NFB Kids*; Nelson, *The Colonized Eye*; Waugh, Baker, and Winton, *Challenge for Change*.

41 Madger, *Canada's Hollywood*; Pendakur, *Canadian Dreams and American Control*.

42 Hart, *The Selling of Canada*.

43 Binnema and Niemi, "Let the Line Be Drawn Now"; Colpitts, "Wildlife Promotions"; Cronin, *Manufacturing National Park Nature*; Deutschlander and Miller, "Politicizing Aboriginal Cultural Tourism"; Loo, *States of Nature*; MacEachern, *Natural Selections*.

44 Apostle, "Canada, Vacations Unlimited"; Francis, *Selling Canada*, 125–76; Gordon, *Time Travel*; Little, *Fashioning the Canadian Landscape*. Key monographs in the history of provincially focused Canadian tourism include: Bradley, *British Columbia by the Road*; M. Dawson, *Selling British Columbia*; Dubinsky, *The Second Greatest Disappointment*; Jasen, *Wild Things*; I. McKay, *The Quest of the Folk*; McKay and Bates, *In the Province of History*; Neatby, *From Old Quebec to La Belle Province*.

45 In the first half of the twentieth century, British Columbia, Alberta, Ontario, Quebec, New Brunswick, and Nova Scotia were the provinces most using film to promote tourism, and thus appear more prominently in the present volume. This book also discusses some tourism films concerning Newfoundland, which has had a unique trajectory in Canadian history. During its 1869 election campaign, Confederation with Canada was a top issue, which voters strongly rejected. In 1907, the colony became a British dominion. In 1934, the indebted dominion suspended self-government, ending 79 years of responsible government, and reverted to roughly a crown colony. Following a wartime economic revival and two close referenda, Newfoundland became Canada's tenth province on 31 March 1949. In 2001, the province's official name changed to Newfoundland and Labrador.

46 Mawani, "From Colonialism to Multiculturalism?" 33.

47 Billig, *Banal Nationalism*. See also Edensor, *National Identity*.

48 Olins, "Branding the Nation." This was part of a special issue of the *Journal of Brand Management* 9, nos. 4/5 (2002) on destination branding, which was followed by a new journal, *Place Branding*, in 2004.

49 Anholt, *Competitive Identity*; Aronczyk, *Branding the Nation*; Aronczyk, "New and Improved Nations"; Dinnie, *Nation Branding*; Potter, *Branding Canada*.

50 Zuelow, "The Necessity of Touring beyond the Nation," 4.
51 Intermediality refers to the complex ways in which various media, including film, borrow from, converge with, and interact with other forms, such as advertising, art, literature, music, performance, and politics. See Pethő, *Cinema and Intermediality*.
52 P. Wolfe, "Settler Colonialism." Contrary to postcolonial studies, settler-colonial studies focus on "colonies where the settlers 'came to stay'" (e.g., North America, Australia, New Zealand, and parts of Africa and Asia) and thus present "distinctive colonial formations with specific dynamics that required separate interrogation" (Carey and Silverstein, "Thinking with and beyond Settler Colonial Studies").
53 Werry, *The Tourist State*, xiv.
54 Lorenzo Veracini argues that settler colonialism "covers its tracks and operates towards its self-supersession" in his "Introducing," 3. Daniel Francis discusses the settler processes of Othering in Canadian history, which led to ersatz representations of Indigeneity (Francis, *The Imaginary Indian*). On settler colonialism and tourism in Canada, see, for example, Grimwood et al., "Settler Colonialism"; Stewart, "Grey Owl in the White Settler Wilderness." On film and settler colonialism, see Lahti and Weaver-Hightower, *Cinematic Settlers*; Limbrick, *Making Settler Cinemas*.
55 Brégent-Heald, "Landscapes, Wildlife, and Grey Owl." As a non-Indigenous scholar of European ancestry, I look at settler-colonial narratives not to *speak* for First Nations peoples, thereby risking further colonization of Indigenous perspectives, but instead aim to problematize past film-tourism networks from a decolonized approach in the present.
56 Wozny, "National Audiovisual Preservation Initiatives."
57 Y. Zimmermann, "What Hollywood Is to America," 101. Rick Prelinger defines sponsored films as those "funded by for-profit and nonprofit entities," which "implies the packaging of information from a particular corporate or institutional perspective" (Rick Prelinger, "The Field Guide to Sponsored Films," National Film Preservation Foundation, 2006, vi, https://www.filmpreservation.org/userfiles/image/PDFs/sponsored2017.pdf).

CHAPTER ONE

1 Hoffman, "What People Want," 77.
2 Ibid. Between the 1890s and his retirement in 1958, Holmes delivered approximately 8,000 illustrated-travel talks and grossed an estimated $53 million (Wallace, "Everybody's Rover Boy," 11). On Howe, see Musser and Nelson, *High-Class Moving Pictures*.

3 Ramsaye, *A Million and One Nights*, 475.

4 "Letter Cliff Denham to Hye Bossin (Managing Editor, *Canadian Film Weekly*)," 3 April 1951, file 1, box 1, Gordon Sparling Fonds, University of Toronto Media Archives (UTMA). See also Eamon, "Farmers, Phantoms and Princes"; Morris, "Images of Canada," 72. Titles in the Living Canada series include *Ice Yachting on the St. Lawrence*; *Montreal on Skates*; *Niagara, the World's Wonder*; *The Outing of the 'Old Tuque Blue' Snow-Shoeing Club of Montreal*. The 1903 catalogue also describes a series of panoramic views as a CPR train travels through Kicking Horse Canyon, called collectively *The Rocky Mountains, Canada*, along with scenes of the logging and fishing industries on the Pacific coast (Urban, *We Put the World before You*). As Paul S. Moore demonstrates, the Living Canada series was also extensively exhibited throughout Canada as part of the CPR's goal to bolster its broader nationalist and settler-colonial imaginaries (P.S. Moore, "Spaces In-Between").

5 Bossin, "Canada and the Film," 29.

6 Although the terms "non-fiction" and "fiction" are anachronistic vis-à-vis early-twentieth-century scenics and story films, I use this distinction for convenience (Peterson, *Education in the School of Dreams*, 65).

7 *MPW*, 16 May 1908, 438.

8 According to Holmes, by "possessing the world through travel," "one may enjoy all the satisfactions of possession without the responsibilities of ownership" (B. Holmes, *The World Is Mine*, ix–x. See also Holmes and Caldwell, *The Man Who Photographed the World*). The German philosopher Martin Heidegger postulated that this shift towards conceiving and grasping the world "as a picture" was what distinguished the "essence of the modern age" (Heidegger, "The Age of the World Picture," 130. See also Crary, *Techniques of the Observer*; Mirzoeff, "What Is Visual Culture"; Schwartz and Przyblyski, *The Nineteenth-Century Visual Culture Reader*).

9 On the emergence of cinema as a continuation of magic-lantern traditions, see Musser, "Towards a History of Screen Practice." Immersive, stationary circular and moving panoramas similarly anticipated the spectacular and spectatorial experience of tourism films (Byerly, "A Prodigious Map beneath His Feet"; A. Griffiths, *Shivers down Your Spine*; Miller, "The Panorama, the Cinema and the Emergence of the Spectacular"; Oettermann, *The Panorama*).

10 Two of the most prominent illustrated-travel lecturers from the 1870s to the 1890s were the Americans John L. Stoddard and Edward L. Wilson, who frequently included Canadian content (Altman, "From Lecturer's Prop to Industrial Product"; Altman, *Silent Film Sound*, 56–8; Barber,

"The Roots of Travel Cinema"; Splinder, "Windows to the American Past"; Stoddard, *Lectures*; E.L. Wilson, *Wilson's Lantern Journeys*).

11 F.E. Lane, "Notes on Lantern Work," 58.

12 Holmes and Stoddard, *Burton Holmes and the Travelogue*, 9. Edison premièred the Vitascope, the first financially viable motion-picture projector in the United States, on 23 April 1896 at New York City's Koster and Bial's Music Hall.

13 Cited in Musser and Nelson, *High-Class Moving Pictures*, 125. Oscar Depue, Holmes's first lantern operator, projectionist, and camera operator, remained with the illustrated lecturer until 1916 (Depue, "My First Fifty Years in Motion Pictures"). Holmes later worked with a number of cameramen, including Lewis Moomaw (1916), Herford T. Cowling (1915–21), Merl LaVoy (1918), Walter Runcie (1923–25), and André de la Verre (1925-34) (Holmes and Stoddard, *Burton Holmes and the Travelogue*, 29).

14 Altman, *Silent Film Sound*, 67. For example, Holmes would typically utter such phrases as "We shall visit" as opposed to, "I have travelled."

15 Musser and Nelson, *High-Class Moving Pictures*, 172, 242. Howe rarely toured with his Travel Festival after 1899, rather managing his several touring companies. For a description of one of Howe's programs, see MPW, 24 June 1911, 1429.

16 MPW, 13 February 1909, 169. See also MPW, 6 February 1909, 145; Musser and Nelson, *High-Class Moving Pictures*, 196.

17 Other American illustrated-travel lecturers c. 1900 included Alexander Black, Frederick T. Burlingham, Bernyce Childs, Dwight L. Elmendorf, Edward John L. Lewis, Burton McDowell, and Evan Northrup. For a typical entertainment, see Chicago Projecting Company, "'Special' Catalog of Motion Picture Machines, Stereopticons, Talking Machines, Accessories and Supplies for Motion Picture Theatres (1908)," in Musser, Jeffery, and Jones, *Motion Picture Catalogs by American Producers and Distributors*, reel 6. See also Musser and Nelson, *High-Class Moving Pictures*, 58–9, 94–5.

18 Bernyce Childs was an illustrated-travel lecturer who presented motion pictures shot on the Pacific coast between San Diego and Nome (Altman, "From Lecturer's Prop to Industrial Product," 70). Philadelphia-born Mary Schäffer based her slide shows and lectures on her exploratory trips to the Rockies and Selkirks in the early twentieth century that focused on the flora, fauna, First Nations communities, and history of the region. The CPR used her photographs and watercolours to entice tourists to the region (Beck, *No Ordinary Woman*, 115. See also Reichwein and McDermott, "Opening the Secret Garden"; S.J. Squire, "In the Steps of 'Genteel Ladies'").

19 Musser and Nelson, *High-Class Moving Pictures*, 81–2.

20 For overviews of the Progressive era, see Diner, *A Very Different Age*; Flanagan, *America Reformed*; McGerr, *A Fierce Discontent*; Muncy, *Creating a Female Dominion in American Reform*; Rodgers, *Atlantic Crossings*.

21 While much of the audience base (and many owners) of nickelodeons were working-class new immigrants, demographics varied by region, city, even venue. Empirical data on attendance during this period are both elusive and highly debated (Singer, "Manhattan Nickelodeons").

22 On the evolution of film exhibition, see Gomery, *Shared Pleasures*. On film as a tool of social uplift, see Uricchio and Pearson, *Reframing Culture*. On the Progressive-era travelogue as "instructive entertainment," see Peterson, *Education in the School of Dreams*.

23 *OLCJ* 1, no. 1 (November 1904), 15.

24 See Endy, "Travel and World Power"; Skwiot, *The Purposes of Paradise*.

25 Kuehnast, "Visual Imperialism and the Export of Prejudice," 185.

26 Aron, *Working at Play*, 127–8; Sears, *Sacred Places*.

27 Jasen, *Wild Things*.

28 The opening of the Erie Canal in 1825 and the (first) Welland Canal in 1832, and of various railways and bridges by c. 1850, greatly increased access to the region, previously reachable only via stagecoach. By c. 1900, better tourist facilities and transportation networks were letting many more visitors see the Falls in short periods. During summers, over ninety regular trains stopped in Niagara Falls daily, while just as many special excursion trains carried thousands of visitors to the region (Dubinsky, *The Second Greatest Disappointment*; Gassan, *The Birth of American Tourism;* Irwin, *The New Niagara*; McGreevy, *Imagining Niagara*; Norris, "Reaching the Sublime").

29 An act of Parliament incorporated the CPR in 1881. The transcontinental line was integral to Prime Minister John A. Macdonald's nationalist vision and formed the bulwark of his National Policy, which included tariff protection for Canadian manufacturers, as well as western settlement (Brégent-Heald, "All Aboard!" 13).

30 In the late nineteenth and early twentieth centuries, the Anglo-Saxon majority in Canada saw itself as a member of the British "race," which prevailed over other communities, including French Canadians. As Philip Buckner summarizes, "To be Canadian was to be British" and "to be British meant to be 'white'" (Buckner, *Canada and the British Empire*, 84. See also S. Carter, "'Britishness,' 'Foreignness,' Women and Land in Western Canada, 1890s–1920s," 46–7). On the CPR and colonization

in the west, see Den Otter, *Civilizing the West*; Hedges, *Building the Canadian West*.

31 Clapperton, "Naturalizing Race Relations."

32 Jessup, "Canadian Artists, Railways, the State and 'the Business of Becoming a Nation'," 183; Jessup, "The Group of Seven and the Tourist Landscape in Western Canada, or The More Things Change ...," 150. Van Horne, the CPR's general manager and vice president, initially promoted tourism on his own but after 1888 gradually delegated it. In 1893, he placed George Ham, an erstwhile journalist and Winnipeg city councillor, in charge, and in 1913 Ham set up a separate publicity branch. Horne retired in 1899, and Thomas G. Shaughnessy succeeded him as the CPR's president (Gibbon, *Steel of Empire*).

33 Hart, "See This World before the Next." For example, Canadian Pacific Railway, *Summer Tours*.

34 Canadian Pacific Railway, *Yoho Valley in the Canadian Rockies and the Glaciers of the Selkirks*, 2 and 7. The Banff Springs Hotel opened in 1888, a year after the CPR's successful lobbying to turn the Banff Hot Springs Federal Reserve, established in 1885, into a National Park. Rocky Mountains Park was renamed "Banff National Park" in 1930. Later National Parks – Glacier (1886), Yoho (1886), Waterton Lakes (1895), and Jasper (1907) – were also accessible by the CPR (Bryce, *The Climates and Health Resorts of Canada*; Hart, *The Selling of Canada*, 26; R.C. Johnson, "Resort Development at Banff"; Marsh, "The Rocky and Selkirk Mountains and the Swiss Connection, 1885–1914").

35 Cocks, *Doing the Town*, 109.

36 The Anglo-American romantic movement in culture and style (1830s–60s) countered the Enlightenment's emphasis on reason and the advent of industrialization, and instead embraced the immediacy of experience. On its connection with the environment, see Oerlemans, *Romanticism and the Materiality of Nature*. On the cultural shifts that precipitated the anti-modernist impulse c. 1900, see Lears, *No Place of Grace*.

37 R. Johnson, *Passions for Nature*, 70. See also Cronon, "Telling Tales on Canvas," 81. On the sublime and picturesque in Canadian landscape imagery, see Little, *Fashioning the Canadian Landscape*; M.J. McKay, *Picturing the Land*.

38 D.E. Nye, *American Technological Sublime*.

39 The Canadian side did industrialize and commercialize, though somewhat later, and not concentrated around the Falls (Irwin, *The New Niagara*, 55). Originally named the Queenston-Chippawa Hydroelectric plant, it was renamed in 1950.

40 Coates, Young, and Bradley, *Moving Natures*. In particular, Lam, "Rails, Trails, Roads, and Lodgings."

41 On the "great picture" genre of the 1850s–80s, consisting of colossal, illuminated canvases displayed in darkened rooms for the paying public, see Cahn, "The Changing Landscape of Modernity." See also Manthorne, "Experiencing Nature in Early Film."

42 Brégent-Heald, *Borderland Films*, 22.

43 *MPW*, 20 June 1908, 528. See also Clegg, "Education by Kinematograph."

44 Hendricks, *Beginnings of the Biograph*, 38.

45 The film is also known as *View from the Gorge Railroad*. Musser, *Before the Nickelodeon*, 66. See also Mathews, "Early Film and American Artistic Traditions," 48.

46 *Boston Herald*, 23 June 1896, 9. Cited in Musser, *Before the Nickelodeon*, 66–7.

47 Niagara Gorge Railroad Company, "Great Gorge Route, most Magnificent Scenic Route in the World." Beginning in 1893, the tourist Niagara Falls Parks and River Railway ran between Chippawa and Queenston via Niagara Falls along the gorge on the Canadian side.

48 *Boston Herald*, 23 June 1896, 9. Cited in Musser, *Before the Nickelodeon*, 66–7.

49 "Edison Films for Projecting Machines and Kinetoscopes, 20 January 1897," in Musser, Jeffery, and Jones, *Motion Picture Catalogs by American Producers and Distributors*, reel 1. *American Falls from above, American Side* can be viewed at http://www.loc.gov/item/00694144 (accessed 28 June 2020).

50 "Edison Films" (September 1902), in Musser, Jeffery, and Jones, *Motion Picture Catalogs by American Producers and Distributors*, reel 2. See also *Circular Panorama of Suspension Bridge and American Falls* (1901).

51 *New York Clipper*, 2 June 1901, 324; No. 105, "Edison Films" (July 1901), in Musser, Jeffery, and Jones, *Motion Picture Catalogs by American Producers and Distributors*, reel 2.

52 "Edison Films" (September 1902), in Musser, Jeffery, and Jones, *Motion Picture Catalogs by American Producers and Distributors*, reel 1; *Scientific American*, 17 June 1899, 397.

53 Dickson's 1896 Niagara series includes *Canadian Falls – Panoramic View from Michigan Central R.R.*; *Lower Rapids, Niagara Falls*; *Niagara Gorge from Erie R.R.*; *Pointing down Gorge, Niagara Falls*; *Taken from Trolley in Gorge, Niagara Falls*; and *Upper Rapids from Bridge*. In April 1895, Dickson had left the Edison Company and joined the new American Mutoscope & Biograph Company.

54 American Mutoscope & Biograph Company, "Picture Catalogue" (November 1902), in Musser, Jeffery, and Jenkins, *Motion Picture Catalogs by American Producers and Distributors*, reel 2.

55 *Cincinnati Enquirer*, 2 November 1896. Cited in Niver, *Biograph Bulletins*, 15.

56 American Mutoscope & Biograph Company, "Picture Catalogue" (November 1902), in Musser, Jeffery, and Jenkins, *Motion Picture Catalogs by American Producers and Distributors*, reel 2.

57 Bottomore, "Taking Views a Perilous Art." Armitage also filmed *Panoramic View of Niagara Falls* (1899) and *Steamship 'Chippewa'* (1899).

58 Schivelbusch, *The Railway Journey*, 15.

59 Singer, *Melodrama and Modernity*, 35.

60 Gunning, "The Whole World within Reach," 36; Altman, *Silent Film Sound*, 87.

61 Bottomore, "The Panicking Audience?"; Tsivian and Taylor, *Early Cinema in Russia and Its Cultural Reception*, 139.

62 Kirby, *Parallel Tracks*, 59.

63 Schivelbusch, *The Railway Journey*, 33, 52–69.

64 The tunnel is located along the picturesque Hudson River in upstate New York (Niver, *Biograph Bulletins*, 29).

65 On phantom rides, see Keiller, "Phantom Rides." Of the 141 pre-1912 railway films, more than fifty involved phantom rides. Most date from 1899 to 1906 and were copyrighted by Edison or Biograph (Niver, *Motion Pictures from the Library of Congress Paper Print Collection*, 381–2).

66 Krows, "Motion Pictures" (December 1938), 328.

67 In addition to promoting British immigration, Hardie's Manitoba films also circulated throughout the Canadian prairies (P.S. Moore, "Spaces In-between." See also Eamon, "Farmers, Phantoms and Princes"; Kula, "Steam Movies," 247).

68 Cecil Hepworth, the son of an illustrated-travel lecturer, founded the Hepworth Manufacturing Company in 1904, which produced scenics, actualities, and comedic shorts (Hepworth, *Came the Dawn*). Williams, Brown, & Earl distributed Hepworth films in the United States (Slide, *Silent Topics*, 6).

69 The titles in the series are *Around Gravel Bay*; *Bridge No. 804, and Daly's Grade*; *Caribou Bridge*; *Down the Western Slope of the Canadian Rockies through Kicking Horse Pass*; *The Eastern Slope of the Rockies, passing Anthracite Station*; *Frazer Canyon, East of Yale*; *The Gap, Entrance to the Rocky Mountains*; *In the Canadian Rockies Near Banff*; *Under the Shadow of Mt. Stephen, Passing Field's Station in the Rocky Mountains*;

and *Up the Big Grade in the Valley of the Kicking Horse Pass*. American Mutoscope & Biograph Company, "Picture Catalogue" (November 1902), in Musser, Jeffery, and Jenkins, *Motion Picture Catalogs by American Producers and Distributors*, reel 2.

70 "Edison Films" (July 1901), in Musser, Jeffery, and Jenkins, *Motion Picture Catalogs by American Producers and Distributors*, reel 2.

71 Ibid. Other titles in Edison's Panoramic Rocky Mountain Series include *Panoramic View between Palliser and Field, B.C.*; *Panoramic View of Albert Cañon*; *Panoramic View of Lower Kicking Horse Valley*; and *Royal Train with Duke and Duchess of York Climbing Mt. Hector*. Many of these films are in the Paper Print Collection, Motion Picture, Broadcasting and Recorded Sound Division (MPBRSD), Library of Congress, Washington, DC (LOC).

72 "Bulletin No. 73," 30 June 1906. Cited in Niver, *Biograph Bulletins*, 250.

73 George C. Hale was a mechanical engineer and entrepreneur from Kansas City, Missouri (Fielding, "Hale's Tours"; Rabinovitz, *Electric Dreamland*; Rabinovitz, "From Hale's Tours to Star Tours").

74 Hayes, "Phantom Carriages," 192; Rabinowitz, "Bells and Whistles," 176.

75 Gittings, *Canadian National Cinema*, 8. See also Brégent-Heald, "All Aboard!"

76 Limbrick, *Making Settler Cinemas*, 2.

77 George Bird Grinnell, a founding member of the Boone and Crockett Club, was the editor-in-chief of *Forest and Stream* 1880–1911. *Rod and Gun* was a Montreal-based periodical established in 1899 and dedicated to fishing and hunting interests in Canada. According to Gail Bederman, red-blooded manhood upheld the discourse of civilization to preserve and perpetuate racial dominance (Bederman, *Manliness and Civilization*). The connection between hunting and hypermasculinity in the late nineteenth and early twentieth centuries did not exclude elite female sportswomen, who were growing in numbers.

78 Mitman, *Reel Nature*, 8–9, 13. Despite distinctions between these categories, I write about "nature," "wilderness," and "wildlife" films interchangeably.

79 Bousé, *Wildlife Films*, 37.

80 In addition to Coe and Bitzer, the other travellers were Dr Herber R. Bishop, a prominent businessman and sportsman; Richard Follett, second vice president of the New England Forest, Fish, and Game Association and manager of the sportsmen's show; C. Everett Johnson, an artist; and F.J. Marion, manager of the Biograph Company. *Moose Hunt in New Brunswick* is in the Paper Print Collection, LOC.

81 The film is also known as *Stalking and Shooting Caribou, Newfoundland*. Biograph Bulletin no. 101, 12 June 1907. Reprinted in Niver, *Biograph Bulletins*, 296–7. See also MPW, 8 June 1907, 221. *Bear Hunt in Canada* (1908), "taken during a recent hunting expedition in the Rocky Mountains," closely parallels these east-coast hunting films. This "interesting picture" offers a "magnificent view of the splendid scenery," and "we see the band of hunters under the care of the Indian guides who take them down the beautiful and picturesque river to the hunting grounds" (MPW, 30 October 1908, 346).

82 On the impact of the tourism industry on fish and game regulations in the northeast, see Parenteau and Judd, "More Buck for the Bang."

83 Gifford Pinchot, chief of the US Forest Service, was the archetypal spokesperson for conservationism, while John Muir, a naturalist and founder of the Sierra Club, spearheaded the preservation movement. Despite some meaningful differences, there was considerable overlap between these two groups during the early twentieth century (S.P. Hays, *Conservation and the Gospel of Efficiency*; Jacoby, *Crimes against Nature*; Warren, *The Hunter's Game*). On the early conservation movement in Canada, see Brown, "The Doctrine of Usefulness"; Foster, *Working for Wildlife*; Girard, *L'écologisme retrouvé*; Loo, *States of Nature*. On hunting and National Parks, see Keller and Turek, *American Indians and National Parks*; Manore and Miner, *The Culture of Hunting in Canada*; Sandlos, *Hunters at the Margin*; Spence, *Dispossessing the Wilderness*. On Indigenous guides and settler-colonial tourists, see Jasen, *Wild Things*, 133–40; Loo, "Of Moose and Men."

84 MPW, 12 March 1910, 336; MPW, 12 March 1910, 371; MPW, 5 August 1911, 299. See also MPW, 16 July 1910, 134.

85 Haskin, "The Popular Nickelodeon," 37. See also Peterson, *Education in the School of Dreams*, 65.

86 Internally consistent, linear narrative structure emerged by 1908. Over the next decade or so, filmmaking became increasingly sophisticated and technical, particularly in lighting and editing. Scenarists and script departments told stories in more effective and complex ways as the industry moved towards production of multiple-reel or feature films after 1913–14 (Gunning, *D.W. Griffith and the Origins of American Narrative Film*, 131; Keil, *Early Cinema in Transition*, 206–9; Musser, *Before the Nickelodeon*, 253–60; Musser, "The Travel Genre," 55–7).

87 Morris, *Embattled Shadows*, 36. See also Ross, "'*Hiawatha*', *The Messiah of the Ojibway* (1903)."

88 McNally, "The Indian Passion Play," 107. The Ojibwa, also known as Ojibwe, Ojibway, and Chippewa, are part of the larger Anishinaabe cultural group. A contemporary of Ralph Waldo Emerson and Henry David Thoreau's, Longfellow was a member of the American romantic movement, which venerated the primeval wilderness and its "noble savages." The writings of American ethnographer and Indian agent Henry Rowe Schoolcraft, whose works attempted to preserve Ojibwa language and traditions as his people's settler-colonial depredations dispossessed them, substantially inspired *Song of Hiawatha.*

89 Stewart, "Hiawatha/Hereafter," 168.

90 Canadian Pacific Railway Company, *Summer Tours to the Upper Lakes*, 22–3. See also Canadian Pacific Railway Company, *A Canoe Trip through Temagaming*; Jasen, *Wild Things*, 85.

91 Urban, *We Put the World before You*, 35, 39. Other US-based filmmakers also adapted *Hiawatha*, often framing it as an American subject, as opposed to Canadian or transnational. The husband-and-wife team of Katharine Ertz-Bowden and Charles Bowden travelled to Desbarats to film the pageant in 1904 and probably used some of Rosenthal's footage for an illustrated lecture. They presented *A Pictorial Story of Hiawatha* on the Chautauqua and Lyceum circuits until 1910. In keeping with the Progressive era's cultural and social milieu, these circuits, active particularly in the rural United States, espoused adult education and moral uplift, emphasizing personal enrichment, social betterment, and public discourse. Newly discovered nitrate film footage from the Bowdens' filmmaking venture was restored and presented at the seventh Orphan Film Symposium at New York University in 2010 (http://www.chicagofilmarchives.org/pres-projects/a-pictorial-story-of-hiawatha-film-restoration-project, accessed 10 December 2020). Carl Laemmle's Independent Moving Picture Company (IMP) produced *Hiawatha* (dir. by William V. Ranous, 1909), filmed reputedly at Minnehaha Falls in Minnesota (*MPW*, 23 October 1909, 563). The following year, IMP released a sequel entitled *The Death of Minnehaha*. In 1913, Frank E. Moore, a self-professed authority on "Indian" culture, produced a four-reel film based on his open-air theatrical production of *Hiawatha*, performed annually on the shores of Lake Chautauqua, New York. Moore described the picture, with its "cast of one hundred and fifty full-blooded Indians," as "a purely American drama written by an American poet and interpreted by true Americans in America" (*MPW*, 1 March 1913, 901; see also *NYDM*, 12 March 1913, 30). The British-based Kinemacolor Company, a precursor to Technicolor, also released a film version of *Hiawatha* (dir. by Edgar Lewis) in 1913.

92 On the history of the Acadian expulsion, see Faragher, *A Great and Noble Scheme*. From the 1850s through the First World War, North American publishers organized much of their fiction around regions, depicting locations far removed from the modern industrial, urbanizing world to appeal to markets searching for local colour or authentic folkways (Brodhead, *Cultures of Letters*; Foote, *Regional Fictions*; Riegel et al., *A Sense of Place*).

93 McKay and Bates, *In the Province of History*, 72. T.C. Haliburton's *The History of Nova Scotia* (1829) and the eighteenth-century writings of Abbé Raynal influenced Longfellow's interpretation of Acadian history (Calhoun, *Longfellow*, 181; N. Griffiths, "Longfellow's Evangeline"). See also Ginette Pellerin's 1996 documentary on the phenomenon for the NFB, https://www.nfb.ca/film/evangelines_quest (accessed 14 May 2015).

94 The British-owned Windsor and Annapolis Railway became the Dominion Atlantic Railway in 1894 after acquiring the Western Counties Railway Company. In 1887, Loran Ellis Baker formed the Yarmouth Steamship Company, which offered speedy service between Boston and Nova Scotia (MacDonald, "Railway Tourism in the 'Land of Evangeline'"; McKay and Bates, *In the Province of History*, 126; J. White, "A Vista of Infinite Development").

95 On the difficulties surrounding narrative structure and challenges relating to articulating temporal and spatial relations, see Keil, *Early American Cinema in Transition*.

96 Later productions also emphasized the landscape's scenic attributes. The Selig Company adapted the poem in *Evangeline: Pictured from a Dramatization of Longfellow's Beautiful Idyll of Arcadia*, in 1911 (release flier, William N. Selig Collection, Academy of Motion Picture Arts and Sciences, Margaret Herrick Library, Beverly Hills, CA [MHL]). Other versions included Fox's *Evangeline* (dir. by Raoul Walsh, 1919) and United Artists' *Evangeline* (dir. by Edwin Carewe, 1929), starring Dolores Del Rio.

97 Bulletin no. 108, 16 September 1907. Reprinted in Niver, *Biograph Bulletins*, 306. See also *MPW*, 14 September 1907, 441; *Billboard*, 21 September 1907, 41.

98 *MPW*, 8 February 1908, 92; *Billboard*, 8 February 1908, 37.

99 *NYDM*, 1 May 1909, 38. Before setting up a studio near Glendale, California, in 1911, Kalem relied largely on outdoor shooting. Its Canadian excursion followed an extended filmmaking trip to Jacksonville, Florida, in the winter of 1908–09 (Brégent-Heald, *Borderland Films*, 191; Morris, *Embattled Shadows*, 40).

100 *MPW*, 20 August 1910, 434. Kalem's Canadian-themed scenic-story films included *The Cattle Thieves* (1909), *The Girl Scout* (1909), *Canadian Moonshiners* (1910), *A Leap for Life, Trappers and Indians in Canada* (1910), *The Perversity of Fate* (1910), and *White Man's Money: The Indian Curse – a Canadian Story* (1910).

101 Brégent-Heald, "The Tourism of Titillation in Tijuana and Niagara Falls," 186.

102 *Variety*, 2 March 1907, 10.

103 *New York Clipper*, 30 March 1907, 156.

104 *MPW*, 13 January 1912, 86, 128, and 152. *A Niagara Honeymoon* was the first in a planned series of Thanhouser productions filmed on location in Niagara Falls. *A Message from Niagara* (1912) used the Falls as a backdrop to stage a morality tale of opium addiction and smuggling. *Niagara the Beautiful* (1912) was a more traditional scenic.

105 See Shaffer, "See America First." In 1893, under President James J. Hill, the GNR became the fifth and northernmost US transcontinental railway. On 11 May 1910, the lobbying efforts of its president, Louis L. Hill, who replaced his father in 1907, resulted in Glacier National Park, straddling the Alberta-Montana border. On the GNR's history, see Hidy, Hidy, and Scott, *The Great Northern Railway*; Strom, *Profiting from the Plains*. On Glacier Mountain National Park, see Shaffer, *See America First*, 59–92.

106 See Brégent-Heald, "All Aboard!"

107 *MPW*, 17 September 1910, 623.

108 Morris, *Embattled Shadows*, 42; Hedges, *Building the Canadian West*, 279–80.

109 Rankin, "With the Edison Players across the Continent," 936.

110 Lears, *Fables of Abundance*, 208. Lears argues that a "therapeutic ethos" emerged as a cultural response to the pressures of industrial and urban life and paved the way for a consumer-based society (Lears, "From Salvation to Self-Realization"). Other key studies in the history of advertising in the early twentieth century include Marchand, *Advertising the American Dream*; McGovern, *Sold American*; Ohmann, *Selling Culture*; Pope, *The Making of Modern Advertising*; Schudson, *Advertising, the Uneasy Persuasion*; Strasser, *Satisfaction Guaranteed.*

111 Walter Dill Scott of Northwestern University's psychology department published *The Theory of Advertising* in 1903, *The Psychology of Advertising* in 1908, and *The Psychology of Advertising in Theory and Practice* in 1913 (Kimmel, *Psychological Foundations of Marketing*, 12).

112 Singer, *Melodrama and Modernity*, 44–9. See also Koszarski, *An Evening's Entertainment*, 182.

113 MPW, 19 November 1910, 1178.
114 *The Life of a Salmon* is in British Film Institute Fonds, Library and Archives Canada, Ottawa (LAC). Canoe races in Victoria were popular in the early twentieth century. On the Empress Hotel, see Reksten, *The Empress Hotel*.
115 MPW, 29 October 1910, 1004; MPW, 5 November 1910, 1045.
116 *Variety*, 24 September 1910, 12; MPW, 23 September 1910, 747–8.
117 MPW, 17 September 1910, 623; MPW, 10 September 1910, 576–7; MPW, 23 September 1910, 747–8. *An Unselfish Love* is available in British Film Institute Fonds, LAC. A complete synopsis appears here: MPW, 17 September 1910, 643.
118 Strathmore History Book Committee, *Strathmore, the Village That Moved*, 30.
119 On white, middle-class female tourists and travellers in this period, see S.J. Squire, "In the Steps of 'Genteel Ladies.'"
120 *The Song That Reached His Heart* is in British Film Institute Fonds, LAC. For a synopsis, see MPW, 22 October 1910, 942.
121 MPW, 12 November 1910, 1116. The title is mistakenly listed as *The Swiss Guard*.
122 *Kinetogram*, 1 November 1910, 6–7, J. Searle Dawley Papers, MHL.
123 S.J. Squire, "Rewriting Languages of Geography and Tourism," 89. The history of the "new woman" is too complex to cover here. For good overviews, see Banner, *American Beauty*, 154–74; Patterson, *Beyond the Gibson Girl*; Peiss, *Cheap Amusements*.
124 MPW, 23 September 1910, 680.
125 Stamp, *Movie-Struck Girls*, 5; Singer, "Female Power in the Serial-Queen Melodrama," 90. On representations of class, see Frank, "Short Takes," 421–2.
126 MPW, 19 November 1910, 1176; Crippen, "Realism and the Photoplay," 14.
127 The Dominion government gave this rural constabulary, established in 1873, sweeping powers to ensure the settlement of the western interior by containing First Nations and Métis peoples in addition to enforcing the law. In 1920, the NWMP absorbed the Dominion Police, the federal police for eastern Canada, and became the Royal Canadian Mounted Police (RCMP) (M. Dawson, *The Mountie*; Graybill, *Policing the Great Plains*; Walden, *Visions of Order*).
128 Emphasis added. MPW, 1 October 1910, 763. A complete synopsis appears in MPW, 15 October 1910, 882.
129 MPW, 15 October 1910, 874.
130 Rankin, "With the Edison Players across the Continent," 937. *Man-to-Man: An Index to Opportunity*, formerly known as *Westward Ho!*

(1907–10), was renamed *British Columbia Magazine* in 1911 and ceased publication in 1915.

131 MPW, 17 September 1910, 623. The other scenic-melodramas directed by J. Searle Dawley in the CPR-Edison series of 1910 were *The Cowpuncher's Glove*, *A Daughter of the Mines*, and *The Ship's Husband*.

132 Cited in Morris, *Embattled Shadows*, 42. In 1912, Dennis would become the assistant to the CPR's president, Lord Shaughnessy, and placed in charge of its Department of Natural Resources.

133 Dench, *Advertising by Motion Pictures*, 99–100.

CHAPTER TWO

1 Bassett, "87% of Human Knowledge Comes by Way of 'Eye Gate,'" 5.

2 Bassett, "87% of Human Knowledge Comes by Way of 'Eye Gate.'" Bassett is referring probably to psychologist Hugo Münsterberg, who proposed in 1916 that "moving pictures appeal not only to the imagination, but … also bring their message to the intellect. They aim toward instruction and information" (Münsterberg, *The Photoplay*, 21. See also Groth, *Moving Images*, 171).

3 MPW, 11 May 1907, 152.

4 Speare, "81 out of 86 Are Buyers after Seeing Motion Picture," 25. Chicago-based Todd Protectograph manufactured cheque-protection machines. Speare wrote and distributed non-theatrically *A Modern Black Art* (1917), a short subject highlighting the benefits of the Todd system to potential customers.

5 Graham, *The Birth of Canadian Film Technology*; Morris, *Embattled Shadows*.

6 ES (January 1922), 6. On the visual-education movement, see Orgeron, Orgeron, and Streible, "A History of Learning with the Lights Off."

7 Rothacker, "Pictures as an Advertising Force," 71. See also Florin, De Klerk, and Vondereau, *Films That Sell*; Groskopf, "Profit Margins."

8 Acland and Wasson, *Useful Cinema*.

9 The Progressive era's most influential spokesperson for democratizing curricula was John Dewey. The philosopher and education reformer argued that democratic teaching, which treats students not as individuals but as members of a community, would guarantee a "worthy, lovely, and harmonious" society (Dewey, "The School and Social Progress," 44). On the various, often-competing groups out to reform education early in the twentieth century, see Reese, *Power and the Promise of School Reform*.

10 Cuban, *How Teachers Taught*, 28, 50; Pattison, "Taking the Movies to School," 7.

11 Dolesé, "The Moving Picture as an Educator," 707. An original member of the [US] National Board of Censorship, Dolesé (née Ruth E. Gould) helped establish an Educational Department within the General Film Company, which was the exclusive distributor for the Motion Picture Patents Company (MPPC). Together with Louis R. de Lorme, she reclaimed reels of educational subjects, including scenics, after they had been returned by the exchanges, and rented them to churches, schools, and other non-theatrical venues. De Lorme went on to form the Public Educational Film Company in June 1915 (Krows, "Motion Pictures" [May 1939], 154–5).

12 *MPW*, 29 January 1910, 119.

13 McClusky, "Place of Moving Pictures in Visual Education," 11.

14 *MPW*, 21 January 1911, 128.

15 The Morrill Act (1862) provided public lands to establish land-grant colleges intended to take both liberal (classical and scientific subjects) and practical (agriculture and the mechanical arts) education to underserved segments of the population. In 1914, the Smith-Lever Act established the Cooperative Extension Service to foster cooperation between the US Department of Agriculture and land-grant colleges in extension work related to agriculture and home economics (Geiger and Sorber, *The Land-Grant Colleges and the Reshaping of American Higher Education*).

16 The original members of the NUEA were Columbia University, Harvard University, Indiana University, Iowa State College, Pennsylvania State College, State University of Iowa, University of California, University of Chicago, University of Colorado, University of Idaho, University of Kansas, University of Michigan, University of Minnesota, University of Missouri, University of North Carolina, University of Oklahoma, University of Pennsylvania, University of Pittsburgh, University of South Carolina, University of South Dakota, University of Virginia, and University of Wisconsin (Dudley, *Historical Sketch of University Extension Division*, 18).

17 Van Hise, "The University Extension Function in the Modern University," 8–10. Headed 1907–26 by Louis E. Reber, Wisconsin's extension division was divided into four departments and then subdivided into bureaux (Curti and Carstensen, *The University of Wisconsin*; Dudley, *Historical Sketch of University Extension Division*, 7; Hoeveler, *John Bascom and the Origins of the Wisconsin Idea*).

18 Dudley, "Cooperation in Visual Instruction," 245.

19 J.H. Wilson, "New Organization Will Stimulate More Intelligent Use of All Visual Aids."

20 "Standards in Visual Instruction Committee Report," February 1921, National Academy of Visual Instruction, box 38, George Kleine Papers, LOC.

21 D.G. Hays, "The New Department of the N.E.A"; D.G. Hays, "Visual Education." In 1932, NAVI and VIAA merged with NEA DVI.

22 Scott, *The Theory of Advertising*, 210; Benjamin, "Science for Sale."

23 Münsterberg, *The Photoplay*, 22, 222. See Grieveson, "Cinema Studies and the Conduct of Conduct," 3–4.

24 Rothacker, "System in Motion Picture Advertising," 71; Rothacker, "The Ne Plus Ultra of Publicity," 21; Rothacker, "Realism in Municipal Advertising," 12. Rothacker co-founded the Industrial Motion Picture Company in 1909, in partnership with Carl Laemmle of the Independent Moving Pictures Company and R.H. Cochrane of the Cochrane Advertising Company. In 1916, after Laemmle and Cochrane left, Industrial became the Rothacker Film Mfg. Co. (See Rothacker Film Manufacturing Co., "Moving Pictures," Chicago History Museum Research Center [CHMRC]). Industrial also published a booklet extolling film for publicity (*Nickelodeon*, 1 December 1910, 313).

25 Dench, *Advertising by Motion Pictures*, 86.

26 Ibid., 93.

27 Clary, "Motion Pictures the Ideal Medium for Resort Advertising."

28 Clary, "Are Motion Pictures Publicity, or Are They Advertising?"

29 Stearns, "Films in Public Service Propaganda," 39.

30 Dench, *Advertising by Motion Pictures*, 97, 50–1.

31 Rothacker Film Manufacturing Co., "Moving Pictures."

32 *Globe*, 2 September 1919, 9.

33 *MPW*, 6 May 1916, 951. Holley was a former engineer for the Northern Pacific Railway and CPR. Established in 1913, the Bureau of Commercial Economics was a non-governmental and "altruistic association using the facilities and instrumentalities of governments, manufacturers and educational institutions in the dissemination of useful information by the graphic method of motion pictures displayed invariably to audiences admitted free" ("Mandate of the BCE," n.d. Records of the National Park Service, Central Files, 1907–1939, General Files, Publicity, Bureau of Commercial Economics [1922], National Archives and Records Administration [NARA]). See also Bureau of Commercial Economics, *Bureau of Commercial Economics*; Savage, "The Eye Beholds."

34 *Globe*, 2 August 1916, 9. See also Backhouse, *Canadian Government Motion Picture Bureau*, 5; Morris, *Embattled* Shadows, 130. The success

of this scheme later inspired H. (Herford) T. Cowling, a cinematographer for Burton Holmes, to propose to the director of the US National Parks Service a "moving picture campaign" of the scenic attractions within the country's national parks to be distributed to theatres via the Bureau of Commercial Economics (H.T. Cowling to Hon. Stephen T. Mather, Director, National Parks Service, 21 January 1922, Records of the National Park Service, Central Files, 1907–1939, General Files, Publicity, Bureau of Commercial Economics [1922], NARA).

35 *RAS*, February 1919, 10. Stark was formerly with the advertising department of the Commonwealth–Edison Company. In June 1916, Essanay sent four cameramen into Canada to begin filming, and the first reels were ready for distribution through the Edison, Essanay, Kleine, and Selig exchanges in July 1917 (B.E. Norrish to F.C.T. O'Hara, 19 February 1918, 2489, vol. 1, RG 20 107, LAC).

36 F.C.T. O'Hara (Deputy Minister, Department of Trade and Commerce) Memorandum, 14 June 1917, 2489, vol. 1, RG 20 107, LAC.

37 *MPW*, 2 February 1918, 724. *RAS* notes similarly: "The film is chiefly educational, though there is much scenic beauty" (May-June 1918, 13). The titles in the series included *Agricultural Opportunities in Western Canada*; *Banff National Park: A Trip through the Great Playground of Canada, Covering an Area of 2,000 Square Miles in the Heart of the Rocky Mountains Park*; *The Great Natural Industries of Canada*; *How Canada and the Farmer Co-operate in Grain Raising*; *Lake Louise*; *Salmon Fishing in New Brunswick*; *Through Canada from Coast to Coast*; *Visiting a Fairyland which Artists of Book and Brush Have Proclaimed the Loveliest Spot in North America*; and *Water Powers of Eastern Canada* (*Motography*, 3 November 1917, 949; B.E. Norrish to F.C.T. O'Hara, 29 November 1919, 2489, vol. 1, RG 20 107, LAC).

38 B.E. Norrish to F.C.T. O'Hara, 29 November 1919.

39 F.C.T. O'Hara to G.E. Foster, 11 May 1917, 2489, vol. 1, RG 20 107, LAC; B.E. Norrish to F.C.T. O'Hara, 19 February 1918, ibid. B.E. Norrish to F.C.T. O'Hara, 29 November 1919.

40 Minister of Trade and Commerce Report, 16 September 1918, 2489, vol. 1, RG 20 107, LAC; *Globe*, 28 August 1919, 4; G.E. Foster Memorandum, 20 April 1918, 2489, vol. 1, RG 20 107, LAC. See Backhouse, *Canadian Government Motion Picture Bureau*.

41 Brégent-Heald, *Borderland Films*, 271–2.

42 *MPW*, 29 August 1914, 1229. See also *MPN*, 7 February 1914, 22; *MPW*, 13 February 1915, 994. Four motion-picture companies were incorporated in Canada prior to the First World War: British American

Film Company (July 1912); Canadian Bioscope Company (November 1912); Conness-Till Company (April 1914); and All-Red Feature Company (July 1914) (Morris, *Embattled Shadows*, 47. See also P.S. Moore, "Nationalist Film-going without Canadian-Made Films?" 52–3).

43 Grau, *The Theatre of Science*, 201.

44 W.H. Weldon, "Evangeline to Be Produced," *Annapolis* [NS] *Spectator*, 30 October 1913, 1. Cited in Constantinides, "The Myth of Evangeline and the Origin of Canadian National Cinema," 66. Run primarily by former members of the New York–based Reliance Company, Canadian Bioscope (incorporated 1912) had its executive offices and studio in Halifax, and its publicity and sales office in New York. By the time *Evangeline* played in American theatres, Canadian Bioscope had completed six more films, although only three (*In the Enemy's Power*, *Mariner's Compass*, and *Saved from Himself*) gained general release. None enjoyed the box-office or critical success of *Evangeline*. The company closed when war broke out (Morris, *Embattled Shadows*, 50–1).

45 MPW, 7 February 1914, 662.

46 MPN, 30 May 1914, 39.

47 MPN, 7 February 1914, 32.

48 MPN, 7 February 1914, 22.

49 The Bowring Company in 1884 launched the Red Cross Line, which offered passenger and freight service between New York, Halifax, and St John's ("Red Cross Line").

50 Canada, Department of the Interior, *Annual Report for the Fiscal Year Ending 31 March 1916*, 3.

51 *Globe*, 17 June 1915, 7; *Globe*, 22 April 1915, 3.

52 Braun and Keil, "Sounding Canadian," 198; P.S. Moore, *Now Playing*, 199–224. See also Steven, "Pleasing the Canadians."

53 Keshen, *Propaganda and Censorship during Canada's Great War*, 36–7.

54 MPW, 1 August 1915, 724; MPW, 9 August 1915, 1229; MPW, 5 September 1914, 1422; MPW, 19 September 1914, 1667; MPW, 3 October 1914, 78; MPW, 12 December 1914, 1563. See also TDS, 23 March 1915, 10; *Globe*, 15 June 1914, 8. Canadian Animated Weekly assumed control of the defunct Montreal-based British American Film Manufacturing Company (Pelletier, "An Experiment in 'Historically Correct' Canadian Photoplays").

55 Rose, *Making 'Pictures in Our Heads'*, 19, 21.

56 *Globe*, 13 March 1918, 15.

57 *Globe*, 7 June 1918, 9; MPW, 14 September 1918, 1572. Established by an order-in-council in February 1918, the DSCR administered employment for honourably discharged members of the Canadian

Expeditionary Force (which fought on the Western Front, in France and Belgium), military hospitals and convalescent homes, pensions, and vocational training. A publicity branch provided information for veterans while generating public interest in "the welfare of the returned soldier" and encouraging "public co-operation in the programme of the commission" (Canada, Department of Soldiers' Civil Re-establishment, *Report of the Work of the Invalided Soldiers' Commission*, 45).

58 *Toronto World*, 23 September 1918, 7. See S. Evans, "Canada's Work for Wounded Solidiers on Film."

59 MPW, 14 September 1918, 1572.

60 CMPD, 10 August 1918; CMPD, 17 August 1918. See also CMPD, 24 August 1918; CMPD, 31 August 1918, 9; *Globe*, 7 June 1918, 9.

61 Edward Bernays, often dubbed the father of public relations, similarly combined the principles of propaganda and psychology, particularly "the conscious and intelligent manipulation of the organized habits and opinions of the masses," to advertising (Bernays, *Propaganda*, 9).

62 RAS, July 1918, 11.

63 Tepperman, "Digging the Finest Potatoes from Their Acre," 131.

64 Ontario, Treasury Department, "Financial Statement of the Hon. T.W. McGarry" (1919), 36. Compared to conventional motion-picture projectors, the Pathéscope was compact, weighed between twenty and twenty-three pounds, and was relatively simple to operate. It also used a special non-inflammable film instead of the common celluloid strip that could ignite, requiring a fireproof booth and licensed operator (Pathéscope Company of America, *Education as Visualization*).

65 Secord, "Canada Teaches Farmers with Films," 13.

66 Ontario, Treasury Department, "Financial Statement," 37.

67 MPW, 16 June 1916, 1819; *Globe*, 13 March 1918, 15. Under the supervision of Don Carlos Ellis, the US Department of Agriculture produced and developed a series of films to be screened throughout the country during the "fall fair" season of 1918 (RAS, October 1918, 8).

68 MPW, 16 June 1916, 1819; MPW, 4 May 1918, 706.

69 Secord, "Canada Teaches Farmers with Films," 13.

70 *Globe*, 30 August 1919, 5.

71 *Globe*, 3 September 1919, 8.

72 *Globe*, 23 August 1919, 8; *Globe*, 6 September 1919, 9.

73 *Globe,* 10 September 1919, 8. See also *Globe*, 9 September 1919, 9.

74 *Globe*, 2 September 1919, 9.

75 EFM, November 1920, 5.

76 A.M. Boggs to F.C.T. O'Hara, 17 September 1917, 2489, vol. 1, RG 20 107, LAC; F.C.T. O'Hara to A.M. Boggs, 19 September 1917, ibid. For more on Boggs, see Serna, "Anita Maris Boggs."

77 Order in Council, P.C. 2307, 19 September 1918; Morris, *Embattled Shadows*, 130.

78 G.E. Foster Memorandum, 20 April 1918, 2489, vol. 1, RG 20 107, LAC; *Globe*, 28 August 1919, 4.

79 *Globe*, 21 May 1918, 3; *Globe*, 13 August 1918, 12; *MPW*, 12 April 1919, 254.

80 H.N. DeWitt to A.K. Maclean, 25 March 1919, RG 20 107, 2489, vol. 1, LAC; F.C.T. O'Hara to G.E. Foster, 11 May 1917, ibid.

81 B.E. Norrish to F.C.T. O'Hara, 14 May 1917, ibid. Beginning in late 1913, Ford's initial films dealt with productivity and rationalizing work practices. This evolved in 1914 into the *Ford Animated Weekly*, a newsreel-type series. The *Ford Educational Weekly* (1916–21), a series of non-fiction one-reelers on a variety of subjects, predominantly industrial and travelogues, also promoted the Ford brand and/or Henry Ford as an altruistic corporate leader. Out of it developed the *Ford Educational Library* (1920–25), which targeted schools and colleges (Grieveson, "The Work of Film in the Age of Fordist Mechanization"; Metcalfe, "Mass Instruction – the Ford Moving Picture Experiment").

82 *MPN*, 3 April 1920, 3160.

83 *Globe*, 28 August 1919, 4; *The Most Picturesque Spot in North America* is at LAC and may be viewed at https://youtu.be/-M6DD-gBQEs (accessed 12 December 2020).

84 Shaffer, *See America First*, 4. See also Brégent-Heald, "All Aboard!"

85 *EW*, 10 May 1919, 60. After leaving Universal, Bach became the sales manager for the W.W. Hodkinson Corporation and later managed the booking department of the Famous Players–Lasky Corporation.

86 Titles include *Apple Time in the Land of Evangeline*; *Building Aeroplanes in Canada*; *Harvest of the Sugar Maple Tree*; *Salmon Fishing on the Skeena*; and *Wooden Shipbuilding in Canada* (Exhibits and Publicity Bureau 1920 Catalogue, n.d., 2489, vol. 1, RG 20 107, LAC).

87 B.E. Norrish to F.C.T. O'Hara, 19 February 1918, 2489, vol. 1, RG 20 107, LAC; Exhibits and Publicity Bureau 1920 Catalogue. While best known for his still photography, Harmon also took moving images of settler colonials' mountaineering expeditions, wildlife and beauty spots (cataracts, glaciers, lakes, mountains, and streams), and sporting activities in and around Banff and Jasper National Parks (Cronin, *Manufacturing National Park Nature*, 58; Harmon, Harmon, and

Robinson, *Byron Harmon, Mountain Photographer*). The Bureau edited the purchased Harmon footage and produced *Thrills a Plenty for the Alpine Climber in the Canadian Rockies* and *Virgin Fields for Explorers (Canadian Rockies)*. *Mt. Assiniboine (Mountaineering Memories)* and *Unblazed Trails* are also based probably on his film work.

88 On commercialism and tourism in the Parks Branch, see Bella, *Parks for Profit*; Brown, "The Doctrine of Usefulness"; Canada and Harkin, *The Origin and Meaning of the National Parks*; Hart, *J.B. Harkin*; Lothian, *A Brief History of Canada's National Parks*.

89 Exhibits and Publicity Bureau 1920 Catalogue.

90 B.E. Norrish to F.C.T. O'Hara, 21 January 1920, 2489, vol. 1, RG 20 107, LAC; *MPW*, 26 April 1919, 557; Exhibits and Publicity Bureau 1920 Catalogue.

91 B.E. Norrish to F.C.T. O'Hara, 11 December 1919, 2489, vol. 1, RG 20 107, LAC.

92 Canada. Parliament. House of Commons. *Debates*, 14th Parliament, 4th Session, Vol. 4 (25 May 1925), 3306.

93 B.E. Norrish to F.C.T. O'Hara, 11 December 1919. C.L. Chester, in collaboration with the editors of the *Outing Magazine*, a periodical about outdoor recreation, produced the Outing-Chester weekly series of one-reel adventure travelogues "showing expeditions to savage lands, in strange places, along untraveled trails" (*Outing Magazine*, September 1918, 346). Released through Mutual, beginning in the summer of 1918, several of its scenics featured Canada: *Mountaineering Memory* (1918) – Mount Assiniboine, BC; *The Unblazed Trail* (1918) – Canadian Rockies; *Getting the Cassiar's Goat* (1919) – a hunting picture filmed in Cassiar County, BC; *From Scales to Antlers* (1919) – northwest Quebec.

94 Canada, Department of Trade and Commerce, *Twenty-ninth Annual Report of the Deputy Minister* (1921), 19; *MPW*, 15 March 1919, 1481; *MPW*, 2 July 1921, 45; B.E. Norrish to F.C.T. O'Hara, 7 February 1918, 2489, vol. 1, RG 20 107, LAC.

95 In December 1918, US President Woodrow Wilson set aside $50,000 to establish, within the Department of Interior's Bureau of Education, the temporary Federal Division of Educational Extension. This unit was to distribute publicity and educational materials such as motion pictures to extension programs, which were soon flooded with war, industrial, and scenic films. Later, the Bureau continued the ad-hoc unit's work through a film-distribution service via university extension divisions. Interior hired William H. Dudley of the University of Wisconsin as a specialist in visual instruction. By 1920, the service had supplied

four million feet of films to thirty-eight distributing centres, including twenty-nine university extension divisions (Bittner, "The University Extension Movement," 27–8, 47. See also McClusky, "Finding the Facts of Visual Education," 395).

96 Frykholm, *George Kleine and American Cinema*; Kleine, *Catalogue of Educational Motion Pictures*; Orgeron, Orgeron, and Streible, "A History of Learning with the Lights Off"; Saettler, *The Evolution of American Educational Technology*, 111, 139.

97 Dudley, "Organization for Visual Instruction," 6.

98 The University of Wisconsin, University of Extension Division, Bureau of Visual Instruction, 1921–22, Educational Use of Films, box 40, George Kleine Papers, LOC.

99 Canada, Department of Trade and Commerce, *Thirty-second Annual Report of the Deputy Minister* (1924), 31–2; Canada, Department of Trade and Commerce, *Thirty-fourth Annual Report of the Deputy Minister* (1926), 46.

100 Motion Pictures and Slides, Catalogue, October, 1922, Visual Instruction Service, North Dakota Agricultural College, University Catalogs, 1920–1927, box 41, Kleine Papers, LOC. This institution is now North Dakota State University. Hollis left extension work to become a film editor at the DeVry Corporation, which Herman DeVry established in 1913 to distribute his portable projector, dubbed a "theatre in a suitcase" (Hollis, *Motion Pictures for Instruction*, 219).

101 Moving Picture Age, *1001 Films*, 56–61. *Moving Picture Age*, formerly *Reel and Slide*, was briefly the official organ of NAVI. It was absorbed in December 1922 by *Educational Screen*, established in late 1921. Ford's Canadian subjects were *Canada's Mountain of Tears* (1919), *God's Handiwork* (1919), *Nature's Echo* (1919), *Thousand Islands in the St. Lawrence River* (1919), and *Are You a Piker? International Good Roads Tour* (1920).

102 Howard, "The Wisconsin Idea," 9.

103 Saettler, *The Evolution of American Educational Technology*, 99–104.

104 Dorris, *Visual Instruction in the Public Schools*, 188–9. Dorris served as president 1927–29 of the NEA DVI (San Francisco State, Department of Geography and Environment, "Anna Dorris," accessed 3 November 2020, https://geog.sfsu.edu/person/anna-dorris); W. Johnson, "Making Learning Easy and Enjoyable").

105 Gregory, "Problems Concerning the Educational Motion Picture," 20.

106 McClusky, "Place of Moving Pictures in Visual Education," 7–8.

107 McClusky, "Finding the Facts of Visual Education," 395.

108 Draft Form of Letters Patent, 17 July 1920, RG 95-1 473, LAC; *CMPD*, 18 September 1926. ASN also operated a full-service laboratory offering release printing for the major Hollywood studios.

109 *CMPD*, 1 March 1934; *CMPD*, 7 March 1953. See also Morris, *Embattled Shadows*, 224–5.

110 E.L. Chicanot, "Behind the Silver Screen," 15 May 1929, 15, file 71, box 2, Gordon Sparling Fonds, UTMA.

111 Peck had been the publicity manager for Canadian Universal Film Company, editor of the *Canadian Moving Picture Digest*, and later manager of the Mutual branch in Montreal (*MPW*, 13 November 1920, 181).

112 R.S. Peck to F.C.T. O'Hara, 18 June 1920, 2489, vol. 1, RG 20 107, LAC; Exhibits and Publicity Bureau Motion Pictures, n.d., ibid.; Canadian Motion Picture Bureau Report, n.d., ibid.

113 R.S. Peck to F.C.T. O'Hara, 8 March 1923, ibid. The name was officially changed on 1 April 1923.

114 Peck, "The Use of Motion Pictures for Governmental Purposes."

115 Peck cited another example from the CPR, which had canvassed passengers on one of its Alaskan steamers to ascertain "how and why [they] had decided to make the trip." "Approximately 60 per cent" did so "because they had seen motion pictures exhibited dealing with" it (Peck, "Publicity Pictures as Used by the Canadian Government," 47).

116 *MPN*, 13 June 1925, 2916. The AMPA was formed in the summer of 1916 to join motion-picture and advertising interests in the film trade.

117 Peck, "Publicity Pictures as Used by the Canadian Government," 45.

118 Brégent-Heald, *Borderland Films*, 65–90. Pierre Berton, the Canadian journalist, popular historian, and broadcaster, in his *Hollywood's Canada*, colourfully explores the American film industry's misrepresentations of Canada in these early northwest melodramas.

119 See Brégent-Heald, "James Oliver Curwood."

120 Peck, "Publicity Pictures as Used by the Canadian Government," 45.

121 *Globe*, 14 February 1929, 4.

122 *MPN*, 13 June 1925, 2916.

123 Bird, "A Man of Talents," 41.

124 *MPN*, 16 May 1925, 2245; *MPW*, 16 May 1925, 361. The production was originally titled *The Comeback*, the title of a novel by M.D.C. Crawford from which it was adapted.

125 *MPW*, 11 July 1925, 149; *MPW*, 4 July 1925, 77. See also the First National advertisement in *MPW* referring to a Maine setting (11 July 1925, 125).

126 *MPW*, 11 July 1925, 149; *PPM* (October 1925), 14.

127 Scenes for *Trail of '98* were filmed in Alaska, and exterior scenes for *The Flaming Forest* in Glacier National Park in Montana on the Canadian border (*MPN*, 10 April 1926, 1589; *FD*, 9 June 1926, 4).

128 The Dominion also apparently supported a second Hoot Gibson feature, *Chip of the Flying U* (dir. by Lynn Reynolds, 1925), filmed partly at the E.P. Ranch, near Pekisko, Alberta, owned 1919–62 by Edward, Prince of Wales (*EH*, 18 July 1925, 66. See also *MPN*, 6 June 1925, 2779). In January 1936 the prince became King Edward VIII, and he abdicated in December and was created Duke of Windsor by his brother, the new King George VI. On the Calgary Stampede and film, see Leeder, "A New Chivalry."

129 The Calgary Stampede took place first in 1912 and again in 1919. As of 1923, it became an annual event, which Weadick managed until 1932. On its early history, see Foran, *Icon, Brand, Myth*; Kelm, "Manly Contests"; Livingstone, *The Cowboy Spirit*. See also Thrift, "To Celebrate the Passing of a Great Era."

130 Gray, *A Brand of Its Own*, 78–9.

131 Calgary Industrial Exhibition Company, "Calgary Exhibition Jubilee and Stampede, annual report, 1925," Calgary Exhibition and Stampede Archives, University of Calgary, Calgary, AB, http://contentdm.ucalgary.ca/cdm/ref/collection/cesa/id/669, accessed 28 November 2017.

132 *Moving Picture Weekly*, 11 February 1922, 19.

133 Calgary Industrial Exhibition Company, "Calgary Exhibition Jubilee and Stampede, annual report, 1925," Calgary Exhibition and Stampede Archives, University of Calgary, Calgary, AB, http://contentdm.ucalgary.ca/digital/collection/cesa/id/611, accessed 3 May 2018.

134 *FD*, 11 October 1925, 11.

135 Canada, Department of Trade and Commerce, *Thirty-fourth Annual Report of the Deputy Minister* (1926), 46.

136 *MPW*, 21 November 1925, 215. F.C.T. O'Hara to Lucien Pacaud, 19 March 1923, file 16613, vol. 1, RG 20, vol. 31, LAC.

137 Memorandum from Raymond S. Peck, 17 August 1925, ibid.; Imperial Conference, Statement by Prime Minister of Canada, 22 October 1925, ibid.

138 See Jarvie, *Hollywood's Overseas Campaign*, 44–67; Segrave, *American Films Abroad*. Imperial Conferences were periodic (1907, 1911, 1917, 1918, 1921, 1923, 1926, 1930, 1936, and 1937) for leaders of the self-governing colonies and dominions of the British Empire to meet and discuss such matters as trade and defence.

139 Statement by Harrison Watson at the Imperial Conference, General Economic Sub-Committee, 1 November 1926, file 16613, vol. 1, RG 20, vol. 31, LAC.

140 FD, 16 March 1927, 6; Canada, Parliament, House of Commons, *Debates*, 16th Parliament, 1st Session, Vol. 2 (6 April 1927), 1995.

141 *Montreal Standard*, 20 May 1939, vol. 198, "Canadian Government Motion Picture Bureau," R202-28-3-E, LAC.

142 Jarvie, *Hollywood's Overseas Campaign*, 44–67; Morris, *Embattled Shadows*, 181–2. In 1938, the British changed the quota law to exclude Dominion productions. See also Chibnall, *Quota Quickies*.

143 Rotha, *Celluloid*, xi.

CHAPTER THREE

1 Corkill, "As the Crane Flies," 716.

2 Stewart, "Grey Owl in the White Settler Wilderness"; Veracini, *Settler Colonialism*; P. Wolfe, "Settler Colonialism."

3 Catalogue of Motion Picture Films Distributed by the National Parks Bureau of Canada, U113-60, pt 1, Universal – Catalogue of motion picture films 1937–1946 (reel T 12919), RG 84 A-2-A, vol. 163, LAC.

4 Canada, Department of Mines and Resources, *Report of Lands, Parks, and Forests Branch for the Fiscal Year Ended March 31, 1939*, 95.

5 Gissibl, Hoehler, and Kupper, "Introduction," 16. See also Binnema and Niemi, "Let the Line Be Drawn Now"; Clapperton, "Naturalizing Race Relations"; Mar, "Carving Wilderness."

6 See Belasco, *Americans on the Road*; D.F. Davis, "Dependent Motorization"; Jakle, *The Tourist*.

7 Aron, *Working at Play*, 183–205, 246–9.

8 Canada, Senate, *Report and Proceedings of the Special Committee on Tourist Traffic*, 1934, 4.

9 Williams was laid off in 1930 during Depression-era budget cuts. Six years later, she published the first history of the Parks Branch – M.B. Williams, *Guardians of the Wild* (MacEachern, "M.B. Williams and the Early Years of Parks Canada").

10 Canada, Department of the Interior, *Report of the Commissioner of Dominion Parks*, Sessional Paper No. 25 (30 June 1915), 4. The Parks Branch's handful of publications in the 1910s began with *A Sprig of Mountain Heather: Being a Story of the Heather and Some Facts about the Mountain Playgrounds of the Dominion* (Ottawa, 1914), http://peel.library.ualberta.ca/bibliography/9259/9.html.

11 United States, Department of the Interior, *Proceedings of the National Parks Conference* (1917), 265.

12 Hart, *J.B. Harkin*, 231–2. The National Parks Act in 1930 changed the name to National Parks and pledged preservation alongside tourism development: "The Parks are hereby dedicated to the people of Canada for their benefit, education and enjoyment, subject to the provisions of this Act and Regulations, and such Parks shall be maintained and made use of so as to leave them unimpaired for the enjoyment of future generations" (Canada, The National Parks Act).
13 MacEachern, "M.B. Williams and the Early Years of Parks Canada," 39. On the promotion of automobile tourism in this period, see Sandlos, "Nature's Playgrounds."
14 Canada, Department of the Interior, *Report of the Commissioner of Dominion Parks, J.B. Harkin* (1920), 7.
15 Canada, Department of the Interior, *Report of the Commissioner, J.B. Harkin* (1923), 112.
16 Canada, Department of the Interior, *Report of the Commissioner, J.B. Harkin* (1925), 67. See also Hart, *J.B. Harkin*, 234, 450.
17 "Canadian Motion Picture Bureau," n.d. (likely 1924), 2489, vol. 1, RG 20 107, LAC.
18 Raymond S. Peck to F.C.T. O'Hara, 29 May 1922, ibid.
19 Raymond S. Peck to F.C.T. O'Hara, 26 December 1923, ibid.
20 Morris, *Embattled Shadows*, 169.
21 Oliver also shot promotional photographs and motion pictures for the CPR and CNR. *Jasper of the Lakes* is at Marjorie B. Oliver Collection, LAC; no copies of Oliver's 1919 film of Waterton are known to exist (Jameson, *W.J. Oliver*, 56, 67).
22 See Jameson, *W.J. Oliver*, 45.
23 Initially called the Buffalo Park Reserve, it became Buffalo National Park in 1913. Little, Brown published Cooper's novel, *The Last Frontier*, in October 1923 (Taves, *Thomas Ince*, 228).
24 Also helping to kill off the buffalo were environmental factors, the introduction of livestock, and agricultural settlement (Colpitts, *Pemmican Empire*; Daschuk, *Clearing the Plains*; Isenberg, *The Destruction of the Bison*).
25 Howard Douglas to W.W. Cory, 15 June 1906, file BU209, vol. 51, pt 1, Parks Canada Files, BNP, RG 84, LAC. Cited in J. Brower, *Lost Tracks*, 39.
26 *WS*, 20 November 1908; *WS*, 7 October 1909; *WS*, 20 September 1911.
27 Mott Lake opened on 1 July 1917 (*WS*, 4 July 1917, 1).
28 J. Brower, *Lost Tracks*, 88.
29 Commissioner to Geo. B. Grinnell, 12 July 1924, file BU232, vol. 53, pt 3, Parks Canada Files, BNP, RG 84, LAC. Cited in J. Brower, *Lost Tracks*, 74.

30 The Department of the Interior would receive a fee of $2,500 plus $250 per buffalo killed (Lothian, *A History of Canada's National Parks,* vol. 4, 32–3; *MPN*, 27 October 1923, 1983). One report claimed the Ince team shot 50,000 feet of film (*MPW*, 26 January 1924, 289). Peter Morris writes that Oliver used some of this footage in *Home of the Buffalo* (1930), which features the round-up and stampeding of bison, for the Parks Branch. It is in Marjorie B. Oliver Fonds, LAC (Morris, *Embattled Shadows*, 170). A sound version was produced in 1934 – *The Return of the Buffalo* – available in Associated Screen News Fonds, LAC.

31 Lothian, *A History of Canada's National Parks,* vol. 4, 33.

32 *MPW*, 26 January 1924, 289; *WS*, 14 November 1923, 1. The trade journals typically suggested eight to ten thousand buffalo rounded up for filming (*MPN*, 27 October 1923, 1983).

33 Paul P. Perry, an Ince cameramen on the shoot, describes in detail the filming of the sequence (Perry, "Stampedes and Camera Pits." See also *EH*, 2 November 1923, 35).

34 *WS*, 28 November 1923, 1.

35 Letter to W.J. Oliver from Thos. H. Ince Corporation, 9 November 1923; Letter to W.J. Oliver from M.B. Williams, 11 November 1923, Correspondence, 1914–1923, vol. 1 (MG 30 D402), William J. Oliver Fonds, R7658-0-4-E, LAC.

36 Letter from J.C. Campbell to W.J. Oliver, 19 November 1923, ibid.

37 *WS*, 17 October 1923, 1.

38 *WS*, 14 November 1923, 3.

39 Ibid., 1.

40 J.M. Davis, *The Gospel of Kindness*; C.E. White, "The Utmost Care, Kindness, and Consideration."

41 *Christian Science Monitor*, 13 October 1923, 1.

42 *MPN*, 15 December 1923, 2778.

43 Ince Statement, record 150, correspondence, 1-1484 and 1-1485, MPPDA Digital Archives, Flinders University Library Special Collections, Adelaide, South Australia, http://mppda.flinders.edu.au/records/150, accessed 3 May 2018.

44 *Calgary Daily Herald*, 10 November 1923, 5, Miscellaneous News Clippings, 1922–1982, M-8119-292, Sheilagh S. Jameson Fonds, Glenbow Archives, Calgary, Alberta. Due largely to the controversy surrounding the 1923 cull, in 1925 the Parks Branch decided to relocate more than 6,000 surplus bison to Wood Buffalo National Park, established in 1922. Plagued by ongoing problems, the herd was destroyed in 1938 and 1939. The park closed in 1939.

45 Ince died shortly after celebrating his birthday on American publishing mogul William Randolph Hearst's yacht, the *Oneida*. Although the official cause of death was a heart attack following acute indigestion, rumours surfaced of a bullet wound inflicted by Hearst on mistaking him for Charlie Chaplin, whom Hearst believed was having an affair with his mistress, Marion Davies (Taves, *Thomas Ince*.) Stromberg formerly worked as a publicist for Ince before starting his own producing company in 1924. He joined MGM the following year (*EH*, 4 July 1925, 28; *MPW*, 12 September 1925, 137).

46 *MPN*, 10 July 1926, 135.

47 Jameson, *W.J. Oliver*, 52.

48 List of Pictures and Dates from Fox News Bulletins, M-8119-269, Fox News Bulletins (1925–1937), Sheilagh S. Jameson Fonds, Glenbow.

49 Letter from George Mitford to W.J. Oliver, 19 January 1928, ibid. Beginning in 1927, Fox began to release synchronous-sound newsreels known as Fox Movietones.

50 Dan E.C. Campbell, "Adventures of a Press Photographer," *Calgary Daily Herald*, 12 October 1929, Clippings 1929–1937, vol. 2 (MG 30-D402), R7658-0-4-E, William J. Oliver Fonds, LAC.

51 On the relationship between automobiles and nature in this period, see Louter, *Windshield Wilderness*.

52 Canada, Department of the Interior, *Report of the Commissioner, J.B. Harkin* (1923), 96.

53 "Will Interest Tourists," n.d., file 173, Scrapbook of Clippings, 1918–1947, vol. 1 (MG 30-D402), R7658-0-4-E, William J. Oliver Fonds, LAC. This article is referring probably to *Motoring in Cloudland* (1926). The Brewster family began an outfitting and packing company based out of Banff in 1900.

54 Canada, Senate, *Report and Proceedings of the Special Committee on Tourist Traffic*, 1934, 16.

55 The film is in Jean-Jacques Joly Fonds, LAC. In 1934, Oliver shot another travel film in the area for the Parks Branch entitled *Waterton*, featuring Harold Long, editor of the *Lethbridge Herald*, along with Oliver's wife, Marjorie, and their daughter, Joan, motoring through the park and enjoying camping, hiking, and other recreational activities. The film is in Marjorie B. Oliver Fonds, LAC.

56 According to one article, Mrs Oliver and her sister, Mrs Foley Martin, play the sisters, while David Cromarty, son of William Cromarty, acting superintendent of Waterton Lakes National Park, plays the friend ("Oliver 'Shoots' Important Scenes for Waterton Film," *Lethbridge Herald*, 29

August 1929, file 173, Scrapbook of Clippings, 1918–1947, vol. 1 [MG 30-D402], R7658-0-4-E, William J. Oliver Fonds, LAC). The film is in Marjorie B. Oliver Fonds, LAC.

57 Canada, Department of the Interior, *Report of the Commissioner of Dominion Parks* (1914), 5. A similar narrative occurs in *Open Skyways in the Rockies* (1929), where tourists motor from Banff to Golden, BC, on the Kicking Horse Trail. It is in Marjorie B. Oliver Fonds, LAC.

58 Sutter, *Driven Wild*, 41–8.

59 Scott, *The Psychology of Advertising*, 7–11.

60 *Department of Highways Nineteenth Report 1936* (Halifax: Provincial Secretary, King's Printer, 1937), PANS. Lerner later founded the International Game Fish Association in 1939. These motion pictures are in Marjorie B. Oliver Fonds, LAC.

61 On the history of skiing in western Canada, see Clayton, "A National Playground Both in Summer and Winter"; Robinson, "Off the Beaten Path?"; Yeo, "Making Banff a Year-Round Park." These motion pictures are in Marjorie B. Oliver Fonds, LAC.

62 The Alpine Club of Canada (ACC), set up in 1906, was the country's leading proponent of mountain climbing and alpinism. On the history of mountaineering and the ACC in Canada's National Parks, see Reichwein, *Climber's Paradise*. These motion pictures are in Marjorie B. Oliver Fonds, LAC.

63 M. Dawson, *Selling British Columbia*, 57–9; Jameson, *W.J. Oliver*, 69.

64 "Thrilling Action Movies of Vancouver Island will be Shown over Canada," 27 June 1930, file 173, Scrapbook of Clippings, 1918–1947, vol.1 (MG 30-D402), R7658-0-4-E, William J. Oliver Fonds, LAC. These two productions are at the BC Archives.

65 MacEachern, *Natural Selections*, 48.

66 Canada, Department of the Interior, *Report of the Commissioner of Dominion Parks* (30 June 1915), 6. On the evolution of wildlife management in Canada, see Loo, *States of Nature*.

67 Canada, Department of the Interior, *Annual Report for the Fiscal Year Ending 31 March 1917*, 7.

68 *Illustrated Canadian Forest and Outdoors* 26, no. 11 (1930), 655. On the emergence of wildlife photography, see Altmeyer, "Three Ideas of Nature in Canada," 30; M. Brower, *Developing Animals*.

69 See also *Playground Sanctuary* (1928?) and *Sanctuary and Playground* (1934), both filmed at Elk Island National Park.

70 See Newsome, Dowling, and Moore, *Wildlife Tourism*.

71 Duffus and Dearden, "Non-Consumptive Wildlife-Oriented Recreation," 215.

72 LH, 2 February 1933, 11.

73 For accounts of Belaney's life, see Billinghurst, *Grey Owl*; Dickson, *Wilderness Man*; Smith, *From the Land of Shadows*. On the development of the Temagami Forest Reserve for timber and tourism in the early twentieth century, see Thorpe, "To Visit and Cut Down."

74 Chapin, "Gender and Indian Masquerade in the Life of Grey Owl"; Krech, *Ecological Indian*.

75 Deloria, *Playing Indian*; Stewart, "Grey Owl in the White Settler Wilderness."

76 Anahareo and McCall, *Devil in Deerskins*; Gleeson, "Blazing Her Own Trail." Grey Owl had been married three times prior to Anahareo. She left him in 1936, and he went on to remarry.

77 Loo, *States of Nature*, 114. See also Braz, "Beaver Voices."

78 Shortt, *A Study in Conviction and Fantasy*, 47; W.H. Corkill, "The Romance of Grey Owl," *Canada's Weekly*, 10 January 1947, 415, vol. 1770, PA272, pt 1, Prince Albert National Park – Grey Owl (Archie Belaney) – Clippings and Correspondence 1931–1938 (reel T 14389), LAC.

79 *The Beaver People* (1928) can be viewed at https://www.nfb.ca/film/beaver_people (accessed 15 December 2020).

80 P. Wolfe, "Settler Colonialism." See also Burow, "Wildlife Conservation."

81 Smith, *From the Land of Shadows*, 90–1.

82 Grey Owl argued that the water conditions in Riding Mountain National Park were detrimental to the beavers (Memorandum by H. Howett, Deputy Minister of the Interior, n.d., vol. 1768. PA174-18. pt 1. Prince Albert National Park – Grey Owl [Archie Belaney] 1931–1937 [reel T 14388], LAC). On the establishment of the park, see Waiser, *Saskatchewan's Playground*, 25–35.

83 Shortt, "A Study in Conviction and Fantasy," 65.

84 Canada, Department of the Interior, *Annual Report for the Fiscal Year Ending 31 March 1931*, 11.

85 The NFB states on its website that *Beaver Family* is from 1930, but Grey Owl was not at the park until 1931. The film can be viewed at https://www.nfb.ca/film/beaver_family (accessed 2 February 2022).

86 Catalogue of Motion Picture Films Distributed by the National Parks Bureau of Canada, U113-60, pt 1, Universal – Catalogue of motion picture films 1937–1946 (reel T 12919), RG 84, A-2-a, vol. 163, LAC; Grey Owl, *Pilgrims of the Wild*.

87 Letter from Gordon Sparling, 3 February 1950, file 197, box 3, Gordon Sparling Fonds, UTMA.

88 For example, the Oscar-winning short subject *Beaver Valley* (1950) features a family of cute and industrious beavers. On Disney's nature films, see Bousé, *Wildlife Films*; Mitman, *Reel Nature*.
89 Cockerell, "Zoology and the Moving Pictures," 369–70.
90 Memorandum, 25 April 1936, vol. 1768, PA174-18, pt 1, Prince Albert National Park – Grey Owl (Archie Belaney) 1931–1937 (reel T 14388), LAC.
91 *LH*, 27 July 1932, 7.
92 *LH*, 18 March 1935, 7.
93 Letter from J.C. Campbell to M.B. Williams, 2 December 1935, R12219-1-5-E, vol. 1, M.B. Williams Fonds, LAC.
94 Letters from J.C. Campbell to M.B. Williams, 4 January and 20 March 1936, ibid.
95 J.B. Harkin to Grey Owl, 24 June 1936, vol. 1768, PA174-18, pt 1, Prince Albert National Park – Grey Owl (Archie Belaney) 1931–1937 (reel T 14388), LAC.
96 Memorandum, 5 July 1937, ibid. The Department of the Interior was dissolved in 1936 and replaced by the Department of Mines and Resources, and the renamed National Parks Bureau was placed under one of its five branches: Lands, Parks and Forests. F.H.H. Williamson succeeded J.B. Harkin and became its controller.
97 Letter to F.H.H. Williamson, Controller, National Parks Bureau from the office of Hugh Eayres, MacMillan Canada, 18 February 1937, vol. 1768, PA174-18, pt 1, Prince Albert National Park – Grey Owl (Archie Belaney) 1931–1937 (reel T 14388), LAC.
98 Irene Moore, "Grey Owl is Ambassador of Great Northland," *Leader Post*, 6 January 1938, vol. 1770, PA272, pt 1, Prince Albert National Park – Grey Owl (Archie Belaney) – Clippings and Correspondence 1931–1938 (reel T 14389), LAC.
99 Letter from F.C. Badgley to C.M. Suggitt, 5 January 1940, file 13, vol. 9, R3608-10-6-E, Grey Owl Series, LAC.
100 Letter from E.H. Morrow to Robert J.C. Stead, 20 January 1938, vol. 1770, PA272, pt 1, Prince Albert National Park – Grey Owl (Archie Belaney) – Clippings and Correspondence 1931–1938 (reel T 14389), LAC.
101 Letter from Robert J.C. Stead to M.U. Bates, 11 January 1945, ibid.
102 M.U. Bates to Robert J.C. Stead, n.d., ibid.

CHAPTER FOUR

1 *MPH*, 22 April 1933, 31
2 Canada, Department of Trade and Commerce, Dominion Bureau of Statistics, "Weekly Bulletin" (7 April 1934), 4.
3 Berkowitz, "A 'New Deal' for Leisure." See also Currell, *The March of Spare Time*.
4 Ogilvie, *The Tourist Movement*, vii.
5 Canada, Senate, *Report and Proceedings of the Special Committee on Tourist Traffic*, 1934, 51.
6 Canada, Department of the Interior, *Annual Report for the Fiscal Year Ending 31 March 1917*, 3.
7 Bratter, *The Promotion of Tourist Travel by Foreign Countries*, 3–5.
8 Canada, Parliament, Senate, *Debates*, 17th Parliament, 5th Session, 295, 312. Dennis hoped that the hearings would underscore the urgent need for Dominion aid to expand tourism in the Maritimes (Kyte, "V-8 and Make and Break"). The final report of the Senate's 1934 Special Committee on Tourist Traffic recommended extending the National Parks into the Atlantic region "as a truly national policy, to embrace all the provinces" (Canada, Senate, *Report and Proceedings of the Special Committee on Tourist Traffic*, 1934, 294).
9 Committee members (all senators) consisted of W.A. Buchanan (Alberta), W.H. Dennis (Nova Scotia), W.E. Foster (New Brunswick), R.F. Green (British Columbia), H.C. Hocken (Ontario), R.B. Horner (Saskatchewan), C. MacArthur (PEI), and G. Parent (Quebec).
10 Canada, Senate, *Report and Proceedings of the Special Committee on Tourist Traffic*, 1934, 8.
11 Ibid., 103–4.
12 Ibid., 77.
13 Ibid., 12.
14 Ibid., 77, 81.
15 Ibid., 133–4.
16 *Catalogue of Motion Pictures Produced by the Canadian Government Motion Picture Bureau*, 3.
17 Canada, Senate, *Report and Proceedings of the Special Committee on Tourist Traffic*, 1934, 151–5.
18 Ibid., 45.
19 The non-commercial CATPB, formed under Dominion charter in 1929, provided a medium of exchange for ideas and information between tourism and publicity bureaux across Canada on improving and promoting

the tourist trade (Stephenson and McNaught, *The Story of Advertising in Canada*, 305–6).

20 Canada, Senate, *Report and Proceedings of the Special Committee on Tourist Traffic*, 1934, 39.

21 Ibid., 291.

22 Ibid., 289.

23 Apostle, "Canada, Vacations Unlimited," 16.

24 Dorland, *So Close to the State/s*, 21.

25 Outline of Important Events in History of Mr. D. Leo Dolan, vol. 1 (Biographical Information), D. Leo Dolan Fonds, MG 30, E259, LAC; Canada, Senate, *Report and Proceedings of the Special Committee on Tourist Traffic* [1934], 45.

26 Memorandum for the Minister, 19 November 1934, vol. 1, Minister Folder 1, D. Leo Dolan Fonds, MG 30, E259, LAC.

27 In 1935, Railways and Canals merged with other departments in the Department of Transport under C.D. Howe. Memorandum for the Minister, ibid.; Memorandum for the Minister, 18 December and 9 May 1935, ibid., Minister Folder 2.

28 "Press Release," 12 December 1936, ibid., Minister Folder 2.

29 Canada, Department of Trade and Commerce, Dominion Bureau of Statistics, "Weekly Bulletin," 25 May 1940, 4.

30 Brégent-Heald, "Five Little Stars."

31 "Canada your Friendly Neighbor Invites You," RG 20-A-5, 1568, T3258-4, LAC.

32 Memorandum for the Minister, 28 December 1934, vol. 1, Minister Folder 1, D. Leo Dolan Fonds, MG 30, E259, LAC.

33 "Canada your Friendly Neighbor Invites You."

34 *Winnipeg Free Press*, 18 July 1934; *Ottawa Citizen*, 18 July 1934, vol. 1, Minister Folder 1, D. Leo Dolan Fonds, MG 30, E259, LAC.

35 "Canada your Friendly Neighbor Invites You."

36 *Ottawa Journal*, 7 March 1935, Newspaper Clippings, vol. 1, D. Leo Dolan Fonds, MG 30, E259, LAC.

37 "Canada your Friendly Neighbor Invites You."

38 Canada, Senate, *Report and Proceedings of the Special Committee on Tourist Traffic* (1934), 42.

39 Memorandum for the Minister, 9 December 1935, vol. 1, Minister Folder 2, D. Leo Dolan Fonds, MG 30, E259, LAC.

40 Rotha, *Celluloid*, 63.

41 *Cinema*, 25 April 1928, "Canadian Government Motion Picture Bureau," vol. 198, R202-28-3-E, LAC.

42 *The Film Daily Yearbook of Motion Pictures – 1929*, 337.
43 *Globe*, 14 February 1929, 4.
44 On the history of the northwest melodrama, see Brégent-Heald, *Borderland Films*.
45 MPN, 19 April 1930, 27.
46 Benelli, "Hollywood and the Travelogue," 6.
47 ES (December 1931), 295. Before becoming "the world's leading authority on travel," in the early 1920s FitzPatrick cut his teeth on such short-subject series as the "Great Authors" and "Great Statesmen" for Charles Urban's Kineto Company (Metro-Goldwyn-Mayer, "James A. FitzPatrick"). He formed FitzPatrick Pictures, Inc., in 1924 and helmed such one-reel music-related series as Famous Music Masters and Famous Melody Series. This evolved into a short-lived Music Travelogue series for Paramount, in which "sound will be recorded simultaneously with the photographic of action at old world landmarks and locales that inspired great masters to create musical masterpieces" (MPN, 25 August 1928, 614). Other FitzPatrick-produced series included American Holidays and Movie Horoscopes.
48 *Hollywood Filmograph*, 6 July 1929, 28.
49 EHW, 6 July 1929, 89. Due to technological difficulties with on-location lip-synchronized recording, sound was applied in post-production in these early TravelTalks. Initially, the orchestra was supervised by Canadian-born conductor and instrumentalist Rosario Bourdon, who was replaced by American composer Nathaniel Shilkret in 1931.
50 *The Film Daily Yearbook of Motion Pictures – 1931*, 704; FD, 29 September 1929, 9.
51 C. Wolfe, "Historicising the 'Voice of God.'"
52 FD, 28 December 1930, 5.
53 Boynoff, "See the World before You Leave it," 4.
54 Studios that used Technicolor, which dominated colour-film production through the 1950s, had to rent the specially built camera, hire a camera operator to work alongside the cinematographer, employ additional lighting equipment, adopt special Max Factor make-up, process and print film at Technicolor's laboratories, and employ Natalie Kalmus, head of its Color Advisory Service, as a consultant (Haines, *Technicolor Movies*).
55 MPD, 31 July 1935, 14.
56 FD, 7 January 1937, 3.
57 FD, 12 August 1935, 2.
58 FD, 19 October 1939, 4.
59 Quigley Publishing Co., *The Box-Office Check-up*, 80.

60 *MGM Shorts Story*, March 1938, 6.

61 *MPH*, 2 April 1938, 44.

62 File 1 (1938), box 16. Office of the President Papers, Archives and Special Collections, University of New Brunswick (UNB).

63 "Newspaper clipping (no title)," 29 April 1939, Louis B. Mayer Bio File and Newspaper Clippings Scrapbook, 1936–1943, Archives and Special Collections, UNB.

64 *Standard* (Montreal), 27 April 1946, in vol. 2, D. Leo Dolan Fonds, MG 30, E259, LAC. See also Brégent-Heald, "Vacationland."

65 *Variety*, 1 September 1937, 16.

66 *FD*, 2 June 1938, 4; *Variety*, 1 September 1937, 16.

67 *BO*, 10 September 1938, 82.

68 *BO*, 1 April 1939, 27.

69 *BO*, 22 October 1938, 96.

70 *BO*, 27 August 1938, 87.

71 *Department of Highways Eighteenth Report 1935* (Halifax, NS: Minister of Public Works and Mines, 1936), Public Archives of Nova Scotia (PANS); Minsky, "Propaganda Bureaus as 'News Services.'"

72 *MPD*, 23 November 1935, 4. Between 1928 and 1937, the New York–based Van Beuren Corporation was best known for its animated short subjects, including treatments of Aesop's Fables. In 1938, McCracken became president of Courier Productions, New York City, which produced documentary short subjects, including two Kodachrome films in Nova Scotia of hunting for the *Field and Stream* film library and another colour film for Warner Bros. of woodcock and grouse shooting (*Department of Industry and Publicity Annual Report 1941* [Halifax: Provincial Secretary, 1942], PANS).

73 *MPH*, 15 August 1936. *Department of Highways Nineteenth Report 1936* (Halifax: Provincial Secretary, King's Printer, 1937), PANS.

74 *FD*, 29 November 1931, 1–2.

75 Felando, *Discovering Short Films*, 20–2.

76 King, "Introduction."

77 Ward, "Extra Added Attractions," 222; King, *Hokum!* 7.

78 *FD*, 21 September 1930, 4.

79 Ward, "Extra Added Attractions," 232.

80 *FD*, 29 November 1931, 5; *MPN*, 17 May 1930, 24.

81 *Variety*, 8 March 1932, 48.

82 *Canadian Cameos: The All-Canadian Sound Shorts, 1936–1937* (Montreal: Associated Screen News, 1937), file 474, box 7, Gordon Sparling Fonds, UTMA. Sparling also helmed the *Sport Chats* series, which would eventually be combined with Canadian Cameos.

83 *Canadian Cameos* brochure, n.d., file 474, box 7, Gordon Sparling Fonds, UTMA.

84 See *Canadian Cameos and Sport Chats: The All-Canadian Sound Shorts for 1935* (Montreal: ASN, 1935), file 473, box 7, Gordon Sparling Fonds, UTMA.

85 *GAM*, 2 March 1937, 8.

86 Allan, "Rhapsody in Two Languages and One Depression"; Jacobs, Hielscher, and Kinik, "Introduction." *Rhapsody in Two Languages* is available for viewing in LAC: https://youtu.be/NKopmAWmatU (accessed 16 December 2020).

87 Don. Buchanan, "*Roundabout* in the Swing," n.d., file 173, Scrapbook of Clippings, 1918–1947, vol. 1 (MG30-D402), William J. Oliver Fonds, R7658-0-4-E, LAC.

88 *GAM*, 25 January 1939, 9.

89 *Canadian Cameos and Sport Chats*; *Kentville N.S., Advertiser and Chronicle*, 14 March 1935, file 72, box 2, Gordon Sparling Fonds, UTMA.

90 *BO*, 27 August 1938, 86.

91 No title, 16 October 1929, vol. 198, Canadian Government Motion Picture Bureau, R202-28-3-E, LAC; Morris, *Embattled Shadows*, 169.

92 Gomery, *The Coming of Sound*.

93 Mees, "A New Substandard Film for Amateur Cinematography."

94 Simonson, "Equipment," 21–3; Wasson, *Everyday Movies*.

95 Slide, *Before Video*; Tepperman, *Amateur Cinema*, 165–7; Wasson, "Electric Homes! Automatic Movies! Efficient Entertainment!"; Wasson, "Modern Ideas about Old Films"; P.R. Zimmermann, *Reel Families*, 29–30.

96 Canada, Department of Trade and Commerce, *Thirty-second Annual Report of the Department of Trade and Commerce* (1924), 31–2.

97 Canada, Senate, *Report and Proceedings of the Special Committee on Tourist Traffic* (1934), 265.

98 Ibid., 84.

99 See, for example, Motion Picture Bureau – National Council YMCA, *Selected Motion Pictures* (1937), 38–46, for its list of Canadian 16-mm scenics available free for rental.

100 Canada, Senate, *Report and Proceedings of the Special Committee on Tourist Traffic*, 1934, 155. See Brégent-Heald, "Vacationland."

101 Morris, *Embattled Shadows*, 167. Sound equipment was being installed at the time of the Senate hearings in 1934.

102 Canada, Senate, *Report and Proceedings of the Special Committee on Tourist Traffic* (1934), 155.

103 Cook and Rahbek-Smith, *Educational Film Catalog*; *International Photographer*, August 1938, 14.

104 BO, 27 August 1938, 86. See also BO, 29 October 1938, 18.
105 Hackett, "National Film Society of Canada, 1935–1951," 138; Acland, "Patterns of Cultural Authority." The NFS was renamed the Canadian Film Institute in 1950.
106 Brison, *Rockefeller, Carnegie, and Canada*; Buxton, *Patronizing the Public.*
107 Acland, "National Dreams, International Encounters," 5.
108 Corbett, *We Have with Us Tonight*, 25. Other Canadian universities implemented continuation or correspondence courses, including British Columbia, McMaster, McGill, Saskatchewan, Toronto, and Western Ontario. The best-known Canadian adult-education program was the Antigonish Movement, emanating from the Extension Department of St Francis Xavier University in Antigonish, Nova Scotia. Established in 1928 under Rev. Dr Moses Coady and Rev. Jimmy Tompkins, it experimented with self-help and co-operative programs to assist workers in agriculture, farming, forestry, and mining during the Depression.
109 Druick, "The Best Teachers and the Best Preachers."
110 EFM, February 1920, 8. See also Grieveson, *Cinema and the Wealth of Nations*, 104; F.K. Lane, "Conservation through Engineering," 34–5; RAS, February 1919, 12.
111 Corbett, "A Brief History of Adult Education in Canada," 8. Carnegie funding also enabled creation of the Banff School of Fine Arts (Reichwein and Wall, *Uplift*, 29).
112 Druick, *Projecting Canada*, 76-77.
113 Acland, "National Dreams, International Encounters," 19–21.
114 Druick and Williams, "Introduction." On the interconnections between the NFS and Grierson, see Acland, "Patterns of Cultural Authority."
115 Corbett, *We Have with Us Tonight*, 151.
116 Druick, *Projecting Canada*, 42. On early cooperation between the CGMPB and Grierson, see Allan, "A National 'as Distinct from Departmental.'"

CHAPTER FIVE

1 Herbert, "Filming Victoria – Canada's 'Little Bit of England,'" 9.
2 Ellis, "John Grierson's First Years at the National Film Board."
3 Field, "Ross McLean."
4 Tallents, "The Birth of British Documentary (Part 1)," 16.
5 Hardy, *Grierson on Documentary*, 12.
6 Ellis, "The Young Grierson in America," 21. See also Charbonneau, "John Grierson and the United States"; Druick, *Projecting Canada*, 45–72.

7 Grierson, "The Documentary Producer," 7.
8 Grierson, "Better Popular Pictures," 227, 230.
9 See Aitken, *Film and Reform*. After resigning from the GPO film unit in 1937, Grierson helped set up the Film Centre, an advisory body to consult on the use of documentary film (Hardy, *Grierson on Documentary*, 19).
10 Rotha, "British Documentary Films Offer American Business Some New Opportunities."
11 Haworth, "Canada to Use Films as Propaganda Aid," 15.
12 *Cinema* (London), 1931, RG 20-C-2-g, R202-28-3-E, CGMPB, LAC.
13 *Citizen* (Ottawa), 3 June 1938; 4 June 1938; 10 June 1938, 19 January 1940; RG 20-C-2-g, R202-28-3-E, CGMPB, LAC. See also *BO*, 23 July 1938, 114.
14 *BO*, 30 July 1938, 95.
15 *BO*, 4 February 1939, 128; Brégent-Heald, "Vacationland," 36.
16 Druick, *Projecting Canada*, 40.
17 Canada, Parliament, House of Commons, *Debates*, 18th Parliament, 4th Session, Vol. 2, 9 March 1939, 1741. On the relationship between the CGMPB and the NFB, see Allan, "A National 'as Distinct from Departmental'"; Ellis, "John Grierson's First Years at the National Film Board."
18 Canada, Parliament, House of Commons, *Debates*, 18th Parliament, 4th Session, Vol. 2, 7 March 1939, 1668; 9 March 1939, 1742.
19 *BO*, 4 February 1939, 128.
20 Canada, Parliament, Senate, *Debates*, 18th Parliament, 4th Session, Vol. 1, 31 March 1939, 98–100.
21 Department of Trade and Commerce – Publicity Branch, 1 November 1939, file A-328, vol. 1, Department of Trade and Commerce Fonds, RG 20-A-3, vol. 575, LAC.
22 Press Release, 21 December 1939, ibid.
23 Boisseau and Markwyn, *Gendering the Fair*, 1; Rydell and Kroes, *Buffalo Bill in Bologna*, 72.
24 Showmanship, n.d., file 49427, vol. 389, Department of Forest Service and Forestry Branch, RG 39, 214-232-5-E, LAC; Department of Trade and Commerce – Publicity Branch," 16 September 1938, ibid.
25 The Dominion Forester, 17 October 1939, ibid.
26 Department of Trade and Commerce – Publicity Branch, 16 September 1938, ibid.; Cowell, "The Canadian Pavilion at the 1939 New York World's Fair and the Development of Modernism in Canada"; Dawn, "Cross-Border Trading."
27 Press Release, 21 December 1939, file A-328, vol. 1, Department of Trade and Commerce, vol. 575, RG 20-A-3, LAC; J.R. Dickson report, 24

November 1939, file 49427, vol. 389, Department of Forest Service and Forestry Branch, RG 39, 214-232-5-E, LAC.

28 Press Release, 21 December 1939, Department of Trade and Commerce.

29 *BSM*, no. 3 (1940), 34; *BSM*, no. 1 (1939), 21; Wasson, "The Other Smal Screen."

30 *FN*, July 1940, 5; *National Board of Review Magazine* (September 1940), 11.

31 *The Case of Charlie Gordon*, *Heritage*, and *Youth Is Tomorrow* (dir. by Stuart Legg, 1939), the latter about youth training, were screened in November 1939 at New York's Museum of Modern Art (MOMA) (Press Release, 28 November 1939, file A-328, vol. 1, Department of Trade and Commerce, vol. 575, RG 20, LAC. See also *BO*, 6 January 1940, 115).

32 By contrast, the British Pavilion screened primarily newsreels about the evolving, threatening situation in Europe. See Grierson, "Propaganda for Democracy"; Swann, *The British Documentary Film Movement*, 138–42.

33 J.R. Dickson to D. Leo Dolan, 30 August 1940, file 49427, vol. 389, Department of Forest Service and Forestry Branch, RG 39, 214-232-5-E, LAC.

34 New York World's Fair – Attendance, 12 November 1940, ibid. See also Robert Stead to Dolan, 29 November 1940, ibid.

35 C.W. Barry to Dolan, 12 November 1940, ibid.

36 Press Release, 21 December 1939, file A-328, vol. 1, Department of Trade and Commerce, vol. 575, RG 20-A-3, LAC.

37 *BO*, 27 May 1939, 113.

38 The King and Queen visited Washington, DC, and Hyde Park, the Roosevelts' mansion on the Hudson River in New York, in addition to attending the world's fair in New York (see Bell, "The Foreign Office and the 1939 Royal Visit to America"; Cull, "Overture to an Alliance";

39 Parmelee, "Canada's Participation in the World's Fair."

40 J. Nye, Jr, "Public Diplomacy and Soft Power."

41 Apostle, "Canada, Vacations Unlimited," 154; Canada, Parliament, House of Commons, *Debates*, 19th Parliament, 3rd Session, Vol. 5, 30 July 1942, 5008.

42 Canada, House of Commons, *Debates*, 19th Parliament, 2nd Session, Vol. 4, 12 November 1941, 4317.

43 Terry, "A Vacation in Canada."

44 Letter from D. Leo Dolan to J.N. Nickell, Assistant Secretary, Essex County Tourist Association, 15 January 1941, Tourism, Propaganda towards the Prevention of Tourist Travel to Canada, RG-20-A-5, 1562, T3200-61, LAC.

45 Letter from K.C. Jones to D. Leo Dolan, 20 March 1941, ibid.

46 Minutes of the Economic Advisory Committee on a discussion concerning the Tourist Trade, 16 March 1940, Tourism, Suggestions and general correspondence re: Advisory Committee on Travel and Tourist Industry, vol. 1563, T3200-75, RG 20-A-5, LAC. The brochure was titled "Plan Your Vacation to Canada as Usual: War Conditions Bring no Restrictions on Travel in Canada."

47 W.S. Thompson, Director of Publicity[,] to D. Leo Dolan, 1 November 1940, Tourism, Suggestions and general correspondence re: Advisory Committee on Travel and Tourist Industry, vol. 1563, T3200-75, RG 20-A-5, LAC.

48 Recommendations made by the Delegates to the Conference of Provincial and Transportation Officials," ibid.

49 Grierson is paraphrasing Walter Lippmann. "John Grierson, 'Relations of the Government to Film Industry in Time of War', An address to the National Board of Review, New York City, 13 November 1941," entry 298, box 1564, OWI Records, NC 148, RG 208, NARA.

50 Goetz, "The Canadian Wartime Documentary." Stuart Legg was the driving force behind both series.

51 *BSM*, no. 6 (1945), 23–4.

52 By 1944, there were eighty-two rural circuits, ten trade-union circuits, and forty industrial circuits. Adamson, "The Educational Film in Canada," 437; Buchanan, "A Canadian Experiment."

53 McInnes, *One Man's Documentary*, 47, 189.

54 *FD*, 27 October 1941, 2. Greene remained head of distribution until 1946.

55 Memorandum, 12 November 1940, Tourism, Suggestions and general correspondence re: Advisory Committee on Travel and Tourist Industry, vol. 1563, T3200-75, RG 20-A-5, LAC.

56 *DNL*, January 1941, 15. *DNL* began in 1940, became *Documentary Film News* in 1948, and folded in 1949.

57 *DNL*, October 1940, 7.

58 The film may be viewed at https://www.youtube.com/watch?v=Vegh2_B20Lo (accessed 27 January 2021).

59 Jessup, "The Group of Seven and the Tourist Landscape in Western Canada," 146.

60 McInnes, *One Man's Documentary*, 177. The film can be viewed at https://www.onf.ca/film/canadian_landscape (accessed 16 December 2020). Its success would launch the NFB's Canadian Artists series.

61 Formed in 1939 with headquarters in Ottawa, Crawley Films was incorporated in 1946 (Forrester, "The Crawley Era").

62 Tepperman, *Amateur Cinema*, 1, 241.
63 Maxim produced *Mag the Hag* in 1925, an early amateur film (Tepperman, *Amateur Cinema*, 20).
64 Of the 150 films listed 1930–44, more than half were travelogues (Kattelle, "The Amateur Cinema League and Its Films," 244–6).
65 MMM, April 1937, 178. The film is available at https://youtu.be/Wcm_Xx-TDqI (accessed 8 January 2022).
66 Crawley, "Cine Canoeing," 388.
67 Crawley, "Three Days of Sequences," 63.
68 Ibid., 63, 77. The silent one-reel scenic also was named best locally produced film in a contest sponsored by the Ottawa branch of the NFS. The judges were J.B. Scott of the CGMPB, President Douglas Leechman of the NFS, and E.W. Harrold of the *Ottawa Citizen* (BO, 6 May 1939, 108).
69 Emphasis added. Crawley, "Three Days of Sequences," 63, 77.
70 Macdougall, "Beyond Observational Cinema," 125.
71 Jessup, "Marius Barbeau and Early Ethnographic Cinema"; Forrester, "The Crawley Era."
72 MMM, December 1939, 608–9. After a showing of *L'Île d'Orléans*, Barbeau apparently convinced the Canadian Geographical Society to sponsor a Crawley film on the history of power in Canada. Following a screening of *Canadian Power* (1939), Grierson contracted the Crawleys to make *Four New Apple Dishes* (1940) to help Nova Scotia sell its surplus (Philips, "The Home Movies People *Pay* to See," 21, 51).
73 MMM, December 1939, 608.
74 MMM, January 1938, 15; MMM, December 1937, 602. Jones also developed a dual turntable to provide musical accompaniment and sound effects, which other amateur filmmakers, including the Crawleys, adopted. Walter Thompson, CNR director of publicity, who briefly headed Canada's Bureau of Public Information during the war, attended one of these screenings. The CNR eventually offered Jones a post as a cinematographer and publicist (MMM, October 1937, 516; MMM, July 1942, 307).
75 MMM, January 1938, 38. A documentary short subject produced by the GPO's film unit under Grierson, *Night Mail* follows a postal-express train through the industrialized landscape, as well as conveying the working conditions of postal workers (Anthony, *Night Mail*).
76 MMM, October 1933, 415; MMM, December 1932, 537; MMM, December 1933, 523.
77 Jones, "Train Trails," 419, 430.
78 Heffernan, "*Hail, British Columbia!*" 100, 118.
79 Ibid.

80 Heffernan, "*Hail, British Columbia!*" 120.

81 D. Leo Dolan to Sir James H. MacBrien, 15 June 1937; Sir James MacBrien to D. Leo Dolan, 18 June 1937, Tourism, Royal Canadian Mounted Police Officers on Duty during Tourist Season, vol. 1562, T3200-47, RG 20-A-5, LAC.

82 *MMM*, March 1942, 92, 113. The NFB incorporated stills from *Hail, British Columbia!* (1941), the Maxim Memorial Award–winning Canadian travelogue, in its contest promotion. See Brégent-Heald, "Come to Canada."

83 *MMM*, March 1942, 128.

84 Coates and Morrison, *The Alaska Highway in World War II*, 52. On Canadian-US relations during this period, see Perras, *Franklin Roosevelt*; Thompson and Randall, *Canada and the United States*, 134–70.

85 *MMM*, June 1942, 259.

86 *MMM*, March 1943, 118.

87 *MMM*, December 1944, 477. This was Gunnell's ninth time on the list.

88 *MMM*, December 1945, 480.

89 Memorandum, 12 November 1940, Tourism, Suggestions and general correspondence re: Advisory Committee on Travel and Tourist Industry, vol. 1563, T3200-75, RG 20-A-5, LAC.

90 *MPD*, 21 August 1939, 15; Boynoff, "See the World before You Leave it."

91 *STR*, 28 March 1942, 29. FitzPatrick also made *Glimpses of Ontario* (1942), a general overview of the province's agricultural, industrial, and scenic attributes.

92 Herbert, "Canada's War Movies," 370. For more on Herbert, see Jenkins, *Celluloid Pueblo*.

93 Memorandum, 12 November 1940, Tourism, Suggestions and general correspondence re: Advisory Committee on Travel and Tourist Industry, vol. 1563, T3200-75, RG 20-A-5, LAC.

94 Herbert, "Filming Victoria," 9–10.

95 *STR*, 18 October 1941, 23; *FD*, 19 December 1941, 7. Herbert probably filmed as well *Peaceful Quebec – At War*. In an article, he details how he shot a travelogue of Quebec during the summer of 1941 and advises amateurs wishing to do the same (Herbert, "I Make a Travelogue in Old Quebec").

96 *MPH*, 21 March 1942, 566.

97 *Exhibitor*, 11 June 1941, 766.

98 Although the seeds of the Good Neighbor Policy were sown in 1928 with President-elect Herbert Hoover's goodwill tour of Latin America, US foreign policy began to shift with Franklin Roosevelt's inauguration in

1933 and accelerated during the Second World War to secure hemispheric defence (Conn and Fairchild, *The Framework of Hemispheric Defense*; Guerrant, *Roosevelt's Good Neighbor Policy*; Pike, *FDR's Good Neighbor Policy*).

99 Executive Order 8840 established the OCIAA on 30 July 1941. In October 1940, Rockefeller created a separate Motion Picture Division under John Hay (Jock) Whitney, which encouraged filmmakers to incorporate more positive representations of Latin America and its citizens (United States, *History of the Office of the Coordinator of Inter-American Affairs*).

100 James and Weller, *Treasure Island*, 225.

101 Cited in Tercero, "First Inter-American Travel Cóngress," 467.

102 Masters, "International Agencies in the Western Hemisphere." In 1948, the Organization of American States (OAS) became the official organ of the Inter-American System. Canada declined to join but did become a permanent observer in 1972 and a full member in 1990.

103 Tercero, "Practical Pan Americanism," 146–7. Tercero died suddenly in July 1939.

104 Canada did not participate in the Golden Gate Exposition because it was already at the New York World's Fair. The International Bureau of Exhibitions, of which Canada is a signatory, does not permit countries to participate in two exhibitions in the same country in the same year (Outline of Important Events in History of Mr. D. Leo Dolan, D. Leo Dolan, vol. 1 [Biographical Information], MG 30, E259, LAC; Telegram from C.D. Howe to Major O.B. Keatings, 18 April 1939, file 721, vol. 1879, R219-100-6-E, LAC).

105 US Department of the Interior, National Park Service, The Policy and Program of the United States Travel Division, RG 5015, 01413, Archives of Ontario (AO). Secretary of the Interior Harold Ickes had in 1937 established a temporary tourism bureau within the National Parks Service, which was itself expanding (United States, Congress, House, Committee on Interstate and Foreign Commerce, *National Travel Board*, 1939).

106 McLennan, "Promoting Tourism, Selling a Nation," 2, 96.

107 United States, Department of the Interior, *Annual Report of the Secretary of the Interior, Fiscal Year Ended June 30, 1941*, 298.

108 Cited in "Statement by the Inter-American Trade and Travel Association," United States, Seventy-sixth Congress, Third Session, *Appendix*, Vol. 86, Part 13 (22 February 1940), 905.

109 Minutes of the Economic Advisory Committee on a discussion concerning the Tourist Trade, 16 March 1940, Tourism, Suggestions and general

correspondence re: Advisory Committee on Travel and Tourist Industry, vol. 1563, T3200-75, RG 20-A-5, LAC.

110 *Detroit Free Press*, 7 September 1940, 12. At the conference, Dolan was made vice president of this organization, composed of officials directing national, state, provincial, and regional tourist and publicity activities throughout the western hemisphere.

111 The USTB was revived in 1947 and renamed the United States Travel Division (United States, Department of the Interior, *Annual Report of the Department of the Interior* 1942, 164. See also "Travel for Relaxation Approved by Washington," 21 January 1942, *New York World-Telegram*, Tourism, North American Travel Conference, vol. 1563, T3200-71, RG 20-A-5, LAC). On tourism's ongoing place in American life during the war, see M. Dawson, "Travel Strengthens America?"

112 *Chicago Daily News*, 23 January 1942, Tourism, Press Articles Received, vol. 1562, T3200-58, RG 20-A-5, LAC.

113 *New York Journal-American*, 2 February 1941, Tourism, North American Travel Conference, vol. 1563, T3200-71, RG 20-A-5, LAC.

114 Payne, *The Official Picture*.

115 Norman A.M. MacKenzie of the University of New Brunswick succeeded Vining as chair, a nominal position. After Grierson resigned from the WIB in 1944, his deputy, Arnold Davidson Dunton, served as general manager until war's end. Prime Minister King then appointed him chair of the CBC, a post he held until 1958.

116 Potter, *Branding Canada*, 80.

117 Letter from Campbell L. Smart to C.H. Payne, 21 November 1942, file A-328, WWII Public Information Committee, External Affairs Canadian Information Division, Department of Trade and Commerce, vol. 575, RG 20-A-3, LAC; Memo from Dana Doten to James Secrest, 16 February 1943, entry 263, box 1430, OWI Records, NC 148, RG 208, NARA.

118 *NYT*, 14 June 1942, 1.

119 Composed of five divisions, the BMP coordinated the production and distribution of newsreel footage and war-information films, both 35-mm and 16-mm, and acted as the central point of contact with the commercial film industry. Mellett was the director of the Office of Government Reports (OGR) in 1939, and in December 1941 President Roosevelt designated him the coordinator of government films. With the establishment of the OWI in 1942, Mellett took over the Bureau of Motion Pictures. Screenwriter and producer Robert Riskin (Oscar winner for writing Frank Capra's *It Happened One Night*, which swept the Academy Awards for 1934) ran the Bureau of Overseas Motion Pictures, which distributed film

materials beyond the western hemisphere (Larson, "The Domestic Motion Picture Work of the Office of War Information").

120 Memorandum to James A. Secrest (Assistant Chief, Bureau of Field Operations) from Dana Doten, Appendix to Report on Canadian Situation, 16 February 1943, entry 263, box 1430, OWI Records, NC 148, RG 208, NARA.

121 Dana Doten to Henry Paynter, Information Division, Office of Emergency Management, 29 August and 3 September 1942, and Dana Doten to George McMillan, 26 November 1942, ibid.

122 Wesley Greene to C.R. Reagan, 11 September 1943, entry 305, box 1581, OWI Records, NC 148, RG 208, NARA. Reagan was a former educator and past president of the National Association of Visual Education Dealers. For more on US non-theatrical distribution of OWI films, see *FN* (March 1942), 1, 7.

123 Emphasis added. H.A. Spencer to (C.H. Payne) Director, Commercial Intelligence Service, Department of Trade and Commerce, 6 January 1944, file A-328, WWII Public Information Committee, External Affairs Canadian Information Division, Department of Trade and Commerce, vol. 575, RG 20-A-3, LAC.

124 Films to be Distributed in the United States, 20 February 1943, entry 305, box 1581, OWI Records, NC 148, RG 208, NARA; Canada's War Films Hit Hard! *BSM* no. 5 (1942): 15–17, 34; pages 15–17 briefly describe these films. See also Wheeler, "War Films in the Classroom," 119.

125 According to Thorson, Jacoby acted as an NFB liaison with New York producers and distributors, as well as various US civic, state, and federal agencies (Canada, Parliament, House of Commons, *Debates*, 19th Parliament, 3rd Session, Vol. 3, 21 May 1942, 2623; 22 May 1942, 2700). The film can be viewed at https://www.nfb.ca/film/high-over-borders (accessed 2 November 2021).

126 Catalogue of 16mm Educational Talking Pictures, 1942–1943, entry 318 Ak–Bu, box 1601, Audio-Film Libraries, OWI Records, NC 148, RG 208, NARA. Other catalogues featuring NFB films in the OWI files include Akin & Bashaw (Denver, CO), Burke's Motion Picture Company (South Bend, IN), Campbell Films (Manhattan, MT), College Film Center (Chicago), and Herbert Studios (Hartford, CT).

127 *ES* (June 1944), 254; Motion Pictures Owned by or Relating to the American Railroads, entry 317, box 1600, OWI Records, NC 148, RG 208, NARA. Carter graduated from the University of Iowa and had worked at University of Chicago Press (*SAH*, October 1945, 26).

128 Canada, Parliament, House of Commons, *Debates*, 19th Parliament, 3rd Session, Vol. 5, 30 July 1942, 5008–9.
129 J.M. Carter, "Films for Tomorrow," *Church Property Administration* 8, no. 4 (1944), 26-9. Cited in ES (September 1944), 302.

CHAPTER SIX

1 US city, state, and regional travel officials formed the National Association of Travel Officials in October 1941 to "build a bridge between private and government efforts" to develop tourism. In November 1945, this body amalgamated with the North American Travel Conference under the latter's name, which became the National Association of Travel Organizations in 1951 (United States, *Destination USA*, 23).
2 *Billboard*, 22 September 1945, 77.
3 Canada – a Tourist Empire, 15 January 1947, item 75, box 3, Tourist Dominion Provincial Conference 1945–1947, GR1968.0310, Provincial Archives of Alberta (PAA).
4 Address to American Automobile Association, n.d., D. Leo Dolan, vol. 1, Speeches, MG 30 E259, LAC.
5 *MPH*, 29 November 1947, 3956; *CMPD*, 28 May 1949, 8. See also *CMPD*, 20 December 1947, 25.
6 Canada, House of Commons Debates, 20th Parliament, 2nd Session, Vol. 5, 30 August 1946, 5618.
7 BO, 9 August 1947, 111. See also *Report of Proceedings, Third Dominion-Provincial Tourist Conference* (Ottawa: King's Printer, 1948), 9, folder 1.3, RG 5 B-6, AO. On the postwar travel boom, see Popp, *The Holiday Makers*.
8 In 1946, Eric Johnston succeeded Will Hays (of the infamous Hays Code) as president of the Motion Picture Producers and Distributors Association and changed its name to the Motion Picture Association of America (MPAA).
9 Kuffert, *A Great Duty*, 73–4.
10 Letter to Dan E.C. Campbell, 10 May 1944, item 129, box 7, Pacific Northwest Tourist Association 1945–1947, GR1968.0310, PAA.
11 Outline of Important Events in History of Mr. D. Leo Dolan, vol. 1 (Biographical Information), MG 30, E259, LAC.
12 Rinden, "Tourism," 5–7. In October 1945, following the disbanding of the Department of National War Services, the CGTB transferred to the Department of Trade and Commerce under minister James A. MacKinnon.
13 Canada, Parliament, House of Commons, *Debates*, 20th Parliament, 1st Session, Vol. 1, 17 September 1945, 242.

14 On the use of tourism in postwar cultural and consumer diplomacy, see Endy, *Cold War Holidays*.

15 Address given by Dolan at the sixth annual meeting of the National Association of Travel Officials, Chicago, 15 November 1946, item 75, box 3, GR1968.0310, PAA.

16 Memo to the Canadian Consuls General at New York and Chicago, n.d., Cooperation with Canadian Consulates in US, CGTB, RG 12-A-1, LAC. Patricia Robb was appointed to the Chicago position, and Veronica O'Meara to New York.

17 Order in Council (P.C. 6300, 28 September 1945) establishing the Canadian Information Service, 28 September 1945, file A-328, vol. 575, RG 20-A3, LAC. A six-member committee – the CBC's general manager, the CIS director, the External Affairs undersecretary of state, the NFB commissioner, the Privy Council Office deputy head, and the Trade and Commerce deputy minister – reported to Parliament through Minister of National Defence Brooke Claxton. The CIS was disbanded in July 1947 and absorbed by External Affairs' Information Division (Hilliker and Barry, *Canada's Department of External Affairs*, 10–11).

18 Canadian Information Service, n.d., file A-328, vol. 575, RG 20-A3, LAC.

19 External Affairs Information Division Advisory Committee, n.d., ibid.; Canadian Information Service, 4 November 1946, ibid.

20 Clearing House Catalogue, ibid. *Field and Stream* was the leading periodical for outdoor enthusiasts and maintained a large circulating library of 16-mm wildlife and game films distributed widely throughout the United States. In 1948, the NFB produced three additional films on sport fishing for that library: *Canadian Smallmouth*, *Coho Salmon on the Fly*, and *Indian Canoe Men*.

21 Letter from Hon. E.C. Manning, Minister of Trade and Industry [and Premier] (Alberta) to D.E.C. Campbell, 25 March 1942, item 142, box 8, GR1968.0310, PAA.

22 Minutes of the first meeting of the tourist advisory board, 24 April 1942, ibid.

23 Minutes from a meeting of the tourist advisory board, 15 December 1944, ibid.

24 $14,500 for departmental advertising and publicity; $10,000 for promotion activities; $10,000 for tourist advertising, together with $4,000 for a booklet, and about $5,000 for 16-mm motion pictures (Letter from D.E.C. Campbell to D. Leo Dolan, 11 March 1946, file 102, box 5, GR1968.0310, PAA).

25 Alberta Government Films Produced by and Available from the Film & Photographic Branch, *Seventh Dominion-Provincial Tourist Conference*, 1952, vol. 1563, T 3200-131, RG 20-A 9, LAC. Crawley Films did the technical sound and editing on both pictures. See Alberta, Department of Economic Affairs, vol. 1 and vol. 4, Crawley Films Limited Fonds, MG 28-III99, LAC. Warner Bros. incorporated scenes from *Autumn in Alberta* for its own *Neighbor Next Door* (dir. by Gordon Hollingshead, 1951), a two-reel Technicolor special associated with the Canadian Cooperation Project (CCP).

26 Alberta, Department of Economic Affairs, *Sixth Annual Report* (1950).

27 British Columbia, Department of Trade and Industry, *Report of the Department of Trade and Industry for the Year Ended December 31st 1944*. See also M. Dawson, *Selling British Columbia*, 44–53.

28 In 1937–38, the BCGTB was the Bureau of Industrial and Tourist Development, which had absorbed the Bureau of Information, founded 1900 (M.C. Holmes, *Publications of the Government of British Columbia,* 225; M. Dawson, *Selling British Columbia*, 80–115).

29 Mortimore, "Clarence Ferris." One of Ferris's earliest productions was *Tourism: A British Columbia Industry* (1940), a silent meta-film showing the BCGTB's activities. Other promotion films include *Vancouver: British Columbia's Island Playground* (1942) and *The Okanagan Valley: British Columbia's Orchard Playground* (1943) (Browne, *Motion Picture Production in British Columbia: 1898–1940*).

30 *TDC*, 8 May 1947, 9; British Columbia, Department of Trade and Industry, *Report of the Department of Trade and Industry for the Year Ended December 31st 1949*.

31 *Summary of Proceedings, Second Dominion-Provincial Tourist Conference* (1948), 15.

32 Ontario, Department of Travel and Publicity, *Report of the Minister of Travel and Publicity, Province of Ontario for the Fiscal year 1946–1947*, 9. Other films include *Lake of the Woods* (1948), *Friendly Invaders* (1949), *Lakehead Nipigon Holiday* (1949), *Muskoka Story* (1949), *Ontario Winter Holiday* (1949), and *Trout Time* (1949).

33 Province of Ontario Tourist Activities for 1952 and Plans for 1953, *Seventh Dominion-Provincial Tourist Conference,* 1952, vol. 1563, T3200-131, RG 20-A 9, LAC. Mary Ainslie, director of the publicity branch, stated that the NFB, to ease customs difficulties, distributed Ontario's 16-mm tourism films throughout the United States to "service clubs, sportsmen's organizations and teacher and pupil groups," as well as to such exhibitions as the Detroit News Travel Show (Ontario,

Department of Travel and Publicity, *Report of the Minister of Travel and Publicity, Province of Ontario for the Fiscal Year 1947–1948*, 11).

34 *Department of Industry and Publicity Annual Report 1947* (Halifax: Provincial Secretary, 1948), PANS.

35 *Province of Nova Scotia, Bureau of Information, Annual Report 1950* (Halifax: Queen's Printer, 1951), PANS. ASN processed approximately 3,000 feet of Courtney's Kodachrome footage, resulting in three films released by Nova Scotia's Department of Industry and Publicity in 1947: *Gateway to the World*, focusing on the port of Halifax during the Second World War; *Happy Valley*, filmed in the Annapolis Valley (a.k.a., the "Land of Evangeline"); and *Spring Fever*, featuring a fishing trip in the Kedgemakooge district.

36 *Department of Industry and Publicity Annual Report 1947* (Halifax: Provincial Secretary, 1948), PANS. For more on Margaret Perry, see https://counterarchive.ca/case-studies/margaret-perry-and-nova-scotia-film-bureau-films (accessed 19 March 2020); Darrell Varga, "Margaret Perry and the Nova Scotia Film Bureau," https://novascotia.ca/archives/nsfilm/perry.asp (accessed 19 March 2020).

37 Emphasis added. Although Perry refers to *Battling 'Blue-Fins'* as a film for "sportsmen," it features both male and female deep-sea anglers, such as the record-breaking husband-and-wife team of John and Georgia Manning from Los Angeles (*Department of Industry and Publicity, Annual Report 1946* [Halifax: Provincial Secretary, 1947], PANS). This area is also where William J. Oliver filmed Michael Lerner in *Warriors of the Deep* (1936) and *Battling the Tuna* (1937), which popularized tuna sport fishing. Perry's *Battling 'Blue-Fins'* is available at https://youtu.be/o_r65StoLt8 (accessed 13 February 2022).

38 *Report of Proceedings, Dominion-Provincial Tourist Conference* (Ottawa: King's Printer, 1947), 68, 85, folder 1.1, RG 5 B-6, AO.

39 *MPH*, 14 December 1946, 35.

40 *Summary of Proceedings, Second Dominion-Provincial Tourist Conference*, 28, 53, 55, folder 1.2, RG 5 B-6, AO.

41 Rommer, "Budge Crawley," 194. See also *CMPD*, 24 February 1951.

42 Dean Walker, "Crawley's and the Sponsored Film," *Canadian Industrial Photography* (January 1960), Crawley Films, box 40, UTMA. Crawley Films also made headway in the American market after the war. Most notably, it produced two series of educational films, one on adolescent development and marriage and the second on family living, for the McGraw Hill Company for distribution to American high schools and postsecondary institutions.

43 "The Critical Issue," 273.

44 *DFN* (January 1947), 7; Grierson, "O Canada! We Stand on Guard for Thee."

45 *CMPD*, 19 July 1947, 18. McLean had been since its inception with the NFB, where he both directed and produced films. He became deputy commissioner in 1943, acting commissioner after Grierson resigned in October 1945 to organize International Film Associates, and commissioner in 1947.

46 McLean, "Canada Serves the Common Cause," 21.

47 Jordan, "Canada's World-wide Films"; Druick, *Projecting Canada*, 74.

48 Cited in Hill, *Canada's Salesman to the World*, 395.

49 Requisition Data – publications, 27 October 1945, U113-60, pt 1, Universal – Catalogue of motion picture films 1937–1946 (reel T 12919), vol. 163, RG 84 A-2-a, LAC.

50 Summary of NFB Report Re Canadian Travel Film Program in the United States as Submitted by H.B. Chandler, 13 October 1960, U117-56-17, pt 1, Universal – Motion Pictures – Wildlife Films 1954–1957 (reel 16203), vol. 2063, RG 84-A-2-A, LAC.

51 Canada, Senate, *Proceedings of the Standing Committee on Tourist Traffic, no.* 2, 31 March 1949, 46.

52 Canada, Senate, *Proceedings of the Standing Committee on Tourist Traffic, no. 1*, 19 February 1948, 16. See also Appendix A, The National Parks of Canada and Their Relation to the Tourist Industry, *Proceedings of the Standing Committee on Tourist Traffic, no. 1*, 21 March 1949, 24.

53 Other films include *Fundy Holiday* (dir. by John E.R. McDougall, 1951), *Point Pelee, Nature Sanctuary* (dir. by Michael Spencer, 1953), *Wardens of Waterton* (dir. by Leslie McFarlane, 1954), and *Land of Bubbling Waters* (1955), (Canadian Travel Film Library [NFB], 1950, *Canadian Travel and Wildlife Films*, LAC). In addition to being a producer, Michael Spencer was chief of the NFB's Liaison Division vis-à-vis other government departments. As of 1951, the CGTB began handling publicity for the Parks Branch (Canada, Department of Resources and Development, *Annual Report for the Fiscal Year ended March 31, 1951*).

54 For example, Canada, Parliament, House of Commons, *Debates*, 21st Parliament, 1st Session, Vol. 3, 7 December 1949, 2874–5.

55 Suspicions regarding Grierson's supposed communist inclinations could be traced back as early as 1942, when US FBI Director J. Edgar Hoover launched an inquiry. On the NFB security scare, see Kristmanson, *Plateaus of Freedom*, 49–85. See also Cox, "The Grierson Files"; G. Evans, *In the National Interest*, 7–9; Whitaker and Marcuse, *Cold War Canada*,

228–52. Both *The Iron Curtain* (dir. by William Wellman, 1948), from Twentieth Century–Fox, and *Operation Manhunt* (dir. by Jack Alexander, 1954) fictionalize the epoch-shaking Gouzenko affair. The films were shot in Ottawa and Quebec, respectively.

56 Wagman, "The Woods Gordon Report."

57 Emphasis added. "The National Film Act of 1950," Government of Canada, National Film Board of Canada, http://onf-nfb.gc.ca/en/about-the-nfb/organization/mandate (accessed 14 April 2020).

58 Canada, Parliament, House of Commons, *Debates*, 21st Parliament, 2nd Session, Vol. 4, 23 June 1950, 4097.

59 Canada, Royal Commission on National Development in the Arts, Letters and Sciences, *Report*, 50 (hereinafter Massey Report). The other commissioners were Georges-Hénri Lévesque, dean of the Faculty of Social Sciences at Laval University; Norman A.M. MacKenzie, president of the University of British Columbia; Hilda Neatby, professor of history at the University of Saskatchewan; and Arthur Surveyer, a civil engineer from Montreal. Members of Canada's cultural elite largely dominated the hearings. On the Massey Commission, see Finlay, *The Force of Culture*; Litt, *The Muses, the Masses, and the Massey Commission*; Massolin, *Canadian Intellectuals*.

60 Druick, "Remedy and Remediation," 160.

61 *Report of Proceedings, Third Dominion-Provincial Tourist Conference* (1948), 44a.

62 Massey Report, 255.

63 M. Dawson, "A 'Civilizing' Industry," 440.

64 Canada, House of Commons, *Debates*, 20th Parliament, 1st Session, Vol. 3, 11 December 1945, 3340; Memorandum to James A. MacKinnon from D. Leo Dolan, 1 November 1945, file T3250-38, vol. 1565, RG 20-A5, LAC.

65 Drafting Recommendations, Educating the Farmer to the Value of the Tourist Business, 15 December 1944, item 142, box 8, Tourist Advisory Board 1940–1944, GR1968.0310, PAA.

66 Report on 1948 Tourist Service Education Week, n.d., file T3610-C-3, vol. 3, RG 20-A-5, vol. 1578, LAC. The CATPB produced "The Visitor Industry Booklet" as a reference guide for industry stakeholders. On the postwar courtesy campaign more broadly, see Dubinsky, "Everybody Likes Canadians."

67 *Summary of Proceedings, Second Dominion-Provincial Tourist Conference* 28, 53, 55, folder 1.2, RG 5 B-6, AO.

68 The NFB released this short subject through Columbia Pictures to more than five hundred Canadian theatres as part of its Canada Carries On series in both English and French to coincide with that year's springtime Tourist Service Week.

69 Canadian Government Travel Bureau, *Travellers' Cheques* (1951–1952), vol. 7, Crawley Films Limited Fonds, MG 28-III99, LAC.

70 Memorandum, 12 November 1940, Tourism, Suggestions and general correspondence re: Advisory Committee on Travel and Tourist Industry, vol. 1563, T3200-75, RG 20-A-5, LAC.

71 Canada, Senate, *Proceedings of the Standing Committee on Tourist Traffic* (1948), 19 February 1948, 10.

72 D. Leo Dolan, "Tourist Activities in 1949 and Plans for 1950," in *Fourth Dominion-Provincial Tourist Conference* (Ottawa: King's Printer, 1949), 3, folder 1.4, RG 5 B-6, AO.

73 National Film Board Report to the Ninth Dominion-Provincial Tourist Conference, *Ninth Dominion-Provincial Tourist Conference*, 1954, vol. 1564, T 3200-131, RG 20 A, LAC.

74 Report on Travel Film Distribution in the United States and Canada, 3 December 1951, *Sixth Dominion-Provincial Tourist Conference*, 1951, vol. 1563, T3200-131, RG 20-A-5, LAC.

75 National Film Board Report to the Ninth Dominion-Provincial Tourist Conference."

76 Ibid.

77 *BSM* 11, no. 7 (1950), 30.

78 J.M. Carter, "The Curriculum Clinic."

79 *Report of Proceedings, Third Dominion-Provincial Tourist Conference* (1948), 6.

80 Letter from Marie L. Kerkmann to Dan E.C. Campbell, 8 January 1946; "*Your Vacation* promotional pamphlet," n.d., item 6, box 1, Solicitations 1939–1947, vol. 2, GR1968.031, PAA.

81 *The Instructor*, Advertising Rate Card, n.d., item 6, box 1, Solicitations 1939–1947, vol. 2, GR1968.031, PAA; Letter from Robert C. Gilboy to Dan E.C. Campbell, 13 September 1946, ibid.

82 *Report of Proceedings, Third Dominion-Provincial Tourist Conference*, 47; *CMPD*, 17 July 1948, 5. See also *BO*, 17 July 1948, 91; *CMPD*, 17 July 1948, 5.

83 H.B. Chandler, Distribution Branch, National Film Board, Canadian Travel Film Programme in the United States, 20 November 1959, *The National Film Board*, item 321, box 37, GR 1968.0310, PAA.

84 Summer Tourist Program in Canada, 1954, *Furnishing of Tourist Promotion and Education Films in National Parks 1954–1955*, U117-57, pt 2, vol. 161, RG 84, A-2-a, LAC.
85 Summer Tourist Program in Canada, 1953, National Film Board of Canada, 1953–1954, item 359, box 17, GR1968.0310, PAA.
86 Agenda, Fifth Dominion-Provincial Tourist Conference, *Fifth Federal-Provincial Tourist Conference, 1950*, vol. 1563, T3200-131, RG 20-A-5, LAC.
87 Summary, *Ninth Dominion-Provincial Tourist Conference*, 1954.
88 Krahn, *Educational Film Guide*, 705; *Department of Industry and Publicity Annual Report 1946* (Halifax: Provincial Secretary, 1947), PANS.
89 New Brunswick Travel Bureau, *Let's Look at New Brunswick* (1951, 1954), Crawley Films Limited Fonds, vol. 5, MG 28-III99, LAC.
90 'Budge' Crawley, "Requisites of Good Travel Films," 27 July 1954, Crawley Films Ltd 1954–1955, PANB. The result was *The Picture Province* (1956), a 16-mm tourism film shot for about $14,000 and highlighting New Brunswick's scenic and recreational attractions. The CGTB's Homer Robinson advised on the script ("Picture Province," Crawley Films Ltd. 1954–1955, PANB). See also Letter from Quentin Brown to R.A. Tweedie, 29 July 1954, and Letter from Graeme Fraser to R.A. Tweedie, 4 August 1954, New Brunswick Travel Bureau, *Picture Province* (1954–1962), vol. 30, Crawley Films Limited Fonds, MG 28-III99, LAC.
91 *Report of Proceedings, Third Dominion-Provincial Tourist Conference* (1948), 44.
92 Report of Select Committee on Canadian Travel Films, 4 December 1951, *Sixth Dominion-Provincial Tourist Conference*, 1951, vol. 1563, T3200-131, RG 20-A-5, LAC.
93 Ibid.
94 Ibid.
95 Established in 1916, the Pacific Northwest Tourist Association (PNWTA) promoted tourism for its member states (Idaho, Montana, North Dakota, Oregon, Washington) and provinces (Alberta, British Columbia, Saskatchewan). Letter from D.E.C. Campbell to W.D. King, Deputy Minister, Department of Trade and Industry, 25 February 1944, item 129, box 7, GR1968.0310, PAA. See also Alberta Post-War Reconstruction Committee, Tourist Trade in Alberta, Appendix 1 to the Report of the Subcommittee on Industry, March 1945, Tourist Dominion Provincial Conference, 1945–1947, item 75, box 3, ibid.

96 Report of the Advertising and Literature Committee – PNWTA, 14 January 1946, Pacific Northwest Tourist Association, 1945–1947, item 129, box 7, ibid. In 1945, Campbell became chair of the PNWTA's Advertising and Literature Committee, which allowed him to advocate for his province throughout the PNW region.

97 See Berton, *Hollywood's Canada*; Collins, "Cooperation, Hollywood, and Howe"; Dorland, *So Close to the State/s*; Madger, *Canada's Hollywood*; Pendakur, *Canadian Dreams and American Control.*

98 *Summary of Proceedings, Fourth Dominion-Provincial Tourist Conference* (1949), 13.

99 Chalmers, "Current Trends in Foreign Trade Policies," 7.

100 American tourists also provided other foreign countries much-needed currency in the two decades following the war, alongside such official reconstruction aid as the Marshall Plan (Fieldston, "Our Dollars Are Celebrities Abroad").

101 Canada, Parliament, House of Commons, *Debates*, 20th Parliament, 4th Session, Vol. 2, 12 February 1948, 1163; 20 February 1948, 1477. See also *CMPD*, 29 November 1947, 11; *CMPD*, 13 March 1948, 3; *MPH*, 29 November 1947, 16.

102 Letter from Eric Johnston to J.J. Fitzgibbons, 21 January 1948, file A-338, vol. 575, CCP of the MPAA, General File, RG 20-A 3, LAC; Memo from Francis Harmon, 8 February 1948, MPAA General Correspondence Files, MHL. See also Brégent-Heald, "Vacationland," 41; D. MacKenzie, "An Early Effort in Cultural Diplomacy."

103 Speech by Francis Harmon, 6 April 1948, MPAA General Correspondence, MHL; Revised budget for CCP, 9 April 1948, ibid.

104 *CMPD*, 17 April 1948, 5; *CMPD*, 28 August 1948, 10.

105 Blake Owensmith, "'How Hollywood is Helping Canada', a transcript of a talk given to members of the Canadian Tourist Association," 14 September 1950, 8-f.79, AMPTP Records, MHL.

106 Letter from Don Henshaw to Blake W. Owensmith, 9 March 1948, MPAA General Correspondence Files, MHL; Studio Facilities Available in Canada for Motion Picture Production and General Information on Canada, September 1948, Canadian Cooperation Reports (1948–1950), AMPTP Records, MHL; Bossin, *Year Book of the Canadian Motion Picture Industry* (1951), 48. The MacLaren Company had developed a working relationship with Hollywood during the war, and Henshaw was active in Canada's Victory Loan drives (A. Dawson, "Motion Picture Production in Canada," 97).

107 Letter from C.D. Howe, 13 July 1948, file A-338, vol. 575, CCP of the MPAA, General File, RG 20-A 3, LAC; Report on the Richardson-Henshaw-Newman Visit, 23 July 1948, MPAA General Correspondence Files, MHL.

108 *STR*, 17 July 1948, 33; *Variety*, 21 July 1948, 20; *CMPD*, 22 October 1949, 5. See also "New York Log," 2–4 March 1948, file A-338, vol. 575, CCP of the MPAA, General File, RG 20-A 3, LAC.

109 Proposed Agenda, Department of Trade and Commerce, CGTB, Dominion-Provincial Tourist Conference, October 1948, file 84-14, box 3152, RG 17, LAC.

110 Letter from Eric Johnston to J.J. Fitzgibbons, 21 January 1948, file A-338, vol. 575, CCP of the MPAA, General File, RG 20-A 3, LAC.

111 Letter from Taylor M. Mills to Herb Butler (Director of Public Relations, Department of Trade and Commerce), 13 April 1948, and Letter from Don Henshaw to A.H. Newman, 13 August 1948, ibid.

112 Studio Facilities Available in Canada for Motion Picture Production and General Information on Canada, September 1948, Canadian Cooperation Reports (1948–1950), AMPTP Records, MHL.

113 Report of American Motion Picture Industry Activities to 30 June 1948, reel 12, General Correspondence Files, MHL; Letter from J.L. Warner to J.J. Fitzgibbons, ibid.; Letter from Edmund Reek to J.J. Fitzgibbons, 28 January 1948, file A-338, vol. 575, CCP of the MPAA, General File, RG 20-A 3, LAC.

114 Letter from E. (Eddie) J. Mannix to J.J. Fitzgibbons, 25 February 1948, and Letter from F. (Fred) C. Quimby to J.J. Fitzgibbons, 24 February 1948, file A-338, vol. 575, CCP of the MPAA, General File, RG 20-A 3, LAC.

115 Holliday, "Gullible's Travels," 23; "Report of T.J. Courtney, Director of the Bureau of Information," in *Department of Industry and Publicity Annual Report 1948* (Halifax: King's Printer, 1949), PANS.

116 *CMPD*, 7 August 1948, 6; Speeches & Conferences Attended by Mr. D. Leo Dolan Where Addresses Given, n.d., D. Leo Dolan "Speeches," vol. 1, MG 30, E259, LAC. *GAM*, 9 July 1948, 2.

117 FitzPatrick TravelTalks MGM Collection, files 88 and 90, box 573, Cinematic Arts Library, University of Southern California (USC); *Report of Proceedings, Third Dominion-Provincial Tourist Conference* (1948), 48. In 1948, James A. FitzPatrick, the self-styled "Voice of the Globe," published his first travel book, with a chapter covering "Conscientious Canada – land of unlimited resources and honest, courageous people!" (FitzPatrick, *Fireside Travels in North America*, 54).

118 Letter from Blake Warwick-Owensmith to D. Leo Dolan, 21 July 1948, file A-338, vol. 575, CCP of the MPAA, General File, RG 20-A-3, LAC.

119 *Report of Proceedings, Third Dominion-Provincial Tourist Conference* (1948), 9 and 64.

120 *Standard* (Montreal), 27 April 1946, in vol. 2, D. Leo Dolan Fonds, MG 30, E259, LAC. Dolan's biographical information also listed the following friends/acquaintances: Howard Strickling, publicity head at MGM; Joan Crawford (Oscar winner, 1945), John Farrow and his wife, Maureen O'Sullivan, and Ned Sparks ("Outline of Important Events," ibid. See also Brégent-Heald, "Vacationland," 42).

121 *MPH*, 17 January 1948, 13. See also Steinhart, *Runaway Hollywood*.

122 *NYT*, 18 June 1948.

123 The Emperor Waltz – billing 1946–1947, Paramount Production Records, 68c.f-55, MHL; Phillips, *Some Like It Wilder*, 90–7.

124 The Emperor Waltz Pressbook, 1947–1948, Paramount Pictures Press Sheets, Group A-7, MHL.

125 *CMPD*, 3 April 1948, 3. Anita Colby, beauty editor for *Photoplay* and "feminine director" at Selznick Studios, in 1947 became an executive assistant to Henry Ginsberg, production head at Paramount, and left there after 18 months to form her own business, Anita Colby, Inc., which advised the major studios (Smyth, *Nobody's Girl Friday*, 87).

126 For example, see *Life*, 17 May 1948, 14.

127 *CMPD*, 4 September 1948, 1; N.W. Squire, "Easy Ace," 129. See also *CMPD*, 22 March 1947, 7. The lodge later named one of its cabins after Crosby, while the Maligne River Anglers Association elected him honorary president, the first foreigner so honoured.

128 J.A. Rigby, Travel and Outdoor Films, NFB to G.E. Ellis, CGTB, 17 October 1950, *Fifth Federal-Provincial Tourist Conference, 1950*, vol. 1563, T3200-131, RG 20-A-5, LAC; *From Tee to Green* is in National Film Board of Canada Fonds, LAC.

129 *Variety*, 25 June 1947, 5; *BO*, 19 July 1947, 123. See also Letter from Arthur J. Krim to J.J. Fitzgibbons, 4 February 1948, MPAA General Correspondence Files, MHL. Eagle-Lion had also distributed the bilingual *Whispering City/La Fortresse* (dir. by Fyodor Otsep, 1947), produced by Quebec Productions Corp. of Montreal. This noirish murder mystery unfolds on the streets of Quebec City and at the nearby Montmorency Falls.

130 *CMPD*, 19 July 1947, 18.

131 *BO*, 27 September 1947, 104; *BO*, 30 August 1947, 118. Rogell planned another Cinecolor drama in Alberta, *Shadow of Time*. Although filming

began there during the spring of 1948, it was never completed (*Variety*, 3 March 1948, 18).

132 CMPD, 12 June 1948, 3.

133 Northwest Stampede, Production Files, Core Collection, MHL.

134 CMPD, 3 July 1948, 5. See also BO, 19 June 1948, 105.

135 NYT, 10 December 1948.

136 Letter from Nat Holt to J.J. Fitzgibbons, 3 February 1948, MPAA General Correspondence Files, MHL.

137 Letter from J.J. Fitzgibbons to Spyros P. Skouras, 4 March 1948, file A-338, vol. 575, CCP of the MPAA, General File, RG 20-A 3, LAC.

138 CMPD, 7 August 1948, 7. See also FD, 23 July 1948, 1, 4.

139 CANADIAN PACIFIC, location report prepared by Lewis J. Rachmil, n.d., 8-f.79, AMPTP Records, MHL.

140 FD, 30 July 1948, 8; BO, 24 August 1948, 107; Gibbon, *Steel of Empire*.

141 BO, 11 September 1948, 101.

142 MPD, 9 March 1949, 2.

143 GAM, 30 April 1949, 10; *Canadian Pacific*, Production Files, Core Collection Files, MHL. The magnificence of the area inspired Nat Holt to film *Cariboo Trail* (dir. by Edwin L. Marin, 1950), another Canadian Western in Cinecolor, featuring Randolph Scott. Though originally slated for a BC shoot, it was filmed in Colorado.

144 Letter from Eric Johnston to C.D. Howe, 29 December 1948, MPAA General Correspondence Files, microfilm roll 12, MHL. See GAM, 3 September 1948, 1.

145 Letter from C.D. Howe, 13 July 1948, file A-338, vol. 575, CCP of the MPAA, General File, RG 20-A 3, LAC.

146 *Report of Proceedings, Third Dominion-Provincial Tourist Conference* (1948), 48.

147 *Report of Proceedings, Fourth Dominion-Provincial Tourist Conference* (1949), 25.

148 Massey Report, 368.

149 GAM, 4 December 1948, 10.

150 Letter from Ross McLean to Francis Harmon, 31 May 1948, file A-338, vol. 575, CCP of the MPAA, General File, RG 20-A 3, LAC. McLean is referring probably to such James Oliver Curwood–inspired Mountie films as *Trail of the Mounties* (dir. by Howard Bretherton, 1947) and *Where the North Begins* (dir. by Howard Bretherton, 1947).

151 Lazarus, "See Canada Plan Success in Part." See also MPD, 10 December 1948, 1.

152 Letter from A.H. Newman to Francis Harmon, 15 December 1948, and Letter from Francis Harmon to Blake Warwick-Owensmith," 29 December 1948, MPAA General Correspondence Files, microfilm roll 12, MHL. By the late 1940s, two Quebec companies were producing feature films – Renaissance Films and Québec Productions Corporation (S. MacKenzie, *Screening Québec*).

153 *Variety*, 13 May 1953, 4.

154 Ibid., 26.

155 Owensmith, "How Hollywood is Helping Canada."

156 Black, "The Photography Is Important to Hitchcock," 546. The script is based on Paul Anthelme's 1902 play, *Nos deux consciences* ("Interoffice communication Warner Brothers from Barbara Keon to Carl Stucke," 29 October 1952, folder 356, Alfred Hitchcock Collection, MHL).

157 Cited in Pratley, "Alfred Hitchcock's Working Credo (1950)," 35.

158 S. MacKenzie, *Screening Québec*, 101. See also Neatby, "Meeting of Minds."

159 Barris, "On the Screen," 8; *MPD*, 5 September 1952, 2. See also Marineau, "Hitchcock's Quebec Shoot."

160 "*I Confess* Pressbook," Production Files, Core Collection Files, MHL. The studio also held the premières in Quebec City and the following day in Montreal.

161 *Niagara* – script (treatment by Charles Brackett, 9/6/51), Charles Brackett Papers, f.27, MHL.

162 "*Niagara* – Pressbook," Core Collection Files, MHL. On the development of Niagara Falls as the favoured destination for honeymooners, see Dubinsky, *The Second Greatest Disappointment*. See also Brégent-Heald, "Dark Limbo."

163 *Niagara Falls Review*, 9 April 1952, 14 April 1952, 2 June 1952, 27 January 1953, Local History Collection, NFPL. See also Brégent-Heald, "The Tourism of Titillation in Tijuana and Niagara Falls," 197.

164 "Vital Statistics on 'NIAGARA,'" Harry Brand (Director of Publicity), *Niagara*, Core Collection Files, MHL.

165 MPAA, *Canadian Cooperation Project: Annual Report* (NY: MPAA, 1953), MHL.

166 Letter from Blake Warwick-Owensmith to Taylor Mills, 20 May 1953, roll 16, MPAA General Correspondence Files, MHL. See also *Variety*, 26 August 1953, 7.

167 CBC Transcript of a John Fisher Report, Projects and Projectors, 13 June 1953, MPPA General Correspondence, reel 12, MHL.

168 *Variety*, 28 April 1954, 6.

169 MPAA, *Canadian Cooperation Project: Annual Report* (1953), MHL.

170 Scenes were also shot at Mammoth Lakes in California's High Sierras. *Rose-Marie* (music by Rudolph Friml and Herbert Stothart, libretto by Otto A. Harback and Oscar Hammerstein II [won Academy Awards 1941, 1945]) premièred on Broadway on 2 September 1924 and ran for 557 performances. In 1928, Joan Crawford (Oscar winner, 1945) starred in the silent *Rose-Marie* (dir. by Lucien Hubbard, 1928); the 1936 musical version (dir. by W.S. Van Dyke) was a vehicle for Nelson Eddy and Jeanette MacDonald (Brégent-Heald, "Primitive Encounters").

171 *Harrison's Reports*, 6 March 1954, 38. See also *MPD*, 3 March 1954, 1, 5.

172 *Rose Marie*, Core Collection Files, MHL.

173 Pressbook for *Saskatchewan*, ibid.

174 Parry, "Homesick but Happy (Alan Ladd)," 43; *MS* (May 1954), 25.

175 Pressbook for *Saskatchewan*, Core Collection Files, MHL.

176 Canada, Parliament, House of Commons, *Debates*, 22nd Parliament, 1st Session, Vol. 4, 25 March 1954, 3321. See also *Hollywood Citizen-News*, 3 March 1954, in *Saskatchewan*, Core Collection Files, MHL. In a title card, Universal-International formally acknowledged "THE SPLENDID RECEPTION ACCORDED THE CAST AND CREW OF 'SASKATCHEWAN' IN CANADA ... THE FRIENDLY COOPERATION, ASSISTANCE AND GENEROSITY OF ALL OUR CANDIAN FRIENDS WAS, AND IS, DEEPLY APPRECIATED." MPAA, *Canadian Cooperation Project; Annual Report* (1953), MHL.

177 Suggested statement for Mr. Ralph R. Moore, Deputy Minister, Province of Alberta, by E.S. Bryant, Director of Publicity, 31 March 1954, item 358, box 16, Films, Ski, etc., 1954, GR1958.0310, PAA.

178 Alberta, Department of Economic Affairs, "Film and Photographic Branch," *Ninth Annual Report* (1953), 8 February 1954, 15.

179 Pressbook for *The Far Country*, Core Collection Files, MHL.

180 MPAA, *Canadian Cooperation Project* (1953), 20–1, MHL.

181 Letter from Ralph Moore to Blake Warwick-Owensmith, 21 August 1953, reel 16, MPAA General Correspondence Files, MHL.

182 Letter from Blake Owensmith to Don Henshaw, 11 November 1953, ibid.

183 MPAA, *Canadian Cooperation Project: Annual Report* (NY: MPAA, 1954), MHL.

184 MPAA, *Canadian Cooperation Project: Annual Report* (NY: MPAA, 1955), MHL.

185 Berton, *Hollywood's Canada*, 172.

186 Canadian Cooperation Reports (1948–1950), AMPTP Records, MHL.

CONCLUSION

1 "Does the Travel Film Pay Off?" 26–27 November 1956, in *Eleventh Dominion-Provincial Tourist Conference*, 156, vol. 1564, T 3200-131, RG 20 A, LAC; H.S. Robinson to T.V. Adams, 21 November 1956, *Eleventh Dominion-Provincial Tourist Conference*, ibid.; *Fourth Dominion-Provincial Tourist Conference*, folder 1.4, (November 1949), 17, 46, RG 5 B-6, AO.

2 "The Story of One Film," in *Eleventh Dominion-Provincial Tourist Conference*, 156. Advertisers and marketers had been employing the "cost per impression" metric to determine the value of or economic feasibility of a particular medium of delivery, such as direct mail, print advertising, radio, film, or television. In this model, the total number of viewers is divided into the expense of production; the more consumers exposed to the advertisement – in this case, a tourism film – the lower the ultimate cost per person.

3 "Travel Film Television – USA," 13 November 1956, in *Eleventh Dominion-Provincial Tourist Conference*, 156. *Rocky Mountain Trout* is in the PAA.

4 *Report of Proceedings, Third Dominion-Provincial Tourist Conference* (Ottawa: King's Printer, 1948), 44, folder 1.3, RG 5 B-6, AO.

5 *BSM* 10, no. 3 (1949), 32. As early as 1943, the NFB had begun televising its film documentaries in New York.

6 *Report of Proceedings, Third Dominion-Provincial Tourist Conference* (1948).

7 MPAA, *Canadian Cooperation Project: Annual Report* (NY: MPAA, 1953), MHL.

8 Travel Film Television – USA, 13 November 1956, *Eleventh Dominion-Provincial Tourist Conference*, 156.

9 Apostle, "The Display of a Tourist Nation," 177.

10 *Maclean's*, 3 August 1957, 1; Croft, "How Leo Lures the Yanks," 22. Dolan died at seventy-one on 12 June 1966.

11 Canada, Senate, *Proceedings of the Standing Committee on Tourist Traffic*, 10 June 1959, 12. *Tourist Go Home* may be viewed at https://www.nfb.ca/film/tourist_go_home (accessed 19 November 2020). See also Apostle, "The Display of a Tourist Nation," 194–6.

12 Solbrig, "Orphans No More," 102.

13 Dubinsky, "Everybody Likes Canadians," 340.

14 Canada, Senate, *Report and Proceedings of the Special Committee on Tourist Traffic* (1934), 23.

15 Parker, "His Majesty, the American Tourist," 40.
16 Scott, *Psychology of Advertising*, 42.
17 *Ottawa Journal*, n.d., and *Saint John Evening Times-Globe*, 4 October 1929, vol. 198, Canadian Government Motion Picture Bureau, R202-28-3-E, LAC.
18 Canada, Senate, *Report and Proceedings of the Special Committee on Tourist Traffic* (1934), 4.
19 *Citizen* (Ottawa), 3 June 1938, 4 June 1938, 10 June 1938, 19 January 1940, CGMPB Scrapbook, RG 20-C-2-g, R202–28–3-E, LAC.
20 Barnouw, *Documentary*, 181.
21 *CMPD*, 30 September 1950.
22 Adamson, "The Educational Film in Canada," 440.
23 Vondereau, "Vernacular Archiving," 52.
24 *Motography*, July 1911, 5.
25 Rotha, *Celluloid*, 46.
26 *DNL*, September 1942, 127.
27 Canada, Senate, *Proceedings of the Standing Committee on Tourist Traffic, No. 1*, 19 February 1948, 15.
28 Baloy, "Spectacles and Spectres."

Bibliography

ARCHIVAL COLLECTIONS

Academy of Motion Picture Arts and Sciences, Margaret Herrick Library, Beverly Hills, CA (MHL)

Alfred Hitchcock Collection
Association of Motion Picture and Television Producers (AMPTP) Records
Charles Brackett Papers
Core Collection Files
J. Searle Dawley Papers
Motion Picture Association of America (MPAA), General Correspondence Files
Paramount Pictures Press Sheets
Paramount Production Records
William N. Selig Collection

Archives and Special Collections, University of New Brunswick, Fredericton, NB (UNB)

Louis B. Mayer Bio File and Newspaper Clippings
Office of the President Papers

Archives of Ontario (AO)

Department of Travel and Publicity
Premier Mitchell Hepburn Correspondence Records

British Columbia Archives, Victoria, BC (BC Archives)

British Columbia Department of Trade and Industry Fonds
Moving Image Records

Chicago History Museum Research Center (CHMRC)

Rothacker Film Manufacturing Co.

Cinematic Arts Library, University of Southern California Los Angeles, CA (USC)

MGM Collection
Twentieth Century-Fox Collection

Glenbow Museum Library and Archives, Calgary, AB (Glenbow)

Sheilagh S. Jameson Fonds

Library and Archives Canada, Ottawa, ON (LAC)

Burton Holmes Collection
Canadian Parks Service Fonds
Crawley Films Limited Fonds
D. Leo Dolan Fonds
Department of External Affairs Fonds
Department of Forest Service and Forestry Branch
Department of Trade and Commerce Fonds
Department of Transport Fonds, Canadian Travel Bureau
Lovat Dickson Fonds
M.B. Williams Fonds
Records of the Department of Industry, Trade and Commerce
William J. Oliver Fonds

Library of Congress, Washington, DC (LOC)

Manuscript Division, George Kleine Papers
Motion Picture, Broadcasting, and Recorded Sound Division (MPBRSD), Paper Print Collection

National Archives and Records Administration, College Park, MD (NARA)

Ford Motor Company Collection, 1903–54
Office of War Information (OWI) Records
Records of the National Park Service, Central Files, 1907–1939, General Files, Publicity Bureau of Commercial Economics (1922)

Niagara Falls Public Library, Niagara Falls, ON (NFPL)

Local History Collection

Provincial Archives of Alberta, Edmonton (PAA)

Audio Visual and Exhibit Services Files
Publicity Bureau Files

Provincial Archives of New Brunswick, Fredericton, NB (PANB)

Department of Tourism Promotions and Marketing Branch Records
New Brunswick Travel Bureau Records

Public Archives of Nova Scotia, Halifax (PANS)

Department of Industry and Publicity

University of Toronto Media Archives, Toronto, ON (UTMA)

Gordon Sparling Fonds

OTHER SOURCES

Acland, Charles R. "National Dreams, International Encounters: The Formation of Canadian Film Culture in the 1930s." *Canadian Journal of Film Studies* 3, no. 1 (1994): 3–26.

– "Patterns of Cultural Authority: The National Film Society of Canada and the Institutionalization of Film Education, 1938–1941." *Canadian Journal of Film Studies* 10, no. 1 (2001): 2–27.

Acland, Charles R., and Haidee Wasson, eds. *Useful Cinema*. Durham, NC: Duke University Press, 2011.

Adamson, Gordon. "The Educational Film in Canada." In *Film and Education: A Symposium on the Role of the Film in the Field of Education*, edited by Godfrey M. Elliott, 437–56.

New York: Philosophical Library, 1948. https://archive.org/details/filmandeducationooellirich/page/n7/mode/2up.

Aitken, Ian. *Film and Reform: John Grierson and the Documentary Film Movement*. New York: Routledge, 2013.

Alberta. Department of Economic Affairs. *Sixth Annual Report*. Edmonton: Department of Economic Affairs, 1950. https://archive.org/details/annualreportofdeo6albe/page/n1/mode/1up.

– *Ninth Annual Report*. Edmonton: Department of Economic Affairs, 1953. https://archive.org/details/annualreportofdeo9albe/mode/1up?q=film.

Allan, Blaine. "A National 'as Distinct from Departmental' Film Board and the Case of *Heritage*." *Canadian Journal of Film Studies* 9, no. 1 (2000): 30–54.

– "Rhapsody in Two Languages and One Depression." *Journal of Canadian Studies* 27, no. 4 (1993): 153–68.

Altman, Rick. "From Lecturer's Prop to Industrial Product: The Early History of Travel Films." In *Virtual Voyages: Cinema and Travel*, edited by Jeffrey Ruoff, 61–76. Durham, NC: Duke University Press, 2006.

– *Silent Film Sound*. New York: Columbia University Press, 2004.

Altmeyer, George. "Three Ideas of Nature in Canada, 1893–1914." *Journal of Canadian Studies* 11, no. 3 (1976): 21–36.

Anahareo and Sophie McCall. *Devil in Deerskins: My Life with Grey Owl*. Winnipeg: University of Manitoba Press, 2014.

Anderson, Benedict. *Imagined Communities: Reflections on the Origin and Spread of Nationalism*. London: Verso, 2016.

Anholt, Simon. *Competitive Identity: The New Brand Management for Nations, Cities, and Regions*. Basingstoke: Palgrave Macmillan, 2006.

– "Nation-Brands of the Twenty-first Century." *Journal of Brand Management* 5 (1998): 395–406.

Anthony, Scott. *Night Mail*. London: BFI, 2007.

Apostle, Alisa. "Canada, Vacations Unlimited: The Canadian Government Tourism Industry, 1934–1959." PhD thesis, Queen's University, 2003.

– "The Display of a Tourist Nation: Canada in Government Film, 1945–1949." *Journal of the Canadian Historical Association* 12, no. 1 (2001): 177–97.

Armatage, Kay. *The Girl from God's Country: Nell Shipman and the Silent Cinema*. Toronto: University of Toronto Press, 2003.

Armatage, Kay, Kass Banning, and Brenda Longfellow. *Gendering the Nation: Canadian Women's Cinema*. Toronto: University of Toronto Press, 1999.

Aron, Cindy S. *Working at Play: A History of Vacations in the United States*. New York: Oxford University Press, 1999.

Aronczyk, Melissa. *Branding the Nation: The Global Business of National Identity*. New York: Oxford University Press, 2013.

– "New and Improved Nations: Branding National Identity." In *Practicing Culture*, edited by Craig Calhoun and Richard Sennett, 105–28. London: Routledge, 2007.

Aydelotte, Winifred. "Your Vacation in Hollywood – and the Cost." *Picture Play Magazine*, June 1935: 12–14, 68.

Backhouse, Charles F. *Canadian Government Motion Picture Bureau, 1917–1941*. Ottawa: Canadian Film Institute, 1974.

Baloy, Natalie J.K. "Spectacles and Spectres: Settler Colonial Spaces in Vancouver." *Settler Colonial Studies* 6, no. 3 (2016): 209–34.

Banner, Lois M. *American Beauty*. Chicago: University of Chicago Press, 1984.

Barber, X. Theodore. "The Roots of Travel Cinema: John L. Stoddard, E. Burton Holmes and the Nineteenth-Century Illustrated Travel Lecture." *Film History* 5, no. 1 (1993): 68–84.

Barnouw, Eric. *Documentary: A History of the Non-Fiction Film*. London: Oxford University Press, 1974.

Barris, Alex. "On the Screen: Hitchcock Makes a Picture and Clashes with His Church." GAM, 27 September 1952, 8.

Bassett, Morton A. "87% of Human Knowledge Comes by Way of 'Eye Gate.'" RAS, March 1918, 5.

Beck, Janice Sanford. *No Ordinary Woman: The Story of Mary Schäffer Warren*. Surrey, BC: Rocky Mountain Books, 2001.

Bederman, Gail. *Manliness and Civilization: A Cultural History of Gender and Race in the United States, 1880–1917*. Chicago: University of Chicago Press, 1995.

Beeton, Sue. *Film-Induced Tourism*. Clevedon: Channel View Publications, 2005.

– "Tourism and the Moving Image: Incidental Tourism Promotion." *Tourism Recreation Research* 36, no. 1 (2011): 49–56.

– *Travel, Tourism and the Moving Image*. Clevedon: Channel View Publications, 2015.

– "Understanding Film-Induced Tourism." *Tourism Analysis* 11, no. 3 (2006): 181–8.

Belasco, Warren James. *Americans on the Road: From Autocamp to Motel, 1910–1945*. Baltimore, MD: Johns Hopkins University Press, 1997.

Bell, Peter. "The Foreign Office and the 1939 Royal Visit to America: Courting the USA in an Era of Isolationism." *Journal of Contemporary History* 37, no. 4 (2002): 599–616.

Bella, Leslie. *Parks for Profit*. Montreal: Harvest House, 1987.

Benelli, Dana. "Hollywood and the Travelogue." *Visual Anthropology* 15, no. 1 (2002): 3–16.

Benjamin, Ludy T., Jr. "Science for Sale: Psychology's Earliest Adventures in American Advertising." In *Diversity in Advertising: Broadening the Scope of Research Directions*, edited by Jerome D. Williams, Wei-Na Lee, and Curtis P. Haugtvedt, 21–42. New York: Psychology Press, 2004.

Berkowitz, Michael. "A 'New Deal' for Leisure: Making Mass Tourism during the Great Depression." In *Being Elsewhere: Tourism, Consumer Culture, and Identity in Modern Europe and North America*, edited by Shelley Baranowski and Ellen Furlough, 185–212. Ann Arbor: University of Michigan Press, 2001.

Bernays, Edward L. *Propaganda*. New York: H. Liveright, 1928. https://archive.org/details/Propaganda1928ByEdwardL.Bernays_201608/page/n2/mode/1up.

Berton, Pierre. *Hollywood's Canada: The Americanization of Our National Image*. Toronto: McClelland & Stewart, 1975.

Billig, Michael. *Banal Nationalism*. Los Angeles: Sage, 1995.

Billinghurst, Jane. *Grey Owl: The Many Faces of Archie Belaney*. Vancouver: Greystone Books, 2003.

Biltereyst, Daniel, Richard Maltby, and Philippe Meers. *The Routledge Companion to New Cinema History*. Abingdon: Routledge, 2019.

Binnema, Theodore (Ted), and Melanie Niemi. "'Let the Line Be Drawn Now': Wilderness, Conservation, and the Exclusion of Aboriginal People from Banff National Park in Canada." *Environmental History* 11, no. 4 (2006): 724–50.

Bird, Carol. "A Man of Talents." *Photoplay*, June 1926, 41, 78.

Bittner, W.S. "The University Extension Movement." *Department of the Interior, Bureau of Education, Bulletin, 1919, No. 84*. Washington, DC: Government Printing Office, 1920. https://eric.ed.gov/?id=ED541420.

Black, Hilda. "The Photography Is Important to Hitchcock." *AC*, December 1952, 524–5, 546–7, 549.

Boisseau, Tracey Jean, and Abigail M. Markwyn. *Gendering the Fair: Histories of Women and Gender at World's Fairs*. Urbana: University of Illinois Press, 2010.

Bolan, Peter, Stephen Boyd, and James Bell. "We've Seen It in the Movies, Let's See If It's True: Authenticity and Displacement in Film-Induced

Tourism." *Worldwide Hospitality and Tourism Themes* 3, no. 2 (2011): 102–16.

Bolan, Peter, and Matthew Kerney. "Exploring Film Tourism Potential in Ireland: From Game of Thrones to Star Wars." *Revista Turismo & Desenvolvimento*, nos. 27/28 (2017): 2149–56.

Bossin, Hye. "Canada and the Film: The Story of the Canadian Motion Picture Industry." In *1951 Year Book: Canadian Motion Picture Industry*, edited by Hye Bossin, 21–41. Toronto: Film Publications of Canada, 1951.

Bottomore, Stephen. "The Panicking Audience? Early Cinema and the 'Train Effect.'" *Historical Journal of Film, Television, and Radio* 19, no. 2 (1999): 177–216.

– "Taking Views a Perilous Art: From *The Phonoscope* (June 1899)." *Film History* 24 (2012): 334–40.

Bousé, Derek. *Wildlife Films*. Philadelphia: University of Pennsylvania Press, 2000.

Boynoff, Sara. "See the World before You Leave it." *Los Angeles Times*, n.d. Reprinted in *Metro-Goldwyn-Mayer Short Story*, October 1939, 4.

Bradley, Ben. *British Columbia by the Road: Car Culture and the Making of a Modern Landscape*. Vancouver: UBC Press, 2017.

Bratter, Herbert Max. *The Promotion of Tourist Travel by Foreign Countries*. Washington, DC: US Government Printing Office, 1931.

Braun, Marta, and Charlie Keil. "Sounding Canadian: Early Sound Practices and Nationalism in Toronto-Based Exhibition." In *The Sounds of Early Cinema*, edited by Richard Abel and Rick Altman, 198–204. Bloomington: Indiana University Press, 2001.

Braz, Albert. "Beaver Voices: Grey Owl and Interspecies Communication." In *Experiencing Animal Minds: An Anthology of Animal–Human Encounters*, edited by Julie A. Smith and Robert W. Mitchell, 51–64. New York: Columbia University Press, 2013.

Brégent-Heald, Dominique. "All Aboard! Travel Films, Railroads, and the North American West, 1897–1910." *American Review of Canadian Studies* 45, no. 1 (2015): 8–25.

– *Borderland Films: American Cinema, Mexico, and Canada during the Progressive Era*. Lincoln: University of Nebraska Press, 2015.

– "'Come to Canada': Wartime Tourism Promotion and the Amateur Film Movement." *Canadian Journal of Film Studies* 13, no. 1 (Spring 2022): 23–48.

– "Dark Limbo: Film Noir and the North American Borders." *Journal of American Culture* 29, no. 2 (2006): 125–38.

– "Five Little Stars: The Dionne Quintuplets, Motherhood, Film and Tourism during the Great Depression." *Historical Journal of Film, Radio and Television* 39, no. 1 (2019): 54–74.

– "James Oliver Curwood: Advertising Canada across the Border." *Journal of Canadian Studies* 52, no. 3 (2018): 691–717.

– "Landscapes, Wildlife, and Grey Owl: Settler Colonial Imaginaries and Tourist Spaces in William J. Oliver's Park Branch Films." In *Cinematic Settlers: The Settler Colonial World on Film*, edited by Janne Lahti and Rebecca Weaver-Hightower, 165–76. London: Routledge, 2020.

– "Primitive Encounters: Film and Tourism in the North American West." *Western Historical Quarterly* 38, no. 1 (2007): 47–67.

– "The Tourism of Titillation in Tijuana and Niagara Falls: Cross-Border Tourism and Hollywood Films between 1896 and 1960." *Journal of the Canadian Historical Association* 17, no. 1 (2006): 179–203.

– "Vacationland: Film, Tourism, and Selling Canada, 1934–1948." *Canadian Journal of Film Studies* 21, no. 2 (2012): 27–48.

Brereton, Pat. "Nature Tourism and Irish Film." *Irish Studies Review* 14, no. 4 (2006): 407–20.

Brison, Jeffrey D. *Rockefeller, Carnegie, and Canada: American Philanthropy and the Arts and Letters in Canada*. Montreal and Kingston: McGill-Queen's University Press, 2005.

British Columbia. Department of Trade and Industry. *Report of the Department of Trade and Industry for the Year Ended December 31st 1944*. Victoria: Government Printer, 1945. https://open.library.ubc.ca/collections/bcsessional/items/1.0319194#p0z-5r0f.

– *Report of the Department of Trade and Industry for the Year Ended December 31st 1949*. https://open.library.ubc.ca/collections/bcsessional/items/1.0340936#p58z-5r0f.

Brodhead, Richard H. *Cultures of Letters: Scenes of Reading and Writing in Nineteenth-Century America*. Chicago: University of Chicago Press, 1993.

Brower, Jennifer. *Lost Tracks: National Buffalo Park, 1909–1939*. Edmonton, AB: Athabasca University Press, 2008.

Brower, Matthew. *Developing Animals: Wildlife and Early American Photography*. Minneapolis: University of Minnesota Press, 2011.

Brown, Robert Craig. "The Doctrine of Usefulness: Natural Resource and National Park Policy in Canada, 1887–1914." In *The Canadian National Parks: Today and Tomorrow*, edited by J.G. Nelson and R.C. Scace, 94–110. Calgary: University of Calgary Press, 1969.

Browne, Colin. *Motion Picture Production in British Columbia: 1898–1940: A Brief Historical Background and Catalogue*. Victoria: British Columbia Provincial Museum, 1979.

Bruno, Giuliana. *Atlas of Emotion: Journeys in Art, Architecture, and Film*. London: Verso, 2002.

– "Site-Seeing: Architecture and the Moving Image." *Wide Angle* 19, no. 4 (1997): 8–24.

Bryce, P.H. *The Climates and Health Resorts of Canada*. Montreal: Canadian Pacific Railway, 1897. https://archive.org/details/cihm_18094/page/n7/mode/2up.

Buchanan, Donald W. "A Canadian Experiment." DNL, June 1942, 87.

Buchmann, Anne. "Planning and Development in Film Tourism: Insights into the Experience of *Lord of the Rings* Film Guides." *Tourism and Hospitality Planning and Development* 7, no. 1 (2010): 77–84.

Buckner, Phillip A. *Canada and the British Empire*. Oxford: Oxford University Press, 2010.

Bureau of Commercial Economics. *Bureau of Commercial Economics: Industrial Information by Means of the Cinematograph*. Philadelphia: Thomson Print, Co., 1914. https://archive.org/details/bureauofcommercioobure.

Burow, Paul Berne. "Wildlife Conservation and Settler Colonialism in the North American West." Engagement, 2017. https://aesengagement.wordpress.com/2017/03/28/wildlife-conservation-and-settler-colonialism-in-the-north-american-west.

Busby, Graham, and Julia Klug. "Movie-Induced Tourism: The Challenge of Measurement and Other Issues." *Journal of Vacation Marketing* 7, no. 4 (2001): 316–32.

Butler, Richard W. "The Influence of the Media in Shaping International Tourist Patterns." *Tourism Recreation Research* 15, no. 2 (1990): 46–53.

– "It's Only Make Believe: The Implications of Fictional and Authentic Locations in Films." *Worldwide Hospitality and Tourism Themes* 3, no. 2 (2011): 91–101.

Buxton, William. *Patronizing the Public: American Philanthropy's Transformation of Culture, Communication, and the Humanities*. Lanham, MD: Lexington Books, 2009.

Byerly, Alison. "'A Prodigious Map beneath His Feet': Virtual Travel and the Panoramic Perspective." *Nineteenth-Century Contexts* 29, nos. 2–3 (2007): 151–68.

Cahn, Iris. "The Changing Landscape of Modernity: Early Film and America's 'Great Picture' Tradition." *Wide Angle* 18, no. 3 (1996): 85–100.

Calhoun, Charles C. *Longfellow: A Re-discovered Life*. Boston: Beacon Press, 2004.

Cammaer, Gerda, and Zoë Druick, eds. *Cinephemera: Archives, Ephemeral Cinema, and New Screen Histories in Canada*. Montreal and Kingston: McGill-Queen's University Press, 2014.

Canada. "The National Parks Act." 20–21 George V, Ch. 33. Assented to 30 May 1930. http://parkscanadahistory.com/publications/national-parks-act-1930.htm.

Canada. Department of the Interior. *Annual Report for the Fiscal Year Ending 31 March 1916*. Sessional Paper No. 25. Ottawa: King's Printer, 1917. http://parkscanadahistory.com/publications/NPBr_annual_reports_1912-21.pdf.

– *Annual Report for the Fiscal Year Ending 31 March 1917*. Sessional Paper No. 25. Ottawa: King's Printer, 1918. http://parkscanadahistory.com/publications/NPBr_annual_reports_1912-21.pdf.

– *Annual Report for the Fiscal Year Ending 31 March 1920*. Sessional Paper No. 25. Ottawa: King's Printer, 1921. http://parkscanadahistory.com/publications/NPBr_annual_reports_1912-21.pdf.

– *Annual Report for the Fiscal Year Ending 31 March 1931*. Ottawa: King's Printer, 1932. http://parkscanadahistory.com/publications/commissioner_report-1931.pdf.

– *Report of the Commissioner of Dominion Parks*. Sessional Paper No. 25. Ottawa: King's Printer, 1914. http://parkscanadahistory.com/publications/NPBr_annual_reports_1912-21.pdf.

– *Report of the Commissioner of Dominion Parks*. Sessional Paper No. 25. Ottawa: King's Printer, 1915. http://parkscanadahistory.com/publications/NPBr_annual_reports_1912-21.pdf.

– *Report of the Commissioner of Dominion Parks*. Sessional Paper No. 25. Ottawa: King's Printer, 1920. http://parkscanadahistory.com/publications/NPBr_annual_reports_1912-21.pdf.

– *Report of the Commissioner of Dominion Parks for the Year Ending March 31, 1912*. Ottawa: Government Printing Bureau, 1912. http://parkscanadahistory.com/publications/commissioner_report-1912.pdf.

– *Report of the Commissioner, J.B. Harkin*. Sessional Paper No. 12. Ottawa: King's Printer, 1923. http://parkscanadahistory.com/publications/NPBr_annual_reports_1922-24.pdf.

– *Report of the Commissioner, J.B. Harkin*. Sessional Paper No. 12. Ottawa: King's Printer, 1925. http://parkscanadahistory.com/publications/NPBr_annual_reports_1925-27.pdf.

Canada. Department of Mines and Resources. *Report of Lands, Parks, and Forests Branch for the Fiscal Year Ended March 31, 1939*. Ottawa: King's Printer, 1940. http://cfs.nrcan.gc.ca/pubwarehouse/pdfs/30918.pdf.

Canada. Department of Resources and Development. *Annual Report for the Fiscal Year ended March 31, 1951*. Ottawa: Minister of Resources and Development, 1951. http://parkscanadahistory.com/publications/ann-rpt-1951.pdf.

Canada. Department of Soldiers' Civil Re-establishment. *Report of the Work of the Invalided Soldiers' Commission, May 1918*. Ottawa: J. de Labroquerie Taché, 1918. https://archive.org/details/reportofworkofinoocanarich/mode/2up.

Canada. Department of Trade and Commerce. "Report of the Deputy Minister." *Thirty-fourth Annual Report of the Department of Trade and Commerce for the Fiscal Year Ending March 31, 1926*. Ottawa: King's Printer, 1926. https://archive.org/details/v2annualdepartme1926canauoft/page/n526/mode/2up.

– *Twenty-ninth Annual Report of the Department of Trade and Commerce for the Fiscal Year Ending March 31, 1921*. Ottawa: Thomas Mulvey, 1921. https://archive.org/details/1922v58i2n2p10_1605.

– *Thirty-second Annual Report of the Department of Trade and Commerce for the Fiscal Year Ending March 31, 1924*. Ottawa: King's Printer, 1924. https://archive.org/stream/1925v61i2p5_1752/1925v61i2p5_1752_djvu.txt.

Canada. Department of Trade and Commerce. Dominion Bureau of Statistics. "Weekly Bulletin." No. 77 (7 April 1934). http://publications.gc.ca/collections/collection_2017/statcan/11-002/CS11-002-77-1934-eng.pdf.

– "Weekly Bulletin." No. 21 (25 May 1940). http://publications.gc.ca/collections/collection_2017/statcan/11-002/CS11-002-8-21-eng.pdf.

Canada. Parliament. House of Commons. *Debates*, 14th Parliament, 4th Session, Vol. 4, 1925. https://parl.canadiana.ca/view/oop.debates_HOC1404_04/1?r=0&s=1.

– *Debates*, 16th Parliament, 1st Session, Vol. 2, 1926–27. https://parl.canadiana.ca/view/oop.debates_HOC1601_02/1?r=0&s=1.

– *Debates*, 18th Parliament, 4th Session, Vol. 2, 1939. https://parl.canadiana.ca/view/oop.debates_HOC1804_02/1?r=0&s=1.

- *Debates*, 19th Parliament, 2nd Session, Vol. 4, 1941–42. https://parl.canadiana.ca/view/oop.debates_HOC1902_04/1?r=0&s=1.
- *Debates*, 19th Parliament, 3rd Session, Vol. 3, 1942. https://parl.canadiana.ca/view/oop.debates_HOC1903_03/1?r=0&s=1.
- *Debates*, 19th Parliament, 3rd Session, Vol. 5, 1942. https://parl.canadiana.ca/view/oop.debates_HOC1903_05/1?r=0&s=1.
- *Debates*. 20th Parliament, 1st Session, Vol. 1, 1945. https://parl.canadiana.ca/view/oop.debates_HOC2001_01/1?r=0&s=1.
- *Debates*. 20th Parliament, 1st Session, Vol. 3, 1945. https://parl.canadiana.ca/view/oop.debates_HOC2001_03/1?r=0&s=1.
- *Debates*. 20th Parliament, 2nd Session, Vol. 5, 1946. https://parl.canadiana.ca/view/oop.debates_HOC2002_05/1?r=0&s=1.
- *Debates*. 20th Parliament, 4th Session, Vol. 2, 1948. https://parl.canadiana.ca/view/oop.debates_HOC2004_02/1?r=0&s=1.
- *Debates*. 21st Parliament, 1st Session, Vol. 3, 1949. https://parl.canadiana.ca/view/oop.debates_HOC2101_03/1?r=0&s=1.
- *Debates*. 21st Parliament, 2nd Session, Vol. 4, 1950. https://parl.canadiana.ca/view/oop.debates_HOC2102_04/1?r=0&s=1.
- *Debates*. 22nd Parliament, 1st Session, Vol. 4, 1953–54. https://parl.canadiana.ca/view/oop.debates_HOC2201_04/1?r=0&s=1.

Canada. Parliament. Senate. *Debates*. 17th Parliament, 5th Session, Vol. 1, 25 January–3 July 1934. https://parl.canadiana.ca/browse/eng/s/debates/17-5.

- *Debates*. 18th Parliament, 4th Session, Vol. 1, 1939. https://parl.canadiana.ca/view/oop.debates_SOC1804_01/1?r=0&s=1.
- *Proceedings of the Standing Committee on Tourist Traffic*. 20th Parliament, 4th Session, Vol. 1. Ottawa: King's Printer, 1948.
- *Proceedings of the Standing Committee on Tourist Traffic*. 20th Parliament, 5th Session, Vol. 1. Ottawa: King's Printer, 1949.
- *Proceedings of the Standing Committee on Tourist Traffic*. 24th Parliament, 2nd Session, Vol. 1. Ottawa: Queen's Printer, 1959.
- *Report and Proceedings of the Special Committee on Tourist Traffic*. Ottawa: King's Printer, 1934.

Canada. Royal Commission on National Development in the Arts, Letters and Sciences. *Report*. (Massey Report.) Ottawa: King's Printer, 1951. http://www.collectionscanada.gc.ca/massey/h5-411-e.html.

Canada, and J.B. Harkin. *The Origin and Meaning of the National Parks of Canada: Extracts from the Papers of the Late Jas. B. Harkin, First Commissioner of the National Parks of Canada*. Ottawa: Queen's Printer and Controller of Stationery, 1961.

"Canada's War Films Hit Hard!" BSM, no. 5 (1942): 15–17, 34.
Canadian Pacific Railway Company. *A Canoe Trip through Temagaming the Peerless in the Land of the Hiawatha*. Montreal: Canadian Pacific Railway, 1900. https://archive.org/details/cihm_03883/page/n5/mode/1up.
– *Summer Tours*. Montreal: Canadian Pacific Railway, 1889. https://archive.org/details/cihm_26756.
– *Summer Tours to the Upper Lakes*. Montreal: Canadian Pacific Railway, 1902. https://archive.org/stream/summertoursvoliioocana#mode/1up.
– *Yoho Valley in the Canadian Rockies and the Glaciers of the Selkirks*. Montreal: Canadian Pacific Railway, 1902. https://archive.org/details/cihm_71236/page/n3/mode/2up.
Carey, Jane, and Ben Silverstein. "Thinking with and beyond Settler Colonial Studies: New Histories after the Postcolonial." *Postcolonial Studies* 23, no. 1 (2020): 1–20.
Carl, Daniela, Sara Kindon, and Karen Smith. "Tourists' Experiences of Film Locations: New Zealand as 'Middle-Earth.'" *Tourism Geographies: An International Journal of Tourism Space, Place and Environment* 9, no. 1 (2007): 49–63.
Carter, J. Margaret. "The Curriculum Clinic: Canadians as They See Themselves." ES, June 1945, 235–7.
Carter, Sarah. "Britishness, 'Foreignness,' Women and Land in Western Canada 1890s–1920s." *Humanities Research: The Journal of the Humanities Research Centre and the Centre for Cross-Cultural Research at the Australian National University* 13 no. 1 (2006): 43–60.
Catalogue of Motion Pictures Produced by the Canadian Government Motion Picture Bureau. Ottawa: King's Printer, 1933. LAC.
Chalmers, Henry. "Current Trends in Foreign Trade Policies: Review of 1947, Part II: British Empire, Latin America, and the Far East." *Foreign Commerce Weekly: A Journal of International Economy*, 21 February 1948: 6–9.
Chan, Brenda. "Film-Induced Tourism in Asia: A Case Study of Korean TV Drama and Female Viewers' Motivation to Visit Korea." *Tourism, Culture and Communication* 7, no. 3 (2007): 207–24.
Chapin, David. "Gender and Indian Masquerade in the Life of Grey Owl." *American Indian Quarterly* 24, no. 1 (2000): 91–109.
Chapman, James. *Film and History*. Basingstoke: Palgrave Macmillan, 2013.
Chapman, James, H. Mark Glancy, and Sue Harper. *The New Film History: Sources, Methods, Approaches*. Basingstoke: Palgrave Macmillan, 2007.

Charbonneau, Stephen. "John Grierson and the United States." In *The Grierson Effect: Tracing Documentary's International Movement*, edited by Zoë Druick and Deane Williams, 13–28. London: British Film Institute, 2014.

Chibnall, Steve. *Quota Quickies: The Birth of the British "B" Film*. London: British Film Institute, 2007.

Clapperton, Jonathan. "Naturalizing Race Relations: Conservation, Colonialism, and Spectacle at the Banff Indian Days." *Canadian Historical Review* 94, no. 3 (2013): 349–79.

Clary, E.J. "Are Motion Pictures Publicity, or Are They Advertising?" RAS, November 1918, 22.

– "Motion Pictures the Ideal Medium for Resort Advertising." RAS, January 1919: 12.

Clayton, Jenny. "'A National Playground Both in Summer and Winter': Civic Groups, Ethnic Organizations, and Tourism Promotion in Revelstoke, BC, 1890–1920." *Histoire sociale/Social History* 49, no. 99 (2016): 389–408.

Clegg, Thomas. "Education by Kinematograph: Future Prospects." MPW, 5 March 1910: 331.

Coates, Colin MacMillan, Jay Young, and Ben Bradley. *Moving Natures: Mobility and the Environment in Canadian History*. Calgary: University of Calgary Press, 2016.

Coates, Kenneth, and William R. Morrison. *The Alaska Highway in World War II: The US Army of Occupation in Canada's Northwest*. Norman: University of Oklahoma Press, 2015.

Cockerell, T.D.A. "Zoology and the Moving Pictures." *Science* 82, no. 2129 (October 1935): 369–70.

Cocks, Catherine. *Doing the Town: The Rise of Urban Tourism in the United States, 1850–1915*. Berkeley: University of California Press, 2001.

Cohen, J. "Promotion of Overseas Tourism through Media Fiction." In *Tourism Services Marketing: Advances in Theory and Practice*. Special conference series, vol. 2, 229–37. Cleveland: Cleveland State University, 1986.

Collins, Maynard. "Cooperation, Hollywood, and Howe." *Cinema Canada* 56 (June-July 1979): 34–6.

Colpitts, George. *Pemmican Empire: Food, Trade, and the Last Bison Hunts in the North American Plains, 1780–1882*. Cambridge: Cambridge University Press, 2014.

– "Wildlife Promotions, Western Canadian Boosterism, and the Conservation Movement, 1890–1914." *American Review of Canadian Studies*, 28, nos. 1–2 (1998): 103–30.

Conn, Stetson, and Byron Fairchild. *The Framework of Hemispheric Defense*. Edited by Dept. of the Army Office of the Chief of Military History. Washington, DC, 1960.

Connell, Joanne. "Film Tourism – Evolution, Progress and Prospects." *Tourism Management* 33, no. 5 (2012): 1007–29.

Constantinides, Zoë. "The Myth of Evangeline and the Origin of Canadian National Cinema." *Film History* 26, no. 1 (2014): 50–79.

Cook, Dorothy Elizabeth, and Eva Rahbek-Smith. *Educational Film Catalog: A Selected, Classified List of 1175 Non-Theatrical Films with a Separate Title and Subject Index*. New York: Wilson, 1936.

Corbett, E.A. "A Brief History of Adult Education in Canada." In *Adult Education in Canada*, edited by J.R. Kidd, 2–10. Toronto: Canadian Association for Adult Education, 1950.

– *We Have with Us Tonight*. Toronto: Ryerson Press, 1967.

Corbin, Amy Lynn. *Cinematic Geographies and Multicultural Spectatorship in America*. Basingstoke: Palgrave Macmillan, 2015.

Corkill, W.H. "As the Crane Flies." *Canada Weekly*, 29 March 1946, 716, in M-8119-292, Miscellaneous News Clippings, 1922–1982, Sheilagh S. Jameson Fonds, Glenbow Archives.

Cowell, Elspeth. "The Canadian Pavilion at the 1939 New York World's Fair and the Development of Modernism in Canada." *Society for the Study of Architecture in Canada Bulletin* 19, no.1 (1994): 13–20.

Cox, Kirwan. "The Grierson Files." *Cinema Canada* 56 (1979): 16–24.

Crary, Jonathan. *Techniques of the Observer: On Vision and Modernity in the Nineteenth Century*. Boston: MIT Press, 1990.

Crawley, F. Radford. "Cine Canoeing." *MMM*, August 1938: 388, 400–1.

– "Three Days of Sequences." *MMM*, February 1940: 62–3, 77.

Crippen, James P. "Realism and the Photoplay." *Motography*, April 1911: 14–16.

"The Critical Issue." *Sight and Sound* 27, no. 6 (fall 1958): 270–9.

Croft, Frank. "How Leo Lures the Yanks." *Maclean's*, 15 July 1953, 22–3, 40.

Cronin, J. Keri. *Manufacturing National Park Nature: Photography, Ecology, and the Wilderness Industry of Jasper*. Vancouver: UBC Press, 2011.

Cronon, William. "Telling Tales on Canvas: Landscapes of Frontier Change." In *Discovered Lands, Invented Pasts: Transforming Visions of the American West*, edited by J.D. Prown, 37–88. New Haven, CT: Yale University Press, 1992.

Croy, W.G. "Film Tourism: Sustained Economic Contributions to Destinations." *Worldwide Hospitality and Tourism Themes* 3, no. 2 (2011): 159–64.

Croy, W.G., and R.D. Walker. "Rural Tourism and Film – Issues for Strategic Rural Development." In *New Directions in Rural Tourism*, edited by D. Hall, L. Roberts, and M. Mitchell, 115–33. Aldershot: Ashgate, 2003.

Cuban, Larry. *How Teachers Taught: Constancy and Change in American Classrooms, 1890–1990*. New York: Teachers College Press, 1993.

Cull, Nicholas J. "Overture to an Alliance: British Propaganda at the New York World's Fair, 1939–1940." *Journal of British Studies* 36, no. 3 (1997): 325–54.

Currell, Susan. *The March of Spare Time: The Problem and Promise of Leisure in the Great Depression*. Philadelphia: University of Pennsylvania Press, 2005.

Curti, Merle Eugene, and Vernon Rosco Carstensen. *The University of Wisconsin: A History, 1848–1925*. Madison: University of Wisconsin Press, 1944.

Czach, Liz. "A Thrill Every Minute! Travel Adventure Film Lectures in the Post-war Era." In *Cinephemera: Archives, Ephemeral Cinema, and New Screen Histories in Canada*, edited by Gerda Cammaer and Zoë Druick, 73–93. Montreal and Kingston: McGill-Queen's University Press, 2014.

Daschuk, James W. *Clearing the Plains: Disease, Politics of Starvation, and the Loss of Aboriginal Life*. Regina, SK: University of Regina Press, 2014.

Davis, Donald F. "Dependent Motorization: Canada and the Automobile to the 1930s." *Journal of Canadian Studies* 21, no. 3 (1986): 106–32.

Davis, Janet M. *The Gospel of Kindness: Animal Welfare and the Making of Modern America*. New York: Oxford University Press, 2016.

Dawn, Leslie. "Cross-Border Trading: Mungo Martin Carves for the World of Tomorrow." *BC Studies* no. 159 (autumn 2008): 7–44.

Dawson, Anthony. "Motion Picture Production in Canada." *Film Quarterly* 5, no. 1 (1950): 83–99.

Dawson, Michael. "A 'Civilizing' Industry: Leo Dolan, Canadian Tourism Promotion, and the Celebration of Mass Culture." *American Review of Canadian Studies* 41, no. 4 (2011): 438–47.

– *The Mountie: From Dime Novel to Disney*. Toronto: Between the Lines, 1998.

– *Selling British Columbia: Tourism and Consumer Culture, 1890–1970*. Vancouver: UBC Press, 2004.

– "'Travel Strengthens America'? Tourism Promotion in the United States during the Second World War." *Journal of Tourism History* 3, no. 3 (2011): 217–36.

Deloria, Philip J. *Playing Indian*. New Haven, CT: Yale University Press, 1999.

Den Otter, A.A. *Civilizing the West: The Galts and the Development of Western Canada*. Edmonton: University of Alberta Press, 1982.

Dench, Ernest A. *Advertising by Motion Pictures*. Cincinnati: Standard Publishing Company, 1916. https://archive.org/details/advertisingbymotoodencrich.

Depue, Oscar B. "My First Fifty Years in Motion Pictures." *Journal of the Society of Motion Picture Engineers* 49, no. 6 (1947): 481–93.

Deutschlander, Siegrid, and Leslie J. Miller. "Politicizing Aboriginal Cultural Tourism: The Discourse of Primitivism in the Tourist Encounter." *Canadian Review of Sociology and Anthropology* 40, no. 1 (2003): 27–44.

Dewey, John. "The School and Social Progress." In John Dewey, *The School and Society: Being Three Lectures by John Dewey*, 19–46. Chicago: University of Chicago Press, 1899). https://archive.org/details/theschoolandsocioodeweuoft/page/n13/mode/2up.

Dickson, Lovat. *Wilderness Man: The Strange Story of Grey Owl*. Toronto: General Paperbacks, 1991.

Diner, Steven J. *A Very Different Age: Americans of the Progressive Era*. New York: Hill and Wang, 1998.

Dinnie, Keith. *Nation Branding: Concepts, Issues, Practice*. London: Routledge, 2015.

Dolesé, Ruth G. "The Moving Picture as an Educator: Its Possibilities at Last to Be Realized," *MPW*, 9 September 1911: 707–8.

Dorland, Michael. *So Close to the State/s: The Emergence of Canadian Feature Film Policy*. Toronto: University of Toronto Press, 1998.

Dorris, Anna Verona. *Visual Instruction in the Public Schools*. Boston: Ginn and Company, 1928.

Druick, Zoë. "The Best Teachers and the Best Preachers: Film, University Extension, and the Project of Assimilation in Alberta, 1917–1936." In *The Institutionalization of Educational Cinema: North America and Europe in the 1910s and 1920s*, edited by Marina Dahlquist and Joel Frykholm, 123–46. Bloomington: University of Indiana Press, 2020.

– *Projecting Canada: Government Policy and Documentary Film at the National Film Board of Canada*. Montreal and Kingston: McGill-Queen's University Press, 2007.

– "Remedy and Remediation: The Cultural Theory of the Massey Commission." *Review of Education, Pedagogy, and Cultural Studies* 29, nos. 2–3 (2007): 159–74.

Druick, Zoë, and Deanne Williams. "Introduction." In *The Grierson Effect: Tracing Documentary's International Movement*, edited by Zoë Druick and Deanne Williams, 1–10. London: British Film Institute, 2014.

Dubinsky, Karen. "'Everybody Likes Canadians': Canadians, Americans, and the Post-World War II Travel Boom." In *Being Elsewhere: Tourism, Consumer Culture, and Identity in Modern Europe and North America*, edited by Shelley Baranowski and Ellen Furlough, 320–47. Ann Arbor: University of Michigan Press, 2001.

– *The Second Greatest Disappointment: Honeymooning and Tourism at Niagara Falls*. New Brunswick, NJ: Rutgers University Press, 1999.

Dudley, William H. "Cooperation in Visual Instruction," *Proceedings of the First National University Extension Conference at Madison, Wisconsin, March 10–12, 1915*, 244–51. https://hdl.handle.net/2027/uva.x030030211?urlappend=%3Bseq=16.

– *Historical Sketch of University Extension Division, the University of Wisconsin and Reminiscences of Associates of Louis Ehrhart Reber, Dean, 1907 to 1926*. Madison: Friends of the University Extension Division, University of Wisconsin, 1944.

– "Organization for Visual Instruction," *Bureau of Education, Department of the Interior*, *Bulletin No.* 7, 1–24. Washington, DC: Government Printing Office, 1921.

Duffus, David A., and Philip Dearden. "Non-Consumptive Wildlife-Oriented Recreation: A Conceptual Framework." *Biological Conservation* 53, no. 3 (1990): 213–31.

Eamon, Greg. "Farmers, Phantoms and Princes: The Canadian Pacific Railway and Filmmaking from 1899–1919." *Cinémas: revue d'études cinématographiques/Cinémas: Journal of Film Studies* 6, no. 1 (1995): 11–32.

Edensor, Tim. "Mediating William Wallace: Audio-visual Technologies in Tourism." In *The Media and the Tourist Imagination: Converging Cultures*, edited by David Crouch, Rhona Jackson, and Felix Thompson, 105–18. London: Routledge, 2005.

– *National Identity, Popular Culture and Everyday Life*. Oxford: Berg Publishers, 2002.

– "Performing Tourism, Staging Tourism." *Tourist Studies* 1, no. 1 (2001): 59–81.

– "Reading Braveheart: Representing and Contesting Scottish Identity." *Scottish Affairs*, no. 21 (1997): 135–58.

Ellis, Jack C. "John Grierson's First Years at the National Film Board." *Cinema Journal* 10, no. 1 (1970): 2–14.

– "The Young Grierson in America, 1924–1927." *Cinema Journal* 8, no. 1 (1968): 12–21.

Endy, Christopher. *Cold War Holidays: American Tourism in France.* Chapel Hill: University of North Carolina Press, 2016.

– "Travel and World Power: Americans in Europe, 1890–1917." *Diplomatic History* 22, no. 4 (1998): 565–94.

Evans, Gary. *In the National Interest: A Chronicle of the National Film Board from 1949 to 1989.* Toronto: University of Toronto Press, 1991.

– *John Grierson and the National Film Board: The Politics of Wartime Propaganda.* Toronto: University of Toronto Press, 1984.

Evans, Suzanne. "Canada's Work for Wounded Soldiers on Film." *Canadian Military History* 19, no. 4 (2010): 41–9.

Faragher, John Mack. *A Great and Noble Scheme: The Tragic Story of the Expulsion of the French Acadians from Their American Homeland.* New York: W.W. Norton & Company, 2005.

Felando, Cynthia. *Discovering Short Films: The History and Style of Live-action Fiction Shorts.* New York: Palgrave Macmillan, 2015.

Field, Alan. "Ross McLean: A Close-Up." DFN, April 1948, 45.

Fielding, Raymond. "Hale's Tours: Ultrarealism in the Pre-1910 Motion Picture." *Cinema Journal* 10, no. 1 (1970): 34–47.

Fieldston, Sara. "'Our Dollars Are Celebrities Abroad': American Tourists, Consumption, and Power after World War II." *Journal of Tourism History* 11, no. 2 (2019): 187–207.

The Film Daily Yearbook of Motion Pictures – 1929. New York: Film Daily, 1929.

The Film Daily Yearbook of Motion Pictures – 1931. New York: Film Daily, 1931.

Finlay, Karen A. *The Force of Culture: Vincent Massey and Canadian Sovereignty.* Toronto: University of Toronto Press, 2004.

FitzPatrick, James A. *Fireside Travels in North America.* St Paul, MN: Brown and Bigelow, 1948.

Flanagan, Maureen A. *America Reformed: Progressives and Progressivisms, 1890s–1920s.* New York: Oxford University Press, 2007.

Florin, Bo, Nico De Klerk, and Patrick Vonderau, eds. *Films That Sell: Moving Pictures and Advertising.* London: BFI/Palgrave, 2016.

Foote, Stephanie. *Regional Fictions: Culture and Identity in Nineteenth-Century American Literature*. Madison: University of Wisconsin Press, 2001.

Foran, Max. *Icon, Brand, Myth: The Calgary Stampede*. Edmonton, AB: Athabasca University Press, 2014.

Forrester, James A. "The Crawley Era." *Cinema Canada*, no. 85 (1982): 22–4.

Foster, Janet. *Working for Wildlife: The Beginning of Preservation in Canada*. Toronto: University of Toronto Press, 1998.

Francis, Daniel. *The Imaginary Indian: The Image of the Indian in Canadian Culture*. Vancouver: Arsenal Pulp Press, 1992.

– *Selling Canada: Three Propaganda Campaigns That Shaped the Nation*. Vancouver: Stanton Atkins & Dosil, 2011.

Frank, David. "Short Takes: The Canadian Worker on Film." *Labour/Le Travail* 46 (2000): 417–37.

Friedberg, Anne. *Window Shopping: Cinema and the Postmodern*. Berkeley: University of California Press, 1993.

Frykholm, Joel. *George Kleine and American Cinema: The Movie Business and Film Culture in the Silent Era*. Basingstoke: Palgrave Macmillan, 2015.

Gassan, Richard H. *The Birth of American Tourism: New York, the Hudson Valley, and American Culture, 1790–1830*. Amherst: University of Massachusetts Press, 2008.

Gaudreault, André, Germain Lacasse, and Jean-Pierre Sirois-Trahan. *Au pays des ennemis du cinéma: pour une nouvelle histoire des débuts du cinéma au Québec*. Quebec: Nuit Blanche, 1996.

Geiger, Roger L., and Nathan M. Sorber. *The Land-Grant Colleges and the Reshaping of American Higher Education*. New Brunswick, NJ: Transaction Publishers, 2013.

Gibbon, John Murray. *Steel of Empire: The Romantic History of the Canadian Pacific*. New York: Tudor Publishing Co., 1937.

Girard, Michel F. *L'écologisme retrouvé: essor et déclin de la commission de La conservation du Canada*. Ottawa: Les Presses de l'Université d'Ottawa, 1994.

Gissibl, Bernhard, Sabine Hoehler, and Patrick Kupper. "Introduction – Towards a Global History of National Parks." In *Civilizing Nature: National Parks in a Global Perspective*, edited by Bernhard Gissibl, 1–27. New York: Berghahn Books, 2015.

Gittings, Christopher E. *Canadian National Cinema: Ideology, Difference and Representation*. London: Routledge, 2013.

Gleeson, Kristin L. "Blazing Her Own Trail: Anahareo's Rejection of Euro-Canadian Stereotypes." In *Recollecting: Lives of Aboriginal Women of the Canadian Northwest and Borderlands*, edited by Sarah Carter and Patricia A. MacCormack, 287–311. Edmonton, AB: Athabasca University Press, 2014.

Gnoth, Juergen. "Branding Tourism Destinations." *Annals of Tourism Research* 25, no. 3 (1998): 761–63.

Goetz, William. "The Canadian Wartime Documentary: 'Canada Carries On' and 'The World in Action.'" *Cinema Journal* 16, no. 2 (1977): 59–80.

Gomery, Douglas. *The Coming of Sound: A History*. New York: Routledge, 2005.

– *Shared Pleasures: A History of Movie Presentation in the United States*. Madison: University of Wisconsin Press, 1992.

Gordon, Alan. *Time Travel: Tourism and the Rise of the Living History Museum in Mid-Twentieth-Century Canada*. Vancouver: UBC Press, 2017.

Graham, Gerald G. *The Birth of Canadian Film Technology*. London: Associated University Presses, 1989.

Grau, Robert. *The Theatre of Science: A Volume of Progress and Achievement in the Motion Picture Industry*. New York: Broadway Publishing Company, 1914.

Gray, James Henry. *A Brand of Its Own: The 100 Year History of the Calgary Exhibition and Stampede*. Saskatoon, SK: Western Producer Prairie Books, 1985.

Graybill, Andrew. *Policing the Great Plains: Rangers, Mounties, and the North American Frontier, 1875–1910*. Lincoln: University of Nebraska Press, 2007.

Gregory, W.M. "Problems Concerning the Educational Motion Picture." *MPA*, January 1922, 20–1, 25–7.

Grey Owl. *Pilgrims of the Wild*. New York: C. Scribner's Sons, 1935.

Grierson, John. "Better Popular Pictures." In *TSMPE* 11, no. 30 (1927): 227–49.

– "The Documentary Producer." *Cinema Quarterly* 2, no. 1 (1933): 7–9.

– "O Canada! We Stand on Guard for Thee." *DFN*, March 1948, 28, 35.

– "Propaganda for Democracy." *Spectator*, 11 November 1938, 799–800.

Grieveson, Lee. *Cinema and the Wealth of Nations: Media, Capital, and the Liberal World System*. Oakland: University of California Press, 2018.

– "Cinema Studies and the Conduct of Conduct." In *Inventing Film Studies*, edited by Lee Grieveson and Haidee Wasson, 3–37. Durham, NC: Duke University Press, 2008.

– "The Work of Film in the Age of Fordist Mechanization." *Cinema Journal* 51, no. 3 (2012): 25–51.

Griffiths, Allison. *Shivers down Your Spine: Cinema, Museums, and the Immersive View*. New York: Columbia University Press, 2008.

Griffiths, Naomi. "Longfellow's Evangeline: The Birth and Acceptance of a Legend." *Acadiensis* 11, no. 2 (1982): 28–41.

Grimwood, Bryan S.R., Meghan L. Muldoon, and Zachary M. Stevens. "Settler Colonialism, Indigenous Cultures, and the Promotional Landscape of Tourism in Ontario." *Journal of Heritage Tourism* 4, no. 3 (2019): 233–48.

Groskopf, Jeremy W. "Profit Margins: The American Silent Cinema and the Marginalization of Advertising." PhD thesis, Georgia State University, Atlanta, 2013.

Groth, Helen. *Moving Images: Nineteenth-Century Reading and Screen Practices*. Edinburgh: Edinburgh University Press, 2013.

Guerrant, Edward O. *Roosevelt's Good Neighbor Policy*. Albuquerque: University of New Mexico Press, 1950.

Gunning, Tom. *D.W. Griffith and the Origins of American Narrative Film: The Early Years at Biograph*. Urbana: University of Illinois Press, 1991.

– "'The Whole World within Reach': Travel Images without Borders." In *Virtual Voyages: Cinema and Travel*, edited by Jeffrey Ruoff, 25–41. Durham, NC: Duke University Press, 2006.

Hackett, Yvette. "National Film Society of Canada, 1935–1951." In *Flashback: People and Institutions in Canadian Film History*, edited by Gene Walz, 135–65. Montreal: Mediatexte Publications, 1986.

Haines, Richard W. *Technicolor Movies: The History of Dye Transfer Printing*. Jefferson, NC: McFarland, 2003.

Hardy, Forsyth. *Grierson on Documentary*. London: Collins, 1946.

Harmon, Byron, Carole Harmon, and Bart Robinson. *Byron Harmon, Mountain Photographer*. Canmore, AB: Altitude, 1999.

Harper, Graeme, and Jonathan Rayner. *Cinema and Landscape*. Bristol: Intellect, 2010.

Hart, E.J. *J.B. Harkin: Father of Canada's National Parks*. Edmonton, AB: University of Alberta Press, 2010.

– "See This World before the Next: Tourism and the CPR." In *The CPR West: The Iron Road and the Making of a Nation*, edited by Hugh A. Dempsey, 151–70. Vancouver: Douglas & McIntyre, 1984.

– *The Selling of Canada: The CPR and the Beginnings of Canadian Tourism*. Banff, AB: Altitude Publishing, 1983.

Haskin, Frederic J. "The Popular Nickelodeon." MPW, 18 January 1908, 36–7.

Haworth, Colin R. "Canada to Use Films as Propaganda Aid." MPH, 26 November 1938, 15.

Hayes, Christian. "Phantom Carriages: Reconstructing Hale's Tours and the Virtual Travel Experience." *Early Popular Visual Culture*, 7, no. 2 (2009): 185–98.

Hays, Dudley Grant. "The New Department of the N.E.A." ES, June 1923, 280–2.

– "Visual Education: Its Scope, Purpose and Value." ES, February 1923, 56–60.

Hays, Samuel P. *Conservation and the Gospel of Efficiency: The Progressive Conservation Movement, 1890–1920*. Cambridge, MA: Harvard University Press, 1959.

Hearon, Fanning. "New Film Sources and How to Get Information about Them." Presented to Proceedings of the Midwestern Forum on Visual Teaching Aids, Chicago, 12–13 May 1939. Cited in ES, June 1939, 195–208.

Hedges, James B. *Building the Canadian West: The Land and Colonization Policies of the Canadian Pacific Railway*. New York: Macmillan, 1939.

Hediger, Vinzenz, and Patrick Vonderau, eds. *Films That Work: Industrial Film and the Productivity of Media*. Amsterdam: Amsterdam University Press, 2009.

Heffernan, Leo J. "*Hail, British Columbia!*" MMM, March 1942, 100–1, 117–20.

Heidegger, Martin. "The Age of the World Picture." In Heidegger, *The Question Concerning Technology and Other Essays*, trans. and ed. William Lovitt, 115–54. New York: Garland, 1977.

Heitmann, Sine. "Film Tourism Planning and Development: Questioning the Role of Stakeholders and Sustainability." *Tourism and Hospitality Planning & Development* 7, no. 1 (2010): 31–46.

Hendricks, Gordon. *Beginnings of the Biograph: The Story of the Invention of the Mutoscope and the Biograph and Their Supplying Camera*. New York: Arno Press 1964.

Hepworth, Cecil M. *Came the Dawn: Memories of a Film Pioneer*. London: Phoenix House, 1951. https://archive.org/stream/camedawnmemoriesoohepw#page/n31/mode/1up.

Herbert, Charles W. "Canada's War Movies." AC, August 1941, 370, 396–7.

– "Filming Victoria – Canada's 'Little Bit of England.'" AC, January 1941, 9–10, 37–8.

– "I Make a Travelogue in Old Quebec." AC, November 1941, 524–5, 543.

Hidy, Ralph Willard, Muriel E. Hidy, and Roy V. Scott. *The Great Northern Railway: A History*. Minneapolis: University of Minnesota Press, 1988.

Hill, O. Mary. *Canada's Salesman to the World: The Department of Trade and Commerce*. Montreal and Kingston: McGill-Queen's University Press, 1977.

Hilliker, John, and Donald Barry. *Canada's Department of External Affairs*. Vol. 2, *Coming of Age, 1946–1968*. Montreal and Kingston: McGill-Queen's University Press, 1995.

Hoeveler, J. David. *John Bascom and the Origins of the Wisconsin Idea*. Madison: University of Wisconsin Press, 2016.

Hoffman, H.F. "What People Want." MPW, 9 July 1910, 77–8.

Holliday, Kate. "Gullible's Travels." *Maclean's*, 15 August 1949, 23–4.

Hollis, A.P. *Motion Pictures for Instruction*. New York: Century Co., 1926.

Holmes, Burton. *The World Is Mine*. Culver City: Murray & Gee, 1953.

Holmes, Burton, and Genoa Caldwell. *The Man Who Photographed the World: Burton Holmes Travelogues, 1886–1938*. New York: Harry N. Abrams, 1977.

Holmes, Burton, and Lothrop Stoddard. *Burton Holmes and the Travelogue: A Life Story as Told to Lothrop Stoddard[,] Son of John L. Stoddard*. Philadelphia: George F. Lasher Printing Co., 1939.

Holmes, Marjorie C. *Publications of the Government of British Columbia, 1871–1947*. Victoria, BC: Provincial Library, 1947. https://www.leg.bc.ca/content-leglibrary/documents/bc1871_1947.pdf.

Howard, Jonas. "The Wisconsin Idea; How It Operates." RAS, September 1918, 9, 14.

Hudson, Simon, and J.R. Brent Ritchie. "Promoting Destinations via Film Tourism: An Empirical Identification of Supporting Marketing Initiatives." *Journal of Travel Research* 44, no. 4 (2006): 387–96.

Hulette, Frank Parker. "An Interview with Thomas A. Edison." MPW, 22 July 1911, 104–5.

Irwin, William. *The New Niagara: Tourism, Technology, and the Landscape of Niagara Falls, 1776–1917*. University Park: Pennsylvania State University Press, 1996.

Isenberg, Andrew C. *The Destruction of the Bison: An Environmental History, 1750–1920*. Cambridge: Cambridge University Press, 2010.

Jacobs, Steven, Eva Hielscher, and Anthony Kinik. "Introduction: The City Symphony Phenomenon, 1920–40." In *The City Symphony*

Phenomenon: Cinema, Art, and Urban Modernity between the Wars, edited by Steve Jacobs, Eva Hielscher, and Anthony Kinik, 3–42. New York: Routledge, 2018.

Jacoby, Karl. *Crimes against Nature: Squatters, Poachers, Thieves, and the Hidden History of American Conservation*. Berkeley: University of California Press, 2001.

Jakle, John A. *The Tourist: Travel in Twentieth Century North America*. Lincoln: University of Nebraska Press, 1985.

James, Jack, and Earle Vonard Weller. *Treasure Island, "the Magic City," 1939–1940: The Story of the Golden Gate International Exposition*. San Francisco: Pisani Publishing, 1941. https://archive.org/details/treasureislandmaoojamerich.

Jameson, Sheilagh S. *W.J. Oliver: Life through a Master's Lens*. Calgary: Glenbow Museum, 1984.

Jarvie, Ian. *Hollywood's Overseas Campaign: The North Atlantic Movie Trade, 1920–1950*. Cambridge: Cambridge University Press, 1992.

Jasen, Patricia. *Wild Things: Nature, Culture, and Tourism in Ontario, 1740–1914*. Toronto: University of Toronto Press, 1995.

Jenkins, Jennifer L. *Celluloid Pueblo: Western Ways Films and the Invention of the Postwar Southwest*. Tucson: University of Arizona Press, 2016.

Jessup, Lynda. "Canadian Artists, Railways, the State and 'the Business of Becoming a Nation.'" PhD thesis, University of Toronto, 1992.

– "The Group of Seven and the Tourist Landscape in Western Canada, or The More Things Change … " *Journal of Canadian Studies* 37, no. 1 (spring 2002): 144–79.

– "Marius Barbeau and Early Ethnographic Cinema." In *Around and About Marius Barbeau: Modeling Twentieth-Century Culture*, edited by Andrew Nurse et al., 269–304. Gatineau, QC: Canadian Museum of Civilization, 2008.

Jewell, Bronwyn, and Susan McKinnon. "Movie Tourism – a New Form of Cultural Landscape?" *Journal of Travel and Tourism Marketing* 24, no. 2 (2008): 153–62.

Johnson, Rochelle. *Passions for Nature: Nineteenth-Century America's Aesthetics of Alienation*. Athens: University of Georgia Press, 2009.

Johnson, Ronald C. "Resort Development at Banff." *Alberta History* 23, no. 1 (winter 1975): 18–24.

Johnson, Wendell. "'Making Learning Easy and Enjoyable:' Anna Verona Dorris and the Visual Instruction Movement, 1918–1928." *TechTrends* 52, no. 4 (2008): 51–8.

Jones, Deborah, and Karen Smith. "Middle-Earth Meets New Zealand: Authenticity and Location in the Making of *The Lord of the Rings*." *Journal of Management Studies* 42, no. 5 (2005): 923–45.

Jones, Hamilton H. "Train Trails." *MMM*, August 1939, 419, 429–30.

Jordan, Isabel M. "Canada's World-wide Films." *SAH*, March 1947, 32–3.

Karpovich, Angelina I. "Theoretical Approaches to Film-Motivated Tourism." *Tourism and Hospitality Planning and Development* 7, no. 1 (2010): 7–20.

Kattelle, Alan D. "The Amateur Cinema League and Its Films." *Film History* 15, no. 2 (2003): 238–51.

Keil, Charlie. *Early American Cinema in Transition: Story, Style, and Filmmaking, 1907–1913*. Madison: University of Wisconsin Press, 2001.

Keiller, Patrick. "Phantom Rides: The Railway and Early Film." In *The Railway and Modernity: Time, Space, and the Machine Ensemble*, edited by Matthew Beaumont and Michael Freeman, 9–84. Bern: Peter Lang, 2007.

Keller, Robert H., and Michael F. Turek. *American Indians and National Parks*. Tucson: University of Arizona Press, 2005.

Kelm, Mary-Ellen. "Manly Contests: Rodeo Masculinities at the Calgary Stampede." *Canadian Historical Review* 90, no. 4 (2009): 711–51.

Keshen, Jeff. *Propaganda and Censorship during Canada's Great War*. Edmonton: University of Alberta Press, 1996.

Khouri, Malek. *Filming Politics: Communism and the Portrayal of the Working Class at the National Film Board of Canada, 1939–46*. Calgary: University of Calgary Press, 2007.

Kim, Sangkyun. "Audience Involvement and Film Tourism Experiences: Emotional Places, Emotional Experiences." *Tourism Management* 33 (2012): 387–96.

– "A Cross-Cultural Study of On-Site Film-Tourism Experiences among Chinese, Japanese, Taiwanese and Thai Visitors to the Daejanggeum Theme Park, South Korea." *Current Issues in Tourism*, no. 8 (2012): 759–76.

Kim, Sangkyun, and Stijn Reijnders. *Film Tourism in Asia: Evolution, Transformation, and Trajectory*. Singapore: Springer, 2018.

Kimmel, Allan J. *Psychological Foundations of Marketing*. London: Routledge, 2013.

King, Rob. *Hokum! The Early Sound Slapstick Short and Depression-Era Mass Culture*. Oakland: University of California Press, 2017.

– "Introduction: Beyond Vitaphone: The Early Sound Short." *Film History* 23, no. 3 (2011): 247–50.

Kirby, Lynne. *Parallel Tracks: The Railroad and Silent Cinema*. Durham, NC: Duke University Press, 1997.

Kleine, George. *Catalogue of Educational Motion Pictures*. New York: George Kleine Company, 1910.

Korstanje, Maximilliano E. "The Portrait of Dean MacCannell: Towards an Understanding of Capitalism." *Anatolia: An International Journal of Tourism and Hospitality Research* 27, no. 2 (2016): 298–304.

Koszarski, Richard. *An Evening's Entertainment: The Age of the Silent Feature Picture, 1915–1928*, vol. 3, *History of the American Cinema*. New York: Scribner, 1990.

Kotler, Philip, Donald Haider, and Irving Rein. *Marketing Places: Attracting Investment, Industry and Tourism to Cities, States and Nations*. New York: Free Press, 1993.

Krahn, Frederic A. *Educational Film Guide*. New York: H.W. Wilson Company, 1951.

Krech, Shepard, III. *Ecological Indian: Myth and History*. London: Norton, 2001.

Kristmanson, Mark. *Plateaus of Freedom: Nationality, Culture, and State Security in Canada, 1940–1960*. Don Mills, ON: Oxford University Press, 2003.

Krows, Arthur Edwin. "Motion Pictures – Not for Theatres." ES 17, no. 10 (December 1938): 325–8.

– "Motion Pictures – Not for Theatres." ES 18, no. 5 (May 1939): 153–6.

Kuehnast, Kathleen. "Visual Imperialism and the Export of Prejudice: An Exploration of Ethnographic Film." In *Film as Ethnography*, edited by Peter Ian Crawford and David Turton, 183–95. Manchester: Manchester University Press, 2004.

Kuffert, L.B. *A Great Duty: Canadian Responses to Modern Life and Mass Culture, 1939–1967*. Montreal and Kingston: McGill-Queen's University Press, 2003.

Kula, Sam. "Steam Movies: Railroads and Moving Images." In *The CPR West: The Iron Road and the Making of a Nation*, edited by Hugh A. Dempsey, 247–57. Toronto: Douglas & McIntyre, 1984.

Kyte, Shelley. "'V-8 or Make and Break': An Investigation of the Development of Tourism in Canada: A Case Study of Nova Scotia." MA thesis, Queen's University, 1997.

Lacasse, Germain, and Pierre Véronneau. *Histoires de scopes: le cinéma muet au Québec*. Quebec: Cinémathèque Québécoise, Musée du Cinéma, 1988.

Lahti, Janne, and Rebecca Weaver-Hightower. *Cinematic Settlers: The Settler Colonial World in Film*. New York: Routledge, 2020.

Lam, Elsa. "Rails, Trails, Roads, and Lodgings: Networks of Mobility and the Touristic Development of the 'Canadian Pacific Rockies,' 1885–1930." In *Moving Natures: Mobility and the Environment in Canadian History*, edited by Colin MacMillan Coates, Jay Young, and Ben Bradley, 275–98. Calgary: University of Calgary Press, 2016.

Lane, F.E. "Notes on Lantern Work." *OLCJ* 1, no. 3 (1905): 58–9.

Lane, Franklin K. "Conservation through Engineering." Department of the Interior. US Geological Survey, Bulletin 705. Washington, DC: Government Printing Office, 1920. https://pubs.usgs.gov/bul/0705/report.pdf.

Larson, Cedric. "The Domestic Motion Picture Work of the Office of War Information." *Hollywood Quarterly* 3, no. 4 (1948): 434–43.

Lazarus, Charles J. "See Canada Plan Success in Part." *MPH*, 11 December 1948, 24.

Lears, T.J. Jackson. *Fables of Abundance: A Cultural History of Advertising in America*. New York: Basic Books, 1994.

– "From Salvation to Self-Realization: Advertising and the Therapeutic Roots of the Consumer Culture, 1880–1930." In *The Culture of Consumption: Critical Essays in American History, 1880–1980*, edited by Richard Wightman Fox and T.J. Jackson Lears, 1–38. New York: Pantheon Books, 1983.

– *No Place of Grace: Antimodernism and the Transformation of American Culture, 1880–1920*. New York: Pantheon Books, 1981.

Leeder, Murray. "'A New Chivalry': The Calgary Stampede on Film." *Luma* 5, no. 20 (2020). https://lumaquarterly.com/issues/volume-five/020-spring/a-new-chivalry-the-calgary-stampede-on-film.

Lefebvre, Martin. "Between Setting and Landscape in the Cinema." In *Landscape and Cinema*, edited by Martin Lefebvre, 19–60. London: Routledge, 2006.

– *Landscape and Film*. London: Routledge, 2006.

– "On Landscape in Narrative Cinema." *Canadian Journal of Film Studies* 20, no. 1 (2011): 61–78.

Lester, Peter. "Cultural Continuity and Technological Indeterminacy: Itinerant 16mm Film Exhibition in Canada, 1918–1949." PhD thesis, Concordia University, 2008.

Limbrick, Peter. *Making Settler Cinemas: Film and Colonial Encounters in the United States, Australia, and New Zealand*. New York: Palgrave MacMillan US, 2010.

Litt, Paul. *The Muses, the Masses, and the Massey Commission.* Toronto: University of Toronto Press, 1992.

Little, J.I. *Fashioning the Canadian Landscape: Essays on Travel Writing, Tourism, and National Identity in the Pre-Automobile Era.* Toronto: University of Toronto Press, 2018.

Livingstone, Donna. *The Cowboy Spirit: Guy Weadick and the Calgary Stampede.* Vancouver: Greystone Books, 1996.

Loo, Tina. "Of Moose and Men: Hunting for Masculinities in British Columbia, 1880–1939." *Western Historical Quarterly* 32, no. 3 (2001): 296–319.

– *States of Nature: Conserving Canada's Wildlife in the Twentieth Century.* Vancouver: UBC Press, 2006.

Lothian, W.F. *A Brief History of Canada's National Parks.* Ottawa: Supply and Services, 1987.

– *A History of Canada's National Parks.* Vol. 4. Ottawa: Supply and Services Canada, 1981.

Louter, David. *Windshield Wilderness: Cars, Roads, and Nature.* Seattle: University of Washington Press, 2010.

Low, Brian John. *NFB Kids: Portrayals of Children by the National Film Board of Canada, 1939–1989.* Waterloo, ON: Wilfrid Laurier University Press, 2002.

MacCannell, Dean. *Empty Meeting Grounds: The Tourist Papers.* London: Routledge, 2002.

– "The Making of *The Tourist.*" *Via Tourism Review* 13 (2018). https://journals.openedition.org/viatourism/2239.

– *The Tourist: A New Theory of the Leisure Class.* New York: Shocken Books, 1976.

– "Tourist Agency." *Tourist Studies* 1, no. 1 (2001): 23–37.

MacDonald, Monica. "Railway Tourism in the 'Land of Evangeline.' 1882–1946." *Acadiensis* 35, no. 1 (2005): 158–80.

Macdougall, David. "Beyond Observational Cinema." In *Principles of Visual Anthropology*, edited by Paul Hockings, 115–32. Berlin: Mouton de Gruyter, 1995.

MacEachern, Alan. "M.B. Williams and the Early Years of Parks Canada." In *A Century of Parks Canada, 1911–2011*, edited by Claire Elizabeth Campbell, 21–52. Calgary: University of Calgary Press, 2011.

– *Natural Selections: National Parks in Atlantic Canada, 1935–1970.* Montreal and Kingston: McGill-Queen's University Press, 2001.

MacKenzie, David. "An Early Effort in Cultural Diplomacy: The Canadian Co-operation Project and Canadian Tourism." *International*

Journal: Canada's Journal of Global Policy Analysis 68, no. 4 (2013): 576–90.

MacKenzie, Scott. *Screening Québec: Québécois Moving Images, National Identity, and the Public Sphere*. Manchester: Manchester University Press, 2004.

Madger, Ted. *Canada's Hollywood: The Canadian State and Feature Films*. Toronto: University of Toronto Press, 1993.

Maltby, Richard. "New Cinema Histories." In *Explorations in New Cinema History: Approaches and Case Studies*, edited by Richard Maltby, Daniel Biltereyst, and Philippe Meers, 3–40. Malden, MA: Wiley-Blackwell, 2011.

Manore, Jean, and Dale G. Miner. *The Culture of Hunting in Canada*. Vancouver: UBC Press, 2007.

Manthorne, Katharine. "Experiencing Nature in Early Film: Dialogues with Church's *Niagara* and Homer's Seascapes." In *Moving Pictures: American Art and Early Film, 1880–1910*, edited by Nancy Mowll Mathews, 55–60. Manchester, VT: Hudson Hills Press, 2005.

Mar, Tracey Banivanua. "Carving Wilderness: Queensland's National Parks and the Unsettling of Emptied Lands, 1890–1910." In *Making Settler Colonial Space: Perspectives on Race, Place and Identity*, edited by Tracey Banivanua-Mar and Penelope Edmonds, 73–94. London: Palgrave Macmillan, 2010.

Marchand, Roland. *Advertising the American Dream: Making Way for Modernity, 1920–1940*. Berkeley: University of California Press, 1985.

Marineau, Jean-Claude. "Hitchcock's Quebec Shoot." *Cinema Canada*, March 1985, 18–19.

Marsh, John. "The Rocky and Selkirk Mountains and the Swiss Connection, 1885–1914." *Annals of Tourism Research* 12, no. 3 (1985): 417–33.

Massolin, Philip. *Canadian Intellectuals, the Tory Tradition, and the Challenge of Modernity, 1939–1970*. Toronto: University of Toronto Press, 2001.

Masters, Ruth D. "International Agencies in the Western Hemisphere." *American Journal of International Law* 39, no. 4 (1945): 713–35.

Mathews, Nancy Mowll. "Early Film and American Artistic Traditions." In *Moving Pictures: The Uneasy Relationship between American Art and Early Film*, edited by Nancy Mowll Mathews, 39–54. New York: Hudson Hills, 2005.

Mawani, Renisa. "From Colonialism to Multiculturalism? Totem Poles, Tourism and National Identity in Vancouver's Stanley Park." *Ariel:*

A Review of International English Literature 35, nos. 1/2 (2004): 31–57.

Mazierska, Ewa, and John K. Walton. "Tourism and the Moving Image." *Tourist Studies* 6, no. 1 (2006): 5–11.

McClusky, Frederick Dean. "Finding the Facts of Visual Education (IV): Free Film and the Non-Theatrical Market for Moving Pictures." *ES* (September 1925): 394–7, 448.

– "Place of Moving Pictures in Visual Education." *University of Illinois Bulletin, Bureau of Educational Research College of Education, Educational Research Circular* 20, no. 46 (16 July 1923): 1–11. https://www.ideals.illinois.edu/bitstream/handle/2142/32924/placeofmovingpic20mccl.pdf.

McGerr, Michael E. *A Fierce Discontent: The Rise and Fall of the Progressive Movement in America, 1870–1920*. New York: Oxford University Press, 2005.

McGovern, Charles. *Sold American: Consumption and Citizenship, 1890–1945*. Chapel Hill: University of North Carolina Press, 2006.

McGreevy, Patrick. *Imagining Niagara: The Meaning and Making of Niagara Falls*. Amherst: University of Massachusetts Press, 1994.

McInnes, Graham. "'Canada Carries On.'" *Maclean's*, 15 March 1941, 19, 26–7.

– *One Man's Documentary: A Memoir of the Early Years of the National Film Board*. Winnipeg: University of Manitoba Press, 2004.

McKay, Ian. *The Quest of the Folk: Antimodernism and Cultural Selection in Twentieth-Century Nova Scotia*. Montreal and Kingston: McGill-Queen's University Press, 1994.

McKay, Ian, and Robin Bates. *In the Province of History: The Making of the Public Past in Twentieth-Century Nova Scotia*. Montreal and Kingston: McGill-Queen's University Press, 2010.

McKay, Marylin J. *Picturing the Land: Narrating Territories in Canadian Landscape Art, 1500–1950*. Montreal and Kingston: McGill-Queen's University Press, 2011.

McLean, Ross. "Canada Serves the Common Cause." *SAH*, May 1947, 20–1, 50–1.

McLennan, Sarah Elizabeth. "Promoting Tourism, Selling a Nation: The Politics of Representing National Identity in the United States 1930–1960." PhD thesis, College of William and Mary, 2015.

McNally, Michael D. "The Indian Passion Play: Contesting the Real Indian in Song of Hiawatha Pageants, 1901–1965." *American Quarterly* 58, no. 1 (2006): 105–36.

Mees, C.E.K. "A New Substandard Film for Amateur Cinematography." TSMPE, 252–8. New York: Society of Motion Picture Engineers, 1923.

Metcalfe, Lyne S. "Mass Instruction – the Ford Moving Picture Experiment." RAS, April 1919, 24–5.

Metro-Goldwyn-Mayer. "James A. FitzPatrick." In *Who's Who at Metro-Goldwyn Mayer*, 191. Culver City, CA: MGM, 1944.

Miller, Angela L. "The Panorama, the Cinema and the Emergence of the Spectacular." *Wide Angle* 18, no. 2 (1996): 34–69.

Minsky, Louis. "Propaganda Bureaus as 'News Services.'" *Public Opinion Quarterly* 2, no. 4 (1938): 677–9.

Mirzoeff, Nicholas. "What Is Visual Culture." In *An Introduction to Visual Culture*, edited by Nicholas Mirzoeff, 1–13. New York: Routledge, 1999.

Mitman, Gregg. *Reel Nature: America's Romance with Wildlife on Films*. Cambridge, MA: Harvard University Press, 1999.

Moore, Paul S. "Nationalist Film-Going without Canadian-Made Films?" In *Early Cinema and the "National,"* edited by Richard Abel, Giorgio Bertellini, and Rob King, 155–63. Bloomington: Indiana University Press, 2008.

– *Now Playing: Early Moviegoing and the Regulation of Fun*. Albany: State University of New York, 2008.

– "Spaces In-between: The Railway and Early Cinema in Rural, Western Canada." In *Rural Cinema Exhibition and Audiences in a Global Context*, edited by Daniela Treveri Gennari, Danielle Hipkins, and Catherine O'Rawe, 73–89. Cham, Switzerland: Palgrave Macmillan, 2018.

Moore, Stephen T. *Bootleggers and Borders: The Paradox of Prohibition on a Canada-US Borderland*. Lincoln: University of Nebraska Press, 2014.

Morgan, Nigel, and Annette Pritchard. *Tourism Promotion and Power*. Chichester: Wiley, 1998.

Morris, Peter. *Embattled Shadows: A History of Canadian Cinema, 1895–1939*. Montreal and Kingston: McGill-Queen's University Press, 1978.

– "Images of Canada." In *Film before Griffith*, edited by John Fell, 67–74. Berkeley: University of California Press, 1983.

Mortimore, G.E. "Clarence Ferris: He Built a Province in Pictures." TDC, 2 November 1952, 4.

Motion Picture Bureau – National Council YMCA. *Selected Motion Pictures, 16 and 35 Silent and Sound, Season 1936–1937*. 23rd Annual

Edition. New York: Motion Picture Bureau National Council YMCA, 1937. https://ia802800.us.archive.org/17/items/selectedmotionpi23moti/selectedmotionpi23moti.pdf.

Moving Picture Age. *1001 Films: A Reference Book for Non-Theatrical Film Users*. 1st ed. Chicago: Class Publications, 1920.

Muncy, Robyn. *Creating a Female Dominion in American Reform, 1890–1935*. New York: Oxford University Press, 2010.

Münsterberg, Hugo. *The Photoplay: A Psychological Study*. New York: D. Appleton & Company, 1916.

Musser, Charles. *Before the Nickelodeon: Edwin S. Porter and the Edison Manufacturing Company*. Berkeley: University of California Press, 1991.

– "Towards a History of Screen Practice." *Quarterly Review of Film Studies* 9, no. 1 (1984): 59–73.

– "The Travel Genre: Moving towards Narrative." *Iris* 2, no. 1 (1984): 47–60.

Musser, Charles, Thomas E. Jeffrey, and Reese Jenkins. *Motion Picture Catalogs by American Producers and Distributors, 1894–1908*. Frederick, MD: University Publications of America, 1984.

Musser, Charles, and Carol Nelson. *High-Class Moving Pictures: Lyman H. Howe and the Forgotten Era of Traveling Exhibition, 1880–1920*. Princeton, NJ: Princeton University Press, 1991.

Neatby, Nicole. *From Old Quebec to La Belle Province: Tourism Promotion, Travel Writing, and National Identities, 1920–1967*. Montreal and Kingston: McGill-Queen's University Press, 2018.

– "Meeting of Minds: North American Travel Writers and Government Tourist Publicity in Quebec, 1920–1955." *Histoire sociale/Social History* 36, no. 72 (2003): 465–95.

Nelson, Joyce. *The Colonized Eye: Rethinking the Grierson Legend*. Toronto: Between the Lines, 1988.

Newsome, David, Ross Dowling, and Susan Moore. *Wildlife Tourism*. Clevedon, UK: Channel View Publications, 2005.

Niagara Gorge Railroad Company. "Great Gorge Route, Most Magnificent Scenic RoutE in the World." Buffalo, NY: Gies, 1900. https://archive.org/details/greatgorgeroutemooniag.

Niver, Kemp R. *Biograph Bulletins, 1896–1908*. Los Angeles: Locare Research Group, 1971.

– *Motion Pictures from the Library of Congress Paper Print Collection, 1894–1912*. Berkeley: University of California Press, 1967.

Norris, Darrell A. "Reaching the Sublime: Niagara Falls Visitor Origins, 1831–1854." *Journal of American Culture* 9, no. 1 (1986): 53–60.

Nye, David E. *American Technological Sublime*. Cambridge: MIT Press, 2007.

Nye, Joseph, Jr. "Public Diplomacy and Soft Power." *Annals of the American Academy of Political and Social Science* 616, no. 1 (March 2008): 94–109.

O'Boyle, Neil. "Place, Peripherality, and Play: Reflections on Film Tourism in Ireland." *Journal of Popular Culture* 52, no. 6 (2019): 1355–71.

Oerlemans, Onno. *Romanticism and the Materiality of Nature*. Toronto: University of Toronto Press, 2004.

Oettermann, Stephan. *The Panorama: History of a Mass Medium*. Trans. Deborah Lucas Schneider. New York: Zone Books, 1997.

Ogilvie, Frederick Wolff. *The Tourist Movement: An Economic Study*. London: Staples Press, 1933.

Ohmann, Richard M. *Selling Culture: Magazines, Markets, and Class at the Turn of the Century*. London: Verso, 1996.

Olins, Wally. "Branding the Nation – the Historical Context." *Journal of Brand Management*, 9, nos. 4–5 (2002): 241–9.

Ontario. Department of Travel and Publicity. *Report of the Minister of Travel and Publicity, Province of Ontario for the Fiscal Year 1946–1947, Sessional No. 48, 1947*. Toronto: King's Printer, 1947. https://archive.org/details/no4ontariosession79ontauoft/page/n3/mode/2up?q=goodwill+tour.

– *Report of the Minister of Travel and Publicity, Province of Ontario for the Fiscal Year 1947–1948, Sessional No. 51, 1948*. Toronto: King's Printer, 1948. https://archive.org/details/no4ontariosession80ontauoft/page/n55/mode/1up.

Ontario. Treasury Department. *Financial Statement of The Hon. T.W. McGarry, Delivered on the 6th March 1919*. Toronto: T.W. Wilgress, 1919. https://archive.org/details/ontariobudget1919onta/page/n3/mode/2up.

Orgeron, Devin, Marsha Orgeron, and Dan Streible. "A History of Learning with the Lights Off." In *Learning with the Lights Off: Educational Film in the United States*, edited by Devin Orgeron, Marsha Orgeron, and Dan Streible, 15–66. Oxford: Oxford University Press, 2012.

– eds. *Learning with the Lights Off: Educational Film in the United States*. New York: Oxford University Press, 2012.

Parenteau, Bill, and Richard W. Judd. "More Buck for the Bang: Sporting and the Ideology of Fish and Game Management in Northern New England and the Maritime Provinces, 1870–1900." In *New England and the Maritime Provinces: Connections and Comparisons*, edited by Stephen J. Hornsby and John G. Reid, 232–51. Montreal and Kingston: McGill-Queen's University Press, 2005.

Parker, Roger Lane. "His Majesty, the American Tourist." *Travel*, November 1939, 40, 50.

Parmelee, J.T. "Canada's Participation in the World's Fair." *Canadian Geographic*, July 1939, 85–7.

Parry, Bert. "Homesick but Happy (Alan Ladd)." MS, November 1953, 42–3, 74–6.

Pathéscope Company of America. *Education as Visualization: The Royal Road to Learning Lies along the Film Highway*. New York: Pathescope Co. of America, 1918. http://archive.org/stream/edvisuaoopath#page/n4/mode/1up.

Patterson, Martha H. *Beyond the Gibson Girl: Reimagining the American New Woman, 1895–1915*. Urbana: University of Illinois Press, 2005.

Pattison, Lindsay. "Taking the Movies to School: Science, Efficiency, and the 'Motion Picture Project' 1929–1939." *History of Intellectual Culture* 6, no. 1 (2006): 1–15.

Payne, Carol. *The Official Picture: The National Film Board of Canada's Still Photography Division and the Image of Canada, 1941–1971*. Montreal and Kingston: McGill-Queen's University Press, 2013.

Peck, Raymond S. "Publicity Pictures as Used by the Canadian Government." ES, January 1926: 45–7.

– "The Use of Motion Pictures for Governmental Purposes." TSMPE, November 1926, 55–60. https://archive.org/stream/transactionsofso25soci.

Peiss, Kathy. *Cheap Amusements: Working Women and Leisure in Turn-of-the-Century New York*. Philadelphia: Temple University Press, 1986.

Pelletier, Louis. "An Experiment in 'Historically Correct' Canadian Photoplays: Montreal's British American Film Manufacturing Co." *Film History* 19, no. 1 (2007): 34–48.

– "The Fellows Who Dress the Pictures: Montreal Film Exhibitors in the Days of Vertical Integration (1912–1952)." PhD thesis, Concordia University. 2012.

Pendakur, Manjunath. *Canadian Dreams and American Control: The Political Economy of the Canadian Film Industry*. Detroit: Wayne State University Press, 1990.

Perras, Galen Roger. *Franklin Roosevelt and the Origins of the Canadian–American Security Alliance, 1933–1945: Necessary, but Not Necessary Enough*. Westport, CT: Praeger, 1998.

Perry, Paul P. "Stampedes and Camera Pits." AC, January 1924, 5–7.

Peterson, Jennifer Lynn. *Education in the School of Dreams: Travelogues and Early Nonfiction Film*. Durham, NC: Duke University Press, 2013.

Pethő, Ágnes. *Cinema and Intermediality*. Newcastle-upon-Tyne: Cambridge Scholars Publisher, 2011.

Philips, Alan. "The Home Movies People *Pay* to See." *Maclean's*, 15 April 1954, 20–1, 51–5.

Phillips, Gene D. *Some Like It Wilder: The Life and Controversial Films of Billy Wilder*. Lexington: University Press of Kentucky, 2010.

Pike, Frederick B. *FDR's Good Neighbor Policy: Sixty Years of Generally Gentle Chaos*. Austin: University of Texas Press, 2013.

Pope, Daniel. *The Making of Modern Advertising*. New York: Basic Books, 1983.

Popp, Richard K. *The Holiday Makers: Magazines, Advertising, and Mass Tourism in Postwar America*. Baton Rouge: Louisiana State University Press, 2012.

Potter, Evan H. *Branding Canada: Projecting Canada's Soft Power through Public Diplomacy*. Montreal and Kingston: McGill-Queen's University Press, 2014.

Pratley, Gerald. "Alfred Hitchcock's Working Credo (1950)." In *Alfred Hitchcock: Interviews*, edited by Sidney Gottlieb, 34–7. Jackson: University Press of Mississippi, 2003.

Quigley Publishing Co. *The Box-Office Check-up: An Annual Produced by the Combined Editorial and Statistical Facilities of "Motion Picture Herald" and "Motion Picture Daily" Devoted to the Records and Ratings of Talent in Motion Pictures of the Year*. New York: Quigley Publishing Co., 1935.

Rabinovitz, Lauren. "'Bells and Whistles': The Sound of Meaning in Train Travel Film Rides." In *The Sounds of Early Cinema*, edited by Richard Abel and Rick Altman, 167–80. Bloomington: Indiana University Press, 2001.

– *Electric Dreamland Amusement Parks, Movies, and American Modernity*. New York, NY: Columbia University Press, 2012.

– "From Hale's Tours to Star Tours: Virtual Voyages and the Delirium of the Hyper-Real." In *Virtual Voyages: Cinema and Travel*, edited by Jeffrey Ruoff, 42–60. Durham, NC: Duke University Press, 2006.

Ramsaye, Terry. *A Million and One Nights; A History of the Motion Picture*. New York: Simon and Schuster, 1964.

Rankin, Norman S. "With the Edison Players across the Continent." *Man-to-Man Magazine* 6–7 (1910): 934–40.

Rattanaphinanchai, Suphapom, and Bongkosh Rittchainuwat. "Film-Induced Tourism in Thailand: An Influence of International Tourists'

Intention to Visit Film Shooting Location." *International Journal of Tourism Sciences* 18, no. 4 (2018): 325–33.

"Red Cross Line: The Great Tourist Route to Halifax, Nova Scotia and St. John's, Newfoundland." New York: Bowring & Co., 1912, Centre for Newfoundland Studies, Memorial University of Newfoundland, St John's. http://collections.mun.ca/cdm/ref/collection/cns/id/143911.

Reese, William J. *Power and the Promise of School Reform: Grassroots Movements during the Progressive Era*. Boston: Routledge & Kegan Paul, 1986.

Reichwein, PearlAnn. *Climber's Paradise*. Edmonton: University of Alberta Press, 2014.

Reichwein, PearlAnn, and Lisa McDermott. "Opening the Secret Garden: Mary Schäffer, Jasper Park Conservation, and the Survey of Maligne Lake in 1911." In *Culturing Wilderness in Jasper National Park Studies in Two Centuries of Human History in the Upper Athabasca River Watershed*, edited by I.S. McLaren, 155–98. Edmonton: University of Alberta Press, 2007.

Reichwein, PearlAnn, and Karen Wall. *Uplift: Visual Culture at the Banff School of Fine Arts*. Vancouver: UBC Press, 2020.

Reksten, Terry. *The Empress Hotel: In the Grand Style*. Vancouver: Douglas & McIntyre, 1997.

Report of Proceedings, Third Dominion-Provincial Tourist Conference (Ottawa: King's Printer, 1948), 44, folder 1.3, RG 5 B-6, AO.

Rhodes, Benjamin D. "The British Royal Visit of 1939 and the 'Psychological Approach' to the United States." *Diplomatic History* 2, no. 2 (1978): 197–211.

Riegel, Christian, Herb Wyile, Karen Overbye, and Don Perkins. *A Sense of Place: Re-evaluating Regionalism in Canadian and American Writing*. Edmonton: University of Alberta Press, 1998.

Riley, Roger, Dwayne Baker, and Carlton S. Van Doren. "Movie Induced Tourism." *Annals of Tourism Research* 25, no. 4 (1998): 919–35.

Riley, Roger, and Carlton S. Van Doren. "Movies as Tourism Promotion: A Push Factor in a Pull Location." *Tourism Management* 13 (1992): 267–94.

Riley, R.W. "Movie-Induced Tourism." In *Tourism: The State of the Art*, edited by A.V. Seaton, 453–8. Chichester: John Wiley & Sons, 1994.

Rinden, Robert W. "'Tourism': Potent Factor in Canadian Economy." *Foreign Commerce Weekly: A Journal of International Economy* (29 December 1945): 5–7, 39–40.

Rittchainuwat, Bongkosh, Eric Laws, Noel Scott, and Suphapom Rattanaphinanchai. "Authenticity in Screen Tourism: Significance of Real and Substituted Screen Locations." *Journal of Hospitality and Tourism Research* 42, no. 8 (2017): 1274–94.

Roberts, Lee. *Film, Mobility and Urban Space: A Cinematic Geography of Liverpool*. Liverpool: Liverpool University Press, 2012.

Robinson, Zac. "Off the Beaten Path? Ski Mountaineering and the Weight of Tradition in the Canadian Rockies, 1909–1940." *International Journal of the History of Sport* 24, no. 10 (2007): 1320–43.

Rodgers, Daniel T. *Atlantic Crossings: Social Politics in a Progressive Age*. Cambridge, MA: Harvard University Press, 2009.

Rojek. Chris, and John Urry. *Touring Cultures: Transformations of Travel and Theory*. London: Routledge, 1997.

Rommer, Joe. "Budge Crawley … Independent Producer." *Home Movies*, May 1953, 194, 206.

Rose, Jonathan W. *Making 'Pictures in Our Heads': Government Advertising in Canada*. Westport, CT: Praeger, 2000.

Ross, Ryan A. "*'Hiawatha,' The Messiah of the Ojibway* (1903): Photographic Stills from the First Dramatic Narrative Film made in Canada." *Canadian Journal of Film Studies* 21, no. 2 (2012): 140–7.

Rotha, Paul. "British Documentary Films Offer American Business Some New Opportunities." *BSM* 1, no. 1 (1938): 25, 27.

– *Celluloid: The Film To-Day*. London: Longmans, Green and Co., 1931.

Rothacker, Watterson G. "The Ne Plus Ultra of Publicity." *Motography*, July 1911, 21.

– "Pictures as an Advertising Force." *Motography*, February 1912, 71–2.

– "Realism in Municipal Advertising." *Motography,* April 1911, 11–13.

– "System in Motion Picture Advertising." *Motography*, May 1911, 71–2.

Rothacker Film Manufacturing Co. "Moving Pictures." Chicago: Rothacker Film Manufacturing Co., 1919.

Ruoff, Jeffrey. *Virtual Voyages Cinema and Travel*. Durham, NC: Duke University Press, 2006.

Rydell, Robert W., and Rob Kroes. *Buffalo Bill in Bologna: The Americanization of the World, 1869–1922*. Chicago: University of Chicago Press, 2013.

Saettler, Paul. *The Evolution of American Educational Technology*. Englewood, CO: Libraries Unlimited, 1990.

Sandlos, John. *Hunters at the Margin: Native People and Wildlife Conservation in the Northwest Territories*. Vancouver: UBC Press, 2007.

– "Nature's Playgrounds: The Parks Branch and Tourism Promotion in the National Parks, 1911–1929." In *A Century of Parks Canada, 1911–2011*, edited by Claire Elizabeth Campbell, 53–78. Calgary: University of Calgary Press, 2011.

Savage, Sean. "The Eye Beholds: Silent Era Industrial Films and the Bureau of Commercial Economics." MA thesis, New York University, 2006.

Schivelbusch, Wolfgang. "Railroad Space and Railroad Time." *New German Critique*, no. 14 (1978): 31–40.

– *The Railway Journey: The Industrialization and Perception of Time and Space*. Berkeley: University of California Press, 1986.

Schudson, Michael. *Advertising, the Uneasy Persuasion: Its Dubious Impact on American Society.* New York: Basic Books, 1984.

Schwartz, Vanessa R., and Jeannene M. Przyblyski. *The Nineteenth-Century Visual Culture Reader*. New York: Routledge, 2004.

Scott. Willard Dill. *The Psychology of Advertising: A Simple Exposition of the Principles of Psychology in the Relation to Advertising.* Boston: Small, Maynard & Co., 1908.

– *The Theory of Advertising: A Simple Exposition of the Principles of Psychology in the Relation to Advertising*. Boston: Small, Maynard & Co., 1904.

Sears, John F. *Sacred Places: American Tourist Attractions in the Nineteenth Century*. Amherst: University of Massachusetts Press, 1998.

Secord, J. Cameron. "Canada Teaches Farmers with Films." *RAS*, January 1919, 13–14.

Serna, Laura Isabel. "Anita Maris Boggs: Historical Invisibility and Gender in the History of Sponsored and Educational Film." *Feminist Media Histories* 1, no. 2 (2015): 135–43.

Segrave, Kerry. *American Films Abroad: Hollywood's Domination of the World's Movie Screens from the 1890s to the Present.* Jefferson, NC: McFarland, 1997.

Shaffer, Marguerite S. "'See America First': Re-envisioning Nation and Region through Western Tourism." *Pacific Historical Review* 65, no. 4 (1996): 559–81.

– *See America First: Tourism and National Identity, 1880–-1940*. Washington, DC: Smithsonian Institution Press, 2001.

Shortt, James. *A Study in Conviction and Fantasy: A.S. Belaney and Grey Owl, 1888–1938*. Ottawa: Parks Canada, 1980. http://parkscanada history.com/series/mrs/378.pdf.

Simonson, Harry. "Equipment." In *Sixty Years of 16mm Film: A Symposium*, 20–24. Evanston, IL: Film Council of America, 1954.

Singer, Ben. "Female Power in the Serial-Queen Melodrama: The Etiology of an Anomaly." In *Silent Film*, edited by Richard Abel, 163–93. New Brunswick, NJ: Rutgers University Press, 1996.

– "Manhattan Nickelodeons: New Data on Audiences and Exhibitors." *Cinema Journal* 34, no. 3 (1995): 5–35.

– *Melodrama and Modernity: Early Sensational Cinema and Its Contexts.* New York: Columbia University Press, 2001.

Skwiot, Christine. *The Purposes of Paradise: US Tourism and Empire in Cuba and Hawai'i*. Philadelphia: University of Pennsylvania Press, 2012.

Slide, Anthony. *Before Video: A History of the Non-Theatrical Film.* New York: Greenwood, 1992.

– *Silent Topics: Essays on Undocumented Areas of Silent Film.* Lanham, MD: Scarecrow Press, 2005.

Smith, Donald B. *From the Land of Shadows: The Making of Grey Owl.* Vancouver: Greystone Books, 2000.

Smyth, J.E. *Nobody's Girl Friday: The Women Who Ran Hollywood.* New York: Oxford University Press, 2018.

Solbrig, Heide. "Orphans No More: Definitions, Disciplines, and Institutions." *Journal of Popular Film and Television* 37, no. 3 (2009): 98–105.

Speare, Jack W. "81 out of 86 are Buyers After Seeing Motion Picture." *RAS*, March 1918, 25–6.

Spence, Mark David. *Dispossessing the Wilderness: Indian Removal, National Parks, and the Preservationist Ideal.* New York: Oxford University Press, 1999.

Splinder, Robert P. "Windows to the American Past: Lantern Slides as Historical Evidence." *Visual Resources: An International Journal of Documentation* 5, no. 1 (1988): 1–15.

Spurr, David. *The Rhetoric of Empire: Colonial Discourse in Journalism, Travel Writing, and Imperial Administration.* Durham, NC: Duke University Press, 1993.

Squire, Nancy Winslow. "Easy Ace." *MS*, October 1946, 52–3, 128–9.

Squire, Shelagh J. "In the Steps of 'Genteel Ladies': Women Tourists in the Canadian Rockies, 1885–1939." *Canadian Geographer* 39, no. 1 (1995): 2–15.

– "Rewriting Languages of Geography and Tourism: Cultural Discourses of Destinations, Gender and Tourism History in the Canadian Rockies."

In *Destinations: Cultural Landscapes of Tourism*, edited by Gregory D. Ringer, 80–100. London: Routledge, 1998.

Stamp, Shelley. *Movie-Struck Girls: Women and Motion Picture Culture after the Nickelodeon*. Princeton, NJ: Princeton University Press, 2000.

Stearns, A.B. "Films in Public Service Propaganda." *RAS*, October 1918, 39–40.

Steinhart, Daniel. *Runaway Hollywood: Internationalizing Postwar Production and Location Shooting*. Oakland: University of California Press, 2019.

Stephenson, H.E., and Carlton McNaught. *The Story of Advertising in Canada: A Chronicle of Fifty Years*. Toronto: Ryerson Press, 1940.

Steven, Peter. "Pleasing the Canadians: A National Flavour for Early Cinema, 1896–1914." *Canadian Journal of Film Studies* 12, no. 2 (2003): 5–21.

Stewart, Fenn. "Grey Owl in the White Settler Wilderness: 'Imaginary Indians' in Canadian Culture and Law." *Law, Culture and the Humanities* 14, no. 1 (2018): 161–81.

– "Hiawatha/Hereafter: Re-Appropriating Longfellow's Epic in Northern Ontario." *Ariel* 44, no. 4 (2013): 159–80.

Stoddard, John L. *Lectures, Illustrated and Embellished with Views of the World's Famous Places and People: Being the Identical Discourses Delivered During the Past Eighteen Years Under the Title of the Stoddard Lectures*, supplementary volume no. 2. Boston: Balch, 1902.

Strain, Ellen. *Public Places, Private Journeys: Ethnography, Entertainment, and the Tourist Gaze*. New Brunswick, NJ: Rutgers University Press, 2003.

Strasser, Susan. *Satisfaction Guaranteed: The Making of the American Mass Market*. New York: Pantheon Books, 1989.

Strathmore History Book Committee. *Strathmore, the Village That Moved: A Story of the Town of Strathmore*. Strathmore, AB: Strathmore History Book Committee, 1986.

Strom, Claire. *Profiting from the Plains: The Great Northern Railway and the Corporate Development of the American West*. Seattle: University of Washington Press, 2003.

Summary of Proceedings, Second Dominion-Provincial Tourist Conference. Ottawa: King's Printer, 1948. https://archive.org/details/summaryofproceedoooodomi.

Susman, Warren A. *Culture as History: The Transformation of American Society in the Twentieth Century*. Washington, DC: Smithsonian Institution Press, 2003.

Sutter, Paul S. *Driven Wild: How the Fight against Automobiles Launched the Modern Wilderness Movement*. Seattle: University of Washington Press, 2015.

Swann, Paul. *The British Documentary Film Movement, 1926–1946*. Cambridge: Cambridge University Press, 1989.

Tallents, Stephen. "The Birth of British Documentary (Part 1)." *Journal of the University Film Association* 20, no. 1 (1968): 15–21.

Taves, Brian. *Thomas Ince: Hollywood's Independent Pioneer*. Lexington: University Press of Kentucky, 2012.

Tepperman, Charles. *Amateur Cinema: The Rise of North American Moviemaking, 1923–1960*. Oakland: University of California Press, 2015.

– "Digging the Finest Potatoes from Their Acre: Government Film Exhibition in Ontario, 1917–1934." In *Hollywood in the Neighborhood: Historical Case Studies of Local Moviegoing*, edited by Katherine Seeley-Fuller, 130–48. Berkeley: University of California Press, 2008.

Tercero, José. "First Inter-American Travel Congress." *Bulletin of the Pan American Union* (August 1938): 465–70.

– "Practical Pan Americanism." *Bulletin of the Pan American Union* (March 1939): 137–50.

Terry, Schuyler B. "A Vacation in Canada." *Hygeia* (April 1941): 291–6.

Thompson, John Herd, and Stephen J. Randall. *Canada and the United States: Ambivalent Allies*. Athens: University of Georgia Press, 2008.

Thorpe, Jocelyn. "To Visit and Cut Down: Tourism, Forestry, and the Social Construction of Nature in Twentieth-Century Northeastern Ontario." *Journal of the Canadian Historical Association*, 19, no. 1 (2008): 331–57.

Thrift, Gayle. "To Celebrate the Passing of a Great Era: Historical Pageantry and Commemoration in the 1925 Calgary Exhibition, Jubilee, and Stampede." *Alberta History* 60, no. 3 (2012): 53–61.

Tooke, Nichola, and Michael Baker. "Seeing Is Believing: The Effect of Film on Visitor Numbers to Screened Locations." *Tourism Management* 17, no. 2 (1996): 87–94.

Tsivian, Yuri, and Richard Taylor. *Early Cinema in Russia and Its Cultural Reception*. Chicago: University of Chicago Press, 1998.

Tzanelli, Rodanthi. *The Cinematic Tourist: Explorations in Globalization, Culture, and Resistance*. New York: Routledge, 2007.

– "Constructing the 'Cinematic Tourist': The 'Sign Industry' of *The Lord of the Rings*," *Tourist Studies* 4, no. 1 (2004): 21–42.

United States. *Congressional Record: Proceedings and Debates of the 76th Congress, Third Session, Appendix, Vol. 86, Part 13, January 3, 1940, to March 5, 1940 (Pages 1–1200)*. Washington, DC: US Government Printing Office, 1940.

United States. Department of the Interior. *Annual Report of the Department of the Interior 1942*. Washington, DC: US Government Printing Office, 1942.

– *Annual Report of the Secretary of the Interior, Fiscal Year Ended June 30, 1941*. Washington, DC: US Government Printing Office, 1941.

– *Destination USA; Report*. Washington, DC: US Government Printing Office, 1973.

– *Proceedings of the National Parks Conference*, Washington, DC: US Government Printing Office, 1917. https://archive.org/stream/proceedingsofnat001917#page/264/mode/1up.

United States. Congress. House. Committee on Interstate and Foreign Commerce. *National Travel Board: Hearing before a Subcommittee of the Committee on Interstate and Foreign Commerce, House of Representatives, Seventy-sixth Congress, First Session, On H.R. 1792 And H.R. 5412, to Encourage Travel in the United States March 28, 1939*. Washington, DC: US Government Printing Office, 1939.

United States. Office of Inter-American Affairs. *History of the Office of the Coordinator of Inter-American Affairs*. Washington, DC: US Government Printing Office, 1947.

United States. President. "Proclamation 2383." *Code of Federal Regulations, Title 3 – The President, 1938–1943 Compilation*. Washington, DC: US Government Printing Office, 1968.

Urban, Charles. *We Put the World before You by Means of the Bioscope and Urban Films*. London: Charles Urban Trading Company, 1903. https://archive.org/details/weputworldbefore00unse/page/n11/mode/2up.

Uricchio, William, and Roberta E. Pearson. *Reframing Culture: The Case of the Vitagraph Quality Films*. Princeton, NJ: Princeton University Press, 1993.

Urry, John. "The 'Consumption' of Tourism." *Sociology* 24, no. 1 (1990): 23–35.

– *Mobilities*. Cambridge: Polity, 2007.

– *The Tourist Gaze*. London: Sage, 1990.

Van Hise, Charles. "The University Extension Function in the Modern University." *Proceedings of the First National University Extension*

Conference at Madison, Wisconsin, March 10–12, 1915, 7–24. https://hdl.handle.net/2027/uva.x030030211?urlappend=%3Bseq=16

Veracini, Lorenzo. "Introducing." *Settler Colonial Studies* 1, no. 1 (2011): 1–12.

– *Settler Colonialism: A Global History*. Basingstoke: Palgrave Macmillan, 2010.

Vonderau, Patrick. "Vernacular Archiving: An Interview with Rick Prelinger." In *Films That Work: Industrial Film and the Productivity of Media*, edited by Vinzenz Hediger and Patrick Vonderau, 59–64. Amsterdam: Amsterdam University Press, 2009.

Wagman, Ira. "The Woods Gordon Report: Accountability, and the Postwar Reconstruction of the National Film Board of Canada." *Journal of Canadian Studies* 42, no. 1 (2008): 83–104.

Waiser, Bill. *Saskatchewan's Playground: A History of Prince Albert National Park*. Saskatoon, SK: Fifth House, 1989.

Walden, Keith. *Visions of Order: The Canadian Mounties in Symbol and Myth*. Toronto: Butterworths, 1982.

Wallace, Irving. "Everybody's Rover Boy." In *The Man Who Photographed the World: Burton Holmes Travelogues, 1886–1936*, edited by Genoa Caldwell, 11–22. New York: Harry N. Abrams, 1977.

Ward, Richard. "Extra Added Attractions: The Short Subjects of MGM, Warner Brothers and Universal." *Media History* 9, no. 3 (2003): 221–44.

Warren, Louis S. *The Hunter's Game: Poachers and Conservationists in Twentieth-Century America*. New Haven, CT: Yale University Press, 1997.

Wasson, Haidee. "Electric Homes! Automatic Movies! Efficient Entertainment! 16mm and Cinema's Domestication in the 1920s." *Cinema Journal* 48, no. 4 (2009): 1–21.

– *Everyday Movies: Portable Film Projectors and the Transformation of American Culture*. Oakland: University of California Press, 2020.

– "Modern Ideas about Old Films: The Museum of Modern Art's Film Library and Film Culture, 1935–39." PhD thesis, McGill University, 1998.

– "The Other Small Screen: Moving Images at New York's World Fair, 1939." *Canadian Journal of Film Studies* 21, no. 1 (2012): 81–103.

Waugh, Thomas, Michael Baker, and Ezra Winton. *Challenge for Change: Activist Documentary at the National Film Board of Canada*. Montreal and Kingston: McGill-Queen's University Press, 2010.

Werry, Margaret. *The Tourist State: Performing Leisure, Liberalism, and Race in New Zealand.* Minneapolis: University of Minnesota Press, 2011.

Wheeler, Edward F. "War Films in the Classroom." *ES* (March 1944): 110–11, 119.

Whissel, Kristen. *Picturing American Modernity: Traffic, Technology, and the Silent Cinema.* Durham, NC: Duke University Press, 2008.

Whitaker, Reg, and Gary Marcuse. *Cold War Canada: The Making of a National Insecurity State, 1945–1957.* Toronto: University of Toronto Press, 1994.

White, Courtney E. "'The Utmost Care, Kindness, and Consideration': The MPPDA versus Allegations of Animal Abuse, 1923–1925." *Cinema Journal* 55, no. 4 (2016): 108–29.

White, Jay. "'A Vista of Infinite Development': Surveying Nova Scotia's Early Tourism Industry." *Journal of the Royal Nova Scotia Historical Society* 6 (2003): 144–69.

Whitehead, Jessica L., Louis Pelletier, and Paul S. Moore. "'The Girl Friend in Canada': Ray Lewis and Canadian Moving Picture Digest (1915–1957)." In *Mapping Movie Magazines: Digitization, Periodicals and Cinema History*, edited by Daniel Biltereyst and Lies Van de Vijver, n.p. Cham, Switzerland: Palgrave Macmillan, 2020.

Williams, M.B. *Guardians of the Wild.* London: T. Nelson and Sons, 1936.

Wilson, Edward L. *Wilson's Lantern Journeys: A Series of Descriptions of Journeys at Home and Abroad: for Use with Photographic Views in the Touroscope, Graphoscope, Stereoscope in the Magic Lantern or the Magic Lantern,* vol. 2. Philadelphia: Wilson, 1884. http://memory.loc.gov/service/gdc/scd0001/2010/20100617002wi/20100617002wi.pdf.

Wilson, J.H. "New Organization Will Stimulate More Intelligent Use of all Visual Aids." *MPA*, June 1920, 20.

Wolfe, Charles. "Historicising the 'Voice of God': The Place of Vocal Narration in Classical Documentary." *Film History* 9, no. 2 (1997): 149–67.

Wolfe, Patrick. "Settler Colonialism and the Elimination of the Native." *Journal of Genocide Research* 8, no. 4 (2006): 387–409.

Wozny, Michele L. "National Audiovisual Preservation Initiatives and the Independent Media Arts in Canada." *Archivaria* 67 (2009): 87–113.

Yeo, William B. "Making Banff a Year-Round Park." In *Winter Sports in the West*, edited by Elise A. Corbet and Anthony W. Rasporich, 87–98. Calgary: Historical Society of Alberta, 1990.

Zimmermann, Patricia Rodden. *Reel Families: A Social History of Amateur Film*. Bloomington: Indiana University Press, 1995.

– "Startling Angles: Amateur Film and the Early Avant-Garde." In *Lovers of Cinema: The First American Film Avant-Garde, 1919–1945*, edited by Jan-Christopher Horak, 137–55. Madison: University of Wisconsin Press, 1995.

Zimmermann, Yvonne. "'What Hollywood Is to America, the Corporate Film Is to Switzerland': Remarks on Industrial Film as Utility Film." In *Films That Work: Industrial Film and the Productivity of Media*, edited by Vinzenz Hediger and Patrick Vonderau, 101–18. Amsterdam: Amsterdam University Press, 2009.

Zuelow, Eric G.E. "The Necessity of Touring beyond the Nation: An Introduction." In *Touring beyond the Nation: A Transnational Approach to European Tourism History*, edited by Eric G.E. Zuelow, 1–18. Farnham: Ashgate, 2011.

Index

www.ingramcontent.com/pod-product-compliance
Lightning Source LLC
LaVergne TN
LVHW041357090826
845264LV00023B/174
* 9 7 8 0 2 2 8 0 1 3 9 3 8 *